BELIEF IN HISTORY

Belief in History

Innovative Approaches to European and American Religion

Editor
Thomas Kselman

UNIVERSITY OF NOTRE DAME PRESS
NOTRE DAME   LONDON

Library of Congress Cataloging-in-Publication Data

Belief in history : innovative approaches to European and
    American religion / editor, Thomas Kselman.
        p. cm.
    Includes bibliographical references.
    ISBN 0-268-00687-3
    1. Europe—Religion. 2. United States—Religion. I.
Kselman, Thomas A. (Thomas Albert), 1948-   .
BL689.B45   1991   90-70862
270—dc20   CIP

Contents

Acknowledgments   vii

Contributors   ix

Introduction • *Thomas Kselman*   1

PART I: RELIGION AND CULTURE

1. Faith as a Concept of Order in Medieval Christendom •
   John Van Engen   19

2. Bodily Miracles and the Resurrection of the Body in the
   High Middle Ages • *Caroline Bynum*   68

3. Alternative Afterlives in Nineteenth-Century France •
   Thomas Kselman   107

4. "He Keeps Me Going": Women's Devotion to Saint Jude
   and the Dialectics of Gender in American Catholicism,
   1929–1965 • *Robert A. Orsi*   137

PART II: RELIGION AND POLITICS

5. The Religious Origins of the Patriot and Ministerial
   Parties in Pre-Revolutionary France • *Dale K. Van Kley*   173

6. The End of Religious Establishment and the Beginning
   of Religious Politics: Church and State in the United
   States • *R. Laurence Moore*   237

PART III: MODELS FOR RELIGIOUS HISTORY

7. Unrethinking the Sixteenth-Century Wars of Religion •
   John Bossy   267

8. Historiographical Heresy: Catholicism as a Model for
   American Religious History • *Jon Butler*   286

Acknowledgments

I would like to thank all the contributors for their cooperation during the long and occasionally tedious process of assembling and publishing this volume. The Department of History and the Institute for Scholarship in the Liberal Arts at the University of Notre Dame provided funds that allowed several of the authors to present preliminary versions of their essays in a friendly and stimulating atmosphere. I would especially like to thank John Van Engen and Phil Gleason, colleagues at Notre Dame who provided support and advice for me as I planned this collection. Finally, thanks are due to John Ehmann and Ann Rice of the University of Notre Dame Press for their work in seeing *Belief in History* through to its publication.

Contributors

John Bossy is professor of history in the University of York. He has published an edition of H. O. Evennett, *The Spirit of the Counter-Reformation* (1968); *The English Catholic Community, 1570–1850* (1976); and *Christianity in the West, 1400–1700* (1985). He is now working on the political history of the wars of religion and the life of Giordano Bruno.

Jon Butler is the Coe professor of American history at Yale University, where he chairs the American Studies Program. He has been a Guggenheim Fellow and is the author of *Power, Authority, and the Origins of American Denominational Order* (1978); *The Huguenots in America: A Refugee People in a New World Society* (1983); and *Awash in a Sea of Faith: Christianizing the American People* (1990).

Caroline Walker Bynum is professor of history at Columbia University. She is a MacArthur Fellow and was elected a Fellow of the Medieval Academy in 1989. She has published *Docere Verbo et Exemplo: An Aspect of Twelfth-Century Spirituality* (1979); *Jesus as Mother: Studies in the Spirituality of the High Middle Ages* (1982); *Holy Feast and Holy Fast: The Religious Significance of Food to Medieval Women* (1989); *Fragmentation and Redemption: Essays on Gender and the Human Body in Medieval Religion* (1990).

Thomas Kselman is an associate professor and chair in the Department of History at the University of Notre Dame. He has been a Guggenheim Fellow, and is the author of *Miracles and Prophecies in Nineteenth-Century France* (1983), and *Death and the Afterlife in Nineteenth-Century France* (forthcoming).

R. Laurence Moore is professor of history at Cornell University. He has been a Fellow of the Rockefeller Foundation and the Woodrow Wilson Center, and is the author of *European Socialists and the American Prom-*

ised Land (1970); *In Search of White Crows: Spiritualism, Parapsychology, and American Culture* (1977); and *Religious Outsiders and the Making of Americans* (1986). He is currently working on a book about the intersections between American religion and American popular culture.

Robert Orsi is associate professor in the Department of Religious Studies at Indiana University. He has received fellowships from the National Endowment of the Humanities and the Fulbright Committee, and is the author of *The Madonna of 115th Street: Faith and Community in Italian Harlem, 1880–1950* (1985). He is currently working on a book about the American devotion to St. Jude.

John Van Engen is professor of history and director of the Medieval Institute at the University of Notre Dame. He has been a Guggenheim Fellow, and is the author of *Rupert of Deutz* (1983) and *The Devotio Moderno* (1988). With the assistance of a grant from the National Endowment of the Humanities he is currently preparing an edition of and commentary on the Brethren of the Common Life.

Dale Van Kley is professor of history at Calvin College. He has received fellowships from the Guggenheim Foundation, the National Humanities Center, the Institute for Research in the Humanities at the University of Wisconsin, and the Newberry Library. He is the author of *The Jansenists and the Expulsion of the Jesuits from France, 1757–1765* (1975), and *The Damiens Affair and the Unraveling of the Ancien Régime, 1750–1770* (1984). He is currently working on a book on the religious origins of the French Revolution.

Introduction

Thomas Kselman

Over the past several years questions about religion and the place of religion in society have drawn increasing attention from scholars and journalists. This concern is in part a reflection of heightened public awareness of the direct and powerful consequences religion can have in domestic politics and international diplomacy. The revolution inspired and led by Shiite Muslims in Iran and the influence of religiously motivated groups on the American political process are just two subjects among many which have made us aware of the salience of religious issues in the contemporary world.[1]

This revived interest in religion has been accompanied by surprise, even shock, among intellectuals and statesmen trained to think and act within a framework in which rational analysis and utilitarian calculations predominate. Confronted by dramatic evidence of the power of religious belief, politicians and diplomats have been forced to take seriously those who claim to have direct knowledge of God's will. Academics have, of course, been able to respond by appealing to a powerful tradition which sees religion as the epiphenomenal expression of economic and social reality. But for many, including the authors represented in this volume, an exclusively functional analysis of religion seems inadequate. Even if religious fervor can be understood in light of social and political concerns, it is not identical with these. As a result of its impact on contemporary affairs we are now more likely to grant religion status as an autonomous force capable of shaping people's lives, their social relations, and political institutions.

Several of the contributors to this volume allude to the importance of religion in contemporary life as part of the background against which their own work should be interpreted. None of the essays, however, makes a simple argument which would reduce current concerns to some set

1

of historical antecedents. There is instead a common conviction that careful historical work can open readers up to the nature and significance of religious belief and thereby contribute to more balanced and nuanced judgments about religion in other contexts, both historical and contemporary.

The essays in this volume also share a concern for redefining the field of religious history so as to broaden its domain and extend its contacts with other disciplines. Influenced by developments in social history and cultural anthropology, historians of religion have made significant advances in the past twenty years. Religious history is now well represented in the major journals and is a topic of lively academic debate. But despite evidence of dynamism, the field remains problematic. Questions about the proper subject matter of religious history and the methods and concepts which ought to be applied are far from being resolved. All of the essays in this volume deal with these issues in some form, and a number of them are explicitly critical of some aspects of recent work in the field. A brief review of religious history as it has emerged over the past several years may help readers see more clearly the direction in which religious history, as represented by the following essays, is moving.[2]

Until the 1950s religious history can generally be identified with the history of institutional churches and formal theology. The publication of the monumental *Histoire de l'église* under the direction of Augustin Fliche and Eugène Jarry exemplifies this approach which looks back to a tradition of church history that developed in universities and seminaries during the seventeenth and eighteenth centuries.[3] In American history Sydney Ahlstrom's *Religious History of the American People,* organized along denominational lines, can be seen as a culminating achievement of this tradition.[4] The emphasis on the concept of "church" in the practice of religious history paralleled the use of "state" in establishing the focus of political history; in both cases traditional historiography sought to organize a narrative around dominant institutions whose progress and decline could be charted and judged. Historians working in this vein assumed that religion could be equated with organized practice and expression, and generally limited themselves to a consideration of Christianity. Church history as written by its foremost representatives had certain strengths; it was sensitive to the power of theological ideas and illuminated the role religious institutions played in political and international affairs. Valuable work is still being done within this tradition, and some historians identified with it, such as Heiko Oberman and Jaroslav Pelikan, have exerted significant influence on religious history defined more broadly.[5] It is impossible, in fact, to imagine someone with an interest in religious history ignoring the importance of churches.

This emphasis on institutional religion contributed to the formation of a paradigm that shaped the ways in which religious history was understood both by those who worked in the field and those whose primary research interests lay elsewhere. I am referring here to "secularization," a tenacious concept that, despite the efforts of critics, will likely survive in some form. Derived initially from the withdrawal of property from church control during the sixteenth century, the term was extended to cover the decline in church attendance and the assumption by the state of charitable and educational functions formerly controlled by religious institutions. In its broadest sense, the concept has been used to describe the erosion of the explanatory power of religious symbols, which are judged as having lost their authority to compel belief.[6]

The story of religious decline attracted intellectuals from a rationalist tradition derived from the Enlightenment, and it is easy to agree with David Wootton when he writes that "the emergence of a secular, irreligious literary culture is one of the major historical developments of the last few centuries."[7] But a number of recent historians, including Wootton, have rooted the origins of atheism in developments within the history of theology; from this perspective, the history of belief merges with the history of unbelief.[8]

Perhaps the most powerful formulation of the paradigm of secularization can be found in the work of Max Weber and Emile Durkheim. Both of these sociologists accepted an evolutionary perspective and observed the disenchantment of the world, increasingly rationalized by science and bureaucracy. But it would be mistaken to identify Weber and Durkheim with an analysis of religion that was exclusively functionalist and reductive. Recent commentators on Weber have complicated our understanding of his concept of "rationalization" and reminded us that it is a process that occurs within religious traditions and can be "frequently disrupted."[9] Durkheim's *Elementary Forms of the Religious Life* can be mined for assertions such as "religion is the product of social causes," but no serious reader of this text would conclude that religious phenomena could be dealt with only by discovering their social constituents. For Durkheim also insisted that "Today we are beginning to realize that law, morals and even scientific thought itself were born of religion, were for a long time confounded with it, and have remained penetrated with its spirit."[10] Both of these thinkers worked extensively with religious materials and were sensitive to the power of religion as a social and historical force. Their work has been appropriated by a positivist tradition of religious sociology but can also be seen as contributing to more recent developments which avoid reductive moves in favor of a more dialectical interpretation of religion and society.[11]

There can be no doubt that studies centered on the concepts of churches and secularization have provided crucial insight into the status of religion in the modern world. But during the 1960s religious history broke free from its close association with churches and began to emphasize adaptive dimensions which allowed religion to be seen more as an active agent in the historical process.[12] In part this development can be seen as reflecting the contemporary skepticism directed at all institutions, but it also resulted from a number of intellectual tendencies which changed the shape of the historical profession.[13]

The emergence of social history in the 1960s was instrumental in shifting the focus away from institutional churches. Curious about the experiences of ordinary people and marginal groups, and frequently inspired by an ideological sympathy for the downtrodden, social history became a powerful force in the profession which even traditional practitioners could not (and did not) ignore. Religious questions were a central problem for this new subdiscipline, a point that can be made by citing the canonical text of E. P. Thompson, *The Making of the English Working Class,* where Methodism is subjected to an extended and hostile analysis. For Thompson, Methodism in the period 1790–1830 "served as ideological self-justification for the master-manufacturers" and was "the desolate inner landscape of Utilitarianism in an era of transition to the work-discipline of industrial capitalism." The emotional release it allowed workers is described as "a ritualised form of psychic masturbation." Despite this rhetorical assault, Thompson does acknowledge that certain features of Methodist belief and practice contributed to working-class consciousness, for "the Methodist political rebel carried through into his radical or revolutionary activity a profound moral earnestness, a sense of righteousness and of 'calling,' a 'Methodist' capacity for sustained organisational dedication and (at its best) a high degree of personal responsibility."[14] This combination of hostility and ambivalence can also be seen in the work of such influential historians as Christopher Hill and Eugene Genovese, both of whom, like Thompson, draw on the Marxist critique of religion. These historians generally associated institutional religion with the ruling classes and distinguished this from more popular forms of religiosity which could empower ordinary men and women to resist oppression and participate in social and political protest movements.[15]

The early emphasis within social history on conflict and protest helped bring into focus the autonomous religious experiences of particular groups which were no longer seen as dependant on institutional churches. Laboring men, peasants, middle-class women, and others were all seen as possessed of unique religious sensibilities. As work proceeded in the 1970s, the emphasis on conflict was augmented and to some extent replaced by a concern for how religious symbols provided a sense of order and meaning for believers. This trend was encouraged by the work of anthropologists, especially by Clifford Geertz, whose understanding of religion as a "cultural system" exerted enormous influence.[16] In the same period French interest in the history of "mentalité" provided continental support for social historians interested primarily in the beliefs and practices of laymen.[17] By the end of the 1970s it seems fair to say that the combination of social history and cultural anthropology had led to the creation of a new field of research, the study of "popular religion."[18]

The concept of "popular religion" has now become central to the work of religious historians, especially those who concentrate on Europe. American historians were a bit slower to absorb the concept, as Jon Butler noted in 1979.[19] But Butler's own work, and the study of Rhys Isaac, who integrated religion into his interpretation of Virginia culture in the eighteenth century, revealed influences similar to those shaping work on Europe.[20] Research on slave religion, revivalism, and witchcraft, and recent surveys by Butler, David Hall, Jay Dolan, and Martin Marty also suggest the emergence of a common perspective on religious history.[21] European history, however, was undoubtedly the most important terrain for religious history in the 1970s. During this decade studies of popular religion were important not only for the study of religious history; they became models for the field of European history broadly defined. Of the many consequences that flowed from works by Natalie Davis, Keith Thomas, Jacques LeGoff, Jean Delumeau, and Carlo Ginzburg, one of the most significant has been elevating religion to a prominent place on the agenda of the historical profession.[22]

There is an additional factor not often discussed that also helps explain current interest in religious history. William McNeill, looking back on his training as a historian during the 1930s, writes that "the greatest defect of what was taught to me as modern European history was the systematic diversion of attention from religious issues." The secular commitments of influential historians such as Carl Becker, Mc-Neill suggests, led the profession to neglect an important dimension of human experience.[23] The expansion of undergraduate and graduate education in the 1950s and 1960s provided many "believers" in the United States with access to training at secular institutions. During the 1960s the historical profession included increasing numbers of men and women who either retained or had only recently abandoned sincere and serious religious commitments. Historical research on religious issues has become for them a way of explaining themselves to their secular colleagues and perhaps to themselves as well. And since religious communities and the beliefs they share are based essentially on historical memories, the deeper understanding of the past that their work encourages will ultimately have consequences for the future of belief and unbelief.

During the decade of the 1980s "popular religion" has continued to inspire much valuable research, but as with previous concepts it has also provoked controversy and is now being widely challenged. Historians, including several represented in this volume, are now more inclined to doubt the radical disjunction between clerical and lay religion assumed by many of those who have worked in this area.[24] They are also more likely to take ideas and institutions seriously, and to retreat from "mentalité," a concept which refers primarily to general attitudes and cultural orientation. Men and women as described in the traditional historiography were capable of formulating ideas and committing themselves to beliefs, a freedom denied to those who are constrained by mental structures that can only be analyzed over the *longue durée*. The concept of "popular religion," originally intended to valorize the religious experiences of ordinary people, can also be read as segregating and patronizing them. The problem, identified years ago by Natalie Davis, of equating "popular religion" with forms of religiosity that are unsystematic, superstitious, and somehow inauthentic, can still be observed in some recent literature.[25]

The criticism of "popular religion" seems to have prepared the way for some new development in religious history, and it is my hope that the essays in this volume will help to shape this field as it moves into the next decade. The title of the volume is intended to suggest that "belief" may be a useful concept that can help us understand and organize current research. Belief is, of course, a familiar term, but one that nonetheless may enable us to integrate perspectives drawn from previous work in the field and current innovations.

Because beliefs are intentional acts, mental states that can be specified by reference to objects, they are necessarily associated with the formulation and expression of specific concepts. Beliefs are available to historians through written texts but can also be approached through ritual behavior, images, and architecture. Even institutional structures can be understood as expressing beliefs about social relations and the distribution of power. Given the broad scope I want to grant belief, it is fair to ask if it has any advantages over some of the previous categories used by religious historians. Unlike "mentalité" or "popular religion" belief assumes an active commitment on the part of the historical actors who are being studied. Belief restores the element of agency to the historical subject, who combines, amends, and rejects elements drawn from the religious environment. Unlike traditional church history, which focused on the ideas and institutions of a clerical elite, belief can be used to cover the relatively unsystematic formulations of laymen without rigidly distinguishing these from the commitments of the clergy. The laity have only rarely been able to engage in the theological discourse of the clergy, but both groups have participated in many of the same rituals and said some of the same prayers, acts that suggest a shared system of beliefs.

In proposing the utility of "belief" my intention is to permit historians to appropriate the results of previous research while avoiding the constraints imposed by previous concepts. Belief may also be capacious enough to allow religious historians to explore some of the new approaches being employed in history and related disciplines. The emphasis in cultural anthropology on the interpretation of symbols has now been complicated by literary criticism's focus on the ways in which meaning is constructed within texts.[26] Reading symbols, literary texts, and rituals in light of these disciplines does not always yield unequivocal results, and practicing historians are known to grumble about being distracted by opaque theory from the empirical work that is central to their discipline. Beliefs as they emerge from interdisciplinary readings of the evidence are not as solid as traditional historians might hope. Recent books by David Sabean and Paul Veyne suggest nonetheless how fruitful these disciplines can be in enriching our understanding of religion. Sabean deals with a number of issues that are familiar to historians of religion, including Communion practices, prophecy, witchcraft, and agricultural rituals, but in his handling they become instruments that allow us to see the varying perceptions of self and community available in German villages from the sixteenth to the eighteenth centuries.[27] Paul Veyne shows how the ancient Greeks developed strategies for reconciling contradictory beliefs about their myths.[28] The historians represented in this volume are not uniformly convinced of the value of theory and techniques drawn from recent anthropology, literary criticism, and critical theory. But these are issues that are relevant to the work of several contributors, for religious history cannot avoid the intellectual crosscurrents that affect historical studies and the liberal arts in general.

Adopting "belief" as a concept for religious history does not, of course, solve a more fundamental definitional problem. What does it mean to qualify this term with "religious"? In other words, what is religion? I am tempted to circumvent this question by citing Leszek Kolakowski's ironic introduction to his recent essay on the philosophy of religion, where he admits that "I am never sure what religion . . . is."[29] But as Kolakowski's own work goes on to show, there is more that can be said on this issue, although it is not one that philosophers or historians seem about to resolve. One recent trend, and one which several of the following essays reflect, has been to make religious experience an irreducible given, worthy of study in its own right. Any definition of religion understood in this light must be self-referential, and any definition that moves outside religion could be castigated as reductive. One purpose of this volume is to suggest that religious beliefs can be taken as a historical given, with their own autonomous force. But as Wayne Proudfoot has suggested, assertions that religion must be understood exclusively in its own terms can easily become a protective strategy for those seeking to defend religious commitments.[30] The empirical nature of historical research, which unfailingly shows religious beliefs and institutions to be bound up with secular reality, may to some extent insulate historians from this charge, but it is one that nonetheless illuminates a tension within the field. This volume reveals an impulse to define a subdiscipline of religious history that is both distinct from and associated with the dominant discipline, a problematic relationship reflected on here, and deserving of further thought.

The essays in this volume reflect the mixture of past and present historical practice, of traditional and innovative concerns, as currently represented in the work of a number of prominent religious historians. Although the essays in this volume begin with an emphasis on the salience of belief, they move in two directions. One group explores how religious beliefs were a crucial vehicle through which people shaped perceptions of self and society. John Van Engen and Caroline Bynum show how medieval theologians struggled to create coherent visions of a Christian society and an embodied self, issues that involved them in complicated strategies that would reconcile beliefs that did not always seem to converge with each other, or with perceptions of current religious practice. Thomas Kselman and Robert Orsi show how beliefs about spirits and saints in the modern era both reflected and shaped social relationships. A second set of essays explores the dialectical relations between religious and political beliefs.[31] Dale Van Kley demonstrates how Jansenist and Jesuit religious discourse played a formative role in the emergence of political ideology just before the French Revolution. Laurence Moore deals with the traditional-sounding problem of church-state relations, but in his view these are mediated by language and belief rather than through formal institutions. Both Van Kley and Moore are concerned with the construction of concepts about citizens, states, and churches, and their appropriate relations and see religious beliefs as crucial in this process. Finally, two essays address the historiography of religion in America and Europe, and suggest some ways in which historians of religion might better describe and analyze religious belief and behavior. John Bossy criticizes the reductionism of recent interpretations of the sixteenth-century wars of religion (including one of his own essays) and argues against what he calls the "categorical anachronisms" that have guided the social history of religion. For Jon Butler, Catholicism offers a potentially useful alternative to Puritanism as a model for thinking about American religion, past and present.

It is my hope that these essays will be read by students of religion — historians, theologians, and social scientists — but the questions they raise about the role of religious belief may also be of interest to general readers. Toward the end of the nineteenth century free-thinkers in both America and Europe looked forward with confidence to an imminent future in which religious belief would fade to insignificance. Such expectations appear naive a hundred years later, and it appears likely that a proper understanding of the twenty-first century will require an appreciation of religious issues. But even were this not the case, a proper understanding of the past will require the kind of reflection on religious belief exemplified in these papers.

NOTES

1. For historical background and an account of the 1979 revolution see Ervand Abrahamian, *Iran between Two Revolutions* (Princeton, N.J.: Princeton University Press, 1982), who stresses the social origins of the recent upheaval in Iran. For a brief study that places more emphasis on the religious

roots of the revolution see Henry Munson, Jr., *Islam and Revolution in the Middle East* (New Haven, Conn.: Yale University Press, 1988). General studies of the role of Islam in contemporary politics include: John Esposito, *Islam and Politics* (Syracuse, N.Y.: Syracuse University Press, 1984), and John Obert Voll, *Islam: Continuity and Change in the Modern World* (Boulder, Colo.: Westview Press, 1982). The international crisis provoked by the Ayatollah Khomenei's call for the execution of novelist Salman Rushdie in February 1989 serves as a reminder of how religious and political concerns remain intertwined and of how volatile this combination can be. For a collection of essays on the religious right in America see Robert Liebman and Robert Wuthnow, eds., *The New Christian Right* (New York: Aldine, 1983). For an overview of the place of religion in contemporary American society see Robert Wuthnow, *The Restructuring of American Religion* (Princeton, N.J.: Princeton University Press, 1988). For an interesting essay on the renewal of interest in religion among contemporary writers of fiction see Dan Wakefield, "And Now, a Word from Our Creator," *New York Times Book Review,* Feb. 12, 1989, pp. 1, 28–29.

2. For other reviews of the field see R. W. Scribner, "Interpreting Religion in Early Modern Europe," *European Studies Review* 13 (1983): 89–105, and Peter Burke, "Popular Piety," in *Catholicism in Early Modern History: A Guide to Research,* ed. John O'Malley (St. Louis, Mo.: Center for Reformation Research, 1988), pp. 113–32.

3. Augustin Fliche and Eugène Jarry, *Histoire de l'église depuis les origines jusqu'à nos jours,* 18 vols. (Paris: Bloud et Gay, 1934–1960). For a review of this tradition see Peter Meinhold, *Geschichte der Kirchlichen Historiographie* (Munich: Alber, 1967). Leopold Van Ranke's history of the papacy can also be seen as falling within this tradition; for selections of his works see George Iggers and Konrad Von Moltke, eds., *The Theory and Practice of History* (Indianapolis: Bobbs-Merrill, 1973). One contributor to this volume remains concerned that "church" history is an impediment to a proper appreciation of the relationship between religion and society. Dale Van Kley has written of "the tendency of most 'secular' historians to relegate ecclesiastical history or 'church' history to a wholly separate and irrelevant category of endeavor and of most ecclesiastical historians to rest content with their ghettolike existence. . . ." In *The Damiens Affair and the Unraveling of the Ancien Régime* (Princeton, N.J.: Princeton University Press, 1984), p. ix.

4. Sydney Ahlstrom, *Religious History of the American People* (New Haven, Conn.: Yale University Press, 1972). For a review of Ahlstrom's work and the tradition it represents see John Lankford, "An End and a Beginning: Reflections on Sydney Ahlstrom's *Religious History of the American People* and the Future of Sociologically Informed Inquiry into Religion in American Life," *Anglican Theological Review* 56 (1974): 463–81.

5. Heiko Oberman, *The Harvest of Medieval Theology: Gabriel Biel and Late Medieval Nominalism* (Cambridge, Mass.: Harvard University Press, 1963);

Jaroslav Pelikan, *The Christian Tradition: A History of the Development of Doctrine*, 5 vols. (Chicago: University of Chicago Press, 1971–1989). Oberman's influence on medieval and Renaissance religious history can be measured in the important volume of essays coedited by him and Charles Trinkaus, *The Pursuit of Holiness in Late Medieval and Renaissance Europe* (Leiden: Brill, 1974). A number of journals, such as *Church History, The Journal of Ecclesiastical History,* and *The Catholic Historical Review,* continue to publish articles that fall within the older tradition of church history. Some recent examples of works that adopt this perspective are: Owen Chadwick, *The Popes and European Revolution* (New York: Oxford University Press, 1981); Austin Gough, *Paris and Rome: The Gallican Church and the Ultramontane Campaign* (New York: Oxford University Press, 1986).

6. For a historical overview see Owen Chadwick, *The Secularization of the European Mind in the Nineteenth Century* (Cambridge: Cambridge University Press, 1975). Hugh McLeod makes judicious use of the concept in his survey *Religion and the People of Western Europe, 1789–1970* (Oxford: Oxford University Press, 1981). Alasdair MacIntyre, *Secularization and Moral Change* (London: Oxford University Press, 1967) analyzes the relationship between declining belief in Christianity and the loss of a sense of moral community. For a collection of essays by sociologists on the problem of secularization see Philip E. Hammond, ed., *The Sacred in a Secular Age* (Berkeley: University of California Press, 1985). Other sociological accounts include: David Martin, *A General Theory of Secularization* (New York: Harper & Row, 1978); Peter Berger, *The Sacred Canopy: Elements of a Sociological Theory of Religion* (New York: Doubleday Anchor, 1967). For additional references and a brief critical review of the concept see Thomas Kselman, "Funeral Conflicts in Nineteenth-century France," *Comparative Studies in Society and History* 30 (1988): 328–30.

7. David Wootton, "Lucien Febvre and the Problem of Unbelief in the Early Modern Period," *Journal of Modern History* 60 (1988): 696.

8. Wootton, "Lucien Febvre and the Problem of Unbelief;" Michael J. Buckley, *At the Origins of Modern Atheism* (New Haven, Conn.: Yale University Press, 1988); James Turner, *Without God, Without Creed: The Origins of Unbelief in America* (Baltimore: Johns Hopkins University Press, 1985). Also relevant here is James Samuel Preus, *Explaining Religion: Criticism and Theory from Bodin to Freud* (New York: Oxford University Press, 1987), which surveys naturalistic views of religion. This work was reviewed by Harry Ausmus in the *American Historical Review* 93 (1988): 1293–94, which provoked an exchange between Preus and Ausmus concerning the perspective historians should adopt in studying religion; see "Communications," *American Historical Review* 94 (1989): 934–35.

9. Scott Lash and Sam Whimster, "Introduction," *Max Weber, Rationality and Modernity*, Scott Lash and Sam Whimster, eds. (London: Allen & Unwin, 1987), p. 8.

10. Emile Durkheim, *The Elementary Forms of the Religious Life* (New York: Free Press, 1967), pp. 87, 472.

11. Wolfgang Schluchter, ed., *Max Webers Sicht des okzidentalen Christentums: Interpretation und Kritik* (Frankfurt am Main: Suhrkamp, 1988), includes essays by Jean-Claude Schmitt, Robert Lerner, Caroline Bynum, Lester Little, and Marvin Becker on the value of Weber's analysis for understanding medieval Christianity. See also the special issue dedicated to the work of Weber of *Archives de Sciences Sociales des Religions* 61 (January-March 1986), especially François Isambert, "Le desenchantement du monde: non sens ou renouveau de sens," pp. 83–104. For a reworking of Weber's ideas see Wolfgang Schluchter, *The Rise of Western Rationalism: Max Weber's Developmental Theory* (Berkeley: University of California Press, 1981). For Weber's references to the "disenchantment of the world" see his essay, "Science as a Vocation," in *From Max Weber*, H. H. Gerth and C. Wright Mills, eds. (New York: Oxford University Press, 1958), pp. 129–56. For an analysis of Durkheim's sociology of religion and a comprehensive bibliography of his work see Steven Lukes, *Emile Durkheim, His Life and Work* (New York: Penguin, 1973). Jerrold Seigel, "Autonomy and Personality in Durkheim: An Essay on Content and Method," *Journal of the History of Ideas* (1987): 483–507, relates the inconsistency and tension within Durkheim's understanding of personality to the development of his religious sociology and to his problematic relationship with a family tradition dominated by a line of rabbis. John Bossy traces the background of Durkheim's equation of religion and society to changes in the ways these words were used during the sixteenth and seventeenth centuries; see his "Some Elementary Forms of Durkheim," *Past and Present*, no. 95 (May 1982): 3–18.

12. In a recent article Claude Langlois sees the 1950s as the period when religious history in France began to shift its interest away from institutional churches; but in France this initiative came from the sociologists of religion, who addressed questions of religious practice which still assumed the central importance of institutional affiliation. See Langlois, "Trente ans d'histoire religieuse," *Archives de Sciences Sociales des Religions* 63 (1987): 91–93.

13. For a stimulating review of recent developments see Peter Novick, *That Noble Dream: The "Objectivity Question" and the American Historical Profession* (New York: Cambridge University Press, 1988), pp. 415–572.

14. E. P. Thompson, *The Making of the English Working Class* (New York: Vintage, 1963), pp. 355, 365, 368, 394.

15. Christopher Hill, *The World Turned Upside Down: Radical Ideas during the English Revolution* (New York: Penguin, 1975); Eugene Genovese, *Roll, Jordan, Roll: The World the Slaves Made* (New York: Pantheon, 1974), pp. 159–284. Genovese states the ambivalence perfectly when he writes that "The living history of the Church has been primarily a history of submission to class stratification and the powers that be, but there has remained, despite all attempts at extirpation, a legacy of resistance that could appeal to certain parts

of the New Testament and especially to the prophetic parts of the Old." Ibid., p. 163. The fascination with and debate over millennial movements is another illustration of how social historians became preoccupied with religious questions during this period. The debate was opened by Norman Cohn, *The Pursuit of the Millennium*, 2nd ed. (New York: Harper & Row, 1961). See Eric Hobsbawm, *Primitive Rebels: Studies in Archaic Forms of Social Movement in the Nineteenth and Twentieth Centuries* (New York: Norton, 1959) for a Marxist perspective on millennialism. For an overview of the literature on this topic see Hillel Schwartz, "The End of the Beginning: Millennarian Studies, 1969–1975," *Religious Studies Review* 2 (1976): 1–14. Millennialism still attracts the interest of scholars; see, for example, Michael Adas, *Prophets of Rebellion: Millenarian Protest Movements against the European Colonial Order* (Chapel Hill: University of North Carolina Press, 1979).

16. Clifford Geertz, "Religion as a Cultural System," in *The Interpretation of Cultures* (New York: Basic Books, 1973). This collection also includes Geertz's essays on "thick description" and the Balinese cockfight, which became ubiquitous in the footnotes of historians publishing in the 1970s.

17. For a programmatic essay on the history of "mentalité" see Jacques Le Goff, "Mentalities: A History of Ambiguities," in Jacques Le Goff and Pierre Nora, eds., *Constructing the Past: Essays in Historical Methodology* (Cambridge: Cambridge University Press, 1985). This collection originally appeared as *Faire de l'histoire* (Paris: Gallimard, 1974). For a selection of relevant articles that originally appeared in the influential journal *Annales: Economies, Sociétés, Civilisations* see Robert Forster and Orest Ranum, eds., *Ritual, Religion, and the Sacred: Selections from the Annales* (Baltimore: Johns Hopkins University Press, 1982). The heir-apparent to Le Goff as the leader of the French school that specializes in these studies is Jean-Claude Schmitt, whose articles have recently been collected in *Religione, Folklore, e società nell'Occidente medievale* (Rome: Laterza, 1988).

18. The concept of "popular religion" was legitimized in a number of essay collections: G. J. Cuming and Derek Baker, eds., *Popular Belief and Practice*, vol. 8 of Studies in Church History (Cambridge: Cambridge University Press, 1972); Bernard Plongeron, ed., *La religion populaire dans l'occident chrétien: approches historiques* (Paris: Beauchesne, 1976); Guy Duboscq, Bernard Plongeron, Daniel Robert, eds., *La religion populaire*, Actes du colloque internationale, Paris, October 17–19, 1977 (Paris: CNRS, 1979); James Obelkevich, ed., *Religion and the People, 800–1700* (Chapel Hill: University of North Carolina Press, 1979). For some of the most influential work in the field see the references in note 22.

19. Jon Butler, "Magic, Astrology, and the Early American Religious Heritage," *American Historical Review* 84 (1979): 317–20.

20. Rhys Isaac, *The Transformation of Virginia: 1740–1790* (Chapel Hill: University of North Carolina Press, 1982).

21. Albert J. Raboteau, *Slave Religion: The 'Invisible Institution' in the*

Antebellum South (New York: Oxford University Press, 1978); Paul Boyer and Stephen Nissenbaum, *Salem Possessed: The Social Origins of Witchcraft* (Cambridge, Mass.: Harvard University Press, 1982); Carol F. Karlsen, *The Devil in the Shape of a Woman* (New York: Vintage, 1989); Paul Johnson, *A Shopkeeper's Millennium: Society and Revivals in Rochester, New York, 1815–1837* (New York: Hill & Wang, 1978); Jon Butler, *Awash in a Sea of Faith; Christianizing the American People* (New Haven, Conn.: Yale University Press, 1990); David Hall, *Worlds of Wonder, Days of Judgment: Popular Religious Belief in Early New England* (New York: Knopf, 1989); Jay Dolan, *The American Catholic Experience* (Garden City, N.Y.: Doubleday, 1985); Martin Marty, *Modern American Religion*, vol. 1: *The Irony of It All* (Chicago: University of Chicago Press, 1986). See also the special issue of *U.S. Catholic Historian* 8 (1989) dedicated to "Spiritualism, Devotionalism, and Popular Religion."

22. Natalie Davis, *Society and Culture in Early Modern France* (Stanford: Stanford University Press, 1975); Keith Thomas, *Religion and the Decline of Magic* (New York: Scribners, 1971); Jacques Le Goff, *Time, Work, and Culture in the Middle Ages* (Chicago: University of Chicago Press, 1980); Jean Delumeau, *La peur en occident* (Paris: Fayard, 1978); Carlo Ginzburg, *Nightbattles: Witchcraft and Agrarian Cults in the Sixteenth and Seventeenth Centuries* (New York: Penguin, 1985; first published in Italian, 1966); idem, *The Cheese and the Worms: The Cosmos of a Sixteenth-Century Miller* (New York: Penguin, 1982; first published in Italian, 1976).

23. William McNeill, "Carl Becker, Historian," *The History Teacher* 19 (1985): 99.

24. R. Po-Chia Hsia, ed., *The German People and the Reformation* (Ithaca, N.Y.: Cornell University Press, 1988) suggests the continuing appeal of studies that use "popular religion" as a paradigm. For critical views of the concept see, for example, Richard Trexler, "Reverence and Profanity in the Study of Early Modern Religion," in Kaspar von Greyerz, ed., *Religion and Society in Early Modern Europe, 1500–1800* (London: Allen & Unwin, 1984), pp. 245–69; Thomas Kselman, "Ambivalence and Assumption in the Concept of Popular Religion," in Daniel Levine, ed., *Religion and Political Conflict in Latin America* (Chapel Hill: University of North Carolina Press, 1986), pp. 24–41; John Van Engen, "The Christian Middle Ages as an Historiographical Problem," *American Historical Review* 91 (1986): 519–52; Edward Peters, "Religion and Culture, Popular and Unpopular," *Journal of Modern History* 59 (1987): 317–30. The important work of William Christian, Jr., is also relevant to this point; see his *Local Religion in Sixteenth-Century Spain* (Princeton, N.J.: Princeton University Press, 1981), esp. pp. 175–80. David Hall, *Worlds of Wonder* also adopts a skeptical perspective about the distance between clergy and people. For a philosophically sophisticated critique of the related concept of "popular culture," see Stuart Clark, "French Historians and Early Modern Popular Culture," *Past and Present*, no. 100 (August 1983): 62–99. Ellen Badone

discusses this issue in an introduction to a volume of essays by contemporary anthropologists, Ellen Badone, ed., *Religious Orthodoxy and Popular Faith in European Society* (Princeton: Princeton University Press, 1989).

25. Natalie Davis, "Some Tasks and Themes in the Study of Popular Religion," in Charles Trinkaus and Heiko Oberman, eds., *The Pursuit of Holiness in Late Medieval and Renaissance Religion* (Leiden: Brill, 1974), pp. 307-36. For an example of a patronizing attitude toward popular religion see Judith Devlin, *The Superstitious Mind: French Peasants and the Supernatural in the Nineteenth Century* (New Haven, Conn.: Yale University Press, 1987).

26. For a collection of essays that explore how historians are dealing with recent trends in anthropology and literary criticism see Lynn Hunt, ed., *The New Cultural History* (Berkeley: University of California Press, 1989).

27. David Warren Sabean, *Power in the Blood: Popular Culture and Village Discourse in Early Modern Germany* (New York: Cambridge University Press, 1984). Sabean would likely quarrel with my conceptualization, for he argues that peasants for most of the period he writes about lacked a sense of the person as "a bounded and integrated motivational structure," that is to say, someone capable of formulating beliefs (p. 35). For Sabean, peasants in early modern Germany employed stories and images which "could be shaped and reshaped in village discourse without anyone necessarily giving assent to them in any specific way (p. 198)." But the point could be reformulated to say that villagers had recourse to a variety of religious beliefs, none of which they accepted unequivocally, to define and defend themselves in the face of a hostile state.

28. Paul Veyne, *Did the Greeks Really Believe Their Myths?* (Chicago: University of Chicago Press, 1988).

29. Leszek Kolakowski, *Religion: If There Is No God . . . On God, the Devil, Sin and Other Worries of the So-Called Philosophy of Religion* (New York: Oxford University Press, 1982), p. 9.

30. Wayne Proudfoot, *Religious Experience* (Berkeley: University of California Press, 1985), esp. pp. xiv–xvii, 228–36.

31. Nathan O. Hatch, *The Democratization of American Christianity* (New Haven, Conn.: Yale University Press, 1989) shows how historians sensitive to the power of religious belief can illuminate crucial relationships between religion and political culture. See also Mark Noll, ed., *Religion and American Politics: From the Colonial Period to the 1980s* (New York: Oxford University Press, 1990).

PART I
Religion and Culture

1

Faith as a Concept of Order in Medieval Christendom

John Van Engen

By the year 800, kings, bishops, and literate churchmen had begun to think of their people as christened and their lands and civilization as "Christendom" (*christianitas*). They knew the difference between a society of the baptized and an assembly of the personally professed. Sermonic diatribes against immorality and indifference together with pessimistic reflections on the approaching endtime both presupposed and disclosed real distance within medieval Christendom between the "merely christened" and the "truly holy." Renewed interest in the people's religion, moreover, has disposed recent historians to focus more sharply upon this gap between prescribed norm and lived reality, prompting some to argue in retrospect for two virtually distinct religious cultures.[1] By this reading, the Christianity of our texts reflects primarily the ideals and impositions of a literate clergy, while the religion of the people should be construed as something conforming more nearly to the modern category of folklore. The question of these illiterate peoples' exact religious allegiance and self-understanding cannot be fully answered – though any sharp distinction between "*christianitas*" and "folklore," most now agree, is anachronistic and would distort their religious consciousness. Aron Gurevich has argued for a certain "low culture" or "parish Catholicism" as the common denominator, and this "mode of consciousness," he believes, can be elicited from Latin texts aimed at the education of the people.[2]

High or low, common or sharply differentiated, the religious culture of medieval Europe went by the self-imposed name of "*christianitas.*" This term is a complex one, often confusing, for in the Middle Ages a single word ("*christianitas*" and its vernacular equivalents) covered at least three interrelated, yet distinct, meanings, distinguished in

English by three different renderings of the same Latin word. In its earliest usage (beginning with the church fathers), *christianitas* referred simply to the quality of being a Christian or professing Christian faith,[3] whence in time it could become for its adherents a form of personal address (*vestra christianitas*); this meaning we render mostly as "Christianity" or the Christian religion. The same Latin word might also refer, second and more specifically, to the rites and rituals, especially the sacramental ministrations, which set most Europeans apart religiously, that which was thought literally to make them Christian and thus to distinguish their observances from the religious cults of other peoples; the English word "christening" derives from the most fundamental of those rites.[4] Finally (though other meanings or nuances could be identified), *christianitas* might also refer to the whole society of Latin Christians and the lands they occupied (what classicizing intellectuals, especially the later Italian humanists, preferred to call "Europe"). This meaning came through most clearly in texts where "Christendom" (same Latin word) was set over against Islam, whether in papal letters or epic poems, and in contexts where high-level political and ecclesiastical relations were at stake within that society.[5]

All three meanings came to overlie one another in medieval Europe from the ninth and especially the eleventh century onwards. Neither "Christianity" nor "Christendom" captures fully the complexity and concreteness signified by this single medieval term; both words, moreover, have acquired a host of additional connotations in the modern world. For us the medieval sense of the term may come to expression more accurately in a phrase: this was "the society of the baptized"—a society in which medieval Europe's unbaptized Jews stood apart as the exception that proved the rule.

This notion of Christendom is inherently paradoxical. The word "*christianitas*" derives, to say it simply, from the Greek translation of a Hebrew title (Messiah) meaning "the anointed one," reserved in Jewish apocalyptic for an endtime figure who would rule over the nations and restore Israel. Around 30 A.D. (according to the form of temporal reckoning that is itself a product of early medieval *christianitas*), certain Jews, distinguished initially as followers of "the way" (Acts 9:2), became convinced that Jesus of Nazareth was this figure, the Christ or Anointed One, and that with his rising from the dead a reign and restoration had begun that would eventually extend to all peoples. Followers of "the way" challenged all peoples to accept the truth of this identification, Jews first and then Gentiles. Yet their own sacred writings suggest at

times that a person would hardly come to this conviction unless moved by God himself. When Peter first professed it, Jesus replied (according to one Gospel account: Matt. 16:17) that it was not flesh and blood but the Father in heaven who had revealed this to him. And Paul, the devout Jew who became the apostle to the Gentiles after a sudden turnaround in his thinking, noted at one point (1 Cor. 12:3) that no one said "Jesus is Lord" except through the Holy Spirit. Yet by the end of the third century a significant minority of Rome's citizens had made this profession publicly, chiefly by undergoing the ritual of baptism; by the end of the fifth century, even more remarkably, this minority had swelled to encompass a significant majority of Rome's peoples; and by the Carolingian era everyone in the Latin West subject to the lordship of a Christian king espoused the faith, ordinarily now as baptized infants with parents or sponsors actually making the profession on their behalf.[6] The onetime Jewish sect had grown into a Gentile consensus; "the way" had become the only way.

Christianitas henceforth embraced all levels from the personal to the social. The distinguishing mark of its adherents, however, remained *faith*, for it was the bond presumed to unite all the baptized individuals in medieval Christendom to Jesus of Nazareth as the Lord Christ. Indeed, baptized Europeans were most commonly called "the faithful," much more commonly than "the Christians."[7] But "faith" was also the ordinary word (in Latin at least) for the bonds between lords and their men as well as for those between husbands and wives, only two among a dozen such social and legal relations, which only added to the rich and sometimes confusing nuances of this term.[8] Building upon a Latin word for "trust" or "confidence" (this latter sometimes separated out as "*fiducia*"), the idea came in the religious realm to include both the contents and the act of professing belief (*quod est* and *quo est* in medieval terminology). With help from Augustine and other church fathers, medieval churchmen came to define "the faith" basically as the Creed and the act of faith as "thinking with assent." From Hebrews 11:1 they learned that faith was a conviction (*argumentum* in Jerome's Latin) about things unseen, containing within it already the kernel (substance) of things hoped for hereafter. All this provided more than enough material for sustained theological reflection. But the most common treatments of faith as such in medieval times focused upon its qualities as a virtue, and indeed as one of the three virtues (with love and hope) essential to a believer.[9]

From time to time medieval writers reflected on what it meant that virtually everyone in Europe was counted among "the faithful" (*fideles*).

It certainly did not mean that everyone was a devout believer and an ardent practitioner. Alexander Murray has found considerable evidence in the sermons of thirteenth-century Italian preachers to show that many townspeople failed to practice the faith and that some proved altogether indifferent to its teachings. Friar Giovanni of Pisa, preaching at Florence in 1305, asked rhetorically how many there were today of these "unfaithful" (*infideli*) who were ignorant and cared nothing about Paradise and all the other unseen matters of the faith.[10] Hugh of Saint Victor, whose "On the Mysteries (or: Sacraments) of the Christian Faith" proved one of the most influential systematic expositions of the early twelfth century, had already distinguished four levels among the faithful: those who simply believed (*sola pietate*), those who tested and confirmed their belief with reason (*approbant*), and those who began to taste inwardly in heart and conscience what they believed. To these he added a fourth set of people "called faithful" only because "they did not oppose the faith," though they observed it more as a customary way of life (*consuetudine uiuendi*) than out of any quality of belief (*uirtute credendi*). They received the sacraments along with the other faithful, but their minds were fixed only on the transient things of this world.[11]

So too in the earliest known medieval treatise dedicated to the subject of faith, a *Mirror of Faith* written for Cistercians about 1140, William of Saint Thierry distinguished three kinds of people (with monks probably foremost in his mind) not troubled by temptation: those possessing the full certainty of an illumined faith, but also those dull of reason (*rationis hebetudo*) and those overwhelmed by negligence or indifference (*negligentiae magnitudo*). The dull and negligent, he observed, professed and assented to the revealed flesh and blood of the faith simply out of custom, never testing spiritually or even knowing (*nescienti*) what the faith was.[12] Yet even in this charge of "infidelity," modern associations tend to distort medieval meanings. Being "unfaithful" was not the same as "disbelieving," though it might include some element of that. As these sources indicate, it referred primarily to someone not focusing upon unseen supernal realities. Identity with Christianity, whether as a matter of custom or of conviction, was uniformly taken for granted as the point of departure for all people called "faithful." When that marvelous gadfly (and adversary of William) Peter Abelard, staged with himself an internal dialogue between "Peter" and "Abelard" on the philosophical issue of personal identity, he asked first what it meant that only "our people" (*gens nostra:* including obviously himself) were endowed with the divine name "Christian."[13]

Faith as a matter of personal conviction is not inherently subject to historical analysis,[14] nor is the issue here to analyze the quality or extent of personal faith in the Middle Ages. What can be attempted — particularly in a volume studying the role of "belief in history" — is to recapture the language and nuances with which contemporary churchmen treated the religious realities of a society in which all were baptized as infants and expected as adults to profess faith in the Christ.[15] The gap between norm and reality was no modern discovery. It inspired preachers and reformers throughout the Middle Ages, and — more importantly for this essay — it provoked churchmen to think about the ways in which faith could refer coherently both to those overtly animated by conviction and to the whole society of the baptized. Their analysis already distinguished implicitly what we may call the ritual, ethical, and cognitive elements involved in professing the faith.

Faith as Sacrament: The Ritual Element

When Charlemagne advanced into Saxony in the 780s, he issued legislation requiring that anyone actively avoiding baptism be subject to penalty of death and that all newborn infants be baptized within one year.[16] For him, and for nearly all subsequent rulers of medieval Europe, kingship and christening manifestly went together. Thirty years later (812), in continuing efforts to reform kingdom and church, Charlemagne questioned his metropolitans about the instruction in baptism they were providing at the level of suffragan bishops and diocesan priests. The king's inquiry elicited some sixty-one letters, tractates, and florilegia,[17] most of them paraphrasing various traditional formularies meant to explain a rite designed for adults. Central to that ritual, as he and all others knew it, was a profession of faith. How that might pertain to infants came up only intermittently in these responses, usually in the form of an appended sentence or paragraph. To justify the practice of baptizing infants Carolingians offered essentially two explanations; these, it is safe to say, remained common throughout the Middle Ages.[18]

First, someone else was understood to make profession of the faith in behalf of the infant. Beginning at an undetermined date (by 400 and common after 500), godparents spoke the necessary threefold "I believe" (*Credo*) in the baptismal liturgy and themselves held (*tenere*) the infants at the font or — standard after the tenth century — received (*suscipere*) them from it; in so doing they obligated themselves to see that the children would be reared in the faith.[19] In this way, without giving up the notion of an individual profession of faith, an initiation rite designed mainly for a special assembly of adult believers was extended to virtually all infants in Western society.[20] Justification for this vicarious profession rested upon a sense of solidarity throughout society and the human race: If newborns entered this world bound to sin by the acts of proto-parents, so they could also commit themselves to the faith through an act of profession made by godparents.[21] The main point of Carolingian regulation, royal or episcopal, was to make sure that godparents were themselves capable of professing the faith, which was defined to mean saying by heart the Lord's Prayer and the Apostles' Creed, and of instructing their godchildren.[22] Charlemagne complained to Bishop Ghaerbald of Liège that the people were embarrassed when confronted by this statute and sought help so they could continue to participate as godparents. The bishop subsequently mandated his priests to check the people on precisely this point (*pleniter instructos habeant de fide*), that is, on their reliability as guarantors or oath-takers (*pro eis fideiussores*) for the faith.[23]

By 800, in sum, this ritual, in which the people plainly expected and wished to participate, may well have outrun for many people any detailed understanding of what was therein vicariously professed. The people affirmed their solidarity with the faith and stood in as guarantors for their godchildren, and this theologians counted as a legitimate vicarious profession of faith. Some theologians at least placed all this in a social and historical perspective. If with the expansion of the church all adults were now counted among the faithful, their children should no less be included in the congregation of Christ. One twelfth-century text of uncertain authorship, apparently recorded in various forms, set it out specifically:

> After the church had spread and gathered the people in among the nations so there was no longer any adult believer found among the faithful who was not one of the faithful, the medicine of salvation was provided as well to their children lest they die before reaching the years of discretion and remain estranged from the company of Christ; thus they are baptized with the sacrament of faith and reconciled to God through the faith of another, just as they were alienated from God through the sin of another. To this end a new form of the sacrament was instituted for catechizing, exorcizing, initiating, and then baptizing infants. The Church listens for the infants and responds to the questions in their behalf until they come to the age of discretion and understand for themselves the sacrament of faith, hope, and charity imposed upon them.[24]

There was a second and in some sense more fundamental way that newborns in medieval Christendom received the faith. Baptism early acquired the name alluded to in this text and in the subtitle for this section; it was the "sacrament of faith." The ancient liturgical rite had included the "giving over" (*traditio*) of the faith as a part of the act of profession, but this notion of "handing over" acquired a new sense in a society of christened infants. In the most widely transmitted and influential of the baptismal explanations from Charlemagne's time, that prepared by Alcuin (well before the emperor's request, indicating again the interest in this issue), the exact meaning assigned this "giving of the faith" remained ambivalent. While it worked best if applied to adults, his explanation also worked well if the "faith" is understood not as the Creed or an act of conscious profession but as the substance (*res*) or point of this ritual act conferred upon and implanted in an infant.[25] Amalarius made it clear in a long section on "children not understanding and yet having the faith" (*De paruulis non intellegentibus et tamen fidem habentibus*) that this was the way contemporaries understood it.[26] The term for this was "*sacramentum fidei*" and the authority for it was none other than Augustine, a passage cited here by Amalarius and everywhere in medieval literature, including Gratian (the textbook for canon law) and Peter Lombard (the textbook for theology). Gratian said simply— summarizing a commonplace and canonizing it for all subsequent lawyers— that it was the "sacrament of faith," not "faith itself," that made infants "faithful."[27] Augustine had argued that infants might not yet have assented (*annuendo*) in their minds or wills to the faith but nonetheless had received (*percipiendo*) the substance of it in the sacrament. In the exposition of baptism in Ivo's *Panormia* this passage appears as the only chapter on the subject "what it is to believe" (*quid est credere*), and the title of the first book of his *Decretum* begins simply, "De fide et sacramento fidei, idest baptismate. . . ." Few passages and few notions proved as influential in establishing the foundations for a society of the baptized: Faith or belief was something which could be conferred upon each infant member of medieval Christendom without conscious assent. All these baptized infants, as Augustine, Gratian, and so many others declared, were to be counted among the "faithful" (*fideles*) by virtue of the sacrament (*ui sacramenti*).[28] Or as a twelfth-century lawyer pointed out (and numerous others like him), even before using it upon attaining the age of reason a child could be said to *have the faith*.[29]

In the ritual of baptism priests made the sign of the cross on an infant with consecrated water. This was understood to leave a permanent "imprint," an invisible and irremovable "mark" on each of the christened. The basic idea had been laid down by Augustine in his dispute with the Donatists, as was the term for this mark (*character*), a word originally denoting a soldier's badge and appropriated by Augustine to designate the Trinitarian confession of faith at baptism, the Christian's distinguishing badge. The word and concept made their way into Western theology slowly,[30] but by the late twelfth century all of Europe's christened were said to bear the "character" of Christian faith, thus marking the faithful off from the infidel. The earliest explicit use of sacramental character in this way, to distinguish the baptized faithful from the infidel, is reported in the teaching of a certain Master Paganus of Corbeil (fl. 1160s–70s).[31] Pope Innocent III (d. 1216), in his widely read commentary on the mass, offered a basic statement of it: The "*character christianitatis*" is a sign of faith distinguishing the faithful from the unfaithful.[32] Guido of Ochelles in 1215–20 went further: This "character" impressed on the soul (*imprimitur animae*) could itself properly be called the sacrament, for it was the sign of faith (*signaculum fidei*) through which the faithful were distinguished from the unfaithful.[33] Peter Lombard had raised the issue only indirectly in his *Sentences,* but most subsequent commentators took a passage in Book IV d.6 as their occasion to comment on this issue. Bonaventure, for instance, noted – in keeping with the main argument of this paper – that "character signified the grace of faith in a certain status (*gratiam fidei secundum aliquem statum*) which distinguished the faithful from the unfaithful or the faithful from each other."[34] Gabriel Biel reviewed all the possible definitions of "character" known to him at the end of the Middle Ages, and after pointing out that the term was found neither in Scripture nor the early fathers, retained it: Character is a certain enabling spiritual power which in the case of baptism places its recipients in the status of the faithful.[35]

On the nature and effect of this "character," how it was imprinted upon the soul at baptism and to what end, later theologians debated endlessly. Bonaventure may be cited as representative of many in the mid-thirteenth century when he described baptismal "character" as preparing people for grace, distinguishing the flock of the Lord, persevering indelibly to preserve people among the faithful, and as orienting them to faith.[36] For historians the images invoked by these theologians convey as much as their conceptual apparatus. William of Paris likened "character" to the consecration of churches or altars, which added no new quality in the strict sense but nonetheless set them apart for divine service.[37] Bonaventure compared character to the arms or insignia of a king (this original Roman sense of the word repeated in nearly every author); it signified adherence to that king's party, even though a particular individual might choose to fight for the other party—as the habit, for instance, signified the religious, even when a certain monk or nun lived irregularly.[38] Gabriel Biel understood it to signify a certain status, as tonsure for clerics or certain marks on clothing for Jews.[39]

Baptism thus impressed upon the soul forever the mark of being in the status of the faithful, thereby predisposing them to act as the faithful. Bonaventure, a Franciscan, thought it disposed them to receive grace from Christ and to be configured to him. Thomas Aquinas, a Friar Preacher, thought that it predisposed the faithful toward participation in ritual worship (the divine cult).[40] At baptism, all agreed, this "character" was inevitably impressed upon a person, unless there was active and conscious resistance (thus, unwilling Jews or Saracens), and it could never be removed, though its saving effects could be obstructed by the unfaithful.[41] With this notion of "character" theologians and lawyers had found a way to name the widespread conviction (certainly quasi-magical for some) that the mark of the cross made upon the forehead and chest at baptism was permanent and irremovable and unrepeatable, and that it predisposed the christened to act as Christians. Indeed it more than predisposed; it obligated. Scotus said simply, as if it were self-evident, that baptism obligated all equally to believe.[42] Yet while theologians claimed that it placed people in the status of the faithful, they stopped short of saying that this literally made them Christians, in the sense of "the saved," for they knew well that heretics also had this "character" imprinted upon them when they received the sacrament of faith.

All the same, when lawyers and theologians said that the sacrament of faith "made" the christened "faithful," they intended more than a signifying or predisposing mark. They meant that the faithful had in some sense received the faith and now possessed it. To explain how this might be, high medieval theologians employed another term, this one borrowed from ancient philosophy and also put into currency in the later twelfth century. "*Habitus*" was understood as an enabling quality of the soul which gave shape to certain virtues, among them the so-called theological virtues of faith, hope, and love. Before the word "*habitus*" gained acceptance, authors also spoke of "*munus*" or gift, claiming that infants had received faith and all the other virtues at christening and were therefore "to be called faithful," though possessing the faith only "in habit" and not yet "in act."[43] It was left to explain in psychological and philosophical terms what this meant and how it could be, a discussion that went on among theologians throughout the Middle Ages and beyond. But on the essential point there was quick agreement: Jurists in the later twelfth century quoted a text ascribed (falsely) to Jerome which declared that "the faith which makes someone faithful is given in the waters of baptism."[44] By 1300 William Ware, an English Franciscan, observed simply that "all theologians agree that in baptism the theological virtues [faith, hope, love] are infused" (*In ista questione est aliquid in quo omnes conueniunt, uidelicet quod in baptismo infunduntur theologice uirtutes*).[45] Jurists followed the theologians at a distance. While Cardinal Hostiensis reported still two opinions on the infusion of the virtues at baptism, Anthonius da Padua in the early fourteenth century regarded it as settled: children are imprinted with the "habit," if not the "use," of the cardinal virtues.[46] Indeed this became a matter of church law: Clement V declared himself for this second view at the Council of Vienne.[47] And a later medieval *summa* for confessors explained that "baptism is called the sacrament of faith because it is conferred in the faith of the church and it confers the habit of faith."[48]

As with the term "character," historians may find the images used in conjunction with the term "habit" as enlightening as the technical terminology. Churchmen commonly likened these infused supernatural virtues to the natural virtues possessed in potency by an infant. As a maturing child acquired the use of memory, intelligence, and the like, so an adult grew into the use of faith and all the other habitual virtues. The most common comparison apparently was to reason, dormant in the child but active in the adult.[49] Richard Fishacre, an English Dominican of the mid-thirteenth century, noted that "infants believe because they have an habitual faith as sleeping persons have eyesight."[50] As a person would wake to see or a child grow to reason, so a christened infant would ordinarily mature to activate an infused faith.

As theologians saw in the conferral of faith at baptism the infusing of a permanent mark and enabler, so high medieval lawyers drew their own consequences from this most fundamental of all Christendom's rites. In the mid-thirteenth century Cardinal Hostiensis asked in his summary of the church's law how infants could enter into obligations apart from their own consent. Baptism, the cardinal explained, was a special case: Because the person's condition was improved by his liberation from the Devil, this was necessarily valid.[51] In his section on vows Hostiensis described those entered into voluntarily—to marry, to go on pilgrimage or crusade, to join the religious life, and the like—and distinguished them from baptism, a necessary vow, meaning it was binding even before it was consciously made.[52] The christened were not only enabled by "habit" and "character" to keep the faith; they were legally bound to do so. "Character" in particular came up for legal discussion because Innocent III used the term in his decretal "*Maiores*" (3.42.3), and jurists subsequently drew out its legal obligations. Thus Innocent IV pointed out that heretics and schismatics, unlike Jews, were to be compelled to keep the faith, since by "character" they were subject to ecclesiastical jurisdiction.[53] By the fourteenth century, in sum, it was received teaching for jurists (Anthonius da Butrio) and theologians (Duns Scotus) alike that baptismal "character" entailed a legal obligation to keep the faith.[54] Gabriel Biel paraphrased Ockham and Alexander of Hales in stating simply that this was a sign which obliged someone to observe the divine law (*signum obligatiuum ad obseruantiam diuinae legis*),[55] just as someone taking up the habit is obligated to observe the laws of the religious.

The test case, the only one possible in medieval Christendom and the one also invoked by theologians and jurists, concerned baptized Jews. The church was clear that they should not be forced to profess the faith, even though popular sentiment, also in a learned and compassionate man such as Cardinal Hostiensis, often ran to the contrary.[56] A canon from the fifth council of Toledo (633), cited throughout the Middle Ages, held, however, that Jews, once baptized, whether by choice or by force, were compelled to keep the faith lest it be rendered vile and contemptible.[57] By the time the high medieval jurists came to consider this case, certain subtleties had been introduced. Compulsion in the strict sense was forbidden, but most held, with Gratian and Hostiensis, that unless there was self-conscious resistance, it entailed a Christian obligation: Baptismal "character" had been imprinted upon the person and would not go away, even if that person chose, to the loss of his soul, not to bring that faith to fruition.[58] Peter the Chanter, at the end of the twelfth century, observed more realistically that such a person might "be forced a little if the princes would allow" (*etiam aliquantum cogere si principes patientur*), but should not be further compelled to observe the faith by way of excommunication![59] Christian masters had in fact a realistic sense of these matters: Thomas argued strongly against the involuntary baptism of Jewish children because their parents might easily persuade them to turn their backs on what they knew nothing about and thus bring further harm upon the faith (*Summa* II/II q. 10 a. 12).

Christian identity became so fully bound up with the baptism of infants that challenges to this practice, rare in the Middle Ages, met with shock and often with force. Several of the sects that arose in the eleventh and twelfth centuries, evangelical or otherwise, repudiated traditional sacramental practice. Peter de Bruis, an iconoclastic reformer and wandering preacher in southern France for nearly twenty years (roughly 1119–39), argued that children could not be saved by the faith of another and that baptism had no saving effect upon them until they reached the age of discretion. To this (and other suspect points) Abbot Peter the Venerable wrote a lengthy response in the 1130s, producing in effect one of the earliest apologies specifically for infant baptism.[60] Later, Waldensians were sometimes charged with denying the efficacy of infant baptism,[61] though this appears to have been true only for one wing affected by contact with the Cathars. In consequence, later theologians standardly reiterated the defense of infant baptism over against all such heretics.[62] These arguments added little theologically to what has already been presented. More striking for the historian is the shock with which these attacks were registered: How could anyone possibly suggest, Peter the Venerable railed, that all the child baptisms the last several hundred years were meaningless and the people therefore probably eternally lost? It would mean there was no Christian, no church, no Christ throughout Europe.[63]

So fundamental was the connection between the "faithful" and infant baptism in European Christendom that the Protestant Reformers likewise took it entirely for granted and reacted with equal or even greater violence against the so-called Anabaptists. Luther noted that baptizing infants was one among several things papists did right and the reformers simply retained[64] – indeed the only sacrament the papists had left untarnished (*illibatum et incontaminatum a constitutionibus hominum*).[65] Luther, like Peter the Venerable, saw baptism everywhere in Europe for a thousand years, a sure sign in itself that these novel rebaptizers had no truth in them; without it there would be no Christendom![66] The whole world knows and sees, he said, that everyone is baptized as a child and because he's a child; these people have attacked something never attacked before.[67] While the reformers were to place their emphasis upon the *promise* signified in baptism,[68] a promise of divine faithfulness understood to eventuate in human faith,[69] even so thorough-going a reformer and critic as John Calvin continued to assume that baptism, though an external rite (*symbolum* in Calvin) not to be confused with the very word or power of God, could be said to confer some distinguishing mark upon an unwitting infant.[70] Indeed Luther retained, to the dismay of other reformers, the notion of an "infant faith" (*fides infantium*). This rested, as Luther noted, upon the faith and prayer of those presenting the child (parents, not godparents) and of the whole church – and identified in this case still as an "infused faith."[71] Calvin, to come full circle, took over the term "*sacramentum fidei*" for that which infants received.[72]

For all their renewed emphasis upon faith as an individual commitment, these reformers could hardly imagine – any more than their medieval predecessors – a religious community that did not include everyone, beginning with infants. Those sectarians who repudiated Christendom, who persisted in claiming that only an adult believer's baptism had any legitimacy, were soon subject to proscription and even capital punishment. It was Huldrich Zwingli in Zurich (who himself went farthest among the magisterial reformers in reducing sacraments to symbolic actions) who first confronted reformers insisting from Scripture that faith must come before baptism. He conceded thinking for a time himself that it would be better to baptize children after they had grown to a mature faith.[73] But he thought better of it and successfully refuted the Anabaptists in public debate. In 1525 the civil magistrates in Zurich ordered the children of sectarians baptized and in 1526 brought the death penalty down on rebaptizers – lay councilmen acting here as kings had before them to protect the solidarity of Christendom.

What moved them is evident from a more colloquial paragraph in Zwingli's treatise. Imagine, he says, that no child was baptized until his sixteenth or eighteenth year or even later, and no one thought much about it anymore. Then if you should ask your neighbors why they reared (or, disciplined: *zuchstu*) their children in such an ungodly (*unchristenlich*) fashion, they might say: But I don't know yet whether or not they'll become Christians. And fresh youths might well retort: What are your admonitions to me? I may or may not become a Christian (*Was gadt mich din warnen an; ich mag ein Christ werden oder nit*).[74] Without the solidarity supplied from infancy by this ritual, the "sacrament of faith" – or the "covenantal promises," as reformers preferred – the order of European Christendom would dissolve.

From "Unformed" to "Formed" Faith: The Ethical Element

To return to our opening question: Would it suffice to say, summing up the preceding section, that "Christendom" in medieval Europe signified primarily that all Gentile infants had received the sacrament of faith? The answer, at one basic level, is yes, for receiving this mark not only stamped these individuals in some mysterious and permanent way. It marked them out for continued involvement in the rituals and obligations entailed by their "character" and "habit." But whether the christened faithful proved full of faith was another matter. And medieval churchmen were not satisfied – returning to Hugh of Saint Victor's distinction – that the form of life alone (*consuetudo uiuendi*) conform to the norms of the faithful: There was to be a quality, a power or virtue (*virtus*), that animated belief from within and put it into practice. In Bishop Ghaerbald of Liege's checklist for priests from around 800, this was the second point: "See that each follows up his faith with works."[75]

For this notion medieval churchmen drew upon a number of scriptural texts, especially those saying that faith without works was dead (*mortua:* James 2:17) and that faith was to be put to work in love (*fides quae per charitatem operatur:* Gal. 5:6). In keeping with these texts – and with numerous other admonitions from Scripture and the Fathers that could be cited – medieval churchmen put primary emphasis, after ritual reception of the faith, upon its virtuous acting out. In his *Admonitio Generalis* of 789 Charlemagne took it in hand to instruct his own delegated officials (*missi*) and bishops in directing and correcting the faithful: To please God and receive his favor it was necessary not only to offer him continuous thanksgiving in worship (*non solum toto corde et ore eius pietati agere gratias incessanter*) but also to be diligent in good works (*sed etiam continua bonorum operum exercitatione eius insistere*).[76] In the earliest extant dossier prepared to argue a case for canonization, that of Gilbert of Sempringham completed just after 1200, the point was made explicitly in a prefatory letter. Even if the faith is in full force these days, unlike the days of the early martyrs, the compiler notes, few in these wicked times put their faith into practice with love; many indeed still oppose the faith, now however in deed (or, way of life: *moribus*) rather than in word, confessing the Christ but denying him in practice – Gilbert, of course, being an extraordinary exception (*fidei specular et exemplar iustitie*) and therefore worthy of canonization.[77]

What Charlemagne and other kings attempted to enforce with public legislation and what the saints were believed to represent in person, early medieval churchmen set out to effect by ecclesiastical and sacramental means, first with the private religious codes known as penitentials. After 1200 churchmen preached the virtues in thousands of sermons, drafted treatises on the vices and virtues (over 5000 items in Latin alone listed by Bloomfield), and employed *Summae confessorum*, a genre that abounded after Lateran Council IV's requirement of annual confession. In recent years historians have focused considerable attention upon these materials and what they can yield for our understanding of moral and social life in the Middle Ages. Here the issue is to integrate this emphasis into notions of faith, particularly faith conceived as a concept of order in a society of the baptized.

Churchmen had to account for two obvious realities. First, belief came in various forms. Sheer unbelief, as Lefevre contended long ago, may have seemed nearly inconceivable. William Peraldus quipped that the person who said there was no God was not just a "fool" (Ps. 14:1); he was insane.[78] Scripture noted – and this text assumed great importance for theologians – that even demons believed in God and trembled (James 2:19). Could this basic belief in God, held even by demons and presumably by everyone else in Europe, also be understood as a form of faith? Second, there were, as noted, many who professed the faith but acted contrary to it; their faith, which failed to issue in practice or works, Scripture called "dead" (*mortua*). In the most influential of the Dominican treatises on the vices and virtues, that by William Peraldus completed about 1250, a section on "kinds (diversity) of faith" devoted greatest attention to the distinction between "dead" and "alive" faith. Plainly, Dominican preachers and confessors had as one of their chief tasks to bring dead faith to life.

Taking these two observations as given realities, that even demons believed in God and that many christened believers failed to practice satisfactorily, theologians set out to devise a terminology that would account for both and for the ritual reality of infused faith. After much debate, stretching from about 1150 into the mid-thirteenth century, masters of theology settled upon the terms "formed" and "unformed" (*informis*) faith, the latter infused into each christened infant as a part of the "habit" of faith. Peter Lombard introduced the issue, and every subsequent schooled theologian had perforce to deal with it. The faith that demons and false Christians hold (not yet making any clear distinction), the Lombard says, is a "quality of mind" (*qualitas mentis*) but one that remains "unformed" because it lacks the shaping effect of love or charity. The question is whether when love is added (in the christened, plainly, not in demons) the faith or quality of mind in this person, now become a good Christian, represents something altogether new. The Lombard (and after a time, nearly all other theologians) opted for the notion of an abiding quality of mind or soul which was formerly unformed and subsequently became formed.[79] Later thinkers became preoccupied with how to allow for the reality of both "unformed" and "formed" faith without projecting two distinct entities in the Christian soul. Differing explanations persisted throughout the Middle Ages,[80] but theologians soon generally linked this "unformed quality" to the infused habit of faith and applied as well Aristotelian notions of potency (unformed) and act (formed). At the end of the Middle Ages Denis the Carthusian prepared a remarkably clear summary of the main positions adopted on the status of unformed faith in the christened soul.[81] Pope Alexander V summarized even more briefly the three main positions adopted by medieval masters.[82] But all agreed that the faith was essentially one and abiding. Thus Richard of Middleton, a Franciscan of the later thirteenth century, noted that in a penitent person charity transformed one and the same faith from the status of unformed to formed.[83]

Setting aside the "faith" of demons, who believed in God but were patently evil – a matter that, admittedly, fascinated many of these theologians – the main issue for historians turns on what these masters regarded as the essential difference, in a society of the baptized, between the formed and unformed character of an abiding and infused faith. All the masters followed essentially one scriptural text (Gal. 5:6) which spoke of a faith-life shaped by love or made manifest in works: Charity was the "form" that was to give shape to the "raw matter" of infused and unformed faith. Faith was the base or foundation; works of love and mercy were the walls, the visible reality.[84] But without the foundation or habit of faith, no work could count as good – as theologians frequently noted, here in a confessor's manual.[85] By the mid-thirteenth century this distinction between a basic infused faith and an active faith formed in love was taken wholly for granted and could appear in almost any setting. One, notably, was the tradition of commentary on Romans 1:17. When it says there that "the just will live by faith" and "the justice of God is revealed therein from faith to faith" (*ex fide in fidem*), medieval commentators found numerous examples (minimally seven in the ordinary gloss) of movement from one species of faith to another, thus from that of the Old Testament to that of the New, and so on. Nicholas of Lyra, a most influential commentator from the early fourteenth century, identified this mainly with the transition from unformed to formed faith, that is, to acts of faith shaped by love and meritorious of eternal life or, in other words, to living and justifying faith[86] – that which made for "true faithful" or "good Christians."

The basic notion is clear and was capable of almost infinite nuance and refinement, chiefly in commentaries on Lombard's *Sentences* (3.25) and in theological *summae* (Thomas: II/II q. 4–6). But it could also be reduced to a practical discriminator – and these medieval masters, also in the texts cited above, always presumed that ongoing world of practice. There it became, in a word, the difference between those persons who were, or who were not, in a state of mortal sin; or put another way, the penitent and the sinner, those absolved and those outside the sacramental state of grace. The lawyers—perhaps in the nature of things—said it most plainly, beginning with Hostiensis and in virtually every subsequent discussion of the obligatory faith: Each baptized person possessed faith as a virtue and was numbered among the faithful until he or she fell into mortal sin.[87] Forming faith meant persuading people to put the faith into practice by way of charity or penance, and restraining or absolving them from mortal sin. Thus Innocent IV noted that lay people gifted with intelligence might look into cognitive matters of the faith, though there was no sin if they did not; the main and sufficient point was that they devoted themselves to good works.[88] At the end of the Middle Ages, Cajetan, commenting upon Thomas's *Summa*, could refer to a person as falling into mortal sin and thus slipping from formed to unformed faith, yet remaining among those counted "faithful."[89]

Just as medieval masters preferred concrete formulas—thus those christened who failed to practice or fell into mortal sin possessed an "unformed" faith—so they also linked supernatural realities with concrete acts. Baptism, we have seen, was the sign of faith conferred. The sign of charity, of faith formed, was penance and the Eucharist—a formula found already in late twelfth-century Schoolmen[90] and repeatedly thereafter. Medieval people communicated infrequently, and then ordinarily only after preparation which included confession and absolution to declare them in a state of grace. The "character" conferred in baptism and the "form of charity" manifest in penance and the Eucharist converged in the practical life of Europe's faithful, as it did in the conceptual apparatus of the masters.

Perhaps the best way to get one last angle on this teaching is to rehearse the views of someone initially trained in it, who subsequently repudiated it: Martin Luther. I cite but a single passage, a commentary on Galatians 5:6 derived from a set of lectures delivered in 1531, a decade after the definitive break. These Sophists (the theological masters), he complains, understand nothing about faith and are therefore forced to fantasize. They say faith does nothing, remains unformed, a blank slate (*tabula*), without charity—as if it were a pouch (*saccus*) to fill with treasure (charity), as if there could be at once and in the same heart infused faith and mortal sin (*fides infusa stat in mortali peccato*). Look out for this, he says. They understand faith as something objective rather than subjective (*Ipsi intelligunt obiective non subiective*). As for those hypocrites who know the faith perfectly well but do not practice it – he perceived fully the point of the distinction – theirs, he says, I simply do not call true faith, for faith in Christ is true when it yields works, as a tree does fruit.[91]

"Implicit" and "Explicit" Faith: The Cognitive Element

The previous two sections have dealt with faith as it pertained to the people of medieval Christendom most immediately, that is, as conferred at christening in a divine and permanent seal, the mark of the cross written invisibly and irremovably on their heads and chests, and then as a way of life made manifest in action, a set of virtues based upon faith but honed and shaped ultimately by penance and charity. But what of the cognitive aspects of the faith, the set of convictions that come to mind as the ordinary meaning of the term "Christian faith"? Here medieval society appears to have accepted, even expected and fostered a chasm between churchmen, who were expected to know the faith and its traditions, and most other people, for whom it was not required.[92] From the later twelfth century onwards, chiefly by way of mendicant preachers and vernacular treatises on pastoral matters, instruction in the faith increased with each passing century, yet without ever overcoming the considerable distance, even within the ranks of the clergy, between educated instructors and uneducated practitioners. Here too post-Reformation emphases and expectations set out, quite intentionally, to reverse earlier medieval assumptions: The earlier age began with ritual and emphasized the ethical but dealt only coincidentally – at least, at the mass level – with the cognitive; the later age focused increasingly on cognitive apprehension, while enforcing matters ethical and (in varying measures) purging ritual. The insistence that everyone, all the christened, know and be able to articulate the faith came to full expression on both sides of the confessional divide in postreformational efforts to catechize the young. Scholars differ on the success of this program, but the program itself and its undeniable effects have plainly influenced the views of those historians who judge that only in the sixteenth and seventeenth centuries was Europe finally "Christianized."[93]

The medieval norm was consistent throughout and represented an outgrowth of the original baptismal rite: The faithful were to know, or at least to recite, the Apostles' Creed and the Lord's Prayer.[94] Disjoined

already by Carolingian times from the baptismal ritual, these two became established as the central marks of those professing Christian faith.
To give but one early example: The royal palace at Aachen lay within
the diocese of Liège, and Bishop Ghaerbald of Liège (785/87–809)–in
one of the earliest extant questionnaires instructing priests how to examine the state of Christianity within their dioceses–insisted that anyone who resisted learning by heart and publicly professing the Prayer
and the Creed, whatever their social rank, be brought before him as in
violation of Christian law and as failing to have the faith that pleased
God.[95] Likewise in Theodulph's influential set of diocesan statutes (more
than fifty extant manuscripts) these two items alone, labeled the foundation of the Christian faith, were required of the people by heart. But
since christening took place in infancy, the only real check on the baptized came at the point when they served as sponsors, as godparents
who would act as guarantors or oath-takers in the faith for the spiritual
children they received from the font–the third point in Ghaerbald's
checklist.[96]

How and when the people were to learn the Creed and the Prayer
is rarely specified in our sources. In the 730s or 740s Abbot Pirmin
of Reichenau appears to emphasize the role of parents, godparents, and
lords, which corresponds to our rough impression of how Christianity
got put in place at the village level. The Council of Mainz (813) foresaw
children being taught the two marks of faith at monasteries or parish
rectories, so they in turn (the children!) could teach them at home, either
in Latin or in the vernacular.[97] Perhaps most importantly, both the
Creed and the Prayer would be heard each Sunday at mass.

Partly owing to the nature of our sources (chiefly diocesan statutes
and conciliar canons), the most common image remains that of priests
being exhorted to teach the Creed and Prayer or exhorting their parishioners to learn them. This holds for the first and most influential of
the new diocesan statutes, that of Paris from around 1200,[98] as it does
for the earliest in England, Stephen Langton's for Canterbury in 1213/
14.[99] The most influential of England's synodical statutes, that prepared
by Bishop Richard Poore for Salisbury in 1217/19, treated the sacraments as the first and main point of the priests' work, then exhorted
the clergy themselves to embody a faith made alive in works and grasped
in the understanding, one which could be passed down from them to
the people–but this, notably, requiring first that archdeacons and rural
deans instruct the priests in simple language, and indeed repeatedly and
in the vernacular.[100] Bishop Poore went on to enjoin his priests to teach

the Prayer, the Creed, and the Ave Maria, suggesting that they gather the children of the village in groups of one or two, for, he observed, parents are dangerously negligent in this regard.[101] The same complaint, that essentially nothing formal on the faith got taught at home by parents or even in the parish by curates, is made at nearly the same time (early thirteenth century) in the sermons of Jacques of Vitry.[102] Two centuries later, on the other hand, there is evidence that elements of the faith were being taught at home: Joan of Arc claimed to have learned them, probably in Latin, from her mother, while a German bishop at Trent claimed that most German-speaking children learned the Creed and the Prayer in the vernacular from their parents.[103] Schmitt has argued that in Romance-language countries (France at least) these marks of the faith were said in Latin and so became ritual chants more than cognitive expressions of learned convictions.[104] All the same, by the end of the Middle Ages, priests were urged to preach expository sermons on the Creed and the Prayer—thus, by way of example, in Breslau in 1406 where the Creed, Prayer, and Salutation were also given in Germanic and Slavic forms.[105] Everyone agreed, in sum, that the christened should know the Creed and the Prayer by heart and as well, after 1200, the Ave Maria, that parish priests should see to their being learned (sometimes in the local tongue) and to the explanation of them, and that adults not become godparents unless they could say the Creed and the Prayer at the font in behalf of their spiritual charges.

With the revival of learning in the twelfth century and the eventual formation of a guild of masters formally committed to "God-talk" (theology), the cognitive aspect of the faith received increased attention from churchmen, and questions arose about how much in reality the faithful should be expected to know. Hugh of Saint Victor, the same who recognized a fourth category of persons "called faithful" by their way of life rather than their quality of belief, addressed at length, and with some annoyance, those at the other extreme, who would not call anyone faithful unless the person understood in depth the mysteries of the faith. This, he observed, they ask of rude souls (*rudibus animis*) who can scarcely comprehend what they see, let alone matters of faith they cannot see.[106] Over against such overweening spirits (the new Schoolmen, we may safely assume), Hugh held that God (literally, "Divine Piety") judged belief according to "devotion," not "cognition," that is, by the measure of love evident in their belief (echoes of the previous distinction).[107] But Hugh's was a nuanced position: He recognized fully that there were many "today" who barely knew (*tenuiter norunt*) and could not think out (*cogitare*) matters of the faith which they nonetheless certainly believed and ardently hoped for.[108]

Even in Peter Lombard's textbook the issue arose only indirectly. But subsequent theologians, following Hugh and Peter, made it a standard part of their expositions under the terms "implicit" and "explicit" faith. Earlier masters had focused primarily upon another question, whether what Old Testament peoples believed could be counted as "faith" even though most (the prophets excepted) had virtually no explicit knowledge of Jesus Christ. The majority of theologians said it could, though it remained a "veiled" faith for all but the prophets. The Lombard then suggested an analogue: This is like those in the church today who are not able to name and distinguish the articles of the Creed, yet believe all that is contained in the Creed; they believe what they do not know (*credunt quae ignorant*), having a faith veiled in mystery.[109] Peter Lombard had taken the main idea and much of his language from a slightly earlier compilation known as the *Summa sententiarum*.[110] Here too there appears the idea that through their superiors the "simple" believe what they do not "know" for themselves, entrusting their faith to those who have responsibility for such matters. While the discussion and the guild of masters who joined in it first made their appearance in the twelfth century, this resolution of the matter stated summarily, it seems, a view most churchmen and intellectuals regarded as self-evident.

When learned masters came to treat the minimal knowledge required of anyone counted among the "faithful," there were at least three contexts in which that discussion might appear. The first occasion arose from Scripture; the most significant verse in this context came from the most famous chapter on faith in the New Testament, Hebrews 11:6 on Enoch: "Sine fide autem impossibile est placere Deo. Credere enim oportet accedentem ad Deum quia est, et inquirentibus se remunerator sit." [But without faith it is impossible to please God. For he that comes to God must believe that he is, and is a rewarder to them that seek him.] The first verse of this chapter, defining faith as the substance of things hoped for and the evidence of things not seen, received careful commentary almost from earliest days; but this verse (6) attracted remarkably little attention in the early medieval West, with most of that centered on how Enoch's faith pleased God. It was the new masters of the eleventh century, so far as I can see, who first perceived its potential. The commentary ascribed to Master Bruno, founder of the Carthusians, noted that for pagans (*gentiles*) it would have sufficed to believe that God was one and rewarded individual acts.[111] Peter Lombard—and we will see this

borne out in another context as well—took a hard line. The standard
set by this verse (believing in one God, who rewarded good) represented
a *sine qua non,* but it would not suffice for salvation.[112] Masters of theology were reluctant to set the standard too low, particularly in regard
to an explicit knowledge of the Christ. Yet later commentators, especially lawyers (including Pope Innocent IV), inclined to interpret this
verse as representing a kind of minimum statement of what was required:
to believe that there is one God and that he rewards the good. Thomas,
characteristically, in his commentary on Hebrews 11:6, tried to reconcile three points: Philosophers (pagans) could know by demonstration
(and therefore not by faith) that God is; Jews believed explicitly that
one God was to be worshipped; and Christians were to believe explicitly (Old Testament Jews only implicitly) in the Christ.[113] By the end
of the Middle Ages some such layered reading of this verse was common, though the standard seems to have gone upwards. Dennis the Carthusian, for instance, argued that both elements noted in the verse were
necessary for salvation, and that implicit in the second (God as rewarder)
was the notion of providence and consequently a plan of salvation.[114]
Most striking of all, the discussion centered around this verse became
a commonplace in the Christian West and extended far beyond the Middle
Ages. About 1611/12 Hugo Grotius, humanist, lawyer, and diplomat,
wrote his first religious treatise and opened with this concept (a God
who rewards) as the minimalist definition of religion, of what Christianity should hold with other religious people and what distinguished
it from atheists.[115]

The second occasion for this discussion arose from Peter Lombard's
remarks (n. 109 above) in Book III d. 25 of his *Sentences,* the standard
textbook for medieval theologians. In very short order Schoolmen understood this as the appropriate place to comment on the "implicit (veiled)
faith" ascribed to the masses of the simple faithful. This essay cannot
follow that teaching through all its later commentators[116] but will simply point up two pertinent matters. First, especially in the early period
(ca. 1150–ca. 1220), masters of theology struggled to agree upon exactly
how much should be required of the faithful; their disagreements reflect
the first flush of the Schoolmen's enthusiasm for cognitive understanding. Peter Lombard himself, to judge from reports of his teachings, held
firmly that the faithful must know something about all twelve articles
of the Creed. When asked how this might apply to the simple or to
shepherds reared in the mountains, he replied the same as to the more
discerning (*discreti*), though possibly in their own language.[117] There

were other masters unwilling to give in too easily to the social and religious realities of a society of the baptized. An unknown master, said in a manuscript to be Alan of Lille, insisted that any adult who had godparents and might stand as a godparent was required to know more than those before and under the law, specifically to know explicitly all the articles of the faith.[118] But most masters saw the situation far more pessimistically. Peter of Poitiers referred to many of the simple as "beasts" who knew little or nothing about the articles of the faith and could be saved only through the faith of their "betters" (*maiorum*) in the church.[119] All the same, while always retaining a distinctly patronizing view of the "simple," later theologians arrived at a kind of rough measure, a balance between implicit and explicit faith, whereby the people should know "roughly" or "in the main" (*grossa*), as Scotus put it, the items specific to Christian faith.[120] The notion of a "rough" (*grossus*) comprehension of the main Christian truths goes back to the early thirteenth century as well, specifically Alexander of Hales.

By the early thirteenth century, theologians seemed content to say that the "simple" must know some articles implicitly and others explicitly. Their real emphasis now lay upon another point, reduced to a phrase that echoed all through the rest of the Middle Ages: Those with implicit faith must "believe whatever the church believes."[121] This basic formula they sought to qualify with various provisions, that the simple *intend* to believe what the church believed, that they hold for *true* whatever the church believed, that they not *disbelieve* anything the church believed, that they stand ready to *learn* or be corrected, and so on. But the meaning was clear, and the saying everywhere. The structure or community of religion which this teaching presupposed is one medieval historians know well from another sphere: the professed religious (or later, chantry priests) bearing the chief burden of prayer and intercession for the faithful. This never meant the faithful were not themselves to pray. So too the full or explicit faith held in trust for them by their ecclesiastical betters (*fides maiorum*: a phrase also found everywhere) never lifted from the common faithful their obligation to believe and to profess their faith as best they could. But the christened in medieval Europe proceeded upon the assumption that there were those who, by virtue of their status in a spiritual and hierarchical society, knew the full faith, as there were those who prayed all day long. The point was to be at one, in intention and confession, with the church conceived as the body of the faithful and led by those "superiors" charged with possessing an explicit knowledge of the faith.

Piling up more quotations from the later Middle Ages on the subject of "implicit faith" would not substantially alter the basic outline provided here, though there were many interesting nuances which this essay cannot take up. It is worth summarizing by way of Thomas's treatment in his *Summa*, owing both to its influence and its clarity. It seems self-evident to him, on the basis of a Pseudo-Dionysian sense of hierarchy, that the greater should illumine the lesser, that the "*maiores*" with explicit faith were to instruct and the "*simplices*" with implicit faith to learn. The simple are to be examined in detail on the articles of the faith only when suspected of heresy and not to be charged with heresy unless they persist in clinging to some falsehood. The errors of the "*maiores*" represent no threat to the entrusted implicit faith of the "*simplices*," because their faith rests ultimately on the church, not only her "betters," and the faith of the church will never fail (*Summa* II/II q.2 a.6). But after the incarnation or the time of grace revealed, all must have an explicit knowledge of the mysteries of Christ, especially those celebrated publicly in worship (*precipue ad ea quae communiter in ecclesia sollemnizantur et publice proponuntur:* II/II q.2 a.7). Neither here nor in his sentence commentary does Thomas indulge in any of those asides on the ignorance of the simple commonly found in these theologians; but he takes wholly for granted the entire structure, an "implicit" faith for the people and an "explicit" faith for prelates and preachers.

The third source for this discussion was provided by the church's law. The definitive and authoritative version of the *Decretales*, issued in 1234, opened with the first canon of the Fourth Lateran Council, which contains a lengthy resumé of the faith. From 1215, therefore, and more particularly from 1234, observing the faith stood as the first point in the church's law, and lawyers were invited to say, in their teaching and in their commentaries, what the people were obliged to observe. The ordinary gloss on this text summarized the theologians: Each Christian was obliged to know the articles of the faith, the clergy explicitly and the people implicitly, meaning, to believe as the church did.[122] In the 1240s Innocent IV introduced a set of distinctions based upon Hebrews 11:6 which all subsequent lawyers took for granted, even when they chose to qualify them. The basic "measure of the faith" binding upon laity (his phrase: *mensura fidei ad quam quilibet tenetur*) is to believe that God is and rewards the good as well as to believe implicitly (i.e., as the church believes) the articles of the faith. But prelates of the church with cure of souls are held to know the articles explicitly, except in the case of poor clerics constrained to work for their food and with no money for study or leisure. They may be dispensed and treated as simple laity except in matters pertinent to the altar; but if they have access to money and masters, they sin unless they progress beyond the laity in explicit knowledge of the faith (*nisi plus proficerent in cognitione distincta fidei quam laici*).[123] Innocent noted in addition—and Hostiensis was to underscore—the "usefulness" of implicit faith for the laity in a legal setting. Even if a person proclaimed some serious error, such as the Father being greater than the Son, so long as he honestly believed this to be what the church held, intended to believe what the church believed, and did not persist in error against the church, he was not to be condemned as a heretic.[124] Unlike Innocent, Hostiensis and later commentators reiterated this point at the beginning of the very next chapter in their commentaries.[125]

Theologians and lawyers drew different consequences from the notion of "implicit faith." Theologians (in varying degrees) sought to protect the many baptized who could not articulate or explain clearly the articles of the faith from the charge of not knowing *unto salvation* the faith they professed. Lawyers understood them to be protected from charges of *heresy*. This protection rested upon an essential precondition: that responsibility for understanding and articulating the faith should be left mainly to churchmen and that the people intend to believe what the collective church believed.

There was undeniably greater emphasis upon cognitive dimensions of professing the faith from the twelfth century onwards and especially from the mid-thirteenth century, when the friars took this matter in hand. All the same, and granting full recognition to mendicant efforts to catechize by way of preaching, teaching, and the confessional, cognitive profession remained largely the preserve of churchmen and, more particularly still, the small number of university educated men. If the simple were held to know the whole faith explicitly, few would be saved—which Bonaventure judged most cruel even to say.[126] So too the lawyers insisted upon cognitive understanding of the faith primarily as necessary to the cure of souls, not in the first instance as an end in itself. So long as the "*maiores*" (the prelates with cure of souls) knew the faith explicitly, the "*minores*" (all the people and lesser clerics without cure of souls) met the requirement if they knew enough to direct their way properly (*ad dirigendum in finem*: the ethical charge of a "formed" faith) and to participate in the church's ritual solemnities.[127]

This brings our discussion back to the first point, the degree to which the habit and character in the souls of the christened faithful had to eventuate in an explicit knowledge as well as an active practice of the faith. Medieval masters became increasingly sensitive to this point and posited one more set of terms distinguishing between the "infused faith" of the christened child and the "acquired faith" (*fides acquisita*) of the mature believer. While parents, godparents, or the church might be said to confess for the child whose infused faith was still implicit and unformed, active adult believers were expected to *acquire* some knowledge of the individual articles of faith—this the foundation for a full catechetical program. Thomas spoke only generally of the difference between infused and acquired virtue, whereas later medieval figures, for instance, Johannes de Breui Coxa, conceded that infused faith was not sufficient to produce explicit faith in the articles.[128] This was particularly evident in the case of those christened children raised outside Christian society, such as among the Saracens. All the same, and here Master John actually reversed the original argument, since all the children of Christendom are pleasing to God they must already possess infused faith.[129] Bringing the soul to acquire and articulate what was already infused—here was the task.

For the people, however, knowledge of the faith was presumed still to come mostly (and here our story comes full circle) by way of ritual practice, acting out their christening. It was at the font that people, as godparents, made formal profession for others. It was in worship that they said the Prayer and sometimes the Creed. It was by way of participating in formal worship (the liturgical seasons and so on) that they assimilated and expressed the essentials of the faith. It was in meeting their annual obligation to confess that they learned about Christ forgiving sins. This Bonaventure stated explicitly in the mid-thirteenth century and employed formally in his explanation of implicit and explicit faith. He conceded that an implicit faith would suffice for the simple faithful. But he required an explicit faith in those matters taught by way of preaching and what he called "ecclesiastical custom and usage": thus knowledge of a Triune God could be expected of anyone making the sign of the cross in the name of Father, Son, and Holy Ghost; knowledge of Christ's life and saving acts of anyone observing church solemnities and priestly activities.[130] In the first decade of the fourteenth century the Dominican Durandus of St.-Porçain made the same point even more firmly, holding the people to be without excuse owing to the rites of the church and vernacular preaching:

> A middling position in the church falls to simple curates and those who
> by office or ministry are to teach others, such as preachers and masters,

and these are held to know explicitly what pertains to their office, that is, the articles in their substance. In difficulties, however, or when attacked by heretics, they must refer to their superiors. The lowest (such as the common people) are held to know or believe explicitly only what is passed on to them by the teaching of their superiors [or betters: *maiorum*] and the common worship [*ritu*] of the church, which is hidden from no one except those obstructed by their own fault. I think, however, that today [or: in modern times, *moderno tempore*] no one can be excused who is ignorant of the articles concerning the Trinity, the incarnation, the resurrection, the ascension, and the coming to judge, since these are made known to everyone in popular preaching [*vulgata predicatione*] through the public worship of the church and the frequent celebration of the feastdays.[131]

This is not to say there was little notion of explicit or cognitive comprehension of the faith among the medieval laity. Joinville tells how King Louis insisted that he know "firmly" (*fermement*) all the articles of the faith and withstand all doubts planted by the devil. The king went on to explain that we must hold firmly (*nous deviens bien croire fermement*) to the faith even when we are only in a position to "say yes" (*encore n'en fussiens-nous certein mais que par oïr dire*). Just as we accept our mother's word about our father and our birth, so we must accept the apostles' word, which we sing each Sunday in the *Credo*, about our faith.[132]

By the end of the Middle Ages the implicit/explicit distinction had extended as well to the area of ethical implementation. A Dominican prior at Basel, John Herolt, prepared a widely copied and frequently reprinted book on "the instruction of Christ's faithful." In explaining to his fellow Dominicans how to recognize and deal with mortal sin he (like many later medieval authors) used the Ten Commandments as one of his guides. About them he says that each of Christ's faithful must necessarily know all of them implicitly, that is, that adultery, stealing, and the like are forbidden; but the laity are not required necessarily to know the commandments explicitly or be able to number them correctly.[133] Again the details are left to those responsible for knowing and overseeing such matters, but the faithful are expected and required to possess a communal sense of the faith and its ethical requirements. Implicit faith seemed to these theologians and lawyers a collective sociological reality, rooted in the people's intention to believe and practice what those charged with responsibility for this religious society believed, practiced, and oversaw. It also seemed the basic way in which the great mass of the simple faithful might be understood to profess the faith that pleased God.

After attempting to understand from within the notion of implicit faith, we may perhaps cast the whole into perspective and conclude this section by considering someone who both knew and repudiated the realities of implicit faith: John Calvin. Commentators appear not to have appreciated fully that his treatment of faith (*Institutes* 3.2.2–3) opens precisely with a vigorous attempt to dismantle this entire theological structure and all that it entailed for the social religiosity of the medieval church. He charges that the Schoolmen's notion of implicit faith had essentially destroyed the faith, decorously covering over the crudest ignorance and dangerously deluding the people.[134] But two points especially drew down his ire. Faith, he said, was rooted in knowledge, not ignorance (*Non in ignoratione, sed in cognitione sita est fides*). And even more importantly (at least to judge from the length and tone of his language), it rested upon knowledge of God and Christ, not reverence for the church (*Fides enim in Dei et Christi cognitione, non in Ecclesiae reverentia iacet*). On this point Calvin railed with the full resources of humanist rhetoric: Does not believing (*credere*) mean understanding (*intelligere*), rather than subjecting your mind obediently (*sensum tuum obedienter submittas*) to the church? Are we saved by proving ourselves ready to embrace whatever the church prescribes, by leaving to the church our faculty for knowing and inquiring? Are we to believe nothing except on condition that such is called the faith of the church—and thus to accept all the errors the church has set forth? Calvin allows for a faith that is "implicit" in the sense of incomplete in this life, but he rejects utterly the received definition: namely, as he puts it, that those believe rightly who glory in their ignorance and so indulge themselves as to assent to the authority and judgment of the church on unknown matters—as if Scripture did not teach everywhere that faith is conjoined with understanding.[135] Here the humanist educator (not unlike the early Schoolmen) and the Protestant reformer have come together to dismiss a faith not borne of knowledge and understanding and not appropriated or generated personally.

For all the harshness of this critique, and the new emphasis upon personal instruction in the truths of the faith, the Protestant reformers retained the Creed, the Prayer, the Commandments, and so on as the essential structure of their own catechisms. The continuity was much greater than what some of the polemics suggest. So too at the level of personal confession, while most Protestants repudiated—it may have been one of the marks of being "protestant" – any simple dependency on what "their superiors" believed, the basic structures could persist in much the same fashion. A magistrate from Strassburg named Carl Mieg said in 1534 of the Tetrapolitan Confession, "I hope that as a layman I won't be trapped into something I don't understand and then forced to confess and believe it."[136] The terms "implicit" and "explicit" faith, along with some of their hierarchical underpinnings, might well be abandoned, but the social and religious realities changed more slowly. It is the historian who must go back to reconstruct this earlier way of seeing faith as a concept of order, as simultaneously inclusive and distinguishing, in a society of the baptized.

Conclusions

Medieval churchmen worked out a remarkably sophisticated conception of how Christendom, a society of the baptized, related to faith, the individual appropriation of that society's religious convictions. It managed to include all save those who self-consciously refused the ritual of christening (the Jewish minority), those outside the lands of christening (Islam), and more ambiguously those who corrupted their christening (the heretics). Yet to be counted among the truly faithful the christened infant had as an adult to put into action and to understand (or at least to articulate in speech) that which had been implanted by the ritual marking of baptism. That many failed to do so, or did so only very imperfectly, was self-evident to these theologians, the social and religious reality which their discussions of faith "formed" and "unformed," "implicit" and "explicit," wholly presupposed.

What remains at issue for historians is not the cleverness or perceptiveness of their categories but the justice and accuracy of labels applied to the religious realities of those our lawyers and theologians regularly called the "simple" (*simplices*) or "lesser" (*minores*) people. This characterization implies, at the very least, a low state of self-conscious practice among most people in medieval Christendom. It also reflects the lofty attitude of these masters – the self-consciousness and occasional arrogance of the intellectually trained, the ecclesiastically ordained, and the socially privileged. Their distinctions rarely took note, except in stock condemnations, of those religious realities now subsumed under the terms "folklore" or "popular religion."

Precisely because faith was understood to encompass all that was "real" religiously, however, faith itself had to encompass in some form all the peoples of European Christendom. In a hierarchical universe which took for granted layers or distinctions of a social, cultural, and religious character, it seemed evident that the notion of faith should also address these differences, that it should be conceived itself as an ordering concept. The concept of faith was understood to embrace, firstly, the entire human person. Christening imprinted the soul with the irremovable mark or "character" of the faithful and infused it with the habit or potency to activate all the Christian virtues. The terms "formed" and "unformed" accounted in turn for the whole spectrum of the *will*, from mortal sin to shaping charity. And the terms "implicit" and "explicit" accounted for the entire range of the *intellect*, from passive (though intentional) conformity up through articulate knowledge of what was believed. Masters of theology recognized that their divisions (see Thomas, *Summa* II/II q.4 a.5, for instance) took in the whole person, together with every possible way that soul, will, and intellect might relate to faith.

They likewise recognized that persons could be called "faithful" or "Catholic" in a number of senses. The distinguishing categories used in this paper were known to these medieval masters, even if the terminology varied. Master Johannes de Brevi Coxa, at the end of the fourteenth century, offered the following set of distinctions in a treatise on faith: "Catholic" might mean, first, any baptized person not stubbornly hostile to the law of Christ, even a child who as yet adhered no more to the law of Christ than to the sect of the Mohammedans! It could additionally mean any rational adult who preserved the faith inviolate and believed without doubting, implicitly or explicitly, all that pertained to it. Or it could mean any person who had transformed their infused habits of faith into acts, and it is these, he says, who are properly called Catholics.[137] This master took "christening" as the foundation and faith in action as the end. Antoninus of Florence (d. 1459), archbishop there during the ascendancy of Cosimo de Medici (d. 1464) and an accomplished canonist, distinguished four kinds of "religious" people in Christendom: those who carry out the basic cultic observances of the faith and this includes all Christendom (or, the whole society of the baptized); those who make their faith manifest in good works, thus all "good Christians"; those given over specially to divine matters, the clergy; and finally those who dedicate their whole selves to God by vow, the religious in the strict sense.[138] Antoninus took over his distinctions (explicitly) from Johannes Andreae, the most influential legal commentator of the fourteenth century, who in turn had borrowed them from Cardinal Hostiensis, himself among the most influential of the thirteenth century.[139] Whether construed as levels of "religion" (as here, and very commonly in medieval texts) or as different forms of faith, the same basic scheme emerges throughout and must have corresponded to a general perception of reality: common cultic observance, ethical implementation, cognitive understanding, and "truly religious," who dedicated themselves to God full time and exemplified all three.

These common assumptions about the workings of religious society in the medieval West entered into and helped shape the formal language about faith. Scholars today taken with notions like "a sociology of knowledge" or "a community of interpretation" should perceive at once what moved these medieval churchmen, what they saw and how it influenced what they were attempting to articulate. All Europeans, save the Jews, were christened and participated at all stages of their lives in the rites designed to inculcate and deepen their "christianizing." That all Europeans bore the "character" and the "habit" imprinted upon them in the sacrament of faith, that each had the potential thereby to act upon the faith and also to understand the world in terms of the faith—this seemed socially, culturally, and religiously self-evident, probably also to many of those "simple" and "lesser" folk who understood nothing of the specialized terminology. That explicit knowledge and full-time practice should be left to specialists seemed a reasonable division of labor in a society which conceived itself as having mainly religious ends. The emphasis upon intentionality with respect to the nonspecialists, of their intending to believe and practice what the church taught and required, fit as well. It represented their basic act of conformity to this society, and it—from the lawyers' and theologians' standpoint—also protected the mass of them from their own religious "simplicity," "crudity," or "errors." While the explanations given by theologians might differ, even substantially on some points, these underlying assumptions about categories of faith shaped for a thousand years the structure of Europe as a society of the christened, one encompassing all those called "the faithful."

NOTES

1. Jean-Claude Schmitt, *Religione, folklore e società nell'Occidente medievale* (Bari 1988), pp. 1–25, has reformulated this position most succinctly and coherently, partly by way of responding to my "Christian Middle Ages" (n. 4 below). A good statement of the issue from this perspective remains the introduction to *Faire Croire: Modalités de la diffusion et de la réception des messages religieux du XIIe au XVe siècle,* Collection de l'Ecole Française de Rome

51 (Rome 1981). Several good essays may also be found in Jean Delumeau, ed., *Histoire veçue du peuple chrétien* (Toulouse 1979).

2. Aron Gurevich, *Medieval Popular Culture: Problems of Belief and Perception* (Cambridge 1988). On methodological issues, see my review in the *Journal of Social History* 24 (1990): 164–67.

3. The word appeared in the earliest post–New Testament writings and was apparently modeled on the Hellenistic Greek term for Judaism (*iudaismos*). Ignatius of Antioch, writing before 110, used the new term (*christianismos*) at least four times and understood it as a way of life ("living in the way of Christianity": *zon kata ton christianismon*). See his epistles *Magn.* 10.1, 10.3; *Rom.* 3.3; *Philad.* 6.1.

4. I underscored this second meaning in "The Christian Middle Ages as an Historiographical Problem," *American Historical Review* 91 (1986): 539–41. "Professing the faith" and "practicing its rituals" were virtually indistinguishable in the common understanding of "*christianitas*," reaching beyond the sacraments to general observances such as the required fasts; thus both meanings are evident in Charlemagne's infamous capitulary concerning the evangelization of the Saxons: "Si quis sanctum quadragesimale ieiunium pro despectu christianitatis contempserit et carnem comederit, morte moriatur. . . ." *Capitularia regum Francorum* in *Monumenta Germaniae Historica, Legum sectio II* (hereafter, *MGH Cap.*), ed. Alfred Boretius (Hannover 1883), p. 68.

5. On this meaning, the most widely studied by historians to date, see Raoul Manselli, "Christianitas," in the *Lexikon des Mittelalters* 2.1915–16, and Van Engen (n. 4 above), p. 540 n. 71 for additional literature. An early and characteristic example may be found in the letter of Pope Alexander III in 1173 concerning Anglo-French rivalries: "Cum de discordia et decertatione quae inter charissimum in Christo filium nostrum Ludovicum illustrem Francorum regem et Henricum Anglorum regem et filios eiusdem regis Anglorum instinctu diabolicae fraudis emersit, toti christianitati et praesertim orientali terrae gravissima videamus pericula imminere. . . ." *PL* 200.962.

6. See Joseph Lynch, *Godparents and Kinship in Early Medieval Europe* (Princeton 1986).

7. A quick check of several recent concordances confirmed this impression. Taking only the nominative plural forms ("*christiani*" as compared with "*fideles*"), the following percentages emerge: in Gregory the Great (11/139), in Anselm of Canterbury (14/30), in Bernard of Clairvaux (30/43), in Thomas Aquinas (96/414). The same percentages carry through in other grammatical forms. While both words were used, these writers plainly designated their people (and themselves) more often as "the faithful" than as "the Christians."

8. Contemporaries were well aware of this and commonly (that is, in nearly all high medieval legal and theological commentaries) listed at the outset nearly a dozen meanings for the word "*fides.*" I cite here the influential legal *summa* of Cardinal Hostiensis: "Quot modis accipiatur fides? Et quidem

XI, nam primo ponitur pro sacramento baptismi . . . , secundo pro castitate tori . . . , tertio pro conuentionali securitate que etiam hosti seruanda est . . . , quarto pro consciencia . . . , quinto pro credulitate secundum quam credimus id quod non uidemus . . . , sexto pro legalitate seu confidentia . . . , septimo pro equalitate et exuberantia actionum . . . , octauo pro legalitate seu fidelitate dolo contraria . . . , nono pro probabili ignorantia . . . , decimo pro simplicitate bona seu innocentia unde dicitur communiter bone fidei homo est . . . , undecimo pro collectione articulorum [the Creed] ut hic. . . ." Hostiensis, *Summa* (Lyon 1537; repr. 1962), p. 4.

9. On the subject of medieval conceptions of faith there is less historical analysis than might be expected; for basic orientation to the theological literature, with bibliography, see Elizabeth Gössmann, *Glaube und Gotteserkenntnis im Mittelalter,* Handbuch der Dogmengeschichte I.2b (Freiburg 1971).

10. "Or mi di, quanti cia di questi infideli? Chi crede oggi i beni invisibili, i beni di paradiso, chissine cura? Non si ne curan le genti. Non sanno che se . . . Ma oggi ne pieno tutto il mondo di questo peccato. . . ." Transcribed by Alexander Murray, "Piety and Impiety in Thirteenth-Century Italy," in G. J. Cumming-Derek Baker, *Popular Belief and Practice* (Cambridge 1972), pp. 83–106, here p. 101 n. 1.

11. "Quartum genus hominum est, quibus credere est solum fidei non contradicere, qui consuetudine uiuendi magis quam uirtute credendi fideles nominantur. Solis enim transeuntibus intenti, nunquam mentem ad futura cogitanda subleuant. Et quamuis fidei christianae sacramenta cum ceteris fidelibus usu percipiunt, quare tamen christianus sit homo uel quae spes christiano sit in exspectatione bonorum futurorum non attendunt. Hi, quamuis nomine fideles dicantur, re tamen et ueritate longe sunt a fide." *De sacramentis* 1.10.4: *PL* 176.332–33.

12. "Negligenti enim et hebeti sufficit interim fides a carne et sanguine reuelata; nec temptatur quia nec *spiritualiter examinatur* [1 Cor. 2:14], quando sufficit ei uel consuetudo assentiendi uel professio confitendi, nescienti utique quid sit fides." *Speculum fidei* 47: ed. Jean Déchanet, *Guillaume de Saint-Thierry, Le Miroir de la Foi,* Sources Chrétiennes 301 (Paris 1982), p. 112.

13. "Dixit A.P., dixit P.A., dixit eidem idem. I [Abelardus]: Cum sit, Petre, Christus Deus a quo Christiani dicuntur, sola est gens nostra, ut estimo, que divini nominis appellatione sit insignita." Charles Burnett, "Peter Abelard *Soliloquium:* A Critical Edition," *Studi Medievali* 25 (1984): 857–95, here 885.

14. In a recent interview concerning the study of religious life in medieval France, Jacques Le Goff stated simply: "Et puis, il y a cette donnée que l'historien ne peut apprehender parfaitement: la foi. Avec tout ce que cela signifie en termes d'épanouissement individuel et collectif." *L'éxpress,* 25 November 1988, p. 76.

15. This social understanding of the faith in medieval Christendom was

first explored by Pierre-Marie Gy, "Évangélisation et sacrements au moyen âge," in *Humanisme et Foi Chrétienne: Mélanges scientifique du centenaire de l'Institut Catholique de Paris*, ed. Charles Kannengiesser-Yves Marchasson (Paris 1976); and his work was developed by Jean-Claude Schmitt, "Du bon usage du *Credo*," in *Faire Croire* (n. 1 above), pp. 337–61.

16. *MGH Cap.*, p. 69.

17. See Susan Keefe, "Carolingian Baptismal Expositions: A Handlist of Tracts and Manuscripts," in Uta-Renate Blumenthal, ed., *Carolingian Essays* (Washington, D.C. 1983), pp. 169–237, and Jean-Paul Bouhot, "Explications du rituel baptismal à l'époque carolingienne," *Revue des études augustiniennes* 24 (1978): 278–301.

18. Fundamental on this subject is A. M. Landgraf, "Kindertaufe und Glaube," in his *Dogmengeschichte der Frühscholastik* (Regensburg 1954), 3.1.279–345. Landgraf focused exclusively on theological issues, but the materials he assembled remain of immense general interest.

19. Lynch (n. 6 above), pp. 120 ff. and passim.

20. Thus in the "*Libellus de mysterio baptismatis*" of Archbishop Magnus of Sens (801–18): "quamuis paruuli per se profiteri non possint, tamen per corda et ora tenentium eos fides confitetur catholica. . . ." *PL* 102.982.

21. Amalarius, the wordy commentator on the liturgy, said it in a sentence: "Potest fieri ut qui alieno peccato sunt ligati, aliena professione soluantur." Ed. J. M. Hanssens, *Amalarii episcopi Opera Liturgica Omnia*, Studi e Testi 138 (Vatican City 1948), p. 249. Hanssens noted that the same idea could be found in a sermon of Augustine (176 = *PL* 38.950). The image there, however, was one of common illness and common healing. Theodulf of Orleans put it this way: "Confessionem suam plane diximus, quia quamuis illi necdum loqui possint, pro illis et confitentur et loquuntur qui eos de lauacro fontis suscipiunt. Nec immerito dignum est ut qui aliorum peccatis obnoxii sunt, aliorum etiam confessione per mysterium baptismatis remissionem originalium percipiant peccatorum." *PL* 105.228.

22. This regulation was repeated endlessly throughout the Middle Ages; one particularly influential and full example is found in Theodulf's capitulary for his diocesan priests: "Commonendi sunt fideles, ut generaliter omnes a minimo usque ad maximum orationem dominicam et symbolum discant. Et dicendum eis, quod in his duabus sententiis omne fidei christianae fundamentum incumbit. Et nisi quis has duas sententias et memoriter tenuerit et ex toto corde crediderit et in oratione saepissime frequentaverit, catholicus esse non potest. Constitutum namque est, ut nullus chrismetur neque baptizetur neque a lauacro fontis alium suscipiat neque coram episcopo ad confirmandum quemlibet teneat, nisi symbolum et orationem dominicam memoriter tenuerit exceptis his, quos ad loquendum aetas minime perduxit." *MGH Capitula episcoporum*, ed. Peter Brommer (Hannover 1984), p. 119. Numerous other examples are translated and discussed in Lynch (n. 6 above), pp. 305–32.

23. Charlemagne's letter to Ghaerbald: "Quibus praecepimus abstinere ut antequam orationem et simbolum scirent et recitare potuissent, neque aliquem de sacro fonte baptismatis suscipere praesumerent. Et ualde erubescentes fuerunt ex hac re et spondere uolebant ut, si concessum eis fuisset, ad tempus hoc improperium a se potuissent auferre." *MGH Cap.,* p. 241. Compare Ghaerbald's statute for his diocesan priests, *MGH Capitularia episcoporum* 1.26.

24. Landgraf (n. 18 above), pp. 290–310, with many additional texts on pp. 288–92. "Postquam ecclesia dilatata est et congregata in gentibus nec inter fideles repertus est aliquis adulte fidei non fidelis, ne paruuli eorum de hac ante rationabiles annos exeuntes alieni remanerent de consortio Christi, provisa est et illis medicina salutis, ut sacramento fidei baptizarentur et per alterius fidem reconcilarentur Deo, sicut per alterius peccatum alienata erant a Deo. Institutum itaque ad hoc nouum sacramentorum genus ad catezizandos paruulos exorcizandos initiandos et demum baptizandos, in quibus pro paruulo audit ecclesia et ad interrogata respondet, donec paruulus ad intelligibiles annos perueniat et sacramenta fidei, caritatis et spei sibi imposita per se intelligat." Here from Codex Bamberg 10, f. 26f. (cited in Landgraf, p. 310); but related to Hugh of Saint Victor, *De sacramentis* 2.6.9: *PL* 176.456 (who often introduced this kind of historical and social perspective, here on infant baptism).

25. "Deinde symboli apostolici traditur ei fides, ut uacua domus et a prisco habitatore derelicta [= Devil driven out by exorcism] fide ornetur et preparetur habitatio Dei. Tunc fiunt scrutinia, ut exploretur sepius an post renuntiationem satanae sacra verba datae fidei radicitus corde defixerit. Tanguntur et nares, ut quamdiu spiritum naribus trahat, in fide accepta perduret. Pectus quoque eodem perunguitur oleo, ut signo sanctae crucis diabolo claudatur ingressus." Alcuin, *Epistolae* 134: *MGH Epistolae* 4.134.

26. "Quamvis paruuli pro aetate non possint intellegere ipsam conuersionem ad Deum atque credulitatem, credimus tamen eos ad Deum conuertere propter conuersionis sacramentum et fidem habere propter fidei sacramentum. . . ." *Opera,* ed. Hanssens (n. 21 above), p. 248.

27. I cite it here as the passage appears in Gratian under the title "Sacramentum fidei, non ipsa fides paruulum facit fidelem": "Nichil est aliud credere quam fidem habere, et per hoc cum respondetur credere paruulus qui fidei nondum habet effectum, respondetur fidem habere propter fidei sacramentum et conuertere se ad Deum propter conuersionis sacramentum, quia et ipsa responsio ad celebritatem sacramenti pertinet. Item: Paruulum, etsi nondum fides illa, que in credentium voluntate consistit, iam tamen ipsius fidei sacramentum fidelem facit, sicut credere respondentur, ita etenim fideles uocantur, non rem ipsam mente abnuendo, sed ipsius rei sacramentum percipiendo." *De cons.* d. 4 c. 76. The original is found in Augustine, *Epistolae 98 ad Bonifacium* 9–10: *CSEL* 34.531–32. The text has come down in various forms, usually shorter than that given by Gratian. See Amalarius, *Opera* (n. 21 above), p. 248; Ivo, *Decretum* 1.187 and *Panormia* 1.56 (possibly Gratian's source); Peter

Lombard, *Sententiae* IV d. 4 c. 4 (12): ed. Brady (Grottaferrata 1981), 2.259. Further references in Landgraf (n. 18 above), p. 286 n. 8.

28. Archbishop Leidrad of Lyons (798–814?) attempted to explain this: "Totum hoc in spe fit ui sacramenti et divinae gratiae quam Dominus donauit ecclesiae cum baptizantur propter uirtutem celebrationemque tanti sacramenti, quamuis suo corde atque ore non agant quod ad credendum confitendumque pertineat; tamen in numero credentium computantur." *PL* 99.868.

29. ". . . credere duobus modis dicitur: Primo sic credere est uti fide; sic iste puer non credit quia non utitur libero arbitrio. Secundo dicitur credere, id est habere credulitatem siue fidem; sic iste puer credit." Roland of Cremona, *Summa*, Codex Paris, Mazar. lat. 795 f. 87 (here quoted from Landgraf [n. 18 above], p. 280 n. 19).

30. Basic orientation in N. M. Haring, "Character, Signum and Signaculum," *Scholastik* 30 (1955): 481–512; 31 (1956): 41–69, 182–212.

31. "M[agister] Paganus dicit, quod sacramentum est caracter, quo distinguuntur fideles ab infidelibus." "Alii vero, ut magister Paganus de Corbolio et alii, dixerunt baptismum esse quemdam karacterem, quo discernuntur baptizati a non baptizatis, qui habet esse in anima ex eo quod corpus abluitur sub forma a Christo prefixa. . . ." Cited from manuscripts in Artur Landgraf, "Die Definition der Taufe," in his *Dogmengeschichte der Frühscholastik* (Regensburg 1955) 3.2.23 n. 4. General orientation to this subject (with bibliography) in Josef Finkenzeller, *Die Lehre von den Sakramenten im Allgemein von der Schrift bis zur Scholastik,* Handbuch der Dogmengeschichte IV.7a (Freiburg 1980), pp. 40–52, 111–18, 209–25.

32. "Signum fidei pro charactere christianitatis accipitur, quo fideles ab infidelibus discernuntur." *De sacro altaris mysterio* 5.5: *PL* 217.892.

33. *Tractatus de sacramentis,* ed. D. van den Eynde (Paderborn 1953), p. 25. Haring (n. 30 above), p. 206 and passim for many additional texts.

34. Bonaventure, *In Sent.* IV d. 6 p. 1 a. 1 q. 2: ed. in *S. Bonaventurae Opera Omnia* (Quaracchi 1889), 4.140–41.

35. "Quia character est quaedam spiritualis potestas ad agendum aliquid secundum certum statum. Nunc autem tantum tria sunt sacramenta, quae ponunt hominem ad certum statum ad aliquid spiritale exercendum. Sic baptismus ponit baptizatum in statum fidelium et membrarum ecelesiae, quo distinguitur ab infidelibus. . . ." Biel, *Collectorium,* ed. W. Werbeck-U. Hofmann (Tübingen 1975), IV/1.249.

36. "Et tangitur quadruplex conditio characteris: quia enim praeparat ad gratiam, ideo principium vitae; quia distinguit gregem Domini, sic sigillum; quia indelebiliter perseuerat, sic custodia; quia specialiter disponit ad fidem, dicitur illuminatio mentis" Bonaventure, *In Sent.* IV d. 3 p. 1 a. 1 q. 1 (ed. Quaracchi 1889), 4.66.

37. *Guilielmi Alverni Opera Omnia* (Paris 1674; repr. 1963), 1.421–26.

38. Bonaventure, *Commentaria in Sent.* IV d.6 (a long discussion of this matter) a. 1 q. 1 (ed. Quaracchi 1889), 4.140–41.

39. Gabrielis Biel, *Collectorium circa quattuor libros Sententiarum* IV d. 6 q. 2: ed. W. Werbeck-U. Hofmann (Tübingen 1975), IV/1.248.

40. ". . . character est quoddam signaculum quo anima insignitur ad suscipiendum [baptism, confirmation] uel aliis tradendum [ordination] ea quae sunt diuini cultus." *Summa theologiae* III q. 63 a. 4 (compare a. 3). See nn. 34 and 36 above for Bonaventure.

41. Thus Cardinal Hostiensis, summarizing much theological and legal discussion: ". . . secus si aliqui coacti ueniant ad baptisum quia tales cogendi sunt fidem quam susceperunt seruare; nam ex quo non contradixerunt characterem receperunt. . . . Tunc ergo characterem sacramentalem imprimit operatio cum obicem uoluntatis non inuenit resistentem expressim. . . . Sed et quamuis impresso characteri non possint baptizati renunciare . . . tamen effectui characteris, idest saluationis, renunciare possunt baptizati . . . ; est ratio quia character semel receptus amitti non potest. . . ." Hostiensis, *Summa* (ed. 1537, repr. 1962), p. 187.

42. *In Sent.* 3.25.1 (ed. Lyons 1639; repr. 1968), 7.1.499.

43. ". . . propter sacramentum fidei, quod paruulus dicitur fidem habere et credere, unde fidelis uocatur, licet fidem et virtutem non habeat in actu sed habitu." Quoted from Codex Bamberg Can. 43 f. 85 by Landgraf (n. 18 above), p. 295 n. 59.

44. "Fides, que fidelem facit, in aquis baptismi datur uel nutritur." On this sentence and its use, see Landgraf (n. 18 above), p. 294.

45. Landgraf (n. 18 above), p. 328.

46. Anthonius at *Decretales* 3.42.3 (ed. Venice 1578; repr. 1967), 3.196: "Nota duas opiones que hodie decisae sunt, an in baptismo paruulorum imprimantur uirtutes, et ultima opinio est quod imprimantur et cardinales et morales quoad habitum, licet non quoad usum. . . ." Cf. Hostiensis at 3.42.3 (ed. Venice 1581; repr. 1965), 3.168.

47. This was then included as the first text in the *Clementines* 1.1 ed. E. Friedberg, *Corpus iuris canonici* (Leipzig 1881), 2.1134.

48. "De primo nota: sine fidei habitu nulli est salus; unde etiam eam paruuli baptizati recipiunt fidei habitum, licet actu fide careant . . . ; baptismus dicitur sacramentum fidei, quia et in fide ecclesiae confertur et fidei habitum confert." Norbert Brieskorn, *Die Summa Confessorum des Johannes von Erfurt* (Frankfurt 1980), p. 841.

49. Thus the jurist Stephen of Tournai: "Sunt etiam qui dicunt fideles dici paruulos, quia fidem habent in habitu, licet non in usu, ut rationem et huiusmodi." J. F. Schulte, *Die Summa des Stephanus Tornacensis über das Decretum Gratiani* (Giessen 1891), p. 278.

50. "Et sic paruuli credunt, quia habent fidem habitualem sicut dormiens uisum." Cited from Vatican Codex Ottobon. lat. 294 f. 69v in Landgraf (n. 18 above), p. 324 n. 84.

51. "Queritur quomodo paruuli qui consentire non possunt obligantur . . . et tenentur astricti ad seruandas omnes sponsiones factas ante baptismum.

. . . Respons.: speciale est in baptismo ut aliquis ignorans obligetur per alium, et est ratio specialitatis, quia per hoc fit melior conditio baptizati cum a potestate et uinculo diaboli liberatur, et sic necesse habet hoc habet ratum. . . ." Hostiensis, *Summa* (ed. Lyon 1537; repr. 1962), p. 186A.

52. "Votum necessitatis dicitur illud quod quis promittit in baptismo, ut abrenunciare satane et pompis eius, tenere fidem, seruare decalogum, et alia sine quibus salus non est. . . . unde cum homo peccat post baptismum dupliciter reus est, et quia peccat in eo quod committit et quia uotum preuaricatur. . . ." Hostiensis, *Summa* (ed. Lyon 1537; repr. 1962), p. 176.

53. "Sed illi qui a gremio ecclesiae diuerterunt, ut heretici et schismatici, ad eam sunt redire cogendi, cum sint de foro ecclesiae, etiam per potentiam secularem . . ." at *Decretales* 3.42.3 (ed. Frankfurt 1570; repr. 1968), p. 456.

54. Thus Antonius da Butrio, commenting on *Maiores* (= Decretales 3.42.3): "Nota hic quod non baptizati non sunt sub iurisdictione ecclesiae, et quod characterem baptismi habentes submittuntur iurisdictioni ecclesiae quoad hoc, ut assumptam fidem seruare compellantur." *Commentarii* (ed. Venice 1578; repr. 1967), 5.196A. For Duns Scotus see n. 42 above.

55. Biel, *Collectorium* (ed. Werbeck-Hofmann), 4.247.

56. Thus Hostiensis on "*Ex litteris*" (= *Decretales* 3.33.2): ". . . et de istis intelligas quod inuiti non coguntur baptizari. . . . Et est hoc contra illos qui furantur paruulos Iudaeorum doli capaces, et postea inducunt ipsos ad baptismum recipiendum, quamuis meo iudicio pie agant et baptismus teneat. . . ." *Commentaria* (ed. Venice 1581; repr. 1965), 3.124. In fairness to the cardinal the teaching of his *Summa*, summarizing standard church teaching, should also be cited: ". . . non coguntur [to be baptized] nam Christi fidem habere non creditur qui ad fidem Christi cogitur precise uenire. . . . Sunt igitur inducendi ad fidem suscipiendam autoritatibus et rationibus blandimentis potius quam asperitatibus, quia coacta servitia non placent Deo. . . . Inducatur ergo beneficentie consolatione vel informatione doctrine ad colendum Deum . . ." (ed. Lyons 1537; repr. 1962), p. 236.

57. "Qui autem iampridem ad Christianitatem coacti sunt . . . , quia iam constat eos sacramentis divinis associatos et baptismi gratiam suscepisse et crismate unctos esse et corporis Domini extitisse participes, oportet ut fidem quam ui vel necessitate susceperint tenere cogantur, ne nomen Domini blasphemetur et fides quam susceperunt uilis ac contemptibilis habeatur." Gratian, *Decretum* d. 45 c. 5 (ed. Friedberg), 1.161–62.

58. Hostiensis, *Summa* (ed. Lyons 1537; repr. 1962), p. 236: ". . . tamen si semel ad fidem peruenerint, idest baptizati fuerint, etiam per iocum, coguntur precise fidem seruare. . . ." Fourteenth-century commentators, such as Anthonius da Butrio and Johannes Andreae, repeated the teaching of Hostiensis but with somewhat less conviction: "Compelli non debet; si compellatur absolute, characterem non recipit. Si compellatur conditionaliter, characterem recipit baptismi, et compellendi sunt ut fidem sic sumptam obseruant." Anthonius de Butrio at *X* 5.6.9 (ed. Venice 1578; repr. 1967), 5.39.

59. Peter the Chanter, *Summa de sacramentis et animae consiliis* 3.259 (c. 21): ed. Jean-Albert Dugauquier, Analecta Mediaevalia Namurcensia 16 (Louvain-Lille 1963), p. 268.

60. *Petri Venerabilis contra Petrobrusianos hereticos,* ed. James Fearns, Corpus Christianorum, Continuatio Mediaevalis 10 (Turnhout 1968), pp. 4, 12–55.

61. Thus the Passauer Anonymous: "De baptismo errant quidam dicentes paruulos non saluari per baptismum; Mt [Mark 16:16]: *Qui crediderit et baptizatus fuerit, salvus erit.* Sed infans non credit, ergo non saluatur. Solucio: Infans baptizatur in fide parentum." See Alexander Patchovsky and Kurt-Victor Selge, *Quellen zur Geschichte der Waldenser,* Texte zur Kirchen-und Theologiegeschichte 18 (Gütersloh 1973), p. 81.

62. Some of that literature reviewed in Landgraf (n. 18 above).

63. ". . . ut cum pene omnes nostre etatis uel memorie in infantia baptizati sint et Christianum nomen assumpserint ac congruo tempore in diuersis gradibus ecclesie prelati sint, nullus episcoporum episcopus, nullus presbiter, nullus diaconus, nullus clericus, nullus monachus, nullus, ut sic loquar, ex tam innumerabili numero saltem Christianus fuerit? . . . Quod si ita est, quanta absurditas sequatur manifestum est. Cum enim tota Gallia, Hyspania, Germania, Italia ac universa Europa a trecentis vel quingentis fere annis nullum nisi in infantia baptizatum habuerit, nullum Christianum habuit. Si nullum Christianum habuit, nec ecclesiam habuit. Si ecclesiam non habuit, nec Christum habuit. Si Christum non habuit, certum est quia periit. Perierunt igitur omnes patres nostri, quia in infantia non potuerunt Christi baptismate baptizari. Peribimus et nos qui uiuimus, qui residui sumus, nisi post Christi etiam Henrici baptismate baptizemur." *Contra Petrobrusianos* (n. 60 above), pp. 13–14.

64. "Wir bekennen aber, das unter dem Bapstum viel Christliches gutes, ia alles Christlich gut sey, Und auch daselbs herkomen sey an uns, Nemlich wer bekennen, das ym Bapstum die rechte heilige schrifft sey, rechte tauffe. . . ." *Von der Widertaufe an zwei Pfarrherrn* in *D. Martin Luthers Werke* (Weimar 1909), 26.147.

65. *De captivitate Babylonica ecclesiae* in *Luthers Werke* (n. 64 above), 6.526.

66. "Aufs vierde, Wo die erste odder kinder tauffe nicht recht were, so wurde folgen, das lenger denn inn tausent iaren keine tauffe und keine Christenheit gewesen were, welchs ist unmuglich, Denn damit wurde der artickel des glawbens falsche sein: Ich glewbe eine heilige Christliche kirche. Denn uber tausent iar fast eitel kinder tauffe gewest ist, Ist die tauffe nu unrecht, so ist die Christenheit so lange zeit on tauffe gewest, ist sie on tauffe gewest, so ist sie nicht Christenheit gewest. . . . Aber weil ynn aller welt durch die gantze Christenheit die kinder tauffe gangen ist bis auff diesen tag, ist kein schein nicht da, das sie unrecht sey, Sondern ein starck anzeigung, das sie recht sey" in *Luthers Werke* (n. 64 above), 26.168–69.

67. "Denn alle welt weis und sihet, das man yderman teuffet, weil er

ein kind ist." "Darumb greiffen sie an, das niemand angriffen hat, auff das sie etwa die ersten sein und ehre einlegen mugen." Ibid., pp. 153, 148.

68. This was no small change, in theological terms, and I do not wish to minimize it. Thus Luther: "At nostra et patrum [Old Testament] signa seu sacramenta habent annexum verbum promissionis, quod fidem exigit et nullo opere alio impleri potest: ideo sunt signa seu sacramenta iustificationis, quia sunt sacramenta iustificantis fidei et non operis, unde et tota eorum efficatia est ipsa fides, non operatio. Qui enim eis credit, is implet ea, etiam si nihil operetur. Inde proverbium illud 'Non sacramentum sed fides sacramenti iustificat.'" *De captivitate Babylonica ecclesiae* in *Luthers Werke* (n. 64 above), 6.532.

69. A good introduction now, with bibliography and texts, by Karl-Heinz zur Mühlen, "Luthers Tauflehre und seine Stellung zu den Taufern," in Helmar Junghans, ed., *Leben und Werk Martin Luthers von 1526 bis 1546, Festgabe zu seinem 500. Geburtstag* (Göttingen 1983), pp. 119–38.

70. "Siquidem Dei signum puero communicatum, velut impresso sigillo, promissionem pio parenti datam confirmat ac ratum esse declarat. . . ." ". . . atque inde se ad certiorem animare fiduciam, quod praesenti oculo foedus Domini filiorum suorum corporibus insculptum cernunt." *Institutio christianae religionis 1559* 4.16.9: ed. P. Barth-G. Niesel, *Johannis Calvini Opera Selecta* (Munich 1936), 5.312, 313.

71. "Hic dico, quod omnes dicunt, fide aliena paruulis succurri, illorum qui offerunt eos. . . . ita per orationem ecclesiae offerentis et credentis, cui omnia possibilia sunt, et paruulus fide infusa mutatur, mundatur et renovatur." *De captivitate Babylonica ecclesiae* in *Luthers Werke* (n. 64 above), 6.538.

72. "Dicimus ergo, quum circuncisionem poentitentiae fideique sacramentum infantibus Deus communicarit, non uideri absurdum si nunc Baptismi participes fiant." *Institutio* 4.16.20 (ed. Barth-Niesel, as n. 70 above), p. 324.

73. "Von der Taufe, von der Wiedertaufe, und von der Kindertaufe," *Huldreich Zwinglis Sämtliche Werke*, Corpus Reformatorum 91 (Leipzig 1927), 4.228. See in general W. P. Stephens, *The Theology of Huldrych Zwingli* (Oxford 1986), pp. 194–217.

74. *Huldreich Zwinglis Sämtliche Werke*, 4.332.

75. "Ut suam fidem unusquisque opere sequatur." Ghaerbald II.2: *MGH Capitularia episcoporum* 1.26.

76. *MGH Cap.* p. 53.

77. "Nunc autem etsi fidei robore opus est, sine qua impossibile est placere Deo [see Heb. 11:6], quanta utilitas consistit in moribus et operibus, *cum fides sine operibus mortua sit* [James 2:20]! Et quidem quanta fuit in illis diebus necessitas exemplis et firmitate fidei quam multi morte sua testati sunt, tantum in his diebus malis, in hoc seculo nequam, credimus expedire ad salutem opera fidei operantis per dilectionem [see Gal. 5:6], quando multi non

uerbis sed moribus fidei contradicunt et confitentes Christum factis negant [see Titus 1:16]." R. Foreville-G. Keir, *The Book of St. Gilbert* (Oxford 1987), p. 4. Just as this passage managed to work in all the key Scripture texts, so the entire paragraph—too long to cite here—is intriguing for our theme.

78. This noted as well by Schmitt (n. 1 above), p. 338.

79. All subsequent discussions have this as their point of departure: "Fides igitur quam daemones et falsi christiani habent qualitas mentis est, sed informis quia sine caritate est. Nam et malos fidem habere cum tamen caritate careant. . . . Si vero quaeritur utrum illa informis qualitas, qua malus christianus uniuersa credit quae bonus christianus, accedente caritate remaneat et fiat uirtus, an ipsa eliminetur et alia qualitas succedat quae uirtus sit, utrumlibet sine periculo dici potest. Mihi tamen uidetur quod illa qualitas quae prius erat remaneat, et accessu caritatis uirtus fiat." *Sent.* 3.23.4 (5), ed. Brady, 2.144.

80. Basic orientation to the first stage of discussion in Georg Engelhardt, *Die Entwicklung der dogmatischen Glaubenspsychologie in der mittelalterlichen Scholastik vom Abaelardstreit (um 1140) bis zu Philipp dem Kanzler (gest. 1236)*, Beiträge zur Geschichte der Philosophie und Theologie des Mittelalters 30 (Münster 1933).

81. *Comm. in Sent.* 3.23 q. 2 (ed. *Opera Omnia*, Tournai 1904), 23. 408–12.

82. "Circa esse fidei informis est considerare eius habitum et usum et defectum. Dixerunt ergo quidam quod adueniente fide formata, tollitur informis totaliter secundum habitum, quia gratia secum affert omnes habitus uirtutum, et impossibile est in eodem esse duos habitus eiusdem speciei. Alii dixerunt quod manet secundum habitum, tollitur secundum actum; non tamen superfluus est habitus, quia disponit ad fidem formatam, et illa per peccatum perdita illuminat ad credendum. Alii dicunt, et est haec opinio communis, quod manet et secundum habitum et secundum actum, sed tollitur secundum defectum. Cum enim ille defectus non sit de substantia eius, non corrumpitur eius substantia per illud quod remouet defectum illum." *Comm. in Sent.* III. 23 q. 6 a. 4 (ed. Toulouse 1652; repr. 1964), 3.181.

83. "Respondeo quod eadem fides in numero potest esse formata et informis temporibus diuersis. In fide enim informi duo sunt, scilicet essentia illius habitus et informitas eius, quae ad eius essentiam non pertinet. Nec est inseparabile accidens illius: Ratione primi non repugnat charitati sed ad eam disponit, sed ratione ipsius informitatis charitati repugnat. Et ideo cum charitas infunditur poenitenti, tollitur informitas praeexistentis fidei, et formatur ipsa fidei essentia, et sic illa eadem essentia fidei in numero, quae ante erat informis, potest fit formata." *Comm. in Sent.* III.23 a. 5 q. 3 (ed. Brixen 1571, repr. 1963), 3.250–51.

84. Numerous texts on this subject were assembled by Landgraf, "Glaube und Werk," in his *Dogmengeschichte der Frühscholastik* (Regensburg 1953), pp. 7–40.

85. "De primo nota: sine fidei . . . actu non est salus adultis discretionem habentibus, nam ubi fidei fundamentum non est, nullius boni operis sequitur aedificium." Brieskorn (n. 48 above), p. 841.

86. "*Ex fide in fidem,* idest, ex fide informi procedendo ad fidem formatam. Licet enim sit idem habitus, tamen dicitur informis sine caritate existens, et superueniente caritate formatur, quia per hoc actus eius efficitur meritorius uite beate, et talis fides formata uiuificat et iustificat perfecte." Quoted here from Heinrich Denifle, *Die abendländischen Schriftausleger bis Luther über Iustitia Dei (Rom. 1:17) und Iustificatio* (Mainz 1905), p. 190, reappearing in texts quoted on pp. 261, 262, 269. On p. 262 an anonymous commentator explains that this latter justifying faith ". . . fideles facit et uere christianos. Fides vero informis, que sociam non habet caritatem, non uiuificat, que est in demonibus et malis christianis."

87. "Species fidei duae sunt: una est formata, quam habet boni et sancti; est et informis, quam habent mali, etiam demones et infideles et existentes in mortali peccato. Et fides istorum caret forma, quia non habent sinceram fidem. . . . Prima est uirtus, a qua dicuntur fideles quicumque baptizantur quousque incidant in mortali. . . . Ideo dicitur fides uera est uirtus quam charitas concomitatur. . . ." *Comm. in Decretales* prologue to 1.1.1 (ed. Venice 1581; repr. 1965), p. 4A.

88. "Item uidetur quod etiam laici quibus Deus dat talentum subtilis ingenii, quod melius faciunt si suum ingenium impendant in cognitione praedictorum, quamuis non uideatur quod peccant etiamsi eis non intendant. Videtur autem eis sufficere quod talenta sibi credita non abscondant in terra, idest in terrenis, sed bonis operibus insistunt." *Comm. in Decretales* ad 1.1.1 (ed. Frankfurt 1570; repr. 1968), p. 2.

89. Cajetan, ad *Summa* 1–2 q. 4 a. 4 (Leonine edition), 8.48, "et de formata informis, cum existens in caritate labitur in peccatum mortale furti vel homicidii manens fidelis."

90. See Nikolaus M. Häring, *Die Zwettler Summe* c. 108, Beiträge zur Geschichte der Philosophie und Theologie des Mittelalters, N.F. 15 (Münster 1977), pp. 158–59.

91. My paraphrase of *D. Martin Luthers Werke* (Weimar 1914), 40/2.34–36, where there is both the recorded lecture form and the smoother published version.

92. This aspect has received most attention recently; see now Gy (n. 15 above) and Schmitt (n. 1 above). Further references in F. W. Oediger, *Über die Bildung der Geistlichen im späten Mittelalter* (Leiden-Cologne 1953), pp. 51–52, in a chapter entitled "Das notwendige Wissen." For evidence of the expected distance between the two groups, see for instance nn. 88 and 123.

93. See, for instance, Gerald Strauss, *Luther's House of Learning: Indoctrination of the Young in the German Reformation* (Baltimore 1978), and Jean Delumeau, *Le catholicisme entre Luther et Voltaire* (Paris 1971). Strauss's pessi-

mistic reading of the visitation records has sparked a debate; compare James Kittelson, "Successes and Failures in the German Reformation: The Report from Strasbourg," *Archive for Reformation History* 73 (1982): 153–75.

94. This had become a routine pronouncement already in the early Middle Ages, though at that time the connection to baptismal catechesis was not yet completely forgotten; see the references in Jaroslav Pelikan, *The Growth of Medieval Theology* (Chicago 1978), p. 12. Just one example, taken from Pirmin of Reichenau's *Scarapsus* c. 32 (early eighth century): "Simbolum et orationem dominicam et ipsi tenite, et filios vel filias vestras docete ut et ipsi teneant. Filiolus, quos in baptismo excepistis, scitote uos fideiussores pro eis apud deum extetisse, et ideo eos docete semper et castigate et corripite, et illos omnes subditus vestros ut subrii et caste et iuste uiuant sepius admonete adque corregite." Ursmar Engelmann, *Der heilige Pirmin und sein Pastoralbüchlein* (Sigmaringen 1976), p. 76.

95. "Primitus ergo, quae christianae legi aduersa sunt, ea proponimus, scilicet qui orationem dominicam et symbolum fidei christianitatis memoriter non tenent neque didicere uolunt, eos notate et ad praesentiam nostram ueniant, seu maiores seu minores siue nobiles siue ignobiles, omnes generaliter ante nos ueniant et dicant orationem dominicam et symbolum apostolorum, ut catholicae fidei plenitudo continetur, quia *impossibile est sine fide placere deo* (Heb. 11:6)." *MGH Capitula episcoporum*, 1.26. The Carolingian evidence assembled and discussed in Lynch (n. 6 above), pp. 305–32.

96. "Ut si patrini vel matrinae, qui infantes de fonte suscipiunt sive masculos sive feminas, si ipsum symbolum et orationem dominicam sciunt, et filios et filias suas spiritales, quos et quas de fonte susceperunt, pleniter instructos habeant de fide, de qua pro eis fideiussores exstiterint." *MGH Capitula episcoporum*, 1.26. For Theodulf's statute and the godparents as guarantors of the faith, see nn. 22 and 23 above.

97. "Symbolum, quod est signaculum fidei, et orationem dominicam discere semper ammoneant sacerdotes populum Christianum, uolumusque ut disciplinam condignam habeant qui haec discere neglegunt siue in ieiunio sive in alia castigatione. Propterea dignum est ut filios suos donent ad scolam, siue ad monasteria siue foras presbyteris, ut fidem catholicam recte discant et orationem dominicam ut domi alios edocere ualeant. Qui vero aliter non potuerit vel in sua lingua hoc discat." Concilium Moguntinense A. 813 c. 45: *MGH Leges* 3.2.1.271–72.

98. "Exhortentur populum semper presbyteri ad dicendam dominicam orationem et *Credo in Deum* et *Salutationem Beate Virginis*." Odette Pontal, ed., *Les statuts synodaux français* (Paris 1971), p. 74. The baptismal section says nothing about this point, also not about sponsors; this appears among the general admonitions.

99. "Quia quilibet christianus adultus dominicam orationem, scilicet Pater noster, et simbolum apostolorum, scilicet Credo in deum, scire debet,

precipimus quod quilibet sacerdos parochianos suos ut hec addiscant studeat ammonere." Canterbury I.32: ed. F. M. Powicke-C. R. Cheney, *Councils and Synods* (Oxford 1964), II.31.

100. "Cum per ministerium (nostrum) ecclesiastica sacramenta tractari et dispensari debeant, necessaria est uobis, filii karissimi [the assembled diocesan clergy], fidei catholice agnitio et professio; quia sine fide impossibile est placere deo, et sicut corpus sine spiritu mortuum est, ita fides sine operibus mortua est [see James 2:20]. Propterea uobis precipimus quod bene uiuendo fidem rectam teneatis, parochianos uestros in articulis fidei, sine qua non est salus, sepius instruentes. Quod ut melius et expeditius fiat a uobis, districte archidiaconis iniungimus quod in capitulis suis expositionem fidei catholice in generali concilio promulgatam sane et simplicibus uerbis instruant et eis illam expositionem frequenter domestico ydiomate sane inculcent. . . ." Salisbury I.3: ed. Powicke-Cheney II.61.

101. "Exhortentur sepius sacerdotes parochianos suos ad discendum simbolum et dominicam orationem et salutationem beate Marie [this borrowed from Paris, as n. 98 above]. Pueros quoque frequenter conuocent et unum vel duos instruant vel instrui faciant in predictis. Et quia parentes circa huiusmodi sunt periculose negligentes, moneantur ut pueros et familiam suam, prout deus eis inspiraverit, instruant in predictis." Salisbury I.5: Powicke-Cheney II.61.

102. From a *Sermo ad pueros et adulescentes:* "Valde sunt necessaria pueris et adolescentibus qui habiles sunt et ydonei ad suscipiendam doctrine eruditionem, sicut cera mollis et tenera facile suscipit sigilii impression. Sed pauci sunt aut nulli qui predicent illis et frangant eis panem doctrine." Cited from manuscript in Schmitt (n. 1 above) 347 n. 35.

103. "Et oultre dist que sa mere luy apprint le *Pater Noster, Ave Maria,* et *Credo,* et que aultre personne que sadicte mere ne luy appris sa creance." *Minute française des interrogatoires de Jeanne la Pucelle,* ed. P. Concoeur (Melun 1952), p. 87. See also *Concilium Tridentinum* 5.1.30, and the careful commentary by Gy (n. 15 above), pp. 567–68.

104. Schmitt (n. 1 above), pp. 350 ff.

105. "Item volumus et statuimus quod in singulis predicacionibus ad populum per predicatores 'Oracio dominica' cum 'Symbolo' exponantur et verbis wlgaribus eis pronunccientur, cum 'Salutacione angelica,' tempore opportuno. . . ." followed by versions of the three texts in Germanic and Slavic forms. Jakub Sawicki, *Concilia Poloniae* (Warsaw 1963), 10.362.

106. "Hoc idcirco commemoramus quia agnouimus quosdam esse minus discretos qui humane possibilitatis mensuram nesciunt, quia suam passibilitatem non attendunt. Et si attendunt, maiori stultitia existimant hoc omnes esse debere, quo se prae ceteris uident amplius aliquid accepisse. Affirmant fidelem nulla ratione esse dicendum qui non magna quaedam et multa et sublimia fidei sacramenta agnoverit, et de maiestate creatoris et de humilitate Salvatoris

quorundam disputationem, profunditatem, rerum gestarum seriem memoria comprehenderit. Ipsam quoque divinitatis naturam rudibus animis, et uix ad ea quae uident sufficientibus, explicandam et corpoream ab incorporea natura subtili quadam consideratione proponunt discernendam." *De sacramentis* 1.10.6: *PL* 176.335–36.

107. "Et beatificandam putant hi [new masters?] fidem ueram id multitudine cognitionis potius quam in magnitudine deuotionis, cum pietas diuina non attendat quanta cognitione credatur sed magis quanta deuotione id quod creditur diligatur." Ibid.

108. "Quanti hodieque in populo Christiano vitae aeternae seculique futuri, quod indubitanter credunt et sperant et ardenter desiderant, formam tamen ac statum ne cogitare quidem vel tenuiter norunt. . . ." *De sacramentis* 1.10.6: *PL* 176.338.

109. "Velata, ut simplicibus quibus revelatum erat, ea esse credenda quae credebant illi maiores et docebant, sed eorum distinctionem apertam non habebant. Sicut et in ecclesia aliqui minus capaces sunt, qui articulos Symboli distinguere et assignare non ualent, omnia tamen credunt quae in Symbolo continentur. Credunt enim que ignorant, habentes fidem uelatam in mysterio. Ita et tunc minus capaces, ex revelatione sibi facta, maioribus credendo inhaerebant, quibus fidem suam quasi committebant." *Sententiae* 3.25.2 (ed. Brady, 1981), 2.155. The most striking part of the distinction appears to echo Jesus' remark to the Samaritan woman (John 4:22): "Vos adoratis quod nescitis; nos adoramus quod scimus."

110. "Alii, quibus magis assentimur, dicunt eos fidem Christi uelatam in mysterio habuisse, et quod alii quibus revelatio erat facta sciebant et credebant, hoc isti, etsi nescirent, credebant. . . . sicut hodie in Ecclesia multi simplices, etsi ita distincte nesciant Trinitatem assignare, credunt tamen, quia in fide et humilitate adhaerent illis qui hoc et faciunt et credunt." *PL* 171.1072.

111. "Si hoc solum credentes gentiles, quod creator unus esset et singulis pro eorum actibus retribueret, satis esset illis." *PL* 153.552.

112. "Et uere sine fide aliquis non potest placere, quia nec potest accedere. . . . Et notandum quod sine hac fide nemo unquam potuit saluari. Haec tamen fides non sufficit ad salutem." *PL* 192.491.

113. Ad Hebrews 11:6: *S. Thomae Aquinatis in omnes S. Pauli apostoli epistolas Commentaria* (Turin 1929), 2.411–12.

114. "Sine horum duorum fide nemo adultus unquam saluari potuit. Nec sufficit fides ista, sed alia multa credere est necesse. Forsitan tamen sufficit ante legem scriptam et item sub lege quantum ad gentiles, quibus sola lex naturalis data erat, nec obligabantur ad legem mosaicam, dummodo implicitam habuerint fidem de adventu incarnationeque Christi. Qui enim credit quod Deus remunerator est, credit providentiam Dei, et per consequens credit modum humanae salvationis, saltem implicite." *Dionysii Cartusiani Opera Omnia* 13.516.

115. "Habet igitur hoc primum in se christianitas, quod religione utitur commune quidem cum multis, non tamen cum omnibus. Impii enim et
quos *athéous* dicimus hoc limite arcentur. Religio autem nulla sine duobus illis
quae ad Hebraeos apostolus commemorat, ut credatur esse Deus, deinde re-
munerari eos, qui ipsi placere studeant." Hugo Grotius, *Meletius sive de iis quae
inter christianos conveniunt epistola,* ed. Guillaume H. M. Posthumus Meyjes
(Leiden 1988), p. 77.

116. That has never been done, except rather cursorily by R.-M. Schultes,
*Fides implicita: Geschichte der Lehre von der Fides implicita und explicita in der
katholischen Theologie* (Regensburg 1920).

117. "De primo, inquid, articulo fuit alia opinio antiquorum [fathers
or masters] et alia Magistri [Lombard]. Fuit enim trita antiquorum quod an-
tiquis ante legem sufficiebant pauciora credere quam modernis. Sufficiebat enim
credere unum Deum esse creatorem omnium, remuneratorem omnium speran-
tium in se. Non enim uisum est eis, quod pastores educati in montibus haberent
aliquam noticiam articulorum. Magistro uisum est quia omnes articulos, scilicet
duodecim in simbolo expressos, tenebantur credere et de omnibus aliquam
noticiam habere. Et adherebat huic verbo: 'Hec est fides catholica, quam nisi
quisque fide firmiter crediderit, saluus esse non potest,' quia *Quicumque uult*
habebant pro simbolo. Cum querebatur ab eo quam noticiam omnium articulorum poterant habere simplices uel pastores in montibus educati, dicebat quia
eamdem quam et discreti, licet forte sub aliis idiomatibus." I. Brady, "Peter
Manducator and the Oral Teachings of Peter Lombard," *Antonianum* 41 (1966):
475. The word 'language' in my paraphrase captures the same ambiguity as
the word 'idiomatibus,' that is, a reference either to the vernacular or to another way of putting things. It is evident that here, as in Lombard's *Sentences,*
the text concerns the veiled faith at once of the "ancients" and of the "modern
simple"; later commentators used the same analogy but generally distinguished
more clearly between the two types.

118. "De christianis adultis et discretis queritur si teneantur credere
duodecim articulos. Ad hoc dicimus quod laici discreti et adulti, idest non
fatui, tenentur duodecim credere implicite, non tamen sicut theologus explicite.
Magister [?] tamen dicebat simplici, ut agricole, sufficere aliquos de articulis
credere et nullos discredere, et credere ecclesiam bene credere, etiam si instrua-
tur paratus sit credere. Nos autem dicimus quod quilibet adultus et discretus
tenetur omnes credere, precipue cum secundum ecclesie consuetudinem si baptizetur adultus proponuntur ei omnes articuli, cum infans, proponuntur simili-
ter et respondent patrini pro eo, ipsum puerum crediturum eos cum peruenerit
ad annos discretionis et patrinus tenetur tunc eum docere. . . . et fides et fidei
cognitio habuit progressum; unde ad plura tenentur moderni quam qui fuerunt
ante legem et sub lege." G. Raynaud de Lage, "Deux questions sur la foi, in-
spirées d'Alain de Lille," *Archives d'histoire doctrinale et littéraire du moyen âge*
14 (1943): 331–32.

119. "Alii uero simpliciores credebant ista sub uelamine, fidem haben-

tes uelatam sicut est etiam hodie; quia quidam bestiales homines sunt, qui non sciunt distinguere articulos fidei nec etiam nominare, qui tamen saluantur in fide maiorum ecclesiae." Peter of Poitiers, *Sententiarum Libri Quinque* 3.22: *PL* 211.1093.

120. "Quilibet tamen habens usum rationis tenetur pro aliquando ad aliquem actum explicitum et maxime ad illa quae sunt grossa ad capiendum, sicut quod Christus natus est et passus et alia quae pertinent ad redemptionem. Sic igitur omnes tenentur ad aliquem actum explicitum pro aliquando et ad alios in generali, ut scilicet credat quod ecclesia credit. Sed ad omnia credenda explicite tenentur maiores in ecclesia, qui praeficiuntur aliis, et tenentur alios in fide instruere uerbo ueritatis et exemplo honestatis . . . aliter cito deficeret fides simplicium." Scotus, *In Sent.* 3.25.1 (ed. Lyons 1639; repr. 1968), 7.499.

121. Thus in an early and clear statement of it by William of Auxerre: "Est ergo sensus, quod prelati debent instruere simplices et simplices debent inniti fidei ipsorum, quia sufficit simplicibus si credunt aliquos articulos fidei explicite et alios implicite. Sed prelati tenentur credere omnes explicite. . . . Credere autem implicite est credere in hoc universali: quicquid credit ecclesia, credere esse uerum." William of Auxerre, *Summa Aurea* 3.12.5, Spicilegium Bonaventurianum 18A (Paris-Grottaferrata 1986), p. 212. Compare nn. 120, 122, 124, 125, 130.

122. "Quilibet christianus debet hoc scire, clerici explicite et laici implicite, scilicet credere tenentur sicut tenet ecclesia."

123. *Commentaria* (Frankfurt 1570; repr. 1968), p. 1A–2.

124. I quote the version from Hostiensis's commentary, which (at least in the available versions) is clearer: "Sed quid prodest laicis fides implicita? Respondeo, si talis ratione motus dicat quod pater filio maior est uel quod tres persone sunt res distantes a se adinuicem uel aliquid aliud simile, dummodo sic credat quia credit ecclesiam sic credere, et suam opinionem fidei ecclesie supponat, nec suum defendat errorem sed paratus sit credere sicut credit ecclesia catholica, nunquam hereticus iudicatur. . . ." *Hostiensis Commentaria* (Venice 1581; repr. 1965), 1.5.

125. I give it here as it appears in the early fourteenth century in Anthonius de Butrio: "Licet quis erret in fide, non debet ut hereticus condemnari uel censeri, dum tamen fidem ecclesie suscipere sit paratus uel se illam tenere fateatur." *Commentarii* (Venice 1578; repr. 1967), 1.7A.

126. Bonaventure saw this clearly, and regarded it not as an act of "ideological control" but as a concession, an act of compassion toward the "simple" who could not otherwise be saved: "Item pauci sint, nisi sint bene periti in theologia, qui sciant articulos symbolorum bene distinguere et numerare. Si ergo omnes tenerentur omnes articulos fidei scire distincte et explicite, pauci saluarentur; quod est ualde crudele dicere." Bonaventure, *In Sent.* 3.25.1.3 (ed. Quarrachi 1887), 3.543.

127. This according to Richard of Middleton in commenting upon *Sent*

3:25: "Minores uero, etsi teneantur explicite credere aliquos articulos qui magis sunt necessarii ad dirigendum in finem et qui in ecclesia solemnizantur communiter . . ." (ed. Brixen 1591; repr. Frankfurt 1963), 3.280.

128. Johannes de Breui Coxa, *De fide* 1: in *Opera Gersoni*, ed. du Pin (Antwerp 1706), 1.808 ff., and esp. 813.

129. Ibid. 814.

130. "Credere autem quosdam implicite, quosdam explicite, hoc est fidei ad salutem necessariae; potest enim fidei simplicium sufficere. Ad illos enim tenentur explicite credendos, quos manifestat eis non solum praedicatio sed etiam ecclesiasticus usus et consuetudo: sicut est de unitate et trinitate, quam possunt nosse ex ipso actu consignationis, consignant enim se in nomine patris et filii et spiritus sancti; sicut est de nativitate, passione, resurrectione et peccatorum remissione, quos cognoscere possunt ex ipsis solemnitatibus, quas ecclesia celebrat, et actibus sacerdotum. Ideo ab horum cognitione et notitia nullus ratione utens excipitur; nec ignorantia excusatur, quia non potest esse talis ignorantia sine negligentia et contemptu. Alios etiam articulos non ita manifestos tenentur utique credere implicite. Implicite autem uoco credere, ut in generali credant universaliter omne quod credit sacrosanta mater ecclesia, ita quod in particulari a nullo illorum dissentiant nec aliquem articulorum discredant." Bonaventure, *In Sent.* 3.25.1.3: (ed. Quaracchi 1887), 3.544. This passage was cited repeatedly by later masters on this subject.

131. "Medii autem sunt in ecclesia curati simplices et qui ex officio uel ministerio habent alios docere, ut praedicatores et doctores, et hi tenentur scire explicite quantum pertinent ad suum officium, hoc est articulos quantum ad substantiam eorum. In difficultatibus autem vel haereticorum impugnationibus debent recurrere ad superiores. Infimi autem (ut communis populus) non tenentur explicite credere uel scire nisi quantum eis traditum est ex maiorum doctrina et communi ritu ecclesiae – qui neminem latet nisi ob culpam suam ab hoc impediatur. Puto autem quod pro moderno tempore nullus potest excusari si ignoret articulum trinitatis, incarnationis, resurrectionis, ascensionis, et adventus ad iudicium, cum ex publico ritu ecclesiae et festiuitatum celebri solemmizatione ut uulgata praedicatione omnibus haec innotescant." *In Sent.* 3.25.1 (ed. Venice 1571; repr. 1964), 2.258A.

132. Jean Sire de Joinville, *Histoire de Saint Louis* VIII.45: ed. Natalis de Wailly (Paris 1874), pp. 25–26. See also Lionel J. Friedman, *Text and Iconography for Joinville's Credo* (Cambridge, Mass. 1958).

133. "Respondeo quod scire precepta dei potest capi dupliciter. Primo scire explicite, hoc est scire precepta dei secundum ordinem, enumerare quid eorum sit primum [etc.]. . . . Secundo modo scire implicite, hoc est scire quod hoc est prohibitum in preceptis dei, non concupiscere rem proximi [etc.]. . . . Sed tenetur scire implicite quod hoc est unum de preceptis decalogi. . . . Sed utrum sit quartum vel octauum hoc laycis de necessitate non tenetur scire. . . . Scire tamen precepta dei ad minus implicite est scientia dei, quam quilibet christianus habere debet" (ed. Strassburg 1490), p. 234.

134. ". . . commentum fabricarunt implicitae fidei, quo nomine cras-
sissimam ignorantiam ornantes, miserae plebeculae cum magna pernicie illu-
dunt. Imo (ut verius et apertius dicam quod res est) commentum hoc veram
fidem non modo sepelit, sed penitus destruit." *Institutio christianae religionis
1559* 3.2.2: ed. P. Barth-W. Niesel, *Johannis Calvini Opera Selecta* (Munich
1968), 4.10.

135. ". . . sed definiunt, rite credere qui in sua inscitia stupent, adeoque
sibi indulgent, modo Ecclesiae authoritati et iudicio de rebus incognitis assen-
tiantur. Quasi vero Scriptura passim non doceat cum fide coniunctam esse in-
telligentiam." Ibid. 3.2.3: p. 11.

136. Quoted by Lorna Jane Abray, "The Laity's Religion: Lutheranism
in Sixteenth-Century Strasbourg," in R. Po-chia Hsia, ed., *The German People
and the Reformation* (Ithaca, N.Y. 1988), pp. 228–29.

137. "Uno modo sumitur catholicus pro omni rite baptisato, qui nulli
contrario legi Christi pertinaciter adhaeret, et in ista descriptione tam adulti
credentes legi Christi quam et paruuli baptisati non plus adhaerentes legi Dei
Christi quam sectae Mahometi comprehenduntur. Alio modo, sumitur catholicus pro omni adulto usum rationis habente, catholicam fidem integram et
inuiolatam servante seu tenente. Seruare autem catholicam fidem integram
contingit omnia quae ad fidem pertinent orthodoxam explicite vel implicite
absque dubitatione credendo. . . . Tertio modo sumitur catholicus pro illo qui
dicto modo seruat catholicam fidem ex habitibus acquisitis, mediante habitu
supernaturali; quia proprius actus fidei catholicae est actus causatus ab habitibus infuso et acquisito. . . . Ideo etiam proprie catholicus est, qui habet tales
actus, qui proprie sunt fides." Johannes de Breui Coxa, *De fide*, in *Opera Gersoni*, ed. du Pin (Antwerp 1706), 1.837–38.

138. "Status religionis denominatur a uirtute quadam morali quae dicitur religio, cuius officium seu actus est exhibere debitum cultum et caeremo-
niam, aliqua offerendo uel faciendo ad Dei honorem, ut sacrificia, oblationes,
inclinationes, et huiusmodi. . . . religio sumitur quadrupliciter: Uno modo
solum pro debito cultu ueri Dei quoad fidem, et sic comprehendit totam christianitatem quae exhibet cultum uero Deo. . . . Secundo sumitur religio pro cultu
ueri Dei non solum per fidem, sed etiam per bona opera . . . et sic religio comprehendit uniuersitatem bonorum christianorum. . . . Tertio sumitur pro statu
clericali quia sunt magis dediti cultui diuino. . . . Quarto sumitur strictissime
pro statu illo qui per emissionem professionis subiicit se praelati imperio, totum se dedicans Deo. . . ." Antoninus, *Summa Theologica* 3.19.1 (ed. Verona
1740; repr. 1959), 3.844.

139. Hostiensis, *Summa Aurea* (ed. Lyon 1537; repr. 1962), p. 173A,
and *Commentaria* at 3.31; Johannes Andreae, *Commentaria* at 3.31 (ed. Siena
1581; repr. 1963), 3.148.

2

Bodily Miracles and the Resurrection of the Body in the High Middle Ages

Caroline Walker Bynum

"The body" has been a popular topic recently for historians of Western European culture, especially for what we might call the Berkeley-Princeton school of Peter Brown, Robert Darnton, Natalie Davis, Stephen Greenblatt, Lynn Hunt, Tom Laqueur, and Elaine Pagels, to name a few.[1] Representing the *Annales* school in this country and deeply influenced by Michel Foucault and Clifford Geertz, these historians have meant by "body" the sexual and gendered body, not a raw biological fact but a cultural construct. They have understood this body, constructed by society, as expressing society's understanding of itself; and they have therefore focused on the history of sexual behavior (both of sexual expressiveness and of its renunciation) and on the ways in which conceptions of the individual as body and of society as body mirror each other so intimately as almost to be the same thing.[2]

In the wake of the appearance of a genuinely new historical topic, self-proclaimed avant-garde journals starting up around the country—for example, *Representations* and *Zone*—have rushed to offer special issues on "the body." The German historian Barbara Duden has begun to compile a bibliography of body history.[3] And the literary critic Francis Barker has offered a stunning and deeply problematical interpretation of Western culture periodized by shifts in the concept of body.[4] Displaying her characteristic wit and insight, Natalie Davis played with—and up to—the current trend by entitling her presidential address to the American Historical Association in December 1987: "History's Two Bodies."[5]

Medievalists too have flocked eagerly to the new topic. The best of them (such as Peter Brown, James Brundage, Joan Cadden, and Joyce Salisbury) have understood how deeply imbedded in the history of medicine and theology the subject should be.[6] But some medievalists (like many modern historians) have reduced the history of the body to the history of sexuality or misogyny and have taken the opportunity to giggle pruriently or gasp with horror at the unenlightened centuries before the modern ones.[7]

Although clearly identified with the new topic, this essay is nonetheless intended to argue that there is a different vantage point and a very different kind of material available for writing the history of the body. Medieval stories and sermons did articulate misogyny, to be sure;[8] doctors, lawyers, and theologians did discuss the use and abuse of sex.[9] But for every reference in medieval treatises to the immorality of contraception or to the inappropriateness of certain sexual positions or to the female body as temptation, there are dozens of discussions both of body (especially female body) as manifestation of the divine or demonic and of technical questions generated by the doctrine of the body's resurrection. If we really care about how medieval people experienced incarnation or embodiment, we must look beyond the history of sexuality and explore as well the mass of texts in which they spoke directly about the place of physicality in human nature and in the divine economy. I shall begin such exploration by describing, first, the flowering of somatic miracles in Western Europe in the twelfth and thirteenth centuries and, second, the lively consideration during this same period in theological circles of the doctrine of bodily resurrection.

At least since Huizinga, historians have been aware of the somatic quality of late medieval piety; and recently Ronald Finucane, Benedicta Ward, Giles Constable, Rudolph Bell and Richard Kieckhefer have explored and explicated it for us in various ways.[10] We encounter this bodily quality most strikingly in certain new miracles, never before reported in the sources, which begin to appear in saints' lives and chronicles in the years around 1200.[11] These miracles, all of which involve bodily transformation in response to religious ecstasy or devotion, include miraculous lactation, mystical pregnancy, and other unusual elongations or swellings of the body. Preeminent among them, of course, are stigmata: the wounds of Christ's passion appearing in the believer and, in female adherents although not in male, bleeding periodically at the day or hour of the crucifixion.[12] Moreover, other bodily expressions of religious enthusiasm which were known earlier in Europe seem to have increased markedly in the twelfth and thirteenth centuries, either in incidence or in reporting or (most probably) in both: for example, outbursts of uncontrollable weeping, ecstatic nosebleeds, levitations and catatonic trances, and miraculous fasting.[13]

Both dead and living bodies took on new significance, in ways modern scholars have not always found sympathetic. The cult of relics (that is, the reverencing of pieces of dead holy people) flourished.[14] Relics were stolen, fought over, displayed, translated, and divided into smaller and smaller bits. The form of reliquaries came increasingly to underline the fact that body parts – that is, arms, fingers, skulls, etc. – were contained within. Exudings of oil or other liquids, or even of manna, from corpses, as well as exhalations of sweet smells (literally, the odor of sanctity) were increasingly reported.[15] Pictures were discovered etched on hearts when holy bodies were prepared for burial.[16] By the early modern period, incorruptibility of the whole cadaver or of a part (that is, remaining lifelike, supple, and without decay for decades after burial) was reported for almost every woman proposed for canonization and for a number of men as well.[17]

The graphic physiological processes of living people were also revered. Holy people spit or blew into the mouths of others to effect cures or convey grace.[18] The ill clamored for the bathwater of would-be saints to drink or bathe in and preferred it if these would-be saints washed seldom and therefore left skin and lice floating in the water.[19] Following Francis of Assisi, several Italian saints kissed lepers' sores; Angela of Foligno, Catherine of Siena, and Catherine of Genoa actually ate pus or lice in an effort to incorporate into themselves the misfortune of those whom society defined as the dead – even indeed the putrefying – among the living.[20]

The new somatic quality of piety extended even to the body of God. Although patristic hymns celebrate the Eucharist as comforting food and inebriating drink, scholars agree that there is, in the church of the first six centuries, no evidence of claims to receive Christ sensually.[21] The years around 1200, however, saw a proliferation of miracles in which the consecrated wafer or the contents of the communion chalice were transformed into bleeding flesh or into blood.[22] In the early fifteenth century Colette of Corbie supposedly received a vision of the Christchild as chopped meat on a platter.[23] A number of thirteenth- and fourteenth-century nuns report choking on the wafer when it became honeycomb or flesh in their throats.[24]

Several characteristics of these miraculous events are worth underlining. The first is simply the somatic quality itself. However problematic body was to late medieval Christians, however clearly a locus of temptation and of pain, it was also the place where divine power was met. The second characteristic of such events – which is in fact another way of making the same point – is their disproportionate incidence in women's lives. Since exegetical, philosophical, scientific, and folk traditions hundreds of years old associated the female with the bodily, the fleshly, the unformed, and the male with the spiritual or rational, formal or structural, it is hardly surprising that women were the most extravagant (although not by any means the sole) practitioners of and participants in somatic religiosity.[25]

Third, one should underline the extent to which these miracles and events have to do with extraordinary breaches or exudings and extraordinary closures. Holy women who did not eat also did not menstruate or excrete, or even (according to one early seventeenth-century account) exude sweat or dandruff.[26] After death many saintly bodies did not putrefy or fragment or give off an ordinary odor of corruption. Yet holy bodies, especially female bodies, flowed outwards – that is, breached body boundaries – in extraordinary effluvia: ecstatic nosebleeds and weepings, periodic stigmatic bleedings, mystical lactations, exudings of sweet smells and curative fluids after death. Related to this is a fourth characteristic. The holy bodies so central in late medieval piety are, exactly in their peculiar conjunction of exuding and closure, liminal (that is, transitional) between life and death.[27] Women who live without eating or excreting display death in life; corpses that exude sweet odors or fresh red blood (instead of the sweat of putrefaction), that return to youthful beauty in the grave and remain unfragmented despite the assault of worms, evidence life in death. What both the living (that is, incorruptible) dead and the unchanging (that is, undecaying) living avoid is corruption. I will need to return to these characteristics in a moment. But now I shall turn to another context within which medieval theorists discussed the embodiment of the human person: the doctrine of the resurrection.

The sentence collections and treatises of the twelfth century, like the Sentence commentaries and quodlibetal questions of the thirteenth, explored and debated the resurrection of the body.[28] All theologians assumed both that the soul was immortal and that the bodies of the saved and of the damned would be regenerated at the Last Judgment.[29] These tenets had become firmly imbedded in Christian teaching through the controversies of the second to fifth centuries C.E.[30] Many subsidiary topics were, however, hotly discussed in the high Middle Ages. These may mostly be grouped under three headings: first, the question of identity – that is, in what sense is the resurrected body the same body as the one that lived before? second, the nature of the risen body – that is, what are the characteristics of the flesh that is to be restored to damned

and blessed alike? third, the *dotes* or gifts (dowries) of the glorified body
—that is, what special benefits will the risen bodies of the saved alone
receive?

Some of the problems raised in connection with these topics have
struck modern scholars as extraordinarily odd. In the early twelfth century, for example, teachers at the school of Laon debated whether food
taken in by the body during its lifetime would become part of the body
and rise at the end. The problem was that if food did not become part
of human nature and rise, we would be limited to the very tiny bodies
passed on from Adam; if food did join the body and rise, the resurrection would be, they said, of *boves et oves* (cows and sheep) rather than
of man.[31] Or, to give a second example: theologians throughout the period,
among them Simon of Tournai, Peter of Capua, and Thomas Aquinas,
debated whether Christ's foreskin and blood rose with him—a problem
made pertinent by the presence in Europe of several shrines claiming to possess the holy foreskin and more than several claiming vials
of Christ's blood.[32]

Another widely discussed issue, which has proven particularly offensive to modern sensibilities, was the problem of eaten embryos—a
special case of the problem of cannibalism.[33] If a person ate another
person (so the argument went, at least by the mid-thirteenth century
when most theologians had decided that digested food does become "of
the substance of human nature"), the common matter would rise in the
one to whom it first belonged. The missing matter would be made up
in the second person from what he or she had eaten that was nonhu-
man. But what (asked Aquinas, pushing the issue) about the case of
a man who ate only human embryos who generated a child who ate only
human embryos? If eaten matter rises in the one who had it first, this
child would, said Aquinas, not rise at all. All its matter would rise elsewhere: either in the embryos its father ate (from which its core of human nature, passed on in the semen, was formed) or in the embryos
it ate. And this conclusion, said Aquinas, violates the doctrine of the
resurrection; thus a new position must be formulated on where the common matter will rise.[34]

Yet other questions, focusing this time on the nature of the resurrected body, included: Can we open and close our eyes in the resurrected body?[35] What age and height will we have in that body?[36] Will
bodies—even mutilated and deformed bodies—rise with all their parts?[37]
Will fat and thin people rise with their characteristic shapes? Will giants
rise as giants, dwarves as dwarves?[38] In which sex will a hermaphrodite

be resurrected?[39] Answers to these questions sometimes merely cautioned against prying into the inscrutable. But they sometimes sketched a sophisticated distinction between, on the one hand, personal characteristics such as body shape or sex, which would be preserved for eternity, and, on the other hand, defects of nature such as dwarfism or hermaphroditism, which would be repaired.

In still other controversies, theologians and preachers explored the nature of the glorified bodies of the blessed. Is Christ's resurrected flesh the paradigm for our resurrection? they asked. If so, did Christ's risen body really eat the boiled fish and honeycomb Luke says he shared with his disciples (Luke 24:42–43)? Should we therefore conclude that we, made like him, will eat in heaven? Surely not, they reasoned; for in what sense then would we, subjected to the indignities of digestion, possess the dowry of impassibility?[40]

Or—to give a final example that brings smiles rather than shudders to modern readers—theologians debated whether the gift of *subtilitas* (which some of them understood as *penetrabilitas*) meant that the glorified body could be in the same place at the same time as another body.[41] The conclusion that it could be was, of course, suggested by gospel stories of Christ passing through closed doors after his resurrection. Answers to the question differed, but all took the physics of the issue seriously. Some, such as Bonaventure and Peter of Trabibus, said a glorified body could penetrate a nonglorified body but not a glorified one. Others, such as Augustinus Triumphus, held that even ordinary bodies could be penetrated by glorified ones only by a miracle.[42]

Serious theological consideration of the resurrection of foreskins and fingernails has seemed almost as bizarre and disconcerting to modern scholars as the sort of miracles I discussed above. Thus historians of philosophy and theology have paid little attention to this aspect of medieval eschatology, preferring to study scholastic discussions of the immortality of the soul. Nonetheless, the little-studied theology of resurrection is useful for understanding medieval conceptions of body, for it reflects the same assumptions that come alive in somatic miracles. In the theology of the resurrection as in miracles of bodily transformation, the person is not (as earlier Platonic definition held) a soul using a body and anxious to escape therefrom; rather the person is an entity in which body and soul are tied together so closely that each expresses the condition of the other.[43] As Aquinas said: ". . . soul and body are one being. So when body is disturbed by some corporeal suffering, soul is of necessity disturbed indirectly as a result [*per accidens*]. . . ."[44]

We are all familiar—through the classic accounts of medieval philosophy by Etienne Gilson and Frederick Copleston—with Aquinas's use of the Aristotelian form/matter dichotomy as a way of explaining that bodily resurrection after the Last Judgment is philosophically necessary.[45] According to Aquinas, the soul as substantial form survives the death of the body but the full person does not exist until body (matter) is restored to its form at the end of time. "Anima . . . non est totus homo et anima mea non est ego."[46] What historians of philosophy have not fully realized, however, is that Aquinas's position was deeply problematic.[47] Thus, in rejecting it, his conservative opponents also insisted that body was crucial to person. Thomas's position did make body philosophically necessary, to be sure; but in some sense it telescoped body into form by holding both that soul is enough to account for individual continuity and that soul is the *forma corporeitatis.*[48] In other words, to Aquinas, it is *soul* that accounts for the "what-ness" of body. Thus any matter which soul informs at the end of time will be *its* body.[49] Logically such a position leads to the conclusion, which Durandus of Saint Pourçain actually voiced in the early fourteenth century, that—although body is necessary for personhood—material continuity is not necessary for resurrection.[50] Durandus argued that God can make the body of Peter out of dust that was once the body of Paul.[51]

Those who opposed Thomas, following an older Platonic or Augustinian tradition, can therefore also be seen (although historians have usually not done so) as giving positive significance to body.[52] Indeed, positing a separate *forma corporeitatis* and assuming material continuity in the resurrection, they struggled to give body a greater substantial reality than did Thomas. Henry of Ghent, for example, held to the theory of a separate *forma corporeitatis* so that the gifts of the glorified body could be understood as real changes *of that body,* not merely as a consequence of change in the soul.[53] Bonaventure wrote, in a sermon on the Assumption of the Virgin Mary:

> Her happiness would not be complete unless she [Mary] were there personally [i.e., bodily assumed into heaven]. The person is not the soul; it is a composite. Thus it is established that she must be there as a composite, that is, of soul and body. Otherwise she would not be there [in heaven] in perfect joy; for (as Augustine says) the minds of the saints [before their resurrections] are hindered, because of their natural inclination for their bodies, from being totally borne into God.[54]

Richard of Middleton and Bonaventure even treated the yearning of soul for body after death as a motive for the saints in heaven: the blessed supposedly pray all the harder for us sinners because they will regain their own deeply desired bodies only when the number of the elect is filled up and the Judgment comes.[55] Proposition 17, condemned at Paris in 1277 ("Quod non contingit corpus corruptum redire idem numero, nec idem numero resurget"), states that a resurrected body cannot be numerically the same as a previously decayed one; the formulation of the condemned position makes clear the conviction of conservative theologians such as Tempier that material continuity is necessary for numerical identity and therefore for resurrection.[56]

In fact one can argue that the condemnation in England of the Thomistic theory of the unicity of form, which implies that continuity of soul (form) is enough to account for personal survival, was owing in part to the threat it posed to the importance of body. Critics of Thomas's position saw that unicity of form implied that a cadaver is not the body and, if this is so, then Christ's body did not lie in the tomb in the *triduum*. With this specific controversy in mind, ecclesiastical authorities at Oxford in 1277 condemned explicitly the argument that a dead body is just a body equivocally (that is, that the word "body" in the two phrases "dead body" and "living body" is merely a homonym).[57]

Commitment to a material component in survival seems indeed to have pulled as a counterweight in the development of the philosophical theory that form accounts for identity. Aquinas, Giles of Rome, and Eustachius of Arras, all of whom articulated a formal theory of identity with varying degrees of explicitness, did not themselves use it in their specific discussions of resurrection. Eustachius stated that God created the glorified body from the same dust it contained earlier.[58] Giles worried about how matter from several bodies could be understood to be in one resurrected body and devoted much attention to questions about the resurrection of eaten food and flesh—matters in which he would presumably have had no interest if he had gone over completely to a formal theory of identity.[59] Aquinas assumed continuity of formed matter (i.e., of body), as his discussion of eaten embryos shows. Displaying both the new identity theory and the assumption that matter does in fact continue, Aquinas said, concerning relics: "The dead body of a saint is not identical to that which the saint held during life, on account of its difference of form—viz., the soul; but it is the same by identity of matter, which is destined to be reunited to its form."[60] So, to Aquinas, the body of Saint Peter in the altar is not really the saint because it has the form not of Peter but of Peter's cadaver; but the dust that lies there will—because it is Peter's cadaver—be reassembled to be reformed by Peter's soul at the end of time. There is still, in fact, material continuity in the resurrection.[61]

Thus the crucial question to which scholastic discussion of the resurrected body returned again and again was not: Is body necessary to personhood? Theologians were so certain it was they sometimes wondered whether resurrection might not be "natural." Peter of Capua, for example, suggested that it was a consequence not of divine grace but of the structure of human nature that body returned to soul after the Last Judgment.[62] The crucial theological question was rather: What accounts for the identity of earthly and risen body? what of "me" must rise in order for the risen body to be "me"?

In their answers, theologians discussed resurrection of foreskins, fingernails, and umbilical cords—issues which have seemed jejune, even preposterous, to modern commentators. Nonetheless, if we take such debates seriously, we find that a profound conception of body is adumbrated here—one in which both innate and acquired physical characteristics, including biological sex and even the marks of human suffering, *are* the person. Theologians agreed that human beings rise in two sexes and with the traces not only of martyrdom but of other particularities as well.[63] Although defects will be repaired in glory and woman's sex can, in Aristotelian terms, be seen as a defect, theologians nonetheless asserted that, for reasons they could not fully understand, God's creation was more perfect in two sexes than in one.[64] Women will rise as women. The short will be reassembled with their own stature. Martyrs (and presumably stigmatics) will return with their wounds as shining scars, all suffering gone and all lack made up but the marks of their experience present for all eternity. What is temporary or temporal, according to this view, is not physical distinctiveness or sex but the change we call corruption (or decay or dissolution) of material being.[65] The bodies of the blessed, endowed with the dowries of *agilitas, claritas* (or beauty), *subtilitas,* and *impassibilitas* (freedom from suffering), will lack exactly that potency, that capacity for change, that to Aristotle characterizes matter.[66]

In the quodlibetal debates of the thirteenth-century schools as in the period's startling new miracles, we thus find three basic assumptions at work. First, body is integral to person and expressive of person, so much so that soul without body is not a person at all. Second (and despite the technical development of a formal theory of identity), material continuity is crucial. Down to the end of the thirteenth century, the majority of scholastic philosophers continue to speak as if persons do not survive unless their *same* material bodies survive. Third, the fundamental religious and cultural problem is decay. Since material continuity is essential for survival, the crucial threat is not separation of body and soul but rather destruction of body. And if corruption or fragmentation or division of body (the transition from whole to part) is the central threat, resurrection (the reassemblage of parts into whole) is the central victory. Small wonder then that closure and exuding, wholeness and division, incorruption and decay are the basic poles around which somatic miracles revolve. If God after the final trumpet will reassemble the person so completely that, as the Gospel promises, "not a hair of your head shall perish" (Luke 21:18), we should not be surprised to find society's saintly heroes and heroines fragmenting and reassembling in this life in extraordinary ways.

My suggestion that the same basic assumptions underlie theological discussion of resurrection and pious veneration of somatic miracle is not merely my interpretation of two aspects of medieval culture. Medieval texts themselves make the connection. For example, Guibert of Nogent's treatise on relics from the early twelfth century, Thomas of Cantimpré's "Life of Christina the Astonishing" from the early thirteenth, and James of Voragine's *Golden Legend* from the 1250s or 60s all indulge in extravagant and sometimes gory descriptions of somatic miracles. All three texts interpret such bodily events in the context of resurrection.

Guibert of Nogent's *De pignoribus sanctorum* has usually been lauded by historians as the beginning of scientific hagiography, a sort of precursor of Valla or Erasmus or Mabillon.[67] And it is true that Guibert criticizes credulous veneration of remains simply because miracles happen there. He does insist that relics be properly documented and that miracles be approved by church authorities. But such arguments are far from Guibert's central concern. What disturbs him most deeply is the practice of moving or dividing the bodies of the saints.[68] Fragmentation is, to Guibert, the ultimate insult and scandal; aiding and abetting it by translating and mutilating holy cadavers strikes him as obscene.[69] Thus the late John Benton was closer to an accurate interpretation of Guibert's *De pignoribus* when he wrote of its author's castration complex.[70] What Benton did not see, however, was that the fear of decay and fragmentation was in no way peculiar to Guibert and had indeed profound theological roots.

The occasion for Guibert's *De pignoribus* was the claim of the monks of Saint Médard to possess the tooth of Christ. Against this claim, Guibert's fundamental argument was theological. He expressed horror and outrage at the notion that any part of Christ (tooth, or umbilical cord, or foreskin) could be left behind on earth to suffer decay. Christ's resurrected body is the paradigm for ours, wrote Guibert; if so much as a drop of his blood or a hair of his head is left behind, how shall we believe that we will rise at the sound of the trumpet? The martyrs bear up under excruciating tortures – and Guibert detailed with fascinated horror splittings of fingernails, hangings by genitals, and other unspeakable persecutions – because they know every particle will return at the end.[71] The eucharistic host, fragmented by human teeth and digestive processes yet in every minute crumb the whole body of Christ, is, argued Guibert, the guarantee that wholeness (that is, nonpartibility and nonpassibility) is God's ultimate promise to humankind. So crucial to salvation was wholeness for Guibert that he argued (in an interesting use of rhetorical theory) that synecdoche, *pars pro toto,* must for Christ be true in a way that went beyond ordinary metaphorical usage.[72]

Thomas of Cantimpré's "Life of Christina the Astonishing" is similarly concerned with remarkable bodily events. Not only does his heroine engage in prodigious austerities, for example, jumping into ovens and icy ponds; she also practices a whole range of holy exudings (both stigmata and miraculous lactations) which have curative effects.[73] And Thomas situates these events in a theology of the resurrection. He reports that another Thomas, abbot of Saint Trond, witnessed Christina take up her feet and kiss their bare soles and say to her body (in language clearly drawn from a popular medieval genre, the "debate between body and soul"):

> O most beloved body! Why have I beaten you? Why have I reviled you? Did you not obey me in every good deed I undertook to do with God's help? You have endured the torment and hardships most generously and most patiently which the spirit placed on you. . . . Now, o best and sweetest body, . . . is an end of your hardship, now you will rest in the dust and will sleep for a little and then, at last, when the trumpet blows, you will rise again purified of all corruptibility and you will be joined in eternal happiness with the soul you have had as a companion in the present sadness.[74]

Themes of bodily division and reassemblage, clearly located within a theology of the resurrection, are also found in James of Voragine's *Golden Legend,* by far the most popular compendium in the later Middle Ages for preachers who wished to reach their audiences with racy yet moral tales. Recent studies of the work have underlined the brutality of its accounts and its archaizing obsession with martyrdom, especially with torture and bodily division.[75] The tale of Saint James the Dismembered, who was cut apart finger by finger and toe by toe, is characteristic. But what strikes me about the *Golden Legend* is not so much the sadism as the *denial* of exactly the dismemberment in which the book simultaneously wallows. Of the 153 chapters devoted to saints, at least 75 have dismemberment as a central motif; but there are only one or two references in all the accounts of the martyrs to the fact that being cut apart might hurt.[76] What is underlined repeatedly is the reassembling of the fragmented body for burial or (particularly in the case of virgin women) the victory of intactness over fragmentation.[77] Although sundered limb from limb, female saints are said to be "whole" because they avoid sexual violation;[78] despite frightful methods of execution, the bodies of both male and female martyrs triumph miraculously over disintegration. For example, the story of Saint Margaret, bound on the rack, beaten with sharp instruments until her bones were laid bare, burned with torches, and plunged into water, describes her body as remaining "unscathed."[79] Burned on the pyre, Saint Theodore renders up his soul, but his body is "unharmed by the fire" (*ab igne illaesum*) and perfumes the air with sweet odor; the wife of Saint Adrian journeys a long distance to join her husband's severed hand with his other remains, which have been preserved from burning by a miraculous rainfall; left by the emperor Diocletian to wolves and dogs, the bodies of two martyrs survive "intact" (*intacta*) until the faithful can collect them for burial.[80] James (or a later interpolator) describes as "unharmed" and "unhurt" Sophia's three daughters, who were fried in a skillet, had their breasts torn off, were stretched on the rack and finally beheaded. In contrast, the emperor Hadrian, who presided over the torture of the three young girls, is said to have "withered away, filled with rottenness" (*totus putrefactus*).[81] Whether or not fragmentation or diminution is characterized as significant (or even in fact as occurring) depends not on what happens to the body physically but on the moral standing of the person to whom the bodily events pertain.

Indeed the fact of bodily division is often denied by exactly the account that chronicles it. The words attributed to James the Dismembered, as he loses his toes, are typical: "Go, third toe, to thy companions, and as the grain of wheat bears much fruit, so shalt thou rest with thy fellows unto the last day. . . . Be comforted, little toe, because great and small shall have the same resurrection. A hair of the head shall not perish, and how much less shalt thou, the least of all, be separated from thy fellows?"[82] The message, with its explicit echoes of Luke 21:18 and of the seed metaphor from 1 Corinthians 15:42–44, is clear.[83] Dismemberment is horrible, to be sure; and even more horrifying is rottenness or decay. But in the end none of this is horrible at all. Beheaded and mutilated saints are "whole" and "unharmed." Severed toes are the seeds from which glorified bodies will spring. God's promise is that division shall finally be overcome, that ultimately there is no scattering.[84] As one of the more conservative contemporary theologians might have said: material continuity *is* identity; for us, as for Christ, the whole will rise and every part is in a sense the whole.[85]

Anthropologists tell us that all cultures deal, in ritual and symbol, with putrefaction; all cultures strain to mask and deny the horror of the period between "first death" (the departure of breath or life) and "second death" or mineralization (the reduction of the cadaver to the hard remains—that is, teeth and bones).[86] And certainly we can see such an effort to give meaning to the process of decay in medieval miracles of effluvia and closure. Miracles of exuding make oil, milk, and blood, whether from cadavers or from the living, curative and therefore generative of life; miracles of inedia in life and incorruptibility in the grave assert living bodies to be changeless and cadavers to be without decay. Moreover, theological debate about the survival of hair and fingernails in the resurrection grapples directly with the fragmentation and change we fear in the tomb. But I think we can look beyond sweeping cultural constants for the peculiar attention paid in medieval piety and doctrine to the problem of decay and material fragmentation. The thirteenth century saw an intense anxiety over the partition of bodies—an anxiety that reached a climax in the papal bull *Detestande feritatis* of 1299.

Historians have long been aware of the background to this anxiety: the frenzy for relics that characterized Western Europe from the ninth century on. They have also stressed the growing practice of dividing bodies—a practice which was prohibited until the ninth century, although the prohibition was not always observed.[87] By the thirteenth century it was common for the privileged to own small bits of saints (fingers or bone chips) to wear as talismans and common also for members of royalty or the high nobility to have their own by-no-means-holy bodies divided in death in order to be buried close to several different saints. What has been less emphasized, however, is the continuing ambivalence with which such practices were fraught.

Two generalizations commonly made about the medieval relic cult are misleading: first, that in popular religion people assumed the relic to be the saint[88] and, second, that popular and elite attitudes toward the saints can be clearly distinguished.[89] It is true that Patrick Geary and Lester Little have discovered rituals in which saints are punished or coerced by humiliating their remains.[90] Nonetheless, popular accounts of apparitions as well as theological discussions of relics make it clear that the saints were understood to be *resident* in heaven, or – if hovering around their earthly remains – in no way coterminous with them. Holy remains were venerated or castigated not because they *were* the saint but because they were the saints' *bodies,* pregnant already with the glory they would receive fully only at the resurrection. The twelfth-century abbot Peter the Venerable explained the point thus: ". . . you ought not to feel contempt for the bones of the present martyrs as if they were dry bones but should honor them now full of life as if they were in their future incorruption."[91]

As Peter Brown has argued in another context, the full ambivalence of medieval attitudes toward relics is present at every level of culture.[92] Throughout the Middle Ages, ecclesiastical authorities sought both to encourage and to tame veneration of body parts. The Fourth Lateran Council legislated against "naked" display of relics for money, and historians have debated whether the disapproval was directed primarily toward relic cult, or toward unprotected display, or toward economic motivation.[93] Canonists and theologians in the same period debated (but did not agree about) whether there could be private property in relics and whether wearing of them by private individuals was acceptably devout.[94] When, in 1299, Boniface VIII legislated against the nobility's practice of dividing bodies for burial *ad sanctos,* he included a prohibition of embalming and boiling bodies and in certain circumstances moving and reburying them. But Boniface's *Detestande feritatis* was not reproduced in the next collection of decretals nor was it enforced in the fourteenth century.[95] And the theological discussion that it occasioned in the schools of Paris echoed a contradiction as old as the church fathers. Those who discussed the bull asserted both that bodily division did not matter because God can reassemble fragments from anywhere and that partition of bodies was an "atrocious and inhuman" practice. The Parisian theologian Gervase of Mount-Saint-Eloi, for example, insisted that, although God could reassemble anything, it was better to bury bodies intact so that they were ready for the resurrection.[96] Roger Bacon, whose work on postponing old age had much influence at the papal court, was aware that death had to intervene between this life and the Last Judgment; but he urged that persons here below should prepare their bodies for resurrection by striving for physical as well as moral equilibrium.[97]

Such inconsistent concerns had characterized the theologians of the first centuries C.E. as well.[98] The fourth-century church historian Eusebius reported that the Romans burned and scattered the bodies of the martyrs of Lyons in order to dash Christian hopes of resurrection.[99] Christian apologists such as Minucius Felix delighted in claiming such repressive measures to be useless because divine power can renew even pulverized dust.[100] The early martyr Ignatius of Antioch hurled in the teeth of his persecutors and even of faltering Christians his confidence that Jesus could overcome the dismemberment and physical destruction of his followers.

> [Let me] become [the prey of] the beasts, that by their means I may be accounted worthy of God. I am the wheat of God, and by the teeth of the beasts I shall be ground, that I may be found the pure bread of God. Provoke ye greatly the wild beasts that they may be for me a grave, and may leave nothing of my body, in order that, when I have fallen asleep, I may not be a burden upon anyone. . . . Fire, and the cross, and the beasts that are prepared, cutting off of the limbs, and scattering of the bones, and crushing of the whole body, harsh torments of the devil—let these come upon me, but only let me be accounted worthy of Jesus Christ.[101]

Nevertheless pious Christians took substantial risks in order to collect the martyrs' bones for reassemblage as well as burial; and Eusebius reports that they grieved when they could not return the mutilated pieces of their heroes and heroines to the earth.[102]

At the level of *exempla* and pious story, we find a similar paradox. Caesarius of Heisterbach, in his collection of miracles, tells of visions in which the pious are invited to take bones from tombs; but he also includes a number of cases of relics that protest their division by bleeding or giving off intense heat.[103] Saints' lives from the early thirteenth century imply much hesitation about bodily partition.[104] James of Vitry, hagiographer of Mary of Oignies (d. 1213), promoted Mary's reputation partly in the hope of improving the value of her finger, which he received as a relic at her death. Thomas of Cantimpré, author of the Supplement to Mary's *Vita* (as of the "Life of Christina the Astonishing" discussed above), delighted in recounting miracles performed by parts of female bodies.[105] But Thomas's account of Mary's life shows a woman who resisted as well as participated in fragmentation. Mary in a sense partitioned herself during her lifetime by pulling out a large hunk of her hair to use as a device to cure the sick;[106] she, however, castigated the prior of Oignies for "cruelly" extracting the teeth of a holy cadaver. After her death she supposedly clenched her own teeth when the same prior tried to extract them as relics. But when he humbly begged her pardon, she shook out a few teeth from her jaw for his use. An old French Life of Saint Barbara tells the story of a decapitated head which asks a priest for communion; Saint Barbara, by her power, then reunites the head with its body, although both parts remain lifeless.[107] Such a story clearly suggests that, death aside, fragmentation itself is an evil to be overcome.

Indeed, not only did preachers and ecclesiastical authorities express reservations about the fragmentation of bodies; popular practice moved symbolically to deny that division actually divided. As partition became ever more common, so did claims that holy bodies do not decay and especially claims that parts of holy bodies are whole or incorrupt. Such emphasis on body *parts* as *whole*, on *severed* flesh as *intact*, is an extravagant and extremely literal use of synecdoche and paradox, as I suggested in discussing the *Golden Legend;* yet we find such extravagance over and over again in thirteenth- and fourteenth-century hagiography. Stories proliferate in which parts of bodies remain incorrupt after burial because of their holy possessor's specific deeds or characteristics. Caesarius of Heisterbach, for example, told of a scribe whose hand remained without decay after death; hagiographers made similar claims for Thomas Aquinas.[108] Incorruption or miraculous reassemblage (sometimes seen in the early Middle Ages as a mark of sinfulness)[109] even came to be taken, by the populace and by some ecclesiastical authorities, as itself a sign of holiness.[110] Caesarius described a robber who had done no good thing during his life except fast but who came to be revered as a martyr after death because five matrons appeared at night, fitted his head back on his shoulders, and laid him out whole on a sumptuous bier.[111]

The years around 1300 were not only years of debate at the papal court about the practice of partitioning corpses and decades of controversy in the schools of Paris and Oxford about how to explain the continuity and identity of body; they were also years in which the division and decay of the human body was an acute issue in other areas of medieval life. Both north and south of the Alps the first dissections were carried out in medical schools, for forensic as well as for teaching purposes. M.-C. Pouchelle has brilliantly demonstrated that they were characterized by an extraordinary sense of the mystery of the closed body and of the audacity required to open it.[112] Recent work in the history of medicine has shown the emergence in the thirteenth century of the notion that the task of physicians is to preserve the body from decay. In some circles, learned medicine (or physic) became centered not on the effort to cure disease but on schemes to return the body (preferably through alchemical manipulation) to its incorrupt state before the Fall.[113]

As Ed Peters has recently reminded us, the same period saw the revival of torture as a judicial procedure. Torturers were, however, allowed only to twist and stretch the body; they were prohibited from maiming or killing it, and thus from breeching or dividing.[114] Indeed so fraught with significance was actual partition that we can often tell, from the kind of bodily division inflicted in the execution, the social class and gender of those executed and the adjudged seriousness of their crimes.[115] The more hideous the offense and the lower the social status of the criminal the more mutilating the punishment: for example, drawing and quartering, or burning (which reduces the body to the tiniest fragments, dust). Moreover, as R. I. Moore and Saul Brody have suggested, the scapegoating of lepers about 1300 was owing not only to increased incidence of the disease but also to conceptualizing of it as living decay and fragmentation. It was because parts broke off the leper's body, because it fragmented and putrefied and became insensate while alive, in other words because it was living death, that it was used as a common metaphor for sin.[116]

Theological debates about resurrection, canonical legislation concerning burial, and hagiographical reports of miracles are not usually related to each other as I have done in this essay. And each has of course its own specific history and context. Debates over the unicity of form and over Christ's body in the *triduum* are related (as the older historiography argues) to the reception of Aristotle in the West. Boniface's bull *Detestande feritatis* must (as new research shows) be placed in the context of ecclesiastical squabbles over rights to bury the French kings as well as in the context of scientific, specifically Baconian, ideas circulating at the papal court.[117] James of Vitry's and Thomas of Cantimpré's accounts of the startling somatic miracles of Mary of Oignies and Christina the Astonishing reflect the specific nature of women's piety in the area of Liège, the ecclesiastical ambitions of the two male hagiographers, and their considerable concern to counter the appeal of Cathar dualism.[118] Nonetheless, if we look only at particular contexts, we run the risk of forgetting the larger configurations which, whether we find them threatening or attractive or merely bizarre, probably first sparked our interest in the Middle Ages. This essay suggests, without in any way denying other historical contexts, that a specific conception of person underlay the new somatic miracles of the thirteenth century, the theological discussion of resurrection, and the practice of and controversy over bodily partition. That conception of person included three assumptions: first, that the human person is a body-soul unity, second, that material continuity is necessary for survival of body and therefore of person, and, third, that the ultimate threat is putrefaction, the ultimate victory not the immortality of the soul but the exact reassemblage of body parts.[119]

Thus "body" was a central problem for pious Christians and scholastic theorists. The current scholarly interest it arouses is entirely appropriate to the medieval evidence. But the problem that body presented most urgently to medieval men and women was not the problem of sexuality or gender, pressing as these issues were. The ultimate problem was death and decay. However odd we may find some of the medieval efforts at solution, it is hard, I think, to claim that they got the problem wrong.

NOTES

The first version of this essay was delivered as a plenary address for the International Conference on Medieval Studies at Kalamazoo, Michigan, in May 1988. It was written while I was a Senior Scholar at the Getty Center for the History of Art and the Humanities in Santa Monica, California. I am grateful to the support staff at the Getty for their help, and especially to Steven Wight, my research assistant, who provided me with ideas as well as references. I would also like to thank Guenther Roth and Stephen D. White for their suggestions.

1. See, for example, Catherine Gallagher and Thomas Laqueur, eds., *The Making of the Modern Body: Sexuality and Society in the Nineteenth Century* (Berkeley: University of California Press, 1987); Peter Brown, *The Body and Society: Men, Women and Sexual Renunciation in Early Christianity* (New York: Columbia University Press, 1988); *Representations 20: Misogyny, Misandry, and Misanthropy* (Fall 1987), especially the articles by Carol Clover and

R. Howard Bloch; Elaine Pagels, *Adam, Eve, and the Serpent* (New York: Random House, 1988). French scholarship has also recently been quite interested in the body. See, for example, Brigitte Cazelles, *Le corps de sainteté d'après Jehan Bouche d'Or, Jehan Paulus, et quelques Vies des XIIe et XIIIe siècles* (Geneva: Droz, 1982); Marie-Christine Pouchelle, *Corps et chirurgie à l'apogée du moyen âge: Savoir et imaginaire du corps chez Henri de Mondeville . . .* (Paris: Flammarion, 1983); and Odile Redon, "Le Corps dans les nouvelles toscanes du XIVe siècle," *Faire Croire: modalités de la diffusion et de la réception des messages religieux du XIIe et XIIIe siècles: table ronde, Rome, 22–23 juin 1979* (Rome and Turin: École française de Rome and Bottega d'Erasmo, 1981), pp. 147–63.

    2. For a brilliant application of this method, see Natalie Davis, "The Sacred and the Body Social in Sixteenth-Century Lyon," *Past and Present* 90 (February 1981), pp. 40–70.

    3. Barbara Duden, *Repertory on Body History: An Annotated Bibliography*, Humanities Working Paper 125 (California Institute of Technology 1987).

    4. Francis Barker, *The Tremulous Private Body: Essays on Subjection* (London and New York: Methuen, 1984). Recent work by the professor of Italian literature Piero Camporesi also stresses the shockingly somatic quality of early modern culture; see Camporesi, *The Incorruptible Flesh: Bodily Mutation and Mortification in Religion and Folklore*, trans. T. Croft-Murray and H. Elsom (Cambridge: Cambridge University Press, 1988). Interest in the body among early modern historians has been greatly stimulated by Mikhail Bakhtin, *Rabelais and His World*, trans. H. Iswolsky (Cambridge, Mass.: M.I.T. Press, 1968).

    5. Natalie Davis, "History's Two Bodies," *American Historical Review* 93, no. 1 (January 1988): 1–30.

    6. See Peter Brown, *The Body and Society;* Joyce Salisbury, "The Latin Doctors of the Church on Sexuality," *Journal of Medieval History* 12 (1986): 279–89, and idem, *Church Fathers and Independent Virgins*, work in progress; Joan Cadden, "Medieval Scientific and Medical Views of Sexuality: Questions of Propriety," *Medievalia et Humanistica*, n.s. 14 (1986): 157–71; and James A. Brundage, *Law, Sex and Christian Society in Medieval Europe* (Chicago: University of Chicago Press, 1987).

    7. This is the viewpoint often found in surveys of women's history. Even so good a literary critic as R. Howard Bloch seems to me to fall into the trap in his "Medieval Misogyny," *Representations* 20 (Fall 1987): 1–24. For other recent work that stresses the negative view of body and of women's bodies in particular, see Jacques Le Goff, "Corps et idéologie dans l'Occident médiéval: La révolution corporelle," in *L'Imaginaire médiéval: Essais* (Paris: Gallimard, 1985), pp. 123–27; and Michel Sot, "Mépris du monde et résistance des corps aux XIe et XIIe siècles," and Jacques Dalarun, "Eve, Marie ou Madeleine? La dignité du corps féminin dans hagiographie médiévale," in *Médiévales* 8 (1985): *Le Souci du corps*, pp. 6–32. Some recent work has argued, in con-

trast, that Christian attitudes contributed toward a positive evaluation of the body; see, for example, the inadequately documented work by Frank Bottomley, *Attitudes Toward the Body in Western Christendom* (London: Lepus Books, 1979) and Prudence Allen, *The Concept of Woman: The Aristotelian Revolution 750 B.C.–A.D. 1250* (Montreal and London: Eden Press, 1985), also inadequately researched but extremely perceptive. Allen views the rise of Aristotle as a victory for sexism but argues that medieval teaching on the resurrection of the body, with its assertion that human beings will rise in two sexes, undercuts the negative Aristotelian position. For a recent study that sees a more positive attitude toward sexuality emerging in the high Middle Ages, see Danielle Jacquart and Claude Thomasset, *Sexualité et savoir médical au moyen âge* (Paris: Presses universitaires de France, 1985). Medievalists usually argue that theological and medical attitudes toward sexuality diverged, with the doctors more positive; see Cadden "Medieval Scientific and Medical Views." I myself have argued in *Holy Feast and Holy Fast: The Religious Significance of Food to Medieval Women* (Berkeley: University of California Press, 1987) (hereafter *HFHF*) that asceticism in the later Middle Ages treated body less as a trap or hindrance than as a means of access to the divine; for a similar point of view, see *Les Miracles miroirs des corps*, ed. Jacques Gélis and Odile Redon (Paris: Presses et Publications de l'Université de Paris-VIII, 1983).

8. Katharine M. Rogers, *The Troublesome Helpmate: A History of Misogyny in Literature* (Seattle: University of Washington Press, 1966); Diane Bornstein, "Antifeminism," in *Dictionary of the Middle Ages,* ed. Joseph Strayer (New York: Scribner's, 1982–), vol. 1, pp. 322–25; Bloch, "Medieval Misogyny."

9. Cadden, "Medieval Scientific and Medical Views"; Brundage, *Law, Sex and Society;* Vern L. Bullough, "Medieval Medical and Scientific Views of Women," *Viator* 4 (1973): 487–93; Jacquart and Thomasset, *Sexualité;* John T. Noonan, Jr., *Contraception: A History of Its Treatment by the Catholic Theologians and Canonists,* enlarged edition (Cambridge, Mass.: Harvard University Press, 1986); Jean-Louis Flandrin, "Contraception, Marriage and Sexual Relations in the Christian West," *Biology of Man in History: Selections from Annales: Économies-Sociétés-Civilisations,* ed. R. Forster and O. Ranum, trans. E. Forster and P. Ranum (Baltimore and London: Johns Hopkins University Press, 1975), pp. 23–47.

10. J. Huizinga, *The Waning of the Middle Ages: A Study of the Forms of Life, Thought and Art in France and the Netherlands in the XIVth and XVth Centuries,* trans. F. Hopman (1924; repr. Garden City, N.Y.: Doubleday, 1956); Ronald C. Finucane, *Miracles and Pilgrims: Popular Beliefs in Medieval England* (Totowa: Rowman & Littlefield, 1977); Benedicta Ward, *Miracles and the Medieval Mind: Record and Event, 1000–1215* (Philadelphia: University of Pennsylvania Press, 1982); Giles Constable, "Miracles and History in the Twelfth Century," presidential address delivered at the Medieval Academy of America meeting, University of California at Los Angeles, 1980, and idem, *Attitudes*

Toward Self-Inflicted Suffering in the Middle Ages, Ninth Stephen J. Brademas Sr. Lecture (Brookline, Mass.: Hellenic College Press, 1982); Richard Kieckhefer, *Unquiet Souls: Fourteenth-Century Saints and Their Religious Milieu* (Chicago: University of Chicago Press, 1984); and Rudolph M. Bell, *Holy Anorexia* (Chicago: University of Chicago Press, 1985).

11. Herbert Thurston, *The Physical Phenomena of Mysticism* (hereafter *PP*) (Chicago: Henry Regnery, 1952); Peter Browe, *Die eucharistischen Wunder des Mittelalters,* Breslauer Studien zur historischen Theologie NF 4 (Breslau: Müller and Seiffert, 1938); Bynum, *HFHF,* and idem, "The Female Body and Religious Practice in the Later Middle Ages," *Zone 3: Fragments for a History of the Human Body* 1 (1989), pp. 160–219.

12. On stigmatization, see: Thurston, *PP,* esp. pp. 69, 95–99, 123; Antoine Imbert-Gourbeyre, *La Stigmatisation: L'Extase divine et les miracles de Lourdes: Réponse aux libres-penseurs,* 2 vols. (Clermont-Ferrand, 1894), which must be used with caution; Pierre Debongnie, "Essai critique sur l'histoire des stigmatisations au moyen âge," *Études carmélitaines* 21.2 (1936): 22–59; E. Amann, "Stigmatisation," *Dictionnaire de théologie catholique,* ed. A. Vacant et al. (hereafter *DTC*) (Paris: Letouzey et Ané, 1909–1950), vol. 14, pt. 1, cols. 2617–19; F. A. Whitlock and J. V. Hynes, "Religious Stigmatization: A Historical and Psychophysiological Enquiry," *Psychological Medicine* 8 (1978): 185–202. On mystical lactations and swellings, see *HFHF,* pp. 122–23, 126, 203–4, 211, 257, 268–69, and 273–75. For stories of pregnant men, which can in this period have both spiritual and comic significance, see Roberto Zapperi, *L'Homme enceint: L'homme, la femme et le pouvoir,* trans. M.-A. Maire Vigueur (Paris: Presses universitaires de France, 1983) and Pouchelle, *Corps,* pp. 142 and 223.

13. Thurston, *PP;* Bell, *Holy Anorexia;* Bynum, *HFHF;* idem, "Women Mystics and Eucharistic Devotion in the Thirteenth Century," *Women's Studies* 11 (1984): 179–214; idem, "Fast, Feast and Flesh: The Religious Significance of Food to Medieval Women," *Representations* 11 (Summer 1985): 1–25; and Peter Dinzelbacher and D. Bauer, eds., *Frauenmystik im Mittelalter,* Wissenschaftliche Studientagung der Akademie der Diözese Rottenburg-Stuttgart 22.–25. Februar 1984 in Weingarten (Ostfildern: Schwabenverlag, 1985).

14. P. Sejourné, "Reliques," *DTC* 13, pt. 2, cols. 2330–65; Nicole Hermann-Mascard, *Les Reliques des saints: Formation coutumière d'un droit,* Société d'Histoire du Droit: collection d'histoire institutionnelle et sociale 6 (Paris: Edition Klincksieck, 1975); Patrick J. Geary, *Furta Sacra: Thefts of Relics in the Central Middle Ages* (Princeton: Princeton University Press, 1978), esp. pp. 152–54; Joan M. Petersen, *The Dialogues of Gregory the Great in Their Late Antique Cultural Background,* Studies and Texts 69 (Toronto: Pontifical Institute of Mediaeval Studies, 1984), pp. 140–50; and E. A. R. Brown, "Death and the Human Body in the Later Middle Ages: The Legislation of Boniface VIII on the Division of the Corpse," *Viator* 12 (1981): 221–70, esp. pp.

223–24. For the argument that German attitudes toward relics differed in important ways from the Western European relic cult, see Lionel Rothkrug, "German Holiness and Western Sanctity in Medieval and Modern History," *Historical Reflections/Réflexions historiques* 15.1 (1988): 161–249.

15. J.-K. Huysmans, *Sainte Lydwine de Schiedam* (Paris, 1901), pp. 288–91, which, however, contains no documentation; Thurston, *PP,* pp. 222–32 and 268–70; Hermann-Mascard, *Les Reliques des saints,* pp. 68–69; Charles W. Jones, *Saint Nicolas of Myra, Bari and Manhattan: Biography of a Legend* (Chicago: University of Chicago Press, 1978), pp. 144–53; and Bynum, "Fast, Feast and Flesh," nn. 22, 81, 82, and 85.

16. Clare of Montefalco's spiritual sisters tore out her heart after her death and found the insignia of the Passion incised upon it; see André Vauchez, *La sainteté en Occident aux derniers siècles du moyen âge d'après les procès de canonisation et les documents hagiographiques,* Bibliothèque des études françaises d'Athènes et de Rome 241 (Rome: École Française de Rome, 1981), p. 408; Camporesi, *Incorruptible Flesh,* pp. 3–15; and Giulia Barone, "Probleme um Klara von Montefalco," in *Religiöse Frauenbewegung und mystische Frömmigkeit im Mittelalter,* ed. P. Dinzelbacher and D. Bauer (Cologne and Vienna: Böhlau, 1988), p. 219. Three precious stones, with images of the Holy Family on them, were supposedly found in the heart of Margaret of Città di Castello; see Life of Margaret, ch. 8, *Analecta Bollandiana* 19 (1900): 27–28. On mystical espousal rings and miraculous bodily elongation, see Thurston, *PP,* pp. 139 and 200.

17. Thurston, *PP,* pp. 233–82, esp. pp. 246–52. Of the 42 saints living between 1400 and 1900 whose feasts are kept by the universal church, there are claims of incorruption in 22 cases and in seven more there are reports of odd phenomena which imply non-decay. Seventeen of the incorrupt are male, but of the six females among the 42 five are incorrupt and for the sixth (Jane Frances de Chantal), who was embalmed, there appears to be a claim for extraordinary survival. There are thus more incorrupt male bodies, but all the female bodies are claimed to be incorrupt. On incorruption, see also [C.] Grant Loomis, "Folklore of the Uncorrupted Body," *Journal of American Folk-lore* 48 (1935): 374–78; Michel Bouvier, "De l'incorruptibilité des corps saints," in *Les Miracles miroirs,* pp. 193–221; João de Pina-Cabral, *Sons of Adam, Daughters of Eve: The Peasant World of the Alto Minho* (Oxford: at the Clarendon Press, 1986), pp. 230–38; and Caroline Bynum, "Holy Anorexia in Modern Portugal," in *Culture, Medicine and Psychiatry* 12 (1988): 259–68.

18. See, for example, the case of Lukardis, *HFHF,* pp. 113–14. See also Life of Lutgard of Aywières, bk. 1, chs. 1–2, and bk. 2, ch. 1, in *Acta sanctorum,* ed. J. Bollandus and G. Henschenius, *Editio novissima,* ed. J. Carnandet et al. (Paris, Palmé, etc., 1863–) (hereafter *AASS*) June, vol. 4 (1867): 192–94; and Life of Benevenuta of Bojano, ch. 10, par. 82, *AASS* October, vol. 13 (1883): 172.

19. Hermann-Mascard, *Les Reliques des saints,* p. 274 n. 21. As examples, see the process of canonization of 1276 for Margaret of Hungary in Vilmos Fraknói, *Monumenta romana episcopatus vesprimiensis (1103–1526),* vol. 1 (Budapest: Collegium Historicorum Hungarorum Romanum, 1896), pp. 237–38, 266, 267 and 288; and the case of Lidwina of Schiedam, "Fast, Feast and Flesh," p. 5.

20. Angela of Foligno, *Le Livre de l'expérience des vrais fidèles: texte latin publié d'après le manuscrit d'Assise,* ed. and trans. M.-J. Ferré and L. Baudry (Paris: Éditions E. Droz, 1927), par. 53, p. 106 (cf. ibid., par. 80, p. 166); Raymond of Capua, *Legenda maior* of Catherine of Siena, in *AASS* April, vol. 3 (1866), pt. 2, ch. 4, par. 155 and 162–63, and pt. 3, ch. 7, par. 412 and 414, pp. 901, 902–3, and 963; Catherine of Genoa, *Il Dialogo spirituale* and *Vita,* ch. 12, ed. Umile Bonzi da Genova, *S. Caterina Fieschi Adorno,* vol. 2: *Edizione critica dei manoscritti cateriniani* (Turin: Marietti, 1962), pp. 422–27 and 140–41. And see Thomas of Celano, First Life of Francis of Assisi, bk. 1, ch. 7, par. 17, in *Analecta Franciscana* 10 (Quaracchi: Collegium S. Bonaventurae, 1941), p. 16; Celano, Second Life, bk. 1, ch. 5, par. 9, in ibid., pp. 135–63; Bonaventure, *Legenda maior* of Francis, pt. 1, ch. 1, par. 5 and 6, in ibid., pp. 562–63; and Bonaventure, *Legenda minor,* ch. 1, eighth lesson, in ibid., pp. 657–58. On leprosy as living decay, see Saul Nathaniel Brody, *The Disease of the Soul: Leprosy in Medieval Literature* (Ithaca, N.Y.: Cornell University Press, 1974), esp. pp. 64 and 79. On Angela, see now the excellent article by Ulrich Köpf, "Angela von Foligno," in Dinzelbacher and Bauer, ed., *Religiöse Frauenbewegung und mystische Frömmigkeit,* pp. 225–49.

21. E. Longpré, "Eucharistie et expérience mystique . . . ," *Dictionnaire de spiritualité, ascétique et mystique, doctrine et histoire,* ed. M. Viller et al. (hereafter *DS*) (Paris: Beauchesne, 1932–), vol. 4, pt. 2, col. 1596.

22. Browe, *Die eucharistischen Wunder.*

23. Peter of Vaux, Life of Colette of Corbie, trans. Stephen Juliacus, ch. 10, par. 84, *AASS* March, vol. 1 (1865), p. 558.

24. *HFHF,* pp. 59–61, 67, 117–19, 131, and 141–42.

25. Bynum, "Female Body and Religious Practice." See also the essays in P. Dinzelbacher and D. Bauer, ed., *Religiöse Frauenbewegung und mystische Frömmigkeit,* which make quite clear the somatic and charismatic quality of female piety, although Dinzelbacher, in a somewhat perverse introduction, seems to deny that there is anything particularly female or worthy of explanation about this. The splendid article by Karen Glente, "Mystikerinnenviten aus männlicher und weiblicher Sicht . . . ," in ibid. suggests that the bodily quality of women's piety is in part a matter of male perception and construction of it.

26. See the 1603 account of the case of Jane Balam, discussed in Hyder E. Rollins, "Notes on Some English Accounts of Miraculous Fasts," *Journal of American Folk-lore* 34.134 (October–December 1921): 363–64; and *HFHF,* p. 211.

27. For this interpretation, I have been influenced by Pina-Cabral, *Sons of Adam.*

28. Richard Heinzmann, *Die Unsterblichkeit der Seele und die Auferstehung des Leibes: Eine problemgeschichtliche Untersuchung der frühscholastischen Sentenzen- und Summenliteratur von Anselm von Laon bis Wilhelm von Auxerre,* Beiträge zur Geschichte der Philosophie und Theologie des Mittelalters: Texte und Untersuchungen 40.3 (Münster: Aschendorff, 1965); Hermann J. Weber, *Die Lehre von der Auferstehung der Toten in den Haupttraktaten der scholastischen Theologie von Alexander von Hales zu Duns Skotus,* Freiburger Theologische Studien (Freiburg: Herder, 1973); Gisbert Greshake and Jacob Kremer, *Resurrectio mortuorum: Zum theologischen Verständnis der leiblichen Auferstehung* (Darmstadt: Wissenschaftliche Buchgesellschaft, 1986), esp. pp. 216–39; A. Michel, "Résurrection des morts," *DTC* 13, pt. 2, cols. 2501–71; A. Challet, "Corps glorieux," *DTC* 3, cols. 1879–1906; and H. Cornélis, J. Guillet, Th. Camelot, and M. A. Genevois, *The Resurrection of the Body* (Notre Dame, Ind.: Fides, 1964). For an indication of the importance of discussion of the resurrection of the body, see the indices to Palémon Glorieux's great study of quodlibetal literature: *La Littérature quodlibetique de 1260 à 1320,* Bibliothèque Thomiste 5 and 21 (Le Saulchoir: Kain, 1925; and Paris: J. Vrin, 1935). Much recent research on patristic and medieval ideas of immortality and resurrection responds to the claim of the Swiss theologian and scholar Oscar Cullmann that the immortality of the soul is a Greek concept not found in the New Testament. For an introduction to this position and the controversy generated by it, see *Immortality and Resurrection,* ed. K. Stendahl (New York: Macmillan, 1965), and *Immortality,* ed. Terence Penelhum (Belmont, Calif.: Wadsworth, 1973).

29. The Fourth Lateran Council (1215) asserted, against the Cathars and other heretics, that "Omnes cum suis propriis resurgent corporibus, quae nunc gestant . . ."; and the Second Council of Lyons (1274) reaffirmed this; see Henry Denzinger, *Enchiridion symbolorum definitionum et declarationum de rebus fidei et morum,* 11th ed., ed. C. Bannwart (Freiburg: Herder, 1911), pp. 189 and 202–3.

30. See A. Michel, "Résurrection des morts"; Ton H. C. Van Eijk, *La Résurrection des morts chez les Pères Apostoliques* (Paris: Beauchesne, 1974); R. M. Grant, "The Resurrection of the Body," *Journal of Religion* 28 (1948): 120–30 and 188–208; Henry Chadwick, "Origen, Celsus, and the Resurrection of the Body," *The Harvard Theological Review* 41 (1948): 83–102; Joanne E. McWilliam Dewart, *Death and Resurrection,* Message of the Fathers of the Church 22 (Wilmington, Del.: Michael Glazier, 1986).

31. Heinzmann, *Die Unsterblichkeit der Seele,* pp. 147–245, esp. pp. 148–55; and Odon Lottin, *Psychologie et morale aux XIIᵉ et XIIIᵉ siècles,* vol. 5: *Problèmes d'histoire littéraire: L'École d'Anselme de Laon et de Guillaume de Champeaux* (Gembloux: J. Duculot, 1959), pp. 35, 265–66, 320–21, 393–96, and vol. 4: *Problèmes de morale,* pt. 1, p. 55. Peter Lombard treats this problem

in *Sententiae in IV Libris Distinctae,* ed. Collegium S. Bonaventurae, Spicilegium Bonaventurianum 4 and 5, 2 vols. (Grottaferrata: Collegium S. Bonaventurae ad Claras Aquas, 1971 and 1981) (hereafter Lombard, *Sentences*), bk. 2,
dist. 30, especially chs. 14–15, vol. 1, pt. 2, pp. 496–505. See also bk. 2, dist.
18, ch. 4, pp. 417–18, dist. 19, chs. 2–6, pp. 422–27, and dist. 20, pp. 427–57.
For a thirteenth-century treatment, see Albertus Magnus, *De resurrectione,* tract.
1, q. 6, art. 9–11, ed. W. Kübel, in *Opera Omnia,* ed. Institutum Alberti Magni
Coloniense, vol. 26 (Münster: Aschendorff, 1958), pp. 254–57. Whether or
not eaten food became flesh was a serious problem for twelfth-century theologians and a favorite locus for discussing the generally vexing problem of
change. For a good summary of the issue, see Kieran Nolan, *The Immortality
of the Soul and the Resurrection of the Body According to Giles of Rome: A Historical Study of a Thirteenth Century Theological Problem,* Studia Ephemeridis
'Augustinianum' 1 (Rome: Studium Theologicum Augustinianum, 1967), pp.
116–23. The close relationship perceived between eating and corruption is undoubtedly connected to the proliferation of miracles of living without eating
in this period, although scholars interested in miracles have not noticed this.

32. Heinzmann, *Die Unsterblichkeit der Seele,* pp. 172, 202–7, and 209–13.
In answer, Thomas Aquinas argued that all Christ's blood rose with him; the
blood in European churches came rather, he said, from desecrated crucifixes
and images; Thomas Aquinas, *Summa theologiae,* ed. Blackfriars, 61 vols. (New
York: McGraw-Hill, 1964–81) (hereafter Aquinas *ST*), 3a, q. 54, art. 3, obj.
3 and reply obj. 3, vol. 55, pp. 26–31. For Guibert of Nogent's preoccupation
with the problem of Christ's umbilical cord, foreskin, tooth, etc., see below
nn. 67–72. For places claiming the relic of the holy foreskin, see Henri Denifle,
*La désolation des églises, monastères et hospitaux en France pendant la Guerre
de Cent Ans,* vol. 1 (Paris: Impression Anastaltique, 1897), p. 167.

33. For disapproving assessments of the medieval interest in this issue,
see H. M. McElwain, "Resurrection of the Dead, theology of" *New Catholic
Encyclopedia,* vol. 12 (New York: McGraw-Hill, 1967), p. 425; and J. A. Mac-
Culloch, "Eschatology," in *Encyclopedia of Religion and Ethics,* ed. J. Hastings,
vol. 5 (New York: Scribner's, 1914), pp. 386 and 391.

34. Michael Allyn Taylor, *Human Generation in the Thought of Thomas
Aquinas: A Case Study on the Role of Biological Fact in Theological Science,*
Ph.D. diss., Catholic University of America, 1982; on thirteenth-century discus-
sions of the cannibalism problem, see also Nolan, *Giles of Rome,* pp. 114–23.

35. Hugh of Saint Victor, *De sacramentis,* II, pt. 18, c. 18, in *Patrologiae
cursus completus: series latina,* ed. J.-P. Migne (hereafter *PL*), vol. 176 (Paris:
Migne, 1854), col. 616.

36. For early discussions of this, see Honorius Augustodunensis, *Eluci-
darium, PL* 172, cols. 1164–65 and 1169. See also the texts edited and discussed in Lottin, *Psychologie et morale,* vol. 5, pp. 321 and 374; and Peter Lombard, *Sentences,* bk. 2, dist. 30, ch. 15, vol. 1, pt. 2, pp. 504–5, and bk. 4,

dist. 44, chs. 2–4, vol. 2, pp. 516–19. The issue is also treated in the compilation by Herrad of Hohenbourg, *Hortus deliciarum*, chs. 850–52, 855, 887, and 1090; see *Hortus deliciarum: Reconstruction*, ed. Rosalie Green et al. (London and Leiden: Warburg Institute/University of London and Brill, 1979), pp. 423–35, 447, and 481.

37. Lombard, bk. 4, dist. 43, ch. 7, art. 2, p. 516, and bk. 4, dist. 44, chs. 2–4, pp. 517–19. On the resurrection of aborted fetuses and monsters, see bk. 4, dist. 44, ch. 8, pp. 521–22. See also the text edited in Lottin *Psychologie et morale*, vol. 5, p. 396. On Albert the Great's discussion of this issue, see Wilhelm Kübel, "Die Lehre von der Auferstehung der Toten nach Albertus Magnus," in *Studia Albertina: Festschrift für Bernhard Geyer zum 70. Geburtstage*, ed. H. Ostlender, Beiträge zur Geschichte der Philosophie und Theologie der Mittelalters, Supplementband 4 (Münster: Aschendorff, 1952), pp. 316–17. Herrad of Hohenbourg (*Hortus deliciarum: Reconstruction*, p. 427, plate 141, number 327) actually includes a miniature of the rendering up of eaten body parts by wild beasts and fish so that these pieces may be reassembled at the resurrection – a motif rare in Western art although common in Eastern; see B. Brenk, "Die Anfänge der Byzantinischen Weltgerichtsdarstellung," *Byzantinische Zeitschrift* 57 (1964): 106–26.

38. Lottin, *Psychologie et morale*, vol. 5, p. 396.

39. Ibid., p. 397.

40. Thomas Aquinas held that risen bodies will have the capacity for touch; see *Summa contra Gentiles*, bk. 4, ch. 84, in *Sancti Thomae Aquinatis Opera Omnia . . .*, vols. 13–15 (Rome: Apud Sedem Commissionis Leoninae, 1918–30) (hereafter *ScG*), vol. 15, pp. 268–69. Risen bodies will not, however, eat: see *ScG*, bk. 4, ch. 83, vol. 15, pp. 262–66. In *Quaestiones disputatae de potentia*, q. 6, art. 8, in *Thomae Aquinatis . . . Opera omnia*, ed. S. E. Frette, vol. 13 (Paris: Vives, 1875), p. 205, Aquinas argues that Christ willed to eat after the resurrection in order to show the reality of his body; see also *ST* 3a, q. 55, art. 6, vol. 55, pp. 56–65. Albert the Great (*De resurrectione*, tract. 2, q. 8, art. 5, p. 278) argues that, in order to demonstrate his resurrected body, the resurrected Christ ate without the food becoming part of his substance; we too could eat that way in the glorified body but have no need to, since we need not demonstrate the resurrection. Weber, *Auferstehung*, pp. 259–60, shows how thirteenth-century theologians vacillated in their treatments of whether there is tasting in heaven. Basic principles conflicted: on the one hand, vegetative functions were seen as eliminated in heaven; on the other hand, as Albert said, "Nulla potestate nobili destituentur."

41. See, for example, Albert the Great, *De resurrectione*, tract. 2, q. 8, art. 2–4, pp. 271–78, and tract. 4, q. 1, art. 15, pp. 337–38. Albert changed his mind on the issue between his treatise on the resurrection and his Sentence commentary; see Weber, *Auferstehung*, p. 331, nn. 329–30.

42. Weber, *Auferstehung*, pp. 331–32. On the *dotes* generally, see Niko-

laus Wicki, *Die Lehre von der himmlischen Seligkeit in der mittelalterlichen Scholastik von Petrus Lombardus bis Thomas von Aquinas,* Studia Friburgensia NF 9 (Freiburg: Universitätsverlag, 1954); and Joseph Goering, "The *De Dotibus* of Robert Grosseteste," *Mediaeval Studies* 44 (1982): 83–109.

43. The burden of Heinzmann's *Die Unsterblichkeit der Seele* is to show the emergence in the twelfth century with Gilbert de la Porrée of a more Aristotelian conception of person over against Platonic definitions of man as soul found, for example, in Hugh of Saint Victor. This argument is, however, to some extent misleading. Although technical definitions may have shifted from Platonic to Aristotelian, thinkers such as Hugh and Bernard of Clairvaux actually treated the human being as an entity composed of body and soul (see note 52 below and Weber, *Auferstehung,* pp. 123 ff.). So indeed did the Fathers. Among patristic treatises on the resurrection, I find only Ambrose's *De excessu fratris sui Satyri,* bk. 2, ch. 20; *PL* 16 (Paris, 1880), cols. 1377–78, adhering to a strictly Platonic definition. For recent revisionist opinion about Augustine's anthropology, see Peter Brown, *The Body and Society,* and Joyce Salisbury, "Latin Doctors."

44. *ST* 3a, q. 15, art. 4, vol. 49, p. 202 (my translation). Aquinas did argue that, without body, the soul in heaven before the end of time would in a certain sense lack memory and other passions; see *ScG,* bk. 2, ch. 81, vol. 13, pp. 504–6.

45. Etienne Gilson, *History of Christian Philosophy in the Middle Ages* (New York: Random House, 1955) and Frederick Copleston, *A History of Philosophy,* vol. 2: *Medieval Philosophy* (Westminster, Md.: Newman Press, 1950), pts. 1 and 2. Even those intellectual historians who have disagreed with Gilson have done so on other grounds than the one I raise here; see Fernand van Steenberghen, *Aristotle in the West: The Origins of Latin Aristotelianism,* trans. L. Johnston (Louvain: Nauwelaerts, 1955) and M.-D. Chenu, *La théologie au douzième siècle,* Études de philosophie médiévale 45 (Paris: J. Vrin, 1957). The basic Catholic position has been to see a growing awareness of and positive appreciation of "nature" and "the natural" in the twelfth century, which prepared for the reception of Aristotle in the thirteenth. For a general discussion of interpretations of thirteenth-century intellectual history, see Steven Ozment, *The Age of Reform 1250–1550: An Intellectual and Religious History of Late Medieval and Reformation Europe* (New Haven, Conn.: Yale University Press, 1980), pp. 1–21.

46. Aquinas, *In epistolam I ad Corinthios commentaria,* c. 15, lectio 2, in *Opera omnia,* ed. Frette, vol. 21 (1876), pp. 33–34: ". . . si negetur resurrectio corporis, non de facili, imo difficile est sustinere immortalitatem animae. Constat enim quod anima naturaliter unitur corpori. . . . Unde anima exuta corpore, quamdiu est sine corpore, est imperfecta. Impossibile autem est quod illud quod est naturale et per se, sit finitum et quasi nihil, et illud quod est contra naturam et per accidens, sit infinitum, si anima semper duret

sine corpore. . . . Et ideo si mortui non resurgunt, solum in hac vita confidentes erimus. Alio modo, quia constat quod homo naturaliter desiderat salutem suiipsius; anima autem, cum sit pars corporis homini, non est totus homo, et anima mea non est ego; unde, licet anima consequatur salutem in alia vita, non tamen ego vel quilibet homo." See Emile Mersch and Robert Brunet, "Corps mystique et spiritualité," *DS*, vol. 2, col. 2352. For a modern position on the survival issue that agrees with Thomas, see Peter Geach, "Immortality," in Penelhum, *Immortality*, pp. 11 ff.

47. Those who have realized this include Norbert Luyten, "The Significance of the Body in a Thomistic Anthropology," *Philosophy Today* 7 (1963): 175–93; Bernardo C. Bazan, "La corporalité selon saint Thomas," *Revue philosophique de Louvain* 81, 4 ser. 49 (1983): 369–409; J. Giles Milhaven, "Physical Experience: Contrasting Appraisals by Male Theologians and Women Mystics in the Middle Ages," paper given at the Holy Cross Symposium "The Word Becomes Flesh," November 9, 1985: and Richard Swinburne, *The Evolution of the Soul* (Oxford: Clarendon Press, 1986), pp. 299–306, esp. n. 9.

48. *ScG*, bk. 4, chs. 80–81, vol. 15, pp. 251–54. Thomas holds that risen body will be reconstituted out of all of the former matter of body, but it is not impossible for it to be reconstituted out of some other matter. Interpretation of this passage has been controversial. See Weber, *Auferstehung*, p. 229, and E. Hugueny, "Résurrection et identité corporelle selon les philosophies de l'individuation," *Revue des sciences philosophiques et théologiques* 23 (1934): 94–106. Hugueny argues that Thomas's thought developed away from the idea of material continuity and toward formal identity.

49. *ScG*, bk. 4, ch. 81, vol. 15, pp. 252–53: "Corporeity, however, can be taken in two ways. In one way, it can be taken as the substantial form of a body. . . . Therefore, corporeity, as the substantial form in man, cannot be other than the rational soul. . . ." See Bazan, "La corporalité selon saint Thomas," pp. 407–8. Bazan says that according to Thomas, "Notre corporalité est toute pénétrée de spiritualité, car sa source est l'âme rationnelle."

50. Durandus of Saint Pourçain, *In Sententias theologicas Petri Lombardi commentariorum libri quatuor* (Lyon: Apud Gasparem, 1556), dist. 44, q. 1, fol. 340v–341r: Utrum ad hoc quod idem homo numero resurgat, requiratur quod formetur corpus eius eisdem pulueribus in quos fuit resolutum." (The printed edition of the commentary is the third and last redaction, moderate in comparison to earlier ones; see Gilson, *History*, p. 774 n. 81.)

51. In answer to the question whether the soul of Peter can be in the body of Paul (which he says is misformulated), Durandus argues (*In Sententias*, dist. 44, q. 1, pars. 4 and 5, fol. 341r): ". . . quaestio implicat contradictionem: quia corpus Petri non potest esse nisi compositum ex materia et anima Petri . . . ergo anima Petri non potest esse in corpore Pauli nec econverso, nisi anima Petri fiat anima Pauli. . . . Restat ergo quod alio modo formetur quaestio . . . : supposito quod anima Petri fieret in materia quae fuit in

corpore Pauli, utrum esset idem Petrus qui prius erat." He concludes (ibid., par. 6, fol. 341r): ". . . cuicumque materiae vniatur anima Petri in resurrectione, ex quo est eadem forma secundum numerum, per consequens erit idem Petrus secundum numero." For the background to Durandus's position, see Weber, *Auferstehung*, pp. 217–53 and 76–78. Weber's basic argument is that there were a number of precursors to Durandus's position, the originality of which has been overestimated.

52. A perceptive exception to the ignoring of positive conceptions of the body among earlier Platonic thinkers is John Sommerfeldt, "The Body in Bernard of Clairvaux's Anthropology," paper delivered at the Kalamazoo Medieval Studies conference, May 1988.

53. Weber, *Auferstehung*, pp. 326–27. The doctrine of the plurality of forms seems to lurk behind much of Franciscan teaching on the gifts (*dotes*) of the glorified body, for thinkers such as Bonaventure and Richard of Middleton hold that body is in some way predisposed for the flowing over of glory into it before it receives the *dotes;* see ibid., pp. 314ff. Such a position tends to give substantial reality to body.

54. Bonaventure, *De assumptione B. Virginis Mariae,* sermon 1, section 2, in *S. Bonaventurae Opera omnia,* ed. Collegium S. Bonaventurae, vol. 9 (Quarrachi: Collegium S. Bonaventurae, 1901), p. 690. See also Aquinas, *ScG,* bk. 4, ch. 79, vol. 15, p. 249, and Aquinas, *De potentia,* q. 5, art. 10, pp. 176–77, which says explicitly that Porphyry's idea that the soul is happiest without the body, and Plato's idea that the body is a tool of the soul, are wrong; the soul is more like God when it is united to the body than when it is separated, because it is then more perfect.

55. Weber, *Auferstehung,* p. 304 n. 197; and see ibid., pp. 266 and 135–36. The Augustinian idea that the soul desires the body so greatly that it is held back from vision of God when it is without the body is also found in Giles of Rome; see Nolan, *Giles of Rome,* pp. 46 and 78.

56. There appears to have been concern generally in the 1270s that the teachings of Aristotle as interpreted by the Arab commentators might lead not only to denial of the immortality of the soul but also to denial of the resurrection of the body. Others among the propositions condemned in 1277 also reflect a concern with the issue of bodily identity, for example, numbers 25 ("Quod Deus non potest dare perpetuitatem rei transmutabili et corruptibili"), 148 ("Quod homo per nutritionem potest fieri alius numeraliter et individualiter"), 155 ("Quod non est curandum de sepultura"), and 178 ("Quod finis terribilium est mors"). See *Chartularium universitatis Parisiensis . . . ,* ed. H. Denifle and A. Chatelain, vol. 1 (Paris: Delalain, 1889), pp. 544–55, and Roland Hissette, *Enquête sur les 219 articles condamnés à Paris le 7 Mars 1277,* Philosophes médiévaux 22 (Louvain and Paris: Publications universitaires de Louvain and Vander-Oyez, 1977), pp. 187, 294, and 307–8. Already in 1270 denial of the resurrection of the body had been condemned; proposition 13 stated "Quod

Deus non potest dare immortalitatem vel incorrupcionem rei corruptibili vel mortali." See *Chartularium univers. Paris.,* vol. 1, p. 487.

57. Debate over whether Christ in the three days was a man went back into the twelfth century. By the mid-thirteenth century, theologians generally agreed that living union was necessary for humanness (i.e., for being a man). Thomas's theory, however, raised the question whether Christ's body on the cross and in the grave were the same body. Giles of Lessines in 1278 raised the issue in a treatise on the unicity of form which he sent to Albert the Great. (Indeed he added the thesis of the equivocality of body to the list of those condemned in 1270, but it is not clear that it was in fact condemned.) Perhaps because of Albert's defense, the unicity of form was not condemned in 1277 in Paris, but in 1277 in Oxford the position was condemned that: ". . . corpus vivum et mortuum est equivoce corpus. . . ." Weber, *Auferstehung,* pp. 76–78 and 150–51. John Quidort (John of Paris) also got into trouble for the implications of his teaching on identity for the body of Christ; see ibid., p. 239. On the condemnation of the doctrine of the unicity of form in England, see *Chartularium univers. Paris,* vol. 1, pp. 558–59; Copleston, *History,* vol. 2, pt. 2, pp. 153–54; and M. Anthony Hewson, *Giles of Rome and the Medieval Theory of Conception: A Study of the De formatione corporis humani in utero* (London: University of London, The Athlone Press, 1975), pp. 6–11. According to Weber, *Auferstehung,* p. 151, both John of Paris and Archbishop Peckham were aware of the implications of these theoretical discussions for the cult of relics.

58. Weber, *Auferstehung,* p. 234.

59. Giles of Rome's Sentence commentary never reaches book 4. His major statement on the resurrection, in the *Quaestiones de resurrectione mortuorum et de poena damnatorum,* has been edited by Nolan, *Giles of Rome,* pp. 69–75, 90–96, 105–13, and 124–30. Giles's position clearly foreshadows Durandus's; see *Quaestiones* in Nolan, *Giles,* pp. 73–74, and Nolan's discussion, pp. 88 and 120. What guarantees the identity of earthly body and risen body (and therefore the identity of person) is not matter but form. As Weber points out, however (*Auferstehung,* pp. 234–36), Giles does not go all the way to Durandus's position. When Giles discusses Christ's body in the *triduum* he makes it clear that, although the body is not man, the material cadaver continues and is Christ's body; Nolan, *Giles,* p. 60. Moreover, like Thomas, Giles devotes much attention to the question of whether the body that rises is a body into which food was converted and to related questions about the resurrection of eaten flesh; see Nolan, *Giles,* pp. 114–23. In his embryological theory, Giles uses form as the principle of identity; see Hewson, *Giles of Rome and Conception.*

60. *ST* 3a, q. 25, art. 6, vol. 50, pp. 202–5.

61. As Weber points out (*Auferstehung,* p. 244), the new identity theory of Durandus, although not condemned, was never fully adopted into theological discourse. More research will be necessary before we know why this is so;

but the argument of my essay suggests that one reason may be the deep roots in pious practice of the assumption of material continuity. I should also point out, however, that attention to the resurrection of the body was lessened once the papacy declared (in the bull *Benedictus Deus* in 1336) that the soul can receive the beatific vision before the resurrection of the body.

62. Heinzmann, *Die Unsterblichkeit der Seele*, p. 208; Weber, *Auferstehung*, pp. 80–106. Simon of Tournai, William of Auxerre, Thomas, Bonaventure, and Giles of Rome all held that the resurrection of the body was both natural and supernatural; see Nolan, *Giles of Rome*, pp. 96–104 and 140.

63. See, for example, the early twelfth-century text edited by Lottin, in *Psychologie et morale*, vol. 5, p. 396, which says: ". . . omnes integro corpore resurgent. Cicatrices uero martirum quas pro Deo passi sunt ibi glorificate ad augmentum glorie ipsorum apparebunt, quemadmodum cicatrices ipsius Christi remanebunt ad maiorem penam malorum et gratiam bonorum, sed non deformant corpora ipsorum quemadmodum in presenti quandoque uidemus dedecentiora corpora esse cicatricibus ipsis." And see Aquinas, *ScG*, bk. 4, ch. 88, vol. 15, pp. 278–79; and *ST* 3a, q. 54, art. 4, vol. 55, pp. 30–35. See also Supplement to *Summa theologiae* 3, q. 96, art. 10, on whether the scars of the martyrs are an *aureole; Supplementum*, compiled and edited by the Brothers of the Order, in *Sancti Thomae Aquinatis Opera omnia*, vol. 12 (Rome: S.C. de Propaganda Fide, 1906), p. 238. In general, thirteenth-century theologians drew on Augustine's *City of God*, bk. 22, ch. 17 (". . . vitia detrahentur, natura servabitur") on this matter; see Weber, *Auferstehung*, p. 79, n. 194.

64. Allen, *Concept of Woman;* Weber, *Auferstehung*, pp. 256–59. Weber quotes Augustinus Triumphus, writing on the resurrection, to the effect that, if persons were to rise in the opposite sex, they would not be the same persons: "Non omnes resurgentes eundem sexum habebunt, nam masculinis sexus et femininus, quamvis non sint differentiae formales facientes differentiam in specie, sunt tamen differentiae materiales facientes differentiam in numero. Et quia in resurrectione quilibet resurget non solum quantum ad id quod est de identitate specifica, secundum habet esse in specie humana, verum etiam resurget quantum ad id, quod est de identitate numerali, secundum quam habet esse in tali individuo. Ideo oportet unumquodque cum sexu proprio et cum aliis pertinentibus ad integritatem suae individualis naturae resurgere, propter quod femina resurget cum sexu femineo et homo cum masculino, remota omni libidine et omni vitiositate naturae" (ibid., p. 258, n. 479). Moneta of Cremona, writing against the Cathars, argued that God created sex difference: see Moneta, *Adversus Catharos et Valdenses Libri quinque* (Rome, 1743: repr. Ridgewood, New Jersey: Gregg Press, 1964), bk. 1, ch. 2, section 4, and bk. 4, ch. 7, section 1, pp. 121 and 315.

65. The resurrected bodies of the damned will be incapable of corruption (i.e., of dissolution or of loss of their matter) but not incapable of suffering. Indeed, scholastic theologians held that the damned also receive their bodies

whole after the resurrection, because only the permanence (i.e., the perfect balance or wholeness) of these bodies insures that their punishment will be permanent and perpetual; see Kübel, "Die Lehre . . . nach Albertus," pp. 316-17.

66. The philosophical significance of this cannot be overestimated. One may simply conclude from it that the Christian notion of a resurrected body is an oxymoron. But one might also reason that Aristotelian notions of body and matter were fundamentally incompatible with Christian doctrine exactly because the Christian conception of body makes possible—indeed necessary—an unchanging body. Already in the second century Tertullian realized that he had to revise drastically the Aristotelian definition of change in order to accommodate it to Christian teaching. See Tertullian, *De resurrectione mortuorum*, ch. 55, ed. J. G. Ph. Borleffs, *Tertulliani Opera*, pt. 2, Corpus christianorum: series latina (Turnhout: Brepols, 1954), pp. 1001-3. Much thirteenth-century discussion of the resurrection of the body seems to realize that Aristotle's notions of change present fundamental difficulties. See Nolan, *Giles of Rome*, pp. 76-89.

67. See Klaus Guth, *Guibert von Nogent und die hochmittelalterliche Kritik an der Reliquienverehrung*, Studien und Mitteilungen zur Geschichte des Benediktiner-Ordens und seiner Zweige, Supplement 21 (Ottobeuren, 1970) and Marie-Danielle Mireux, "Guibert de Nogent et la critique du culte des reliques," in *La Piété populaire au moyen âge*, Actes du 99ᵉ Congrès National des Sociétés Savantes Besançon 1954: Section de philologie et d'histoire jusqu'à 1610, vol. 1 (Paris: Bibliothèque Nationale, 1977), pp. 293-301. I thank Thomas Head for calling my attention to Guibert's treatise as particularly relevant to my topic.

68. Guibert, *De pignoribus*, bk. 1, *PL* 156 (Paris, 1853), cols. 611-30.

69. Guibert argues that Mary must have been assumed bodily into heaven, because otherwise the vessel which bore Christ's body (and by implication then Christ's body itself) would experience corruption, and such a conclusion would be scandalous; *De pignoribus*, bk. 1, ch. 3, cols. 623-24. At the same time, Guibert opposes elaborate coffins which retard decay and thinks corpses should be allowed to return to "mother earth"; ibid., chs. 3-4, cols. 624-30. Clearly decay is a highly charged phenomenon for Guibert. Thus he does not wish cadavers to be disturbed. It would seem to be exactly because he desires bodily reassemblage and finds it so counter-intuitive (because putrefaction is, to him, so horrifying) that he seeks such extravagant guarantees that all particles of the body will rise at the Last Judgment.

70. John F. Benton, ed., *Self and Society in Medieval France: The Memoirs of Abbot Guibert of Nogent* (New York: Harper Torchbook, 1970), Introduction, pp. 26-31.

71. For Guibert's fascination with the details of bodily torture, see *De pignoribus*, bk. 4, ch. 1, cols. 668-69. Indeed so worried is Guibert about tor-

ture and bodily division that he does not wish to espouse a eucharistic theory that equates the sacrifice of the mass with the crucifixion. Guibert does not wish Christians to be reminded of the dividing of Christ's body; the body on the altar is rather, he argues, the body of the resurrection. See *De pignoribus,* bk. 2, ch. 6, col. 648; also bk. 3, ch. 2, obj. 6, col. 654.

72. In *De pignoribus,* bk. 2, ch. 2, cols. 632–34, Guibert argues that if I destroy a fingernail, I claim that I, not merely a part of me, am hurt. We call friends or relatives "ourselves." How much more is all of Christ included in the *me* of *Qui manducat me* (John 6:58)? Those who eat the Eucharist eat the *totus Christus;* they eat not a part of Christ but the *universitas* of the substance. "Quod si particulas illas illum esse negas, partem pro toto, et totum pro parte poni posse forsitan ignoras, synecdochice nempe non solum loqui Scripturas, sed ipsos quosque illitteratos et vulgares hac figura sermonum uti, nulli non perspicuum. . . . *Qui manducat me vivit propter me.* . . . Est enim dicere: Qui exterius meum, carnem videlicet et sanguinem, manducat, vivit ex eo ipso quod interiorem hominem illuminando vivificat. Cum ergo fieri non possit ad litteram, ut totus ab aliquo manducetur, nisi pars pro toto accipiatur, secundum interiorem sensum indifficulter id agitur, praesertim cum fides corporis ita habeatur ut quod minutatim porrigitur, totum in suis minutiis teneatur" (ibid., col. 632a–c). On synecdoche in twelfth-century hagiography, see also Cazelles, *Le corps de sainteté* (note 1 above), pp. 48 ff.

73. Thomas of Cantimpré was generally interested in somatic phenomena. He wrote four lives of women saints (Mary of Oignies, Christina *Mirabilis* [the Astonishing], Margaret of Ypres and Lutgard of Aywières), all of which are characterized by extravagant bodily miracles. On his *Bonum universale de apibus,* ed. Georges Colvener (Douai, 1627), a collection of miracle stories, many of which display a concern for body, see Henri Platelle, "Le Recueil des miracles de Thomas de Cantimpré et la vie religieuse dans les Pays-Bas et le nord de la France au XIIIᵉ siècle," in *Assistance et Assistés jusqu'à 1610,* Actes du 97ᵉ Congrès National des Sociétés Savantes, Nantes, 1972 (Paris: Bibliothèque Nationale, 1979), pp. 469–98, and Alexander Murray, "Confession as a Historical Source in the Thirteenth Century," in *The Writing of History in the Middle Ages: Essays Presented to Richard William Southern* (Oxford: at the Clarendon Press, 1981), pp. 275–322, esp. pp. 286–305. Thomas also wrote on female physiology; see *Die Gynäkologie des Thomas von Brabant: Ein Beitrag zur Kenntnis der mittelalterlichen Gynäkologie und ihrer Quellen,* ed. C. Ferckel (Munich: Carl Kuhn, 1912), an edition of part of book 1 of Thomas of Cantimpré's *De naturis rerum;* there is a new edition by Helmut Boese, *Liber de natura rerum: Editio princeps secundum codices manuscriptos,* vol. 1: *Text* (New York and Berlin: De Gruyter, 1973).

74. Life of Christina the Astonishing, ch. 5, number 36, pars. 47–48, *AASS* July, vol. 5, pp. 658–59; trans. Margot H. King, *The Life of Christina Mirabilis,* Matrologia latina 2 (Saskatoon: Peregrina, 1986), pp. 27–28. Eliza-

beth A. Petroff discusses this passage briefly but with characteristic insight in *Medieval Women's Visionary Literature* (Oxford: Oxford University Press, 1986), p. 36. On the genre of debates between body and soul, to which this passage clearly belongs (although to my knowledge students of Christina's *Vita* have not noticed the point), see Robert W. Ackerman, "*The Debate of the Body and Soul* and Parochial Christianity," *Speculum* 37 (1962): 541–65.

75. See Giselle Huot-Girard, "La justice immanente dans la *Légende dorée*," *Cahiers d'études médiévales* 1 (1974): 135–47; Alain Boureau, *La Légende dorée: Le système narratif de Jacques de Voragine (+1298)* (Paris: Éditions du Cerf, 1984); Sherry L. Reames, *The Legenda Aurea: A Reexamination of Its Paradoxical History* (Madison: University of Wisconsin Press, 1985); and Marie-Christine Pouchelle, "Représentations du corps dans la Légende dorée," *Ethnologie française* 6 (1976): 293–308. Pouchelle underlines the fear of division I mention below and emphasizes the role of body as avenue to God that I discussed in *Holy Feast and Holy Fast*. André Vauchez, "Jacques de Voragine et les saints du XIIIᵉ siècle dans la Légende dorée," in *Legenda Aurea: Sept siècles de diffusion: Actes du colloque international . . . à l'Université du Quebec à Montreal 11–12 mai 1983*, ed. B. Dunn-Lardeau (Montreal and Paris: Bellarmin and J. Vrin, 1986), pp. 27–56, gives an interpretation opposed to that of Boureau and Reames.

76. Boureau, *La Légende dorée*, pp. 60–61 and 115–33.

77. On stories of early Christians reassembling the bodies of the martyrs, see below note 101.

78. Of the 153 chapters (many of which tell several stories), 91 chapters treat martyrs; the majority of the martyrs discussed are not merely killed but in some way dismembered. According to my rough count, 23 of 24 female martyrs defend their virginity (12 die). There are only 6 cases of male saints whose virginity is threatened (only one dies). In contrast there are 48 temporary resurrections of men, only 9 of women. It almost seems as if women's stories are not safely concluded until the women are dead and intactness is finally affirmed forever. Men, on the other hand, are allowed to return to a condition of bodily change in order to finish unfinished business. On virginity as the central female virtue, see Clarissa Atkinson, "'Precious Balsam in a Fragile Glass': The Ideology of Virginity in the Later Middle Ages," *Journal of Family History* 8.2 (Summer 1982): 131–43.

79. James of Voragine, *Legenda aurea vulgo historia lombardica dicta*, ed. Th. Grässe, 3rd ed. (Breslau: Koebner, 1890), pp. 400–403.

80. Ibid., pp. 740–41, 597–601, and 601–2.

81. Ibid., pp. 203–4. It is worth noting that Sophia is said to have gathered up the remains of her daughters and buried them, with the help of bystanders; she was then buried with her children. This chapter, not found in the 1283 manuscript, is probably a later interpolation but is fully in the spirit of the other chapters; see Boureau, *La Légende dorée*, pp. 27–28.

82. James of Voragine, *Legenda aurea,* ed. Grässe, pp. 799–803; trans. G. Ryan and H. Ripperger, *The Golden Legend,* 2 parts (London: Longmans, Green: 1941), pt. 2, p. 719.

83. James also uses the seed metaphor in his discussion of the death of the contemporary saint, Peter Martyr; see *Legenda aurea,* ed. Grässe, p. 282: "Sic granum frumenti cadens in terram et infidelium manibus comprehensum et mortuum uberem consurgit in spicam, sic botrus in torculari calcatus liquoris redundat in copiam, sic aromata pilo contusa odorem plenius circumfundunt, sic granum sinapis contritum virtutem suam multipliciter demonstravit." The metaphor was extremely important in the earliest Christian discussions of resurrection; see A. Michel, "Résurrection des morts," cols. 2515–32.

84. Boureau, *La Légende dorée,* p. 126, makes something of the same point when he emphasizes that the torture itself is not the fundamental concern of these passages: "En construisant une échelle des peines, on s'est situé dans la perspective du bourreau, alors que la seule orientation pertinente est celle de la Providence." Cazelles, *Le corps de sainteté,* pp. 48–61, also stresses that stories of division of saintly bodies tend to underline their non-bodiliness.

85. Another place where the concern with part/whole is present in medieval theology and popular practice is in eucharistic doctrine and devotion. For a discussion of the intense emphasis in miracle stories and saints' lives on masticating (fragmenting) Christ's body in the wafer, see *HFHF,* chapter 2. The stress in such stories on the fragmenting of the host is matched by an intense sense that it remains fertile and whole as a symbol of the believer and of the community of the church. For the importance of these themes in late medieval drama, see Leah Sinanoglou, "The Christ Child as Sacrifice: A Medieval Tradition and the Corpus Christi Plays," *Speculum* 48 (1973): 461–509.

86. Louis-Vincent Thomas, *Le cadavre: de la biologie à l'anthropologie* (Brussels: Éditions complexe, 1980).

87. See note 14 above.

88. Geary, *Furta sacra,* p. 39, says: "The relics *were* the saint. . . . they were . . . the reality symbolized since they referred not beyond themselves but to themselves, as the saint residing among his followers." See also ibid., p. 162; and Stephen Wilson, "Introduction," to *Saints and Their Cults: Studies in Religious Sociology, Folklore and History,* ed. Wilson (Cambridge: Cambridge University Press, 1983), p. 11. For certain Greek fathers who said that touching the bones of the martyrs was participating in their sanctity, see H. Leclercq, "Martyr," *Dictionnaire d'archéologie chrétienne et de liturgie,* ed. F. Cabrol and H. Leclercq, vol. 10, pt. 2 (Paris: Letouzey et Ané, 1932), col. 2452. The fifth-century church historian Theodoret tells of a hermit named James who collected relics in a casket in order to live, and die, near them; see Leclercq, "Martyr," col. 2457. Nonetheless it seems significant that medieval texts do *not* say the bones are the saint and that an awareness of the bones as bones or dust is pervasive in the literature of the Middle Ages. See below n. 91. The point

I wish to stress is the inconsistency and ambivalence of medieval attitudes.

89. Peter Brown, in *The Cult of the Saints: Its Rise and Function in Latin Christianity* (Chicago: University of Chicago Press, 1981), has described the assumption, found in older scholarship, that popular and elite attitudes are separate and distinguishable and has delivered trenchant criticism against it.

90. Patrick Geary, "L'humiliation des saints," *Annales-économies-sociétés-civilisations* 34 (1979): 27–42; idem, "La coercition des saints dans la practique religieuse médiévale," in Pierre Boglioni, ed., *La Culture populaire au moyen âge*, Études presentées au 4ᵉ colloque de l'Institut d'Études médiévales de l'Université de Montréal, 2–3 avril 1977 (Montreal: l'Aurore, 1979), pp. 145–61; and Lester Little, "La morphologie des malédictions monastiques," *Annales-économies-sociétés-civilisations* 34 (1979): 43–60.

91. *Sermo Petri Venerabilis . . . in honore sancti illius cuius reliquiae sunt in presenti, PL* 189, cols. 1001–3; reedited by Giles Constable, in "Petri Venerabilis sermones tres," *Revue bénédictine* 64 (1954): 269–70. One can find such expressions all through the Middle Ages. For example, one early epitaph reads: "Nil iuvat, immo gravat, tumulis haerere piorum/ Sanctorum meritis optima vita prope est . . . :" and another: "Haec tenet urna tuum venerandum corpus Vincenti abbatis/ Set tua sacra tenet anima, caeleste sacerdos/ Regnum mutasti in melius cum gaudia vite." See H. Leclercq, "Martyr," cols. 2457 and 2508. Gregory the Great in the *Dialogues*, bk. 4, ch. 50, *PL* 77, col. 412, tells his interlocutor that the souls of the dead benefit from the burial of their bodies in church chiefly because their relatives, coming daily to the holy place, will be reminded by the sight of their tombs to pray for them. In the *Morals on Job*, Gregory argues that we shall remain as dust until the end of time, but then we will flower like Aaron's rod; *Moralia*, bk. 14, ch. 55, *PL* 75, col. 1075. And see note 102 below.

92. See note 89 above. For a sophisticated argument about the difficulty of separating levels of culture, see John Van Engen, "The Christian Middle Ages as an Historiographical Problem," *American Historical Review* 91 (1986): 519–52.

93. Hermann-Mascard, *Les Reliques des saints*, pp. 212–17; and Pierre Duparc, "Dilaceratio corporis," *Bullétin de la Société Nationale des Antiquaires de France 1980–1981* (Paris: Boccard, 1981), pp. 360–72.

94. Hermann-Mascard, *Les Reliques des saints*, pp. 313–39.

95. Duparc, "Dilaceratio corporis," p. 365.

96. E. A. R. Brown, "Death" (note 14 above), pp. 238–40.

97. See note 113 below.

98. For Roman prohibitions on moving cadavers (which are usually seen by historians as a significant cause of Christian discomfort with the fragmentation of martyrs' bodies), see Hermann-Mascard, *Les Reliques des saints*, pp. 26–42, 62 ff., and Philippe Ariès, *The Hour of Our Death*, trans. H. Weaver (New York: Knopf, 1981), pp. 29–51.

99. Eusebius, *The Ecclesiastical History*, bk. 5, ch. 1, ed. H. Lawlor and

J. Oulton, 2 vols., Loeb Classical Library (London and Cambridge, Mass.: Heinemann and Harvard University Press, 1932; repr. 1973), vol. 1, pp. 435–37. Throughout bk. 5, ch. 1, Eusebius displays a fascination with the details of torture similar to that found in James of Voragine.

100. Minucius Felix, *Octavius*, chs. 11, 34, 37–38, trans. R. E. Wallis in *Ante-Nicene Fathers: Translations of the Writings of the Fathers Down to A.D. 325*, ed. A. Roberts and J. Donaldson, vol. 4 (Edinburgh, 1885; repr. Grand Rapids: Eerdmans, 1982), pp. 178–79, 194, and 196–97; on this passage see Arthur Darby Nock, "Cremation and Burial in the Roman Empire," *Harvard Theological Review* 25.4 (1932): 334. The accounts of both Eusebius and Minucius Felix imply, of course, that some Christians did assume that bodily partition threatened resurrection.

101. Ignatius of Antioch, *Epistle to the Romans*, trans. A. Roberts and J. Donaldson in *Ante-Nicene Fathers*, vol. 1, pp. 75 and 104. The textual tradition of Ignatius is very complicated, but this sentiment occurs in all versions of his letters.

102. Eusebius reports this in the same passage where he cites with scorn the Roman conviction that scattering bodies prevents resurrection; he also tells us that the Romans had to post guards to prevent the faithful from stealing the remains to bury them; see *Ecclesiastical History*, bk. 5, ch. 1, vol. 1, pp. 435–37. For stories of early Christians caring for remains, see Hermann-Mascard, *Les Reliques des saints*, pp. 23–26. James of Voragine repeats such stories in *The Golden Legend*.

Many scholars have pointed out that a belief in resurrection tends to emerge in situations of persecution, for adherents want to claim that those who die for the faith will be rewarded in another life with the good fortune they have clearly in some sense been denied in this life. Lionel Rothkrug gives a more profound version of this argument when he suggests that, to Jews of the Maccabaean period and to early Christians, resurrection was a substitute for the burial owed to the pious; see Rothkrug, "German Holiness and Western Sanctity" (note 14 above), pp. 215–29. Thus early Christians could adhere to the hope of resurrection and yet display intense concern for the remains (relics) of their heroes.

103. For bones inviting their disturbance, see Caesarius of Heisterbach, *Dialogus miraculorum*, dist. 8, chs. 85–87, ed. J. Strange, 2 vols. (Cologne: Heberle, 1851), vol. 2, pp. 151–55; for resisting, see dist. 8, chs. 53 and 60, vol. 2, pp. 125–26 and 133. To Caesarius, the bones both are and are not the saint; he says: "Although the souls of the saints always contemplate the divine face, nevertheless they have regard for their bodies, and when they see us devoted to them, they have much delight in this" (ibid., dist. 8, ch. 87, vol. 2, p. 155). He also tells (*Dialogus*, ed. Strange, dist. 8, ch. 88, vol. 2, pp. 155–56) of bones which sort themselves out so that the false relics are eliminated.

104. Robert Grosseteste indeed seems to have forbidden division of his

corpse on his deathbed; see E. A. R. Brown, "Death," pp. 227 and 243. Guibert of Nogent in the *De pignoribus* tells several earlier tales which are intended to indicate that relics do not wish to be dismembered; see *De pignoribus,* bk. 1, ch. 4, cols. 626–30.

105. On Mary of Oignies, see Bynum, *HFHF,* pp. 115–24; and Laura Dushkes, "Illness and Healing in the *Vitae* of Mary of Oignies," M.A. thesis, University of Washington, 1988. For a miracle worked by Mary's finger, see Thomas of Cantimpré, *Supplementum,* ch. 3, pars. 15–17, *AASS* June, vol. 5 (Paris, 1867), pp. 577–78.

106. Thomas of Cantimpré, *Supplementum,* ch. 1, pars. 6–7, pp. 574–75. The hairs, which effected two cures, are repeatedly called a "relic." Thomas recounts an occasion on which they came alive for almost a whole hour; ibid., par. 7, p. 575.

107. For Mary of Oignies's teeth, see ibid., ch. 3, par. 14, pp. 577. For the incident of the head in the Life of Barbara, see Cazelles, *Le corps de sainteté,* pp. 55–56.

108. Caesarius, *Dialogus,* dist. 12, ch. 47, vol. 2, p. 354; see also Bynum, "Female Body and Religious Practice," nn. 149–50. On Aquinas, see E. A. R. Brown, "Death," p. 234 n. 48.

109. L. Thomas, *Le cadavre,* pp. 39–44 and 199; Ariès, *Hour of Our Death,* p. 360. We find in Guibert of Nogent an ambivalence about decay that is characteristic of medieval writers: on the one hand, it is horrible (and therefore cannot touch the bodies of Christ or Mary); on the other hand, it is a return to "mother earth" and should not be inhibited by elaborate coffins. See above note 69.

110. See Bouvier, "De l'incorruptibilité."

111. Caesarius, *Dialogus,* dist. 7, ch. 58, vol. 2, pp. 76–79.

112. Pouchelle, *Corps et chirurgie,* pp. 132–36. She claims that the earliest official dissections (in 1315) were dissections of female bodies. The dissections to which she refers were clearly not the first dissections or autopsies of any sort. Dissections arising out of embalming or for the purpose of determining the cause of death in legal cases were practiced at least from the early thirteenth century; dissections of the human body for teaching purposes were practiced at Bologna about 1300. See Walter Artelt, *Die ältesten Nachrichten über die Sektion menschlicher Leichen im mittelalterlichen Abendland,* Abhandlungen zur Geschichte der Medizin und der Naturwissenschaften 34 (Berlin: Ebering, 1940), pp. 3–25; Mary Niven Alston, "The Attitude of the Church Towards Dissection Before 1500," *Bulletin of the History of Medicine* 16 (1944): 221–38; Ynez Viole O'Neill, "Innocent III and the Evolution of Anatomy," *Medical History* 20.4 (1976): 429–33; Nancy G. Siraisi, "The Medical Learning of Albertus Magnus," in James A. Weisheipl, ed., *Albertus Magnus and the Sciences: Commemorative Essays, 1980* (Toronto: Pontifical Institute of Medieval Studies, 1980), p. 395; and Jacquart and Thomasset, *Sexualité,* p. 49.

113. Agostino Paravicini Bagliani, "Rajeunir au Moyen Âge: Roger Bacon et le mythe de la prolongation de la vie," in *Revue médicale de la Suisse romande* 106 (1986), pp. 9–23, and idem, "Storia della scienza e storia della mentalità: Ruggero Bacone, Bonifacio VIII e la teoria della 'prolongatio vitae,'" in *Aspetti della Letteratura latina nel sècolo XIII: Atti del primo Convegno internazionale di studi dell' Associazione per il Medioevo e l'Umanesimo latini (AMUL) Perugia 3–5 ottobre 1983*, ed. C. Leonardi and G. Orlandi, Quaderni del Centro per il Collegamento degli Studi Medievali e Umanistici nell' Università di Perugia, 15 (Florence and Perugia: "La Nuova Italia," 1985), pp. 243–80; and, for useful background on thirteenth-century notions of "physic," see Faye Marie Getz, "Medicine at Medieval Oxford," in *The History of Oxford University*, vol. 2 (Oxford: at the Clarendon Press), forthcoming.

114. Edward Peters, *Torture* (Oxford: Blackwell, 1985), pp. 67–68.

115. J. G. Bellamy, *The Law of Treason in England in the Later Middle Ages* (Cambridge: Cambridge University Press, 1970), pp. 9, 13, 20–21, 26, 39, 45–47, 52, and 226–27. As Bellamy points out (ibid., p. 227), historians often know the nature of the crime only from the type of execution inflicted. We know, for example, that a homicide had been adjudged petty treason in fourteenth-century England if the male perpetrator was drawn and hung, or the female perpetrator burned. See also Camporesi, *Incorruptible Flesh*, pp. 19–24.

116. Saul N. Brody, *The Disease of the Soul: Leprosy in Medieval Literature* (Ithaca, N.Y.: Cornell University Press, 1974), pp. 64–66, 79, 85–86. See also R. I. Moore, *The Formation of a Persecuting Society: Power and Deviance in Western Europe, 950–1250* (New York: Blackwell, 1987), pp. 58–63; idem, "Heresy as Disease," in *The Concept of Heresy in the Middle Ages (11th–13th Century: Proceedings of the International Conference, Louvain, May 13–16, 1973*, ed. W. Lourdaux and D. Verhelst (Louvain: University Press, 1976), pp. 1–11; and Camporesi, *Incorruptible Flesh*, pp. 90–96.

117. E. A. R. Brown, "Death"; and Paravicini Bagliani, "Rajeunir au Moyen Âge," and "Ruggero Bacone, Bonifacio VIII e la teoria della 'prolongatio vitae.'"

118. See Bynum, *HFHF*, pp. 252–53.

119. I have argued elsewhere that these three assumptions are present *mutatis mutandis* in current philosophical discussion and popular culture: see "Material Continuity, Personal Survival and the Resurrection of the Body: A Scholastic Discussion in Its Medieval and Modern Contexts," *History of Religions* 30 no. 1 (August 1990): 51–85, and *Fragmentation and Redemption: Essays on Gender and the Human Body in Medieval Religion* (New York: Urzone, 1991), Introduction and ch. 7.

3

Alternative Afterlives in Nineteenth-Century France

Thomas Kselman

Medievalists may not all agree with Jacques Le Goff about the importance of the use of purgatory as a noun in the twelfth century, but to judge by a number of recent books, historians increasingly accept his claim that "Ideas about the other world are among the more prominent features of any religion or society."[1] Le Goff proposes that the geography of the afterlife provides "the framework within which society lives and thinks," and that changes in the map of the next world constitute a "crucial intellectual revolution," a change in "life itself." Through the work of Le Goff and others we are now beginning to perceive changes in the map of the afterworld, a new field of research that promises to enlarge our understanding of religious belief and its connections with the development of social and political attitudes. The study of alternative afterlives also bears on questions that are becoming increasingly important in the borderlands between social and intellectual history, questions about self-conception which previous generations have thought about by reflecting on the status of the self after death.

Historians have discussed the birth of purgatory and the decline of hell, and the landscape of heaven has recently been described in a survey that covers 2000 years of history.[2] These and other works show how the three-tiered model of heaven-purgatory-hell constructed during the Middle Ages was challenged by the Reformation and subjected to a broad rationalist critique during the Enlightenment. But in France the success of the Counter-Reformation limited the impact of the Reformers' critique of Purgatory, and the skepticism of the Enlightenment reached only a literate elite. The abbé Meslier (1664–1729) provides a good illustration of the restricted audience for alternative afterlives in the eighteenth century. This curé of Etrépigny in Champagne believed that after death "I shall be nothing." But he never shared his atheism with his parishioners, so as not to deny them the consolation of hope in an afterworld better than this one.[3] For most French men and women it was only in the nineteenth century that orthodox Catholicism lost what Michel Vovelle has called its "hegemonic position, its quasi-monopoly" over images of the afterlife.[4] Despite the pioneering work of Charlton, Vovelle, and Ariès, we still lack a detailed understanding of the alternatives that competed with Catholicism.[5]

During the nineteenth century in France a number of different conceptions of the afterlife were proposed by philosophers and social theorists. But unlike the eighteenth century, discussion of these was not limited to a literate elite. Alternative afterlives were part of a public debate that took place in newspapers and journals as well as philosophical treatises. Organizations were founded that attempted to spread new ideas about the afterlife to a broad audience. These alternative afterlives were unable fully to replace the Catholic model inherited from the Middle Ages. But by posing a public challenge to the received tradition they altered the ways in which French men and women thought not only about the next world, but also about the nature of the self and human destiny.

There were three general alternatives to Catholicism in the nineteenth century: spiritualism, positivism, and spiritism.[6] The first two, spiritualism and positivism, have long been recognized as major philosophical schools and legitimate subjects for historians of ideas. The relations of spiritualism and positivism to political developments in France have been explored, and some historians have also treated their religious dimensions.[7] By comparison, very little is known about French spiritism, a philosophical and religious system that originated in the occult traditions of the eighteenth and early nineteenth centuries and emerged as a coherent and public alternative to Catholicism in the 1850s. In this essay I will deal briefly with spiritualist and positivist speculation on the afterlife, concentrating on the issues of self-conception and human destiny. But most of my attention will be focused on spiritism, for the ideas it propagated allow us to see in a new light personal and religious anxieties that were characteristic of the nineteenth century.

Spiritualism, as developed by its most influential representative, Victor Cousin, was not philosophically innovative, and has not been treated kindly by recent commentators. James Kloppemberg, for example, describes Cousin's philosophy as "a thin verbal wallpaper covering the cracks between science and religion."[8] Nonetheless, through the influence he exerted on French education, Cousin ranks as one of the major figures in nineteenth-century French intellectual life. Cousin's understanding of the afterlife falls within the tradition of deism that had emerged in the Enlightenment. Spiritualists believed that the annihilation of the self at death would seriously undermine a philosophical system in which the individual is the primary source of value. This is especially the case if, as Cousin and his followers observed, rewards and punishments were not equitably distributed during the lifetimes of individuals. The theodicy proposed by spiritualists to explain this discrepancy required an afterlife to ensure that ultimately all individuals received what they deserved.[9] Spiritualists generally assumed the existence of a just God, and their reflections on immortality proceeded from this starting point. In a moving letter to Mme Swetchine written in 1857, Alexis de Tocqueville revealed his most deeply felt religious convictions, which can be taken as a concise statement of spiritualist belief.

> I firmly believe in another life, since God who is sovereignly just has given us such an idea; in this other life, I believe in the remuneration of good and evil, since God has permitted us to distinguish between them and the freedom to choose; but beyond these clear notions everything that is beyond the limits of this world appears to me clouded in a darkness that frightens me.[10]

De Tocqueville's letter suggests a combination of earnestness and anxiety that may not be typical; Cousin's affirmations are generally more self-confident, though this is perhaps because they were published in philosophical treatises. But de Tocqueville's statement, because it appears in his personal correspondence, is perhaps a more telling witness to the quality of spiritualist belief. In the more systematic form provided by Cousin, spiritualism became the basis for philosophical instruction within the French university system for most of the nineteenth century and influenced both academic philosophy and the opinions of the educated elite.[11]

A second general alternative to the Catholic afterlife offered a more radical solution. A number of theorists that I label positivists rejected the idea of an immortal soul and restricted the afterlife to existence in the memories of those still alive. I would extend this term to include people who were not explicitly attached to the philosophical system of Auguste Comte, such as Ernest Renan and Auguste Blanqui. All of these shared a conviction that modern science offered no evidence for the existence of a disembodied spiritual life and that a new basis for self-understanding and morality had to be formulated that focused on the achievement of this-worldly progress.[12] As with the spiritualists, positivists clearly drew on Enlightenment thought, especially that of Condorcet, and like the spiritualists they attempted to find institutional vehicles, such as organizations of free-thinkers and Masonic lodges, for the diffusion of their ideas to a broader audience.[13]

Spiritualists and positivists shared a critical attitude toward the Catholic afterlife, which they saw as a program to frighten people into the churches on the basis of doctrines that undermined confidence in human reason and earthly progress. But when compared with Catholic doctrine, the work of these thinkers seems like arid theorizing. Catholic writers may have argued about some of the specific features of the afterworld but at least they offered believers a clear model of their future based on the long-standing distinctions between heaven, purgatory, and hell. As Le Goff and the Vovelles have suggested, this scheme offered substantial consolation, for despite the fear of hell exploited by many preachers, purgatory was a place that most believers could aspire to, thus preserving in them hope in salvation and eternal bliss. And alongside this doctrine the church elaborated a rich variety of purgatorial devotions that allowed mutual support between the living and the dead.[14] Spiritism never achieved the intellectual legitimacy accorded Cousin, Comte, and their followers, but it was nonetheless potentially a more dangerous competitor, for it provided believers both with a clearer outline of the next world and with rituals which allowed them to explore it.

The development of French spiritism paralleled the spiritualist movements in America and Great Britain which have been described by R. Laurence Moore and Janet Oppenheim.[15] In France, as in England and America, spiritism offered a way "to synthesize modern scientific knowledge and time-honored religious traditions concerning God, man and the universe."[16] French, English, and American spiritists read each others' journals, attended international congresses, and were members of the same associations.[17] Perhaps the best example of such contacts is the French philosopher Henri Bergson, who gave the presidential address to the English Society for Psychical Research in 1913, a speech in which he defended the immortality of the soul on the basis of apparitions of the dead.[18] But French spiritism, while it confirms much of what Oppenheim and Moore have argued in their work, also differs in interesting ways that can help illuminate the religious landscape of France.

A comprehensive history of French spiritism would take us back well before the nineteenth century, to the occult ideas of the late eighteenth century, to the belief in spirit-possession that spread from the mountains of southern France in the late seventeenth century, to the magical practices and Neoplatonism of the Renaissance, and beyond.[19] Spiritists made broad claims about their own genealogy, and sought to legitimize themselves by claiming Pythagoras, Plato, and Jesus as precursors. But the immediate origins of the movement are clearly located in three speculative traditions that flourished during the first half of the nineteenth century.

Socialism, Swedenborgianism, and mesmerism were not discrete and coherent schools of thought.[20] Perhaps the best way to grasp the tendency of these elements to overlap is by recalling some of the enthusiasms taken up and abandoned in turn by Charles Baudelaire. Jules Fleury recalls him in the 1840s as devoted to Swedenborg one day and to the Polish mystic Hoene-Wrónski the next.[21] Attracted to the work of Edgar Allen Poe, Baudelaire's first translation of the American, "Révélation magnétique," described an experiment in which a hypnotist "magnetised" a dying man, whose soul was unnaturally retained for weeks in the body. This story first appeared in the socialist paper *La liberté de penser* in 1848.[22] Baudelaire's dabbling in mysticism, science, and politics reveals a religious skeptic searching for new beliefs that would satisfy his doubt. These were typical concerns of the age, and for many writers social and religious speculation necessarily involved consideration of the afterlife.[23]

The afterlives imagined by socialists have not played a prominent role in current interpretations of this movement. Recent social historians such as William Sewell and Bernard Moss have added a great deal to our understanding of early French socialism, which they describe as influenced by traditions of corporate solidarity and political radicalism, and by the expanding influence of merchant capitalism.[24] Edward Berenson in his recent work, *Populist Religion and Left-Wing Politics in France, 1830–1852*, has now added a religious dimension to socialism that previous historians had neglected.[25] But for Berenson the Christianity of Louis Blanc, Pierre Leroux, and others is essentially a medium for the expression of political and social ideals, and it seems fair to say that he is interested in religion primarily because of its political consequences.

Without discounting the value of this argument, it nevertheless reflects a functionalist view of religion that limits our understanding of the significance and quality of religious belief. The figure of Alphonse

Esquiros, who figures in Berenson's account of populist religion, illustrates this problem. Esquiros is presented by Berenson as a typical representative of social-democratic ideology in the 1840s. He is critical of the domination of capital and a vigorous defender of the right to work. As editor of the most important social-democratic paper outside of Paris he was responsible for the spread of radical ideas into the countryside around Marseille. All of this is true, but there are additional elements in Esquiros's career that arguably belong in a work seeking connections between religious belief and political ideology.

In addition to his career as politician and journalist, Esquiros was also a novelist, a historian, a playwright, and a theologian. In his literary work he displays an interest in metempsychosis, an idea which he explores more fully in a pamphlet published both in Marseille and Paris during the Second Republic, *De la vie future au point de vue socialiste* (The afterlife from the socialist point of view).[26] In this essay Esquiros argues that a future life is "a truth of natural history," that can be established by reason and observation. Death is another birth, following which our lives will continue, first on this planet, and then perhaps on others. Our future lives will not be exclusively spiritual, for we will retain a body composed of a subtle matter with which we will experience all our earthly sensations, as well as some new ones which are not specified. The continued life of the body is essential for Esquiros, who asserts that "I don't believe in the immortality of the soul; I believe in the immortality of man."[27] Esquiros explicitly links the future life to his political ideals, for "Belief in philosophic immortality is the most secure boundary from which one can defend against the invasion of brutal strength. Let the persecuters attack their victims; time will seize them by the throat and strangle them. . . . The doctrine of the immortality of the soul is a revolutionary doctrine, a democratic doctrine."[28]

For Esquiros, working for the social-democratic republic was possible only because he was convinced that all those who participated in the struggle would someday personally enjoy the fruits of their labor. The certainty of a future life was necessary to his ideology as a shield against despair in a battle that was difficult, and which might cost socialists their lives. Charles Fourier shared this perspective, but was even more daring in his speculation about the afterlife. Jonathan Beecher, in his recent biography of Fourier, argues that his cosmological system was neither a joke nor an aberration, as previous scholars had claimed.[29] Fourier himself saw his doctrine of immortality as "one of the pivots of the harmonian system: it would be a scrawny runt without the solution of this problem. . . ."[30] Fourier began his argument by reflecting on the desire for immortality that can be observed as a general characteristic of humanity. It can be seen, for example, in a veiled manner in the regrets of old people who wish that they could start their lives over again, but possessed of all the wisdom of their experience. In Fourier's system such a desire is a clue to human destiny, for God would not have allowed for such an attraction unless it were to be in some way fulfilled.[31] Starting from this desire, Fourier proposed that we return to life armed with our experience, in a series of reincarnations that will last for 80,000 years. Half of these lives (810 of the total of 1620) will be on earth, the other in a vague extra-mundane state comparable to sleep.

Pierre Leroux has recently drawn attention as a socialist whose influence was undervalued by previous historians.[32] With Leroux, as with Fourier, the afterlife plays a central role in his ideology. In his two-volume work, *De l'humanité*, which first appeared in 1840, Leroux emphasizes the relationship between individual perfection in an afterlife and social progress.[33] Leroux's version of the afterlife is rooted exclusively in earthly society, for unlike Fourier he does not postulate any "trans-mundane" existences. Our future lives will be lived on earth, and they will be very much like our current existence.[34] Leroux's formulation of the afterlife made him liable to attacks from Catholics and spiritualists that he was a pantheist, and some passages in his work suggest an understanding of immortality as the absorption of the self into a larger whole. "You *are*, thus you *will be*. Because, being, you participate in being, that is to say the eternal and infinite being."[35] But Leroux was explicitly critical of the materialist tradition and defended a self, a "moi," that endured and took on successive corporal forms in which previous experience was present, but not explicitly remembered. Individual lives, although not recalled in detail, were nonetheless incorporated into the self. He compared this process to the experience of sleep, a period when

> our ideas, our sensations, our sentiments from the previous day, are transformed and incarnated in us, become us. . . . Sleep regenerates us, and we leave it more alive and strengthened, but with a certain forgetfulness. In death, which is a greater forgetting, it seems that our life is digested and elaborated in a manner that, while effacing itself in its phenomenal form, is transformed in us, and augments, in passing by this latent state, the potential force of our life. . . . We have been, we no longer remem-

ber the forms of this existence; and nevertheless we are, by our virtual-
ity, precisely the result of what we have been, and always the same being, but enlarged.[36]

Socialists such as Fourier, Leroux, and Esquiros all rejected materialism as demoralizing, and postulated individual immortality as necessary in a social philosophy that sought the reconciliation of individual and social progress. Not all socialists accepted such an argument;
Proudhon and Saint-Simon, for example, attempted to construct a moral
system without reference to future lives. The socialism of these skeptics, and the atheism of Marx and Engels, have contributed to a tendency among contemporary intellectuals to assume a clear polarity in
which conservative political and social ideologies are aligned with a belief in personal immortality, whereas a commitment to social change
is associated with denial of an afterlife. But socialist reflection on personal immortality during the nineteenth century testifies to the powerful appeal this doctrine still exercised even among some of those radically critical of the social and ecclesiastical systems.

Although socialists sometimes made general references to mesmerist
experiments, the afterlives they described were essentially speculative
derivations from their philosophical principles. But during the first half
of the nineteenth century similar claims about the afterlife were made
on the basis of testimony from travelers to the next world. This direct
access to the afterlife was an integral part of the Swedenborgian and
mesmermist movements that flourished in the Romantic era and prepared
the way for the séances which were the central ritual of the spiritist
movement of the 1850s.[37]

Alphonse Cahagnet, a mesmerist active in the 1840s and 1850s,
was a transitional figure whose work links the diffuse ideas and practices of the Romantic era to the spiritist movement of the 1850s. Cahagnet began his career as a hypnotist-healer whose "somnambules" gave
medical advice to clients. But Cahagnet was familiar with the occult
tradition and its defense of the spirit world, as presented in works of
Saint-Martin and Swedenborg. In the late 1840s his "somnambules" began
to report meetings with angels, and then with the dead, and to carry
messages back and forth between this world and the next. By 1848 spirit
communications had become more important in his work than healings
and formed the basis of his first book, *Arcanes de la vie future dévoilés.*
Cahagnet claimed that mesmerists had become too preoccupied with
physical phenomena and hesitated to report on the evidence of spiritual

forces and their implications. The interviews with his "somnambules" transcribed and published in *Arcanes* established a new program for mesmerist research.

> This work will offer you the proof of a world better than ours, where you will exist after having left your body in the here-below, and where an infinitely good God will reward you a hundredfold for the evils that it was useful for you to suffer in this world of pain. I am going to prove that your relatives, your friends wait for you impatiently, that you can, while in this world, enter into communication with them, speak with them, and obtain information that you will judge necessary; in order to do this, it is not necessary to deny the existence of the soul, or abandon all good will and justice in order to obtain the desired proofs; by somnambulism you will have as much proof as you will desire.[38]

For Cahagnet, mesmerist contact with the spirit-world provided a theodicy, guaranteed family solidarity beyond the grave, and ensured the truth of its claims by an appeal to empirical evidence and scientific method. The clear statement of this potent mixture of religious and family sensibilities, legitimized by science, make Cahagnet a key figure in the early history of French spiritism, a fact already accepted by Emma Hardinge Britten, an English devotee who published a comprehensive history of the European movement in 1884.[39] But Cahagnet, according to Britten, was a John the Baptist in relation to the personalities who came after him, an analogy she doesn't complete, but which suggests something of the millennial mood that attached to spiritism in France and elsewhere.

Spiritism in France became an organized movement in the 1850s, in response to the immediate stimulus provided by news of the "turning tables" of the United States and England. To judge by the journalistic response and the anxiety of the clergy, large numbers of French men and women repeated the practices of Americans and British by sitting around a table and invoking spirits that answered by rappings or by taking possession of one of the assistants, who became a medium through which they communicated with this world.[40] The best documented of these séances is the series of invocations that occurred in the home of Victor Hugo, in exile on the island of Jersey, between September 1853 and October 1855.[41] Of course, it would be impossible to claim that these sessions, conducted in the presence of and frequently transcribed by one of the literary giants of the nineteenth century, were completely typical. But the practices of Jersey and the questions considered were not all or even primarily initiated by Hugo. The first experiments were introduced by Delphine de Girardin, the wife of the liberal journalist and a prominent figure in Parisian society. Arriving on Jersey in early September, visibly weakened by the cancer that would soon kill her, she described the séances of Paris and arranged the circle of participants according to her previous experiences in the capital. Victor Hugo was at first skeptical, and only gradually let himself be absorbed into the spirit conversations. Finally, the séances were open to frequent visitors from the Continent, a detail which may help explain why the events on Jersey resemble those that occurred elsewhere.

The initial questions posed to the spirits of Jersey were tests in which the participants asked the table to tell them what they were thinking or what they had written. The results were disappointing, but on the evening of September 11, a breakthrough occurred. In answering a series of questions about the thoughts of the participants a spirit was identified as Léopoldine Hugo, the much-loved daughter who had drowned in a boating accident soon after her marriage in 1846. From this point on Victor Hugo was a regular and active assistant. Over the next few months a number of topics were discussed with the spirits, but by 1854 literature and literary gossip were the dominant subjects as writers from the past, including Shakespeare and Moliére, acknowledged the genius of Hugo and dictated new works.

Political circumstances as well as family sentiment may help explain Hugo's fascination with the turning tables. Exiled from France following the collapse of the Second Republic, which he had supported, it was undoubtedly consoling for Hugo and his circle to receive assurances from beyond about their ultimate success; even the spirit of Napoleon III, traveling during the emperor's sleep, paid a call to Jersey to confess his guilt and ask pardon. There was some talk among family members that the séances might be a distraction from the political work to be done, but isolated on Jersey in the face of Napoleon's apparent triumph, Hugo did not have many options.[42] Fascination with spiritism as a distraction from political defeat was clearly at work in Paris as well. In 1853 the socialist playwright Eugène Nus and some former collaborators on the paper *Démocratie pacifique* came across an article on spirit rappings in an American newspaper. Bored and disillusioned, they immediately began to experiment, and the tables responded with messages that showed the spirit world to be in accord with their socialist convictions.[43] The existence of a spirit world had been affirmed by a number of prominent socialists prior to 1850; in the face of political defeat some disciples began to make regular contact with the next world and were thereby reassured about the ultimate success of their principles.

Family and political concerns provide an important background for understanding the Jersey séances, but for Hugo and his friends the experiments were significant because they illuminated the ultimate context within which all personal and social problems could be resolved. The cosmology revealed by the spirits provided Hugo and the other questioners with guidance and reassurance on fundamental religious and metaphysical problems.

Hugo was repelled by the doctrine of eternal punishment, but he was equally anxious that good and evil men not share the same fate. The afterlife as revealed by the spirits reconciled the need for reward and punishment with the rejection of hell. On September 13 a spirit confirmed Hugo's belief that there is no hell, and on September 29 (a day when Victor Hugo was not present), a spirit from Jupiter, in response to a series of leading questions, affirmed that "depending on whether their conduct is good or bad, human beings after their death are on happy or unhappy planets."[44] These ideas were familiar to Hugo from his contacts with the socialists and mystics who had considered the problem of evil from a non-Christian perspective during the Romantic decades of the 1830s and 1840s. Pierre Leroux was, for example, a friend who passed through Jersey late in September and with whom Hugo had serious discussions about the phenomena.[45] Mme Hugo, addressing the spirits in December 1853 asserted that the key revelations about the immortality of the soul and its extraterrestrial reincarnations on other planets were already established dogma among the Hugo circle. As was typical on Jersey among both humans and spirits, her comment concluded with an adulatory bow in Hugo's direction. "You see, she told the spirit, that insofar as men are concerned, his thought preceded your revelation."[46]

The Jersey séances, and those in France as well, may not have communicated original ideas, but they did offer what was apparently direct empirical evidence of an afterlife. But when questioned about publishing the transcripts of the séances, the most impressive of all the spirits, L'Ombre de Sépulcre, hesitated, and ordered that they be shown only to those who already believed.[47] The Hugo circle accommodated itself willingly to this advice. Some of what transpired on Jersey appeared in a book by Auguste Vacquerie in 1863, but Hugo himself never published a word about the séances, a surprising reticence for a writer whose productivity and vanity are as legendary as his genius. One reason for Hugo's hesitancy was the doubt that he periodically experienced about the precise nature of the phenomena. Perhaps, he speculated, there were no spirits, and the sessions only produced thoughts that were circulating among the participants. The fact that some of the poetry dictated by the spirits resembled his own verses clearly favored this position. On a more philosophic plane, Hugo may have been concerned that the revelations would somehow diminish the sublimity and mystery that he valued in his vision of the universe.[48]

The spirits did not reveal themselves exclusively to the left. The imperial family had a number of sessions with the famous Scottish medium Daniel Douglas Home in 1857. The Empress Eugénie was convinced that her father had squeezed her hand during one séance, and the emperor was also favorably impressed.[49] The vogue of turning tables, widely commented on during the 1850s, was broad enough to include the emperor and his most famous opponent. Flaubert's decision to ridicule spiritism as one of the fads adopted by his representatives of bourgeois fatuity, Bouvard and Pécuchet, is further evidence of spiritism's cultural impact.[50] By the 1860s public as well as private séances were a familiar part of the Paris social scene, a point that can be illustrated by describing the performances of the Davenport brothers, two American mediums whose spirit show was a much-discussed topic of conversation in September 1865.

The Davenports' act consisted in letting themselves be tied by ropes inside an armoire, which was then closed.[51] Then, ostensibly while they were bound, spirits were evoked that played guitars, tambourines, and other instruments. The reports in *Le Temps*, the leading liberal journal of the day, were consistently skeptical, and made an explicit comparison between the Davenports' tricks and those performed by magicians, including the famous Robert Houdin, who claimed no supernatural assistance. While the Davenports were performing, the magician Robin was providing similar entertainment, at a lower price than the twenty francs charged by the Americans, at the Paris Hippodrome. Robin, in fact, was drawing crowds in part by claiming he could perform the same feats and therefore refute the claims of the spiritists, a posture that led some of their followers to try and disrupt his act. The first séance of the Davenports was disorderly, with members of the audience leaping onto the stage trying to verify that no fraud was being committed. The show ended in chaos when one skeptic mounted the stage and claimed to show how the brothers were able to escape from their bonds using the folding seat in the armoire. The crowd began shouting, and the French translator and master of ceremonies responded by promising to return the admission fees. The disorder led the police to enter the room and force everyone to leave.

The next evening the Davenports' experiments were repeated, but only before an audience of invited guests, each of whom paid an admission fee of thirty francs, which amounts to more than the average worker would earn in a week. With no journalists present, the performance went smoothly, but *Le Temps* commented ironically that had the problems continued, another session would have been scheduled again, and the admission fee doubled. Responding to this sarcasm, the Davenports arranged a third performance, to which they invited a number of journalists. This time no problems occurred, and even *Le Temps* admitted its representative was unable to discover the trick. But despite the lack of clear evidence that would provide a natural explanation for the performance, the paper continued to doubt. One contributor to *Le Temps* asked why the Davenports continued to require the presence of armed guards at their performances, a security measure unnecessary at the performances of Houdin. His explanation addressed the central issue in the public controversy over spiritism. The need for protection was the result of "the highly unusual pretension of the Davenport brothers, who don't want to be conjurers, but mediums. The guitars which grate, the tambourines which wander . . . obey supernatural powers."[52] The article concluded by demanding to know why powerful spirits would need the crude material security provided by police and why the authorities should be defending fraud when political and civil liberties were being denied.

The experiments on Jersey have suggested that spiritism offered some hope of resolving difficult philosophical and religious questions. The Davenport show and the general attention given spiritism in the press and in literature during the 1850s and 1860s reveal public fascination with spirit manifestations. The intellectual and popular appeal of the movement was based in large part on the work of two French thinkers, Allan Kardec and Camille Flammarion.

Kardec was born Hippolyte-Léon-Denizard Rivail in Lyon in 1804; the son of a lawyer, he was educated at the Protestant school of Pestalozzi in Geneva, and apparently suffered from religious prejudice because of his Catholicism. Rivail moved to Paris in 1824, where he ran his own school for almost a decade. When financial troubles forced him to close he worked as a lycée teacher and wrote a number of manuals to prepare students for state examinations.[53] During the 1830s and 1840s Rivail also kept abreast of developments in mesmerism and starting in 1854 he began attending the séances of a number of Paris mediums; in 1856 Rivail, now known as Allan Kardec, names he bore in previous existences, published *Le livre des esprits,* a work which became the most important document of the spiritist movement and which is still in print after dozens of reeditions over the past century.[54] In 1858 Kardec founded *La Revue Spirite,* a journal which he edited until his death in 1869 and which was the official publication of Kardec's Société des Etudes Spirites. Kardec's work as both publicist and organizer resulted in the creation of a network that his followers claimed may have linked as many as 600,000. This estimate may be exaggerated, but if we take into account the enormous success of his many books and the attention he received in the press, it is clear that Kardec was an influential thinker.[55] He is still revered by spiritists, who have made his tomb in Père Lachaise cemetery a shrine whose popularity rivals that of Edith Piaf's (who was also a spiritist).

At his death in 1869 Kardec was eulogized by Camille Flammarion (1842–1925), a scientist and author whose career suggests the powerful appeal of spiritist ideas in the second half of the nineteenth century.[56] As a child Flammarion prepared for the priesthood, but was forced to leave the *petit séminaire* of Langres following a financial crisis in his family. As an apprentice engraver in Paris, Flammarion continued to educate himself and eventually won a position at the Paris Observatory. In 1862 he began a publishing career which lasted sixty years and included over seventy books. Flammarion's works were an important factor in the success of the firm established by his brother and which continues to be a force in the world of French publishing.[57]

Flammarion is perhaps best known for his defense of the doctrine of extraterrestriality. Starting with *La pluralité des mondes* in 1862, Flammarion consistently argued for the existence of intelligent life on other planets, including the sun.[58] As Michael Crowe has recently shown, the concept of extraterrestriality was at the center of nineteenth-century astronomy. As founder and first president of France's *Société astronomique,* an organization which attracted primarily amateurs with an interest in recent scientific discoveries, Flammarion was a key figure in the popularization of astronomy. He also served in the 1860s as editor of the popular *Magasin pittoresque,* and as a writer for the newspaper *Le Siècle.* He presented his ideas through the genres of philosophical dialogues and fiction as well as in popular accounts of science, such as his *Astronomie populaire.*[59]

Kardec and Flammarion were not alone in their work, and a number of other authors also gained notoriety for describing afterlives that shared common ground with the spiritist movement.[60] But Kardec and Flammarion were the most prominent, and it is their work that is seen as the basis for the contemporary spiritist movement.[61] Under their leadership spiritism developed into a public statement of beliefs already seen at work in the séances on Jersey. Personal immortality, reincarnation on earth, and the transmigration of souls to other planets, where they experienced moral progress or decline based on their inclination and will, were the key elements in spiritist cosmology. Kardec and Flammarion, however, chose to emphasize certain features in their system which distinguish their work from the previous loosely formulated Romantic tradition and from British and American spiritualism as well. These distinctions can help illuminate the changing features of French religion in the nineteenth century.

First of all, the spiritist movement of the 1850s appears to have retreated from the commitment to social progress evident in the earlier period. The socialists (Esquiros, Fourier, Leroux) who speculated about the afterlife were inspired by a vision in which social progress remained a central concern, and they understood individual progress in the afterlife to be conditioned by the collective experience of the human race. Although Kardec retains a few references to social progress, he emphasizes instead the ways in which spiritist doctrines justify the fate of individuals in this world.[62] In the earlier period the doctrine of immortality was consoling because it guaranteed that the individual would participate in the future glory for which he worked. Spiritism in the 1850s looked backward as well as forward and saw earthly existence as expiation for personal imperfection. Human lives are not conditioned so much by social circumstances as they are by individual moral choices made in previous existences. Not surprisingly, spiritism in the 1850s found many of its recruits in the middle classes, a fact which Kardec noted with pride and tried to use as an advertisement for the movement.[63]

Spiritism in the 1850s also took a more ambiguous position on the material conditions of the afterlife. During the first half of the century the afterlife was frequently described as a material as well as spiritual existence; influenced by Swedenborg, thinkers such as Fourier,

Esquiros, and Cahagnet proposed that embodied selves would continue to experience physical sensations and even have sexual relations in their future existences. Kardec was also unable to imagine a self that was exclusively spiritual, but his conceptualization of the self was more complicated and ambiguous than that of his predecessors.

Kardec proposed that the individual in his earthly life consists of a physical body, a spiritual soul, and a third element he called the *périsprit,* composed of an ethereal matter that mediates between the soul and the body.[64] This entity, an ancestor of the astral body that figures largely in the thought of Shirley MacLaine and her New Age colleagues, resembles the body and allows the self to continue to interact with earthly beings and other spirits. It was the *périsprit* that spiritists used to explain the ghostly apparitions and the physical manifestations of the séances. But the *périsprit* is without sex; in future reincarnations it can assume the body of either male or female and the choice is an indifferent one.[65] Furthermore, as the self continues to progress through the universe, it eventually is freed from the need to seek embodiment and survives as a combination of *périsprit* and soul. In the final stages of development, even the matter of the *périsprit* disappears, and all that remains is the spiritual soul.[66] This formulation suggests that Kardec was torn between a vision in which the essential self resided in a spiritual soul and one which emphasized the importance of material continuity as the basis for personal identity. In her essay in this volume Caroline Bynum shows how this debate can be traced in philosophical and devotional writings of the Middle Ages, and she concludes that medieval Christianity, for all its "spirituality" retained a sense of self that included a positive interpretation of corporality.[67] It may be that skepticism directed against specific Christian doctrines such as the resurrection of the body in fact undermined the corporal sense of self; spiritualists such as Cousin certainly have a more ethereal view of the afterlife and of the permanent self than is found in orthodox Christianity. But the writings of Swedenborg and those influenced by him suggest a continuing desire to envision the afterlife as a corporeal as well as spiritual existence. Kardec's *périsprit* reveals a confused and hesitant attitude about the definition of matter and spirit and their relationship to one another; it thereby illuminates a struggle over the conception of self which was being worked out within the systems of religious belief available in the nineteenth century.[68]

Finally, French spiritism is distinctive in its emphasis on the astronomical context of future lives and in its alienation from Christianity. In England psychology, biology, and physics all played a role in the debates surrounding the spiritualist movement, but in France it was the sidereal revolution, the growing realization that the universe included countless stars, that had the greatest impact on speculation about the afterlife.[69] To judge on the basis of Flammarion's experience, this may be due in part to the enduring predominance and clarity of the Catholic model of the next world. Although they debated the implications both of extraterrestrial life and spiritualist experiments, English Christians, on the whole, showed themselves able to accommodate themselves to these positions.[70] In France, where Christianity was expressed almost exclusively within the Catholic church, there was less space available for debate and discussion about these questions. At the age of eighteen, when Flammarion began to ask himself questions about the location of heaven, hell, and purgatory, whose existence seemed incompatible with his knowledge of the universe, he found no one within the church able to deal effectively with his problems.[71] Previous thinkers, including Fourier and Reynaud, had already speculated that the physical universe could be viewed as the site of future lives. Flammarion adopted this position as capable of reconciling his knowledge of the physical universe and his commitment to immortality, and his scientific expertise provided it with a legitimacy that worked to the advantage of the spiritist movement. But in France such a position required him to move away from the church, and from Christianity.[72]

How are we to interpret the evidence of spiritism in nineteenth-century France? Traditional lines of analysis are certainly a useful starting point. We can argue, with Oppenheim, Moore, and Ariès, that, in an age marked by religious skepticism, the growing prestige of science, and greater affectivity between family members, spiritism provided scientific sanction for reassuring beliefs about the future of the self and the eternal solidarity of the family. A more hostile and functionally oriented analysis might stress the escapism implicit in spiritist practice and doctrine. Oppressed workers, and later bored middle classes, sought relief and entertainment by imagining a world better than this one. From the perspective of the history of religion, spiritism illustrates the continuing spread of doubt about the afterworld preached by orthodox Christianity, whose God was willing to condemn people to eternal punishment for even momentary and trivial lapses.

All of these approaches help us understand spiritism, but I believe they should be supplemented by applying some insights drawn from recent work in intellectual history. Influenced by linguistic theory and literary criticism, historians of ideas have questioned our reading of texts, which can no longer be seen as yielding univocal and unambiguous meanings, nor as bearing an uncomplicated relationship to a nonlinguistic reality to which they refer.[73] Spiritist texts, in their attempt to describe a ghost-world with the help of scientific language and thereby solve once and for all profound metaphysical problems concerning the self and its destiny, seem to me especially appropriate for this kind of analysis.

Devotees of spiritism not only read the extensive publications produced by Kardec, Flammarion, and others. They actively responded to them, and their own experiences became part of the spiritist literature. In his later years Flammarion's published works are increasingly taken up with the reports he received from correspondents eager to share with him stories about ghosts, haunted houses, second sight, and telepathy.[74] The audience that Flammarion appealed to was responding to an author who experimented with a number of genres, including imaginative fiction, as vehicles for expressing his ideas about death and human destiny. Flammarion was not the only writer in the spiritist tradition drawn to fiction. Esquiros included a long ghost story as a preface to his philosophical essay on the future life.[75] Fourier's early writings, for all their seriousness, were presented as a parody in which the truthful elements would be protected by a veil of more absurd inventions that would draw the attention of critics.[76]

With this blurring of genres in mind, I would like to conclude with the suggestion that spiritist texts can be understood if we associate them with the *conte fantastique,* a literary form roughly equivalent to the Victorian ghost story popular throughout the nineteenth century. Literary critics who have grappled with defining this genre focus on its combination of psychological realism and supernatural incident. According to Pierre-Georges Castex, the fantastic is characterized by "a brutal intrusion of mystery into the framework of real life."[77] For Tzvetan Todorov the fantastic is "the hesitation experienced by someone who knows only natural laws when he confronts an event apparently supernatural."[78] Todorov's analysis is especially interesting, for he proposes that uncertainty is at the core of the fantastic; as soon as a character can determine the exact nature of the experience, the story is no longer fantastic. Although the *conte fantastique* has a history of its own, these general characteristics can be found in stories written throughout the nineteenth century by authors including Charles Nodier, Prosper Mérimée, Théophile Gautier, and Guy de Maupassant.[79] Of course, the stories of Poe, as translated by Baudelaire, also fall within this genre.[80]

The fantastic element in many of these stories includes contact with the dead, who are met in a dreamlike state. In its classic form, as represented by Gautier's "La cafetière," a young man joins a party of ghosts who descend from their pictures in the bedroom he occupies at a friend's house. He dances and falls in love with one of them, a young woman named Angela, who then disappears as the morning light comes through the windows. After the young man is awakened, he passes off his experience as an illusion and begins to sketch aimlessly at breakfast. His friend identifies the sketch as his sister, who died two years previously.[81] The appeal of this *conte fantastique* rests on its ability to combine the experience of belief and doubt in contemplating death and the afterlife. But the choice of a genre that is explicitly imaginative creates a distance between the reader and this experience; the possibility of an afterlife, and of contact with the dead, is implicitly denied by being expressed in a story that is invented. Many spiritist texts, especially Kardec's, promise a more direct experience of the afterworld. But Kardec also leaves room for doubt by noting inconsistencies in the spirit messages and looking to the future for the confirmation that will eliminate the skepticism his doctrines provoke. Flammarion is even more willing to accept uncertainty, as suggested in the titles of his works, which refer to the infinite, the unknown, and the mysterious.[82] Hugo's hesitancy to publish the results of the Jersey séances resonates with Flammarion's implicit acknowledgment that, despite their volume and overt self-confidence, his writings were unable to uncover the secrets of the universe.

A similar ambiguity can be observed in the Davenport performances. Critics made a particular point of comparing the tricks of the Davenports with those produced by magicians who claimed no supernatural powers, a position repeated by skeptics in subsequent cases in France and elsewhere. This skeptical posture, and the evidence it employed, can help undermine supernaturalist claims, but it passes over the question of what drew audiences to the performances of both mediums and magicians, and assumes that a sharp distinction existed between the two in the minds of audiences. Was this in fact the case? Were those who attended the shows of Robin, and later Houdin, drawn exclusively because they admired the art these men employed in making guitars strum and tambourines sound without any apparent physical action on their part? We know that in the eighteenth century performers in the fairs of Paris still played on doubts people had about the explanations for their magical acts.[83] And even if the audience assumed that the performers were using "natural" means, what accounts for their fascination with the pretense that the person in fact responsible for the trick could not be seen to have done anything? In England, the famous relationship between Arthur Conan Doyle and the magician Houdini shows us that someone convinced of the mediumistic powers of a performer can deny even the explicit disavowal of such powers by the performer. I am willing to accept the skeptical argument that natural means were used in the performances of both mediums and magicians, but the appeal of these acts may nonetheless be in part the result of an audience's desire to contemplate, within the context of a performance, the possibility of spiritual reality.

We will never know for sure what went on in the minds of the readers of *contes fantastiques* and of spiritist literature, nor can we be certain of the attitudes of the audiences that attended public séances and magic shows. But we do know that many French men and women were drawn to these in an age of declining religious practice and public discussion about the fate of the self after death. These texts and performances suggest an odd psychological state in which artist and audience agree to consider immortality, the afterlife, and relations with the beyond in carefully limited circumstances (in the pages of a book, in a theater, or at the movies) that I take as characteristically modern.

NOTES

1. Jacques Le Goff, *The Birth of Purgatory* (Chicago: University of Chicago Press, 1986), p. 1.

2. Le Goff, *The Birth of Purgatory;* Michel and Gaby Vovelle, *Vision de la mort et l'au-delà en Provence d'après les autels des âmes du Purgatoire* (Paris: Colin, 1970); D. P. Walker, *The Decline of Hell: Seventeenth-Century Discussions of Eternal Torment* (Chicago: University of Chicago Press, 1964); Colleen McDannell and Bernhard Lang, *Heaven: A History* (New Haven: Yale University Press, 1988). See also Geoffrey Rowell, *Hell and the Victorians: A Study of the Nineteenth-Century Theological Controversies Concerning Eternal Punishment and the Future Life* (Oxford: Clarendon Press, 1974). For an interesting work comparing near-death experiences, including glimpses of the afterworld, in medieval and modern times, see Carol Zaleski, *Otherworld Journeys* (New York: Oxford University Press, 1985). Zaleski, however, passes very quickly over the nineteenth century.

3. John McManners, *Death and the Enlightenment* (Oxford: Clarendon Press, 1981), p. 161. For a recent edition of Meslier's works see his *Oeuvres complèts: Préface et notes par Jean Deprun, Roland Desné, Albert Soboul* (Paris: Anthropos, 1970).

4. Michel Vovelle, *La mort et l'occident de 1300 à nos jours* (Paris: Gallimard, 1983), p. 532.

5. D. G. Charlton, *Secular Religions in France, 1815–1870* (New York: Oxford University Press, 1963) includes material on beliefs about the afterlife, and his work remains a valuable starting point for the study of alternatives to Catholicism. In addition to *Vision de la mort et l'au-delà en Provence*, written with Gaby Vovelle, Michel Vovelle's works include: *Mourir autrefois: Attitudes collectives devant la mort aux XVIIᵉ et XVIIIᵉ siècles* (Paris: Gallimard, 1974); *La piété baroque et déchristianisation en Provence au XVIIIᵉ siècle* (Paris: Seuil, 1978); *La mort et l'occident de 1300 à nos jours*. Philippe Ariès' works include *The Hour of Our Death* (New York: Knopf, 1981), and *Images of Man and Death* (Cambridge, Mass.: Harvard University Press, 1985). For a review essay on the work of Vovelle and Ariès see Thomas Kselman, "Death in Historical Perspective," *Sociological Forum* 2 (1987): 591–97.

6. There is some possibility for terminological confusion, since in France *spiritualisme* describes something very different from American and English "spiritualism." Because French philosophers such as Cousin had already adopted the term *spiritualisme* to describe their deist position, those interested in communication with the dead chose *spiritisme* to describe their philosophy. On the choice of terms see Allan Kardec, *Le livre des esprits*, 15th ed. (Paris: Didier, 1865), pp. iii–v.

7. For a useful introduction that emphasizes ways in which these philosophical traditions shaped French moral education see Phyllis Stock-Morton, *Moral Education for a Secular Society: The Development of Moral Laique in Nineteenth-Century France* (Albany: State University of New York Press, 1988). See also: William Logue, *From Philosophy to Sociology: The Evolution of French Liberalism, 1870–1914* (DeKalb, Ill.: Northern Illinois University Press, 1983). Standard works include: Felix Ravaisson, *La philosophie en France au XIXᵉ siècle*, 2nd ed. (Paris: Hachette, 1885); Hippolyte Taine, *Les philosophes classiques du XIXᵉ siècle*, 7th ed. (Paris, 1895); J. Gunn, *Modern French Philosophy* (London: Unwin, 1922); Emile Bréhier, *The History of Philosophy*, vol. 6: *The Nineteenth Century* (Chicago: University of Chicago Press, 1968); Walter M. Simon, "The 'Two Cultures' of the Nineteenth Century: Victor Cousin and Auguste Comte," *Journal of the History of Ideas* 17 (1956): 311–31.

8. James Kloppenberg, *Uncertain Victory: Social Democracy and Progressivism in European and American Thought, 1870–1920* (New York: Oxford University Press, 1986), p. 17. For an introduction to Cousin see Alan Spitzer, *The French Generation of 1820* (Princeton: Princeton University Press, 1987), pp. 71–96. See also Stock-Morton, *Moral Education*, pp. 33–44.

9. Cousin's defense of immortality can be found in his *Du vrai, de beau, et du bien* (Paris, 1856), pp. 412–22. See also his pamphlet, *Philosophie populaire* (Paris: Didot, 1848).

10. The French text reads: "Je crois fermement à une autre vie, puisque Dieu qui est souverainement juste, nous en a donné l'idée; dans cette autre vie, à la rémunération du bien et du mal, puisque Dieu nous a permis de les distinguer et nous a donné la liberté de choisir; mais au-delà de ces notions claires, tout ce qui dépasse les bornes de ce monde me parait enveloppé de ténèbres qui m'épouvantent." In Alexis de Tocqueville, *Oeuvres complètes,* vol. 15 (Paris: Gallimard, 1983), p. 315.

11. For philosophical defenses of immortality that resemble those of Cousin see Jules Simon, *La religion naturelle* (Paris, 1856); Charles Renouvier *Essais de critique générale—deuxième essai* (Paris: Ladrange, 1859), pp. 565–689. On the philosophical influence of these thinkers see Stock-Morton, *Moral Education,* pp. 47–59. Emile Ollivier, the liberal prime minister during the closing days of the Second Empire, expressed sentiments similar to those of de Tocqueville in his will; see Jacques Gadille, "On French Anticlericalism: Some Reflections," *European Studies Review* 13 (1983): 138.

12. For Comte's religious doctrine see the collection of his work edited by Gertrud Lenzer, *Auguste Comte and Positivism: The Essential Writings* (New York: Harper, 1975), pp. 393–98, 442–76; for a brief discussion of Cousin's understanding of subjective immortality see Pierre Arnauld's introduction to Auguste Comte, *Catéchisme positiviste* (Paris: Flammarion, 1966), pp. 19–20. For Renan's position see his *L'avenir de la science,* in *Oeuvres complètes,* vol. 3 (Paris: Calmann-Levy, 1949), pp. 982–1018; for Blanqui see *L'éternité par les astres* (Paris: Baillière, 1872).

13. On organizations of free-thinkers see: Jacqueline Laloulette, "Les enterrements civils dans les premières décennies de la Troisième République," *Ethnologie française* 13 (1983): 111–28; Thomas Kselman, "Funeral Conflicts in Nineteenth-Century France," *Comparative Studies in Society and History* 30 (1988): 325–27; Patrick Hutton, *The Cult of the Revolutionary Tradition: The Blanquists in Politics, 1864–1893* (Berkeley: University of California Press, 1981), pp. 51–53. For the shift of the Masons from theism to atheism during the 1860s see Gérard Gayot, *La franc-maçonnerie française* (Paris: Gallimard, 1980), pp. 226–29.

14. Michel et Gaby Vovelle, *Vision de la mort et l'au-delà en Provence.* The anticlerical Paul Parfait provides an extensive list of Catholic devotions in his *L'arsenal de la dévotion* (Paris: Decaux, 1876); see especially pp. 73–107.

15. R. Laurence Moore, *In Search of White Crows: Spiritualism, Parapsychology, and American Culture* (New York: Oxford University Press, 1977); Janet Oppenheim, *The Other World: Spiritualism and Psychical Research in England, 1850–1914* (New York: Cambridge University Press, 1985). On English spiritualism see also: Logie Barrow, *Independent Spirits: Spiritualism and English*

Plebians, 1850–1910 (New York: Routledge and Kegan Paul, 1986); Alex Owen, *The Darkened Room: Women, Power and Spiritualism in Late Victorian England* (London: Virago, 1989). For a survey of the movement that concentrates on revealing the fraudulent practices of the mediums see Ruth Brandon, *The Spiritualists* (New York: Knopf, 1983).

16. Oppenheim, *The Other World*, p. 59.

17. Paris was the site, in 1900, of a "Congrès spirite et spiritualiste" that drew an international audience, including the biologist Alfred-Russell Wallace, the British scientist credited along with Darwin for discovering the principle of natural selection. See *Le Temps*, Sept. 18, 1900, p. 4.

18. Henri Bergson, "Fantômes de vivantes," in *Mélanges* (Paris: PUF, 1972), pp. 1002–19. For Bergson's involvement with the controversial medium Eusapia Palladino see ibid., pp. 673–74. The Nobel prize-winning biologist Charles Richet also worked closely with the British spiritualists in the late nineteenth and early twentieth century; see Brandon, *The Spiritualists*, pp. 96–97, 132–47.

19. For the occult aspects of the Enlightenment see Robert Darnton, *Mesmerism and the Enlightenment in France* (New York: Schocken, 1970); Auguste Viatte, *Les sources occultes du Romantisme*, vol. 1 (Paris: Champion, 1965); Clark Garrett, *Respectable Folly: Millenarianism and the French Revolution in France and England* (Baltimore: Johns Hopkins University Press, 1975). On spirit-possession see Clark Garrett, *Spirit Possession and Popular Religion: From the Camisards to the Shakers* (Baltimore: Johns Hopkins University Press, 1987). For the Renaissance see D. P. Walker, *Spiritual and Demonic Magic: From Ficino to Campanella* (Notre Dame, Ind.: University of Notre Dame Press, 1975).

20. Perhaps the expansion of knowledge about Eastern religions should be added as a fourth strain of thought that helps explain the emergence of spiritism. A review of the index in the basic work by Raymond Schwab, *The Oriental Renaissance: Europe's Discovery of India and the East, 1680–1880* (New York: Columbia University Press, 1984; first published in French, 1950) suggests that virtually every thinker considered in this essay was influenced by the texts of Indian religion that began appearing in the late eighteenth century and which gave added support to the doctrine of metempsychosis. For the career of Anquetil-Duperron, whose translations of the Upanishads began appearing in 1786, see Jean-Luc Kieffer, *Anquetil-Duperron: L'Inde en France au XVIIIᵉ siècle* (Paris: Les Belles Lettres, 1983).

21. Jules Fleury, *Souvenirs et portraits de jeunesse* (Paris, 1872), pp. 132–33. On Hoene-Wrónski (1776–1853), see Andrzej Walicki, *Philosophy and Romantic Nationalism: The Case of Poland* (Oxford: Clarendon Press, 1982), pp. 107–21.

22. *Oeuvres complètes de Charles Baudelaire: Traductions: Histoires extraordinaires par Edgar Poe* (Paris: Conard, 1932), pp. 269–83, 456.

23. For general treatments of the Romantic era and its religious preoccupations see Paul Bénichou, *Le temps des prophètes: Doctrines de l'âge romantique* (Paris: Gallimard, 1977); Georges Gusdorf, *Du néant à Dieu dans le savoir romantique* (Paris: Payot, 1983); Bernard M. G. Reardon, *Religion in the Age of Romanticism* (Cambridge: Cambridge University Press, 1985). For a more idiosyncratic view of the period, stressing the importance of concerns about transcendance and the afterlife, see Philippe Muray, *Le 19ᵉ siècle à travers les âges* (Paris: Denoel, 1984). For specific treatments of the influence of spiritual currents on authors see Jacques Borel, *Séraphita et le mysticisme balzacien* (Paris: Corti, 1967); Auguste Viatte, *Victor Hugo et les illuminés de son temps* (Montreal: Les Editions de l'Arbre, 1942).

24. William H. Sewell, *Work and Revolution in France: The Language of Labor from the Old Regime to 1848* (Cambridge: Cambridge University Press, 1980); Bernard Moss, *The Origins of the French Labor Movement: The Socialism of Skilled Workers, 1830–1914* (Berkeley: University of California Press, 1976). For an older work that remains standard see Frank Manuel, *The Prophets of Paris* (New York: Harper Torchbook, 1965).

25. Edward Berenson, *Populist Religion and Left-Wing Politics in France, 1830–1852* (Princeton: Princeton University Press, 1984).

26. Alphonse Esquiros, *De la vie future au point de vue socialiste* (Paris: Comon, 1850). For a recent study of Esquiros's literary work see Anthony Zielonka, *Alphonse Esquiros (1812–1876): A Study of His Works* (Paris: Champion-Slatkine, 1985). For biographical details see J. P. Van der Linden, *Alphonse Esquiros, de la bohème romantique à la république sociale* (Paris: Nizet, 1948).

27. Esquiros, *De la vie future,* p. 110.

28. Ibid., pp. 119, 121.

29. Jonathan Beecher, *Charles Fourier: The Visionary and His World* (Berkeley: University of California Press, 1986), pp. 318–52. For a concise presentation of his ideas about immortality see Charles Fourier, *Théorie de l'Unité Universelle,* in *Oeuvres complètes,* vol. 3 (Paris, 1841), pp. 304–46. Michel Nathan, in *Le ciel des Fourièrists: Habitants des étoiles et réincarnations de l'âme* (Lyon: Presses Universitaires de Lyon, 1981), traces the influence of Fourier on later thinkers.

30. *Théorie de l'Unité Universelle,* p. 309.

31. Fourier's dependence on an argument that moves from the subjective experience of a human sentiment to an affirmation of a supernatural truth identifies him with a Romantic theological tradition that can be seen clearly in the work of Chateaubriand. Fourier's argument here resembles Chateaubriand's defense of the immortality of the soul; see *Génie du christianisme,* vol. 1 (Paris: Flammarion, 1966; first published 1802), pp. 197–220.

32. Jacques Viard, *Pierre Leroux et les socialistes européens* (Paris: Actes Sud, 1982); idem, "Les origines du socialisme républicain," *Revue d'Histoire Moderne et Contemporaine* 33 (1986): 133–47. For Leroux's role as cofounder

of the influential journal *Le Globe* see Spitzer, *The French Generation of 1820,* pp. 97–128. For the influence of Leroux on writers including George Sand and Victor Hugo see David Owen Evans, *Le socialisme romantique: Pierre Leroux et ses contemporains* (Paris: Rivière, 1948).

33. Pierre Leroux, *De l'humanité, de son principe, et de son avenir* (Paris: Perrotin, 1840).

34. Leroux, *De l'humanité,* vol. 1, p. 242.

35. Ibid., p. 244.

36. Ibid., pp. 289–90.

37. For the importance of Swedenborgianism see Auguste Viatte, *Les sources occultes du romantisme,* vol. 2 (Paris: Champion, 1965); idem, *Victor Hugo et les illuminés de son temps,* pp. 33–53; Frank Paul Bowman, "Illuminism, Utopia, Mythology," in *The French Romantics,* D. G. Charlton, ed. (Cambridge: Cambridge University Press, 1984), vol. 1, p. 8; Jacques Borel, *Séraphita et le mysticisme balzacien.* McDannell and Lang have now provided an able summary of Swedenborg's system in *Heaven: A History,* pp. 181–227. Swedenborg's works were newly translated into French during the nineteenth century; see his *L'Apocalypse réveilée,* trans. J. P. Moët and J. A. T. Tull (Paris: Treuttel et Wurtz, 1823), and *Arcanes célèstes,* 7 vols. (St. Amande et Paris, 1841–1854), edited and published by J. F. E. Le Boys des Guays. For a selection of his work in English see George F. Dole, ed., *Emmanuel Swedenborg: The Universal Human and Soul-Body Interaction* (New York: Paulist Press, 1984). For mesmerism see Darnton, *Mesmermism,* pp. 67–72, Auguste Viatte, *Victor Hugo et les illuminés de son temps,* pp. 10–25.

38. Louis Alphonse Cahagnet, *Arcanes de la vie future dévoilés* (Paris: Baillière, 1848), p. xii.

39. Emma Hardinge Britten, *Nineteenth-Century Miracles* (New York: Lovell, 1884), pp. 42–44.

40. For the history of spiritism see Jean Vartier, *Allan Kardec: La naissance du spiritisme* (Paris: Hachette, 1971). David Hess provides a useful discussion of the context of the French movement in "Spiritism and Science in Brazil: An Anthropological Interpretation of Religion and Ideology," Ph.D. diss., Cornell University, 1987. Hess's concern with French spiritism, and particularly with the figure of Allan Kardec, is based on the importance of the movement in modern Brazil, where Kardec's version of spiritism is a major force in the religious life of the country. For critical comments on the movement from contemporaries see: Emile Littré, "Du tables parlantes, des esprits frappeurs et autres manifestations de ce temps-ci," *Revue des Deux Mondes* 1 (1856): 847–72; Adrien Delandre, "La magie et les magiciens au XIXe siècle," *Revue Contemporaine* 32 (1857): 5–32, 251–84; for the responses of the church see Abbé J. Cognat, "De l'évocation des esprits," *L'Ami de la religion* 163 (Jan. 14, 1854): 109–15; Louis Veuillot, *L'Univers,* July 26, 1852; P. A. Matignon, S.J., *Les Mort et les vivants* (Paris: Le Clere, 1863).

41. For a complete edition of the texts and a useful introduction by Jean and Sheila Gaudin see Victor Hugo, *Oeuvres complètes,* Jean Massin, ed., vol. 9, pt. 2 (Paris: Le Club Français du Livre, 1971), pp. 1167–1492. For a brief narrative of the events see Hubert Juin, *Victor Hugo, 1844–1870* (Paris: Flammarion, 1984), pp. 297–329. Hugo's experiments are also treated in Maurice Levaillant, *La crise mystique de Victor Hugo (1843–1856)* (Paris: Corti, 1954).

42. For the fears that the tables would distract the Hugo circle from its political responsibilities see Hugo, *Oeuvres complètes,* vol. 9, pt. 2, p. 1185.

43. Eugène Nus, *Choses de l'autre monde,* 5th ed. (Paris: Librairie des sciences psychologiques et spirites, n.d.).

44. Hugo, *Oeuvres complètes,* p. 1233.

45. Ibid., p. 1170.

46. Ibid., p. 1174.

47. Ibid., pp. 1181, 1255.

48. Hugo wrote on December 17, 1854: "Ce monde sublime veut rester sublime; mais ne veut pas devinir exact, ou du moins il veut que son exactitude sublime ne nous apparaisse qu'énorme et confuse dans de prodigieuses échappées d'ombre et de lumière; il veut être notre vision et non notre science. . . . Dès que nous commençons à voir un peu distinctement, le monde mysterieux se ferme. Il faut que nous ne soyons sûrs de rien, c'est là l'expiation humaine. Chaque fois que l'homme, submergé à vaul'eau dans les ténèbres, ruisselant de toutes les écumes de l'abime et de la nuit, parvient a se cramponner au bord de la barque de foi et sort de l'obscurité à mi-corps, l'ombre qui est dans la barque lui fait lâcher prise, et le rejette au gouffre, et lui dit: Va, homme, lutte, souffre, roule, nage, doute! *E pur si muove!* Et pourtant je crois! et pourtant je crois! et pourtant je crois! à toi, mon âme, à vous, mon Dieu!." Ibid., p. 1178.

49. *Lettres familières de l'Impératrice,* vol. 1 (Paris: Le Divan, 1935), pp. 141–42; Dr. E. Barthez, *The Empress Eugénie and Her Circle* (New York: Brentano's, 1913), pp. 137–43.

50. According to Flaubert, the popularity of the turning tables was encouraged by the press, which reported the events as a serious matter. See *Bouvard et Pécuchet* (Paris: Gallimard, 1979), pp. 277–301. Spiritism and the related systems of Swedenborgianism and mesmerism also were frequent elements in the popular genre of the *conte fantastique.* See Pierre-Georges Castex, *Le conte fantastique en France de Nodier à Maupassant* (Paris: Corti, 1982).

51. For a brief description of the Davenports' performances see Arthur Conan Doyle, *The History of Spiritualism* (New York: Doran, 1926), pp. 211–29. Doyle, of course, was an advocate of the Davenports, but his remarks are nonetheless of interest, for he points out that their public performances marked an important stage in the diffusion of the movement to a mass audience.

52. *Le Temps,* Sept. 19, 1865, p. 1.

53. Vartier, *Allan Kardec,* pp. 27–39; Yvonne Castellan, *Le spiritisme,* 5th ed. (Paris: Presses Universitaires de France, 1974).

54. According to the *Catalogue des imprimés* of the Bibliothèque National, *Le livre des esprits* went through 35 editions between 1857 and 1889. For an extensive analysis of the content see Hess, "Spirits and Scientists." According to Hess *Le livre des esprits* can be seen as a kind of "Pestalozzian textbook." A condensed version of this work, published as *Qu'est-ce que le spiritisme?* went through 14 editions between 1859 and 1881. Kardec also published a guide for mediums, *Le livre des médiums,* which went through 18 editions between 1861 and 1885. Other popular works include: *Caractères de la révélation spirite,* 31 editions between 1868 and 1881; *L'évangile selon le spiritisme,* 14 editions between 1864 and 1880; *Résumé de la loi des phénomènes spirites,* 31 editions between 1864 and 1881; *Le spiritisme à sa plus simple expression,* 33 editions between 1862 and 1884.

55. For the spiritist assessment of their numbers see Vartier, *Allan Kardec,* p. 308. My argument for the significance of the spiritist movement rests less on the numbers officially enrolled and more on the cultural influence that resulted from the publication and discussion of spiritist literature, which clearly reached an audience well beyond those inscribed in the Société des Etudes Spirites.

56. Camille Flammarion, *Mémoires* (Paris: Flammarion, 1911), pp. 494–98.

57. Flammarion, *Mémoires.*

58. See, for example, Camille Flammarion, *La pluralité des mondes,* 33rd edition (Paris: Flammarion, 1885?), pp. 315–29. For the publishing history of this work, which went through at least thirty editions between 1862 and 1882, see Michael Crowe, *The Extraterrestrial Life Debate, 1750–1900* (Cambridge: Cambridge University Press, 1986), p. 652.

59. Flammarion, *Mémoires,* pp. 298–300, 325–32. See also Crowe, *Extraterrestrial Life Debate,* pp. 378–86, 612–13, who notes that *Astronomie populaire* went through seventy editions by 1885. In *Récits de l'infini,* 11th ed. (Paris: Flammarion, 1885) Flammarion presents his ideas in the form of dialogues between Lumen, a spirit who describes the universe and the afterlife, and his earthbound friend, Quaerens. This work went through twelve editions between 1873 and 1892. Flammarion also published *Les habitants de l'autre monde* (Paris: Ledoyen, 1862), a work which presents messages from spirits including Socrates, Lammenais, and Delphine de Girardin. Later in his life Flammarion expressed skepticism about the evidence from séances and disavowed a work on astronomy which he had written with the help of Galileo. See *Le Temps,* July 18, 1899, p. 2. But Flammarion continued to believe in the spirit world, in the possibility of demonstrating its existence with empirical evidence, and in contacts between the worlds of the living and the dead. See *L'Inconnu et les problèmes psychiques: Manifestations des mourants, apparitions, télépathie, communications psychiques, suggestion mentale, vue à distance; le monde des rêves, la divination de l'avenir* (Paris: Flammarion, 1900). The title of this work suggests the range of evidence that Flammarion thought could

be brought to bear on the question of the afterlife. He also believed haunted houses proved the existence of a spirit-world, and engaged in a public controversy with the composer Saint-Saëns, who disputed the possibility of a personal soul, in the *Nouvelle Revue*, Dec. 15, 1900. See Flammarion, *Haunted Houses*, trans. (New York: Appleton, 1924). In his final work, *La mort et son mystère*, 3 vols. (Paris: Flammarion, 1920–1922), Flammarion continued to argue for an immortal soul on the basis of ghostly apparitions and occult phenomena, which he believed should be understood as natural rather than supernatural manifestations.

60. The most important of these was Jean Reynaud, who was active in the Saint-Simonist movement of the 1830s and served during the Second Republic as a deputy in the Constituent Assembly, an undersecretary of state for education and a councilor of state. During the 1830s Reynaud published a series of articles on extraterrestrial life and the transmigration of souls in the *Encyclopédie nouvelle* of Pierre Leroux; these were revised and published together as *Terre et ciel* (Paris: Furne, 1854). Flammarion read and was influenced by Reynaud, whose work went through three editions in the 1850s and was considered serious enough to be condemned by a church council at Périgueux in 1857. See Jean Reynaud, *Réponse au concile de Périgueux* (Paris: Furne, 1858). Another influential figure was Louis Figuier, a doctor who, like Flammarion, gained a reputation as a popularizer of modern science. Following the death of his son Figuier was converted to spiritism and his work, *Le lendemain de la mort, ou la vie future selon la science* (Paris: Hachette, 1871), went through ten editions by 1894. For other works in the tradition of Flammarion and Reynaud see Crowe, *Extraterrestrial Life Debate*, pp. 407–23.

61. Castellan, *Le spiritisme*, a contemporary apology for spiritism published in the "Que sais-je?" series of the Presses Universitaires de France, treats Kardec as the founder of the movement, as does Vartier, *Allan Kardec*.

62. See, for example, *Le livre des esprits*, p. 331, where Kardec comments on a spirit communication: "L'humanité progresse par les individus qui s'améliorent peu à peu et s'éclairent; alors, quand ceux-ci l'emportent en nombre, ils prennent le dessus et entrainent les autres." From Kardec's perspective, social progress would result primarily from individual enlightenment rather than collective action.

63. Allan Kardec, "Propagation du Spiritisme," *Revue Spirite* 1 (1858): 241. But it is important to note significant working-class support for the movement as well, especially in Lyons; see "Le Spiritisme à Lyon," *Revue Spirite* 3 (1861): 290.

64. Kardec, *Le livre des esprits*, pp. 58–62; idem, Allan Kardec, *Qu'est-ce que le spiritisme?*, 19th edition (Paris: Librairie des sciences psychologiques, n.d.), p. 113.

65. Kardec, *Le livre des esprits*, p. 88.

66. Ibid., pp. 79–81.

67. Caroline Bynum, "Bodily Miracles and the Resurrection of the Body in the High Middle Ages." See also Caroline Bynum, *Holy Feast and Holy Fast: The Religious Significance of Food to Medieval Women* (Berkeley: University of California Press, 1987), especially pp. 299–302.

68. Flammarion reveals a similar distaste for corporal existence in his obsessive preoccupation with the image of a female eating, a sight which never failed to disgust his spiritual contacts. Michel Nathan, "Les métamorphoses de la fëminité dans l'oeuvre de Camille Flammarion," in *La femme au XIXe siècle*, 2nd ed. (Lyon: Presses Universitaires de Lyon, 1979), pp. 123–36.

69. On the importance of the sidereal revolution see Crowe, *Extraterrestrial Life Debate*, p. 41.

70. Oppenheim, *The Other World*, especially pp. 67–85.

71. Flammarion, *Mémoires*, pp. 168–88.

72. Flammarion was active in Jean Macé's anticlerical Ligue de l'Enseignement in the late 1860s; see his *Mémoires*, pp. 384–85. Léon Denis, who succeeded Kardec as the leader of the spiritist organization, was overtly hostile to Catholicism; see Castellan, *Le Spiritisme*, pp. 70–72.

73. For a brief introduction to these questions see Dominick La Capra, *History and Criticism* (Ithaca: Cornell University Press, 1985). For a collection of essays on the theory and practice of the new intellectual history see Dominick La Capra and Steven Kaplan, *Modern European Intellectual History* (Ithaca: Cornell University Press, 1982). Michael Ermath, "Mindful Matters: The Empire's New Codes and the Plight of Modern Intellectual History," *Journal of Modern History* 57 (1985): 506–27 offers a critical and somewhat hostile appraisal of the new approaches. For a more sympathetic reading of a number of recent works in the field see John Toews, "Intellectual History after the Linguistic Turn: The Autonomy of Meaning and the Irreducibility of Experience," *American Historical Review* 92 (1987): 879–907.

74. Flammarion, *La mort et son mystère*, vol. 1, p. 19, reports having received 4106 letters between 1899 and 1919, many of which were reproduced in this three-volume work.

75. "Confessions d'un curé de village," in *De la vie future*, pp. 9–59.

76. Nathan, *Ciel des fouriéristes*, p. 32.

77. *Conte fantastique*, p. 8.

78. *Introduction à la littérature fantastique* (Paris: Seuil, 1970), p. 29.

79. For some recent collections of these see: Charles Nodier, *La Fée aux Miettes, Smarra, Trilby* (Paris: Gallimard, 1982); Prosper Mérimée, *Carmen* (Paris: Flammarion, 1973), which includes the *conte fantastique*, "Les Ames du Purgatoire"; Théophile Gautier, *La Morte amoureuse, Avatar, et autre récits fantastiques* (Paris: Gallimard, 1981); Guy de Maupassant, *Contes fantastiques complets* (Paris: Marabout, 1983).

80. Baudelaire, *Histoire extraordinaires par Edgar Poe* (Paris: Conard, 1932).

81. Théophile Gautier, "La cafetière," in *La morte amoreuse*, pp. 47–57. This story first appeared in *La Cabinet de lecture*, May 4, 1831.

82. Flammarion, *Récits de l'Infini, L'Inconnu, La mort et son mystère*.

83. Robert Isherwood, *Farce and Fantasy: Popular Entertainment in Eighteenth-Century Paris* (New York: Oxford University Press, 1986), pp. 51–55.

4

"He Keeps Me Going": Women's Devotion to Saint Jude Thaddeus and the Dialectics of Gender in American Catholicism, 1929–1965

Robert A. Orsi

Devotion to Saint Jude Thaddeus, patron saint of hopeless cases, began in an incident at Our Lady of Guadalupe Church, a Mexican national parish in South Chicago, in the spring of 1929. Our Lady of Guadalupe was a new church, built in 1928 by Claretian missionaries, a Spanish order of men who had assumed as one of their concerns the care of Spanish-speaking migrants in North American cities. The church was located in an ethnically mixed neighborhood, and representatives of the community's many different Catholic cultures had participated in its dedication ceremonies. South Chicago was dominated in these years by slaughterhouses and steel mills, and crisscrossed by train tracks. In prosperous times, a gritty cloud of cinders and dust darkened the streets even in the middle of the afternoon. These were not prosperous times, however, so the air was clearer, but the neighborhood was shadowed by economic crisis. Shrine historians emphasize the grim mood in South Chicago in the early months of 1929.[1]

Visitors to the church in these hard times could bring their prayers and petitions to two saints whose statues stood on a small side altar to the right of the central image of *Nuestra Señora de Guadalupe*. Saint Thérèse of Liseux, the Little Flower, occupied the place of prominence above this side altar, and off to one side on a detached pedestal stood a large statue of Saint Jude Thaddeus, who was at this time virtually unknown in American Catholicism.[2]

137

Most of the people kneeling before the two statues were women, although the story of the Shrine's origins does not make this explicit. Popular piety in American Catholic culture has largely been the practice and experience of women, just as it has always been publicly dominated by male religious authorities.[3] As the devotion to Saint Jude eventually took shape in Chicago, it too became women's practice. Jude is identified by his devout with particular women in their lives. The minority of men who participate in the cult point back to their mothers, wives, or sisters when they talk about the first times they prayed to the saint. As one man told me, "I lived on Ashland Avenue [in Chicago]. My mother lived on Ashland Avenue for forty-five years. She called on Saint Jude whenever she had a problem, and I have followed in her footsteps."[4] Women have characteristically assumed special responsibilities in the practice of the cult; they were thought to be in a particularly close relationship with Jude not accessible to men, and as a result their prayers were believed to be more powerful and efficacious.

The clergy at various American Catholic shrines, well aware of this feature of the devotions over which they presided, have often seemed embarrassed by it; and they have sometimes worried that they were exploiting women to raise funds for clerical projects.[5] During the 1930s, the founder of Chicago's enormously popular Sorrowful Mother novena tried to goad men into attending services in greater numbers by offering them a reward of cigarettes, and the director of Jude's shrine warned in 1958 that prayer is "not only the practice of pious women and innocent children but a deadly earnest necessity for all equally."[6] But it is mainly women who appear in a pictorial essay on the shrine prepared in 1954.[7] However unacknowledged this participation is officially, the legend of the founding of Jude's shrine takes on new meaning, and raises new questions, when it is glossed with the fact of women's central role in the cult.

Thérèse was a celebrated figure, beloved for her "little way" of sanctity, the path of submission, humility, and silence. Contemporary authors have discovered another Thérèse, fiercely independent and spiritually innovative, but this was not the figure of the Catholic popular imagination in 1929. "Thérèse of Lisieux," writes Monica Furlong, "sweet, childlike, obedient, tragic, has been until recent times a cherished icon of Catholic womanhood," cast in "one of the favorite moulds of traditional female sanctity, the mould of virginity, of suffering, of drastic self-abnegation."[8] It is more difficult to determine how people understood Saint Jude, but I have asked his contemporary devout, many of whom have participated in his cult since its early years, and they most often emphasize his manly qualities. I was told that Jude "is tall, handsome, with a cleft in his chin"; "looks like Saint Joseph"; "[looks like] a very loving big brother or father"; "is quiet, soft-spoken, sure of himself"; "is very handsome — he looks like Jesus." One woman described him as "a great man, who is close to God and has a pull with him." Another said the saint is "a powerful healer. He looks like Christ. He looks like a man who wants you to test him on whatever the petitions may be." A sixty-eight-year-old woman whose devotion to Jude began twenty-five years ago gave me a longer description:

> I picture St Jude as a man to be of 5 feet and between 9 to 11 inches in height with a good and average build. He gives the appearance of a very kindly, loving, and caring person with a Big Heart. He looks like a very humble and courageous man, with a very Fatherly disposition, and compassion for all mankind particularly those who are desperate for help. His very close resemblance to his Cousin Jesus is simply outstanding and beautiful.[9]

The statue of Jude in Chicago, consistent with an older iconographical tradition, shows the saint holding in his arms a small image of Jesus' face, so that when the devout look at Jude they are looking into the faces of two men, a transposition of the familiar depiction of the Madonna and Child. The belief that Jude was an Apostle further identifies him with the church and its male authorities. One of my sources made this identification explicit: "Sometimes when I pray to him for something I need desperately it seems like he is standing right next to me in Mass vestments."[10]

Legends about the origins of devotions to particular saints, in Western and Eastern cultures, point to the supernatural influences determining the site of the devotion, and this is true of the account preserved at the shrine in Chicago as well. During Holy Week of 1929, the story goes, visitors to the church began gathering at the base of Jude's statue in ever greater numbers. So insistent was their devotion to the unknown Apostle that the clergy finally decided, on Holy Saturday, to reverse the two statues, giving Jude the place of prominence over the side altar, where he remains today. The cult of Saint Jude begins in this reversal. According to shrine chroniclers, this spontaneous expression of devotion to Jude was a sign that the saint himself had willed Chicago, an industrial city of immigrants in the middle of the United States, as the location of the modern revival of his cult.

The clergy had less supernatural reasons for preferring Jude to the

Little Flower. Jude's cult was founded by Father James Tort, an ambitious and savvy young priest from Barcelona who is described in an early profile as a "little high-pressure" man.[11] The Claretians needed some means of supporting their various enterprises in the United States, and Tort must have realized that only limited help would come from Chicago's formidable Cardinal, George Mundelein, who believed that priests should finance and support their own endeavors.[12] Although there is no evidence of this, Tort surely knew that popular devotions were a well-tried and promising source of funds, but at the same time he also must have been aware that there was already a local cult of the Little Flower at a nearby Carmelite parish in Chicago, as well as a thriving national devotion based in Oklahoma City.[13] Jude, on the other hand, had the singular advantage of truly being the "unknown saint," as he is identified in the early years at the shrine.

Devotion to Saint Jude took shape then somewhere between the desires of the devout and the ambitions of the clergy. For our purposes it is not important whether or not this legend it true: this is how the shrine imagines its founding. The story of the switched statues, however, does raise the two interconnected sets of questions with which this essay is concerned, one having to do with the language and structures of gender in religious traditions and the other with the nature and practice of popular religion. But before I outline these issues, we need to look at how women think about this saint's place in their lives.

"An Ongoing Relationship"

The most obvious characteristic of devotion to Saint Jude is the impulse of the devout toward narrative. Because Jude is the "hidden saint," as the shrine presents him, obscured in history by the unfortunate popular misidentification of him with Judas, the devout promise that they will make his actions in their lives public so that others will learn of him. This is the reason for all the discursive practices associated with the cult, from the long letters women write to the shrine to the simple thank-you notices that appear in the classified sections of local newspapers around the country. Women entered the world of the cult knowing that their connection with Jude would sooner or later give them the chance to describe in some public forum the most awful experience of their lives.

This transformation of experience into narrative took (and still takes) many forms. Women told their stories to other women, to strangers in hospitals, to family members, to needy colleagues at work. Jude's older devout, the women whose devotion dates to the early years of the cult's history, structure their autobiographies with reference to the saint's place in their lives; Jude has been their constant and trusted companion, they believe, every day, and at every major crisis or turning point in their experience. They reconstruct their lives with reference to Jude, imagining themselves in relation to this Other. Hagiography here takes on a new connotation: these women do not write and talk *about* the saint but about themselves and the saint together.

The following narrative was prepared in response to a request I made through the shrine's mailing list for stories of women's devotion to Jude. The woman writing is sixty-two years old, married, and the mother of two adult children who live close to her in a small New England town.

"I am writing," she begins, "because Saint Jude has been sharing all of my burdens, giving me peace of mind and generally being with me for more than 30 years." She first encountered the devotion in 1954, when "a crippled man" appeared at her door selling religious articles. "At that time I was 29 years old, newly married, pregnant, and living in my husband's family's house with my mother-in-law," a situation that was causing her some unhappiness. Jude's devout typically can remember the circumstances of their initial meeting with the saint, and they privilege this moment in their autobiographies: after encountering Jude, things change; something new happens. As another woman wrote to the shrine about her first meeting with Jude in 1941, "I never heard of this wonderful Saint, and it makes me feel like a different person since I know about him."[14]

Saint Jude intervened in the tense situation developing between the young woman and her mother-in-law. The couple was able to find their own home, and shortly afterwards their first child, a boy, was born. "From that time on, I very seldom made a decision or took any action in my life without asking Saint Jude for his guidance."

"How has he helped my family?" she asks. She has been married for thirty-four years, and even though "our life together was not perfect, all problems were minor and handled quickly by prayer to Saint Jude." Jude helped her raise her son and daughter, "particularly when [they] were teenagers and out on their own . . . I would ask Saint Jude to care for them while I could not, and he always did!" Although her husband is "not as verbal or demonstrative in his devotion to Saint Jude as I am," he has seen what the saint has done for them and "I feel he also trusts Saint Jude for our future and is thankful for our past."

Jude helped her advance over the years from her first job as a "typist" to the position of managing executive of a town, the post from which she has recently retired. "I could not have accomplished this had Saint Jude not been with me all the way, putting the correct words and actions into my head when I required assistance." She has always told her friends and co-workers about Jude, and she kept shrine prayer cards in her desk to give to people who needed them. She has a statue of Jude on her bedroom dresser, and "in times of great stress I light a vigil light in front of this statue. . . . I feel my prayers are always answered, altho' my requests are not always granted." She closes her story, "I feel I have been very privileged to have Saint Jude with me always to help carry my burdens and share my joys."

The sense here at the end is of a partnership between Jude and this woman: Jude has helped her bear her own burdens, he has not miraculously taken them away. As another woman wrote me, "I am sure I pester Saint Jude too much, but he keeps me going and he never fails, although I try to help myself first."[15]

There was a postscript to the letter of the New England mother, appended three months later. "Before I completed this correspondence last June, my husband was diagnosed as having bladder cancer! I will not go into detail, but with the constant help of Saint Jude we have had the best summer I can remember." Although the future is uncertain, she says at the end, "I have complete confidence that Saint Jude will care for us both."[16]

Since the founding of the devotion in Chicago in 1929, many thousands of American Catholic women have lived in what another correspondent called "an ongoing relationship" with the saint.[17] They have carried his picture in their purses, set his statue up in their homes in places where, as they say, they can look into his "soft, sympathetic," "penetrating," "compassionate" eyes when they need to and have talked to him as they go about their days.[18]

These older women encountered Jude during the "heyday of devotionalism" in American Catholic culture, in Jay Dolan's phrase, from the 1920s to the 1960s, an extraordinarily creative period in the history of American Catholic popular piety when women and clergy, sometimes together, frequently at odds with each other, experimented with devotional forms and structures in response to the community's changing needs and perceptions.[19] Jude's cult grew rapidly in these years, moving along dispersed tracks of narrative exchange in neighborhoods and across the country. The devotion existed primarily in women's conversations with each other. As one woman explained to me:

> I share my devotion to Saint Jude with all [the] members in my family and try to promote devotion to [among?] my friends and have succeeded. I have a friend who was terrified because the doctor discovered a lump on her breast and she came to me because I just had my right breast removed and I gave her the [Saint Jude] prayerbook and told her she must have faith in Saint Jude and she will come thru.[20]

Jude here is the medium for the exchange of confidences, shared fear and discomfort, and the occasion for the expression of support; and through conversations like this the devotion to Saint Jude became one of American Catholicism's most important and visible popular cults.

Hopeless Cases

The women who entered the world of Jude's devotion, seeking his face on medals and prayer cards, addressing his statue on their night tables, were impelled by fear and need. Jude was called upon only when all other help, divine and human, had failed. But what constitutes "hopelessness"? What kind of social or cultural experience is a crisis defined as "desperate"?

The hagiographical autobiography cited above offers some indication of what women meant by a hopeless situation: Jude helped in times of personal transition (from single to married, at the threat of impending widowhood), cultural change (during adolescence in the difficult 1960s), sickness, uncertainty, and when a beloved significant other turned away either in sickness, death, incapacity, powerlessness, or rejection. These were not "private" (as opposed to "public") occasions: Jude was called upon at just those moments when the effects and implications of changing historical circumstances (economic distress, the evolution of new medical models and authorities, and war, to cite just three of the recurring situations described by the devout) were directly and unavoidably experienced within the self and family.

"Crisis"—these situations of hopelessness—always has specific historical coordinates. There has been a tendency in discussions of the cult of saints to construe the entreaties of the devout as perennial: people have always gotten sick, this argument goes, and sick people always desire to be better, and this is why they pray to saints. But "crisis" itself is a cultural construction: people construe their unhappiness, experience their pains, talk about their sicknesses, and search for the appropriate intellectual, moral, and emotional responses to their dilemmas in socially and culturally bound ways. Because Jude stands at the intersection of the "private" and "public," praying to him became the way women encountered, endured, imagined, thought about, and learned the appropriate responses to "crisis." The cult offered women a critical catechesis in ways of living.

Women came to Jude as sisters, daughters, mothers, aunts—in other words, as figures in socially constructed and maintained kinship roles. The women who first turned to the saint in the late 1920s and 1930s belonged to an important transitional generation in American Catholic history. Historians have noted the beginnings of the dissolution in these years of the immigrant enclaves, the intricately constructed honeycombs of mutual responsibility and support in urban Catholic neighborhoods. Once the immigrant family had been the primary source of economic stability and social security, shaping an individual's fundamental choice of job, spouse, and residence; now the children of immigrant parents were confronted with new challenges and possibilities in a changing social and economic world.[21]

This new generation of American-born or raised Southern and Eastern Europeans had also begun to entertain new kinds of ambitions: the power and authority of immigrant parents, often not explictly denied, had begun to wane as their children entered a work world in which their parents could be of limited support and assistance. The woman whose autobiography we have studied began her work life as a typist, a position which required skills lacking in the immigrant generation. The period was marked by conflict between the generations in these Catholic ethnic communities as younger people sought greater autonomy in choosing companions, work, spouses, residence. In southern and eastern European immigrant communities, tension and anger over changing roles and expectations and distress over the loosening of traditional authority would be most sharply focused on young women.[22]

The letters written by women to the Chicago shrine over the years reflect these particular conflicts and special pressures. Jude was called upon when women were unable successfully to negotiate among contradictory cultural assignments and responsibilities: to help resolve conflicts over the choice of a spouse, for example, or to assist young women in their efforts to live their married lives in a newer, more American idiom as their husbands' partners, to aid them in finding and keeping jobs, and in securing adequate childcare while they worked.[23]

The devotion began in the experience of the Depression, flourished during the Second World War, and continued to grow in the postwar years; this is the public chronology of the cult. But these historical periods were experienced by the devout in particular ways, and the letters of need and gratitude written by women to the shrine and published in the *Voice of Saint Jude* constitute a running gloss on the recent past, disclosing the inner history of these years. During the Depression women wrote about their grief at their husbands' unemployment and their own dismay at not being able adequately to meet the household responsibilities they believed were theirs.[24] Women took their husbands to the shrine and prayed there with them, reestablishing through Jude a bond that was otherwise threatened. "We are praying," one woman wrote, "that my husband will hold his job and make good."[25]

In the late 1940s and throughout the 1950s, women brought to Jude their fears of the pain of childbirth or their terrible unhappiness at not being able to have children. A woman confided to the readers of the letters page of the *Voice of Saint Jude* in April 1952:

> During my pregnancy I was quite ill; and I was in such great fear of the pain I would have to endure when the baby would arrive. Yet with Jude's help I had the strength to see my illness through, and at the actual birth I suffered so little that I could hardly believe it was all over and I was the mother of a beautiful child.[26]

Another women wrote that she had become "obsessed with fear" before her daughter's birth, but that she "wore [Jude's] medal (even on the delivery table) and put my fear and anguish in his hands."[27] Many women named their children Jude or Judith in gratitude for the saint's help.[28]

During the 1950s, when married women began looking for work outside the home again in greater numbers, the devout turned to Jude for assistance in dealing with the new problems they were facing. This is how one woman understood this particular moment in her life:

> I applied for a secretarial position [after being away from this work for five years] and while on the way to this job I prayed to Saint Jude who granted me this job. To this day and forever I shall thank him. Also granted was the guidance he gave me to get my boy started in kindergarten. For three weeks my boy cried when I took him and attempted to leave him in the room. The teachers and I had given up. One day as I was taking him home a stranger saw me crying and taking my boy home. She told me to pray to Saint Jude for help which I did and on the second day

my boy went to class without a fear. I shall always be grateful and say a prayer for this stranger and Saint Jude.[29]

Single women turned to Jude for help in finding good husbands and then for assistance in dealing with the inevitable family tension that erupted over their choices. Younger women wrote that Jude helps "through all the frustrations and problems of being a teenager."[30] Mothers asked him to guide them in responding to the needs and values of their maturing children: "show me the right way to help my son" one woman prayed to the Saint during a family crisis.[31] Older women sought Jude's assistance in caring for dying parents, living with the loneliness of widowhood, and facing the problems of aging.

Women understood themselves to be accomplishing something when they turned to Saint Jude: in partnership with him, they changed things, found work, settled problems.[32] The least helpful way of reading this devotion would be to try to account for what happens after prayer in the way that last century's scientists "explained" the cures at Lourdes. More important is to consider how these women created and sustained a world in relation to Jude, how they imagined reality and its alternatives, and how they constructed this world in their devotions. The stories women told about themselves and Saint Jude were not static recapitulations of experience, explained by referring to the economic crisis of the Depression or the physical threats of the social pressure to have children after the war. The narrative process is central here: the letters do not represent the recasting of experience in another, "symbolic," key, but the reexperiencing of experience in a new way.

We have seen that the women believed themselves to be "different persons" after encountering Jude. Without Jude's help, one woman wrote me, "I don't think I would be as a good a person."[33] The world and the self are remade in relation to Jude, but what is the world and who is the self so constituted?

New and Better Persons: Questions of Gender in the Devotion to Saint Jude

Women who say that they became new persons in their encounters with Jude at the most desperate moment in their lives are alerting us to a central feature of devotionalism studied specifically as women's practice. Feminist historians for the last two decades have been struggling with fundamental issues of the study of women's history: Is this the history of domination? resistance? of women's culture or women's sphere, as an earlier division had it? Joan Scott has recently suggested that a new approach to women's history entails a new understanding of politics and subjectivity as well as a new analysis of gender. Drawing on poststructuralist understandings of subjectivity, Scott writes that "identities and experiences are variable phenomena . . . discursively organized in particular contexts or configurations." From this perspective gender is defined as culturally sanctioned and maintained "knowledge about gender differences."[34]

Religious traditions, with their considerable institutional and psychological authority, are highly privileged expressions of what is considered true and real (at least to certain segments of modern society), and devotionalism, which was the way most Catholics engaged their tradition in the mid-twentieth century, served as the site of particularly compelling discursive organizations of truth about gender. Religious sanctions were applied and divine approbation given to specific presentations of "maleness" and "femaleness" in the various media, official and popular, of American Catholicism. Women were positioned in a certain way in relation to the sacred, and this position was said to reflect and reveal women's fundamental identity.

What world of meaning, then, did women enter when they turned to Jude and imagined him looking at them with sympathy and understanding? The first task here will be to indicate some of the characteristic patterns of behavior, clusters of symbols, and affective responses (Geertz's "moods and motivations") that comprised American Catholic devotionalism in the middle years of this century. "Woman" was constructed in the tropes and metaphors of devotional culture in specific ways. When women prayed to the saint, practiced the cult, and discovered or created new selves in the process, they were learning by an intimate pedagogy the religiously consecrated cultural grammar of gender, and they were taking shape as selves within the gendered forms and structures with which reality is constituted by religious traditions.

Women entered the world of Jude's devotion at particularly difficult times, as we have seen: in their own perceptions, the world had become unhinged, everything was upside down, and they were feeling desperate, hopeless, and abandoned. Once we have identified some of the levels of meaning in the devotional construction of "woman," can we go on to say that at such desperate moments women were located in (and even located themselves in) a particular ordering of the world? To borrow a term from the structuralist study of ideology, are women "interpellated" here into the organization of gender characteristic of devotional culture?

The second part of the discussion that follows suggests another more dialectical possibility for understanding women and popular religion. Gender is not a static social category into which people are *fitted*. As Scott notes, constructions of gender emerge out of highly conflictual and open-ended cultural processes and so bear the marks of contradiction, dissent, resistance, repression. We will have to consider whether or not devotional culture is marked in this way as well, opening the way for creativity amid its fissures. But we need to begin with the world that women entered through Jude's eyes.

"Why Should a Voice Like Mine Be Heard?" Women in American Catholic Devotional Culture

The devotion to Saint Jude does seem to have reproduced in another register the characteristic structures of male-female relations during the Depression. Susan Ware observes that there was a clear division of men and women's roles in the United States in this period, with women assigned primary responsibility for the maintenance, economic and moral, of the home. "Women had complete responsibility for the domestic sphere and played a crucial role in holding families together against the disintegrating forces of the Depression."[35] Threatened by their increasing inability to fulfill this sustaining role in hard times, women turned to religion for "consolation," as Ware puts it, and church attendance rose. William Chafe suggests that this inward turning and search for religious consolation and security reinforced women's traditional roles.[36] A number of studies of American working people have shown that workers tend to hold themselves responsible for losing their jobs, even in periods of manifest economic crisis, and evidence from the Depression suggests that women blamed their men for their inadequate support. One man remembers his feelings in Bethlehem, Pennsylvania, in the 1930s: "I think Roosevelt's program saved the self-respect and the sanity of a lot of men."[37]

Seen against this background, Jude appears to be a further expression of the resentment and disorientation women experienced when their husbands lost their jobs, on the one hand, as well as another way of saving male sanity and self-respect, on the other. Nowhere in the published letters (or in my conversations with the devout about these times) is there any expression of anger against an economic system that could make families feel hungry and threatened. Instead, women prayed to Jude for his help in finding work for their husbands; and when at last, often after long, sustained periods of searching, the latter did find jobs, their wives explicitly attributed their success to Jude, not to the men's skill, diligence, or dedication, or to changes in the economy. "I started a Novena on Easter Sunday so my husband would find work," one woman informed the shrine. "I am so happy to say that he went to work the other day. I am sure that without Saint Jude's help he would have failed to secure employment."[38] This is the characteristic structure of Depression narratives: they open with an incomprehensible event (unemployment), describe the woman's turning to Saint Jude, and end in an incomprehensible event (finding work), reinforcing—by finding religious meaning in—an alienated understanding of the social process. There is a pervasive sense of passivity throughout: men are fired, men are hired. "Some time ago," another woman wrote the shrine in 1935, "I asked you to remember my husband in your prayers for the novena [sic] that he might secure work. At the same time I prayed hard and placed Saint Jude's picture in my front window and asked him to call my husband to work. A few days later he was called to work."[39]

Women were turning here to a male to help men, so that the devotion reproduced and confirmed female dependence on, and silent, unobtrusive support of, men. The public life of Jude's cult was male dominated. The Claretian rationale for the devotion was to provide financial support for young boys attending the order's seminary in Momence, Illinois. Pictures of seminarians regularly appeared in the *Voice of Saint Jude*, along with photographs of clergy and the other major group of males publicly identified with the cult, the Chicago Police. Tort founded the Police Branch of the Saint Jude's League in 1932 both to secure Jude's protection for the police and to involve the latter in his various fundraising efforts. Several times a year the Chicago Police marched in full dress uniform around the shrine, or, after 1948 when a special meeting hall was opened for the fraternal organization in the Claretian building in the Loop, around the Claretians' downtown church. One thousand policemen received communion together at the shrine in 1936, five thousand on October 27, 1946. Pictures of these events routinely appeared in the *Voice*.[40]

Women were participating then in a devotion to a male saint, officially understood to derive his power from his kinship relationship with Jesus, a devotion that was publicly represented, not by women (with the unintentional exception of the pictorial history cited earlier), but

by priests, boys destined for the clergy, and armed adult men.[41] The
devout supported this structure out of a strong sense of duty: once Jude
had acted for them, they understood themselves to have acquired a life-
long debt. One man told me that his mother sent a donation to the shrine
even during the most difficult days of the Depression in thanksgiving
for something Jude had done for her and in support of the boys in the
seminary.[42]

American-born or raised women, the daughters of the immigrants,
were thus initiated into understandings of themselves as women common in Irish and southern and eastern European Catholic cultures: bound
by duty and need to a male religious figure who was thought to be particularly responsive to their prayers, women acted in the cult as the strong,
quiet, invisible centers of emotional, moral, and practical order and stability in their homes.[43] One way of understanding devotionalism in this
period is as the disciplining of a new generation of Catholic women.
As a priest writing in another popular devotional periodical, *Little Flower
Magazine,* warned: "How much then there is for the [Catholic] women
of America to do in their own gentle, womanly way. They must be the
custodians of modern society to drive from it all sham and sin and falsehood; to scorn evil and love good; women of good lives, of intelligence,
of tender feeling; women with pity and mercy, the living images of God's
tenderness; an unsparing devotion to the happiness of others."[44]

There was a great deal of uneasiness in devotional culture that young
Catholic women "in these days of movies, automobiles, trolleys, golf,
sensational magazines, woman suffrage and women in business, sport,
etc." (as these days were defined by Martin Scott, S.J., writing in the
influential devotional journal *Ave Maria*) were not living up to the ideal
of "the Catholic woman." The intensity and venom with which young
women were imagined and criticized in devotional culture during these
transitional years reflects this fear. "The ranks of the Magdalens will
be recruited by numbers all too great," the editors of *Ave Maria* feared
in 1927, because of the atmosphere in "stores and shops and factories
and offices," and against this they urged "early training and parental control."[45] If women fall, according to Msgr. Thomas Riley, so does culture, because conscience is but "everyman's nagging wife."[46]

The discipline of economic hardship during the Depression was
welcomed by some Catholic writers as an antidote to the dreams of young
women. Mothers, wrote Nellie Ivancovich in *Ave Maria,* who are responsible for "building that citadel of the Church and of society, the
Christian home," have been threatened of late by their own ambitions

in "pagan and materialistic culture." But this is changing: "The many reasons that drew a large number of women away from the home—money, pleasure, prosperity—have failed in these days of depression, and people are learning that in the search for advantages something of much greater value has been lost—the proper care and training of the children." Fortunately, although mothers have been failing, the "ideal of perfect motherhood, a memory or a vision of 'Mother' as she was or might have been," has persisted.[47]

There were two categories of women in devotional culture: old women who had been broken by time and labor and young women who needed to be broken by time and labor. Older mothers are always tired, beaten, sad, and silent; young women are always rebellious, dangerous, wild. Rosie, a young bride in "Jim Graney's Wife," a short story published in *Ave Maria* in 1920 by Helen Moriarity, is an idle, rebellious red-haired beauty, "intoxicated with life, vain of the beauty which had captivated sober Jim Graney, selfish with youth's supreme and thoughtless egotism." She is contrasted in the story with Jim's mother, whose life is characterized by "self-sacrifice." One afternoon, Jim comes home and finds Rosie out with friends and his mother lying in a heap on the floor, crushed by overwork. When Rosie comes home, Jim exiles her forever from his house.

Rosie responds by indenturing herself as a servant to her own mother's family, and the transformation of the young woman by suffering begins. "Time . . . laid a devastating hand on her bright hair, ruthlessly took the lilt out of the gay voice, and set the giddy feet on duty's rugged path." She slaves for her family, converting their slovenly home into the cleanest dwelling in the neighborhood, but "in the process she herself became little more than an indistinguishable blur. A bent, pale little drudge, with red work-worn hands, the hair that was once her pride drawn back into a dull knot at the back of her head, she bore slight resemblance to the radiant, round-cheeked beauty that had charmed the heart out of sober Jim Graney."

As it turns out, Jim prefers red hands to red hair. His mother dies, and Jim, wounded in a railroad accident, is lying on his bed when he hears a "timid voice" asking him if he wants supper. At first he cannot recognize his wife, but when he does, he yields to the "tender touch of Rosie's toughened but capable hand." They reunite, raise many children together, and at the end of the story, gay young Rosie has become a "popular and beloved matron."[48]

Rosie and her sisters were treated harshly in devotional culture in these years. Inevitably wild and dangerous, they were frequently shown luring their "sober" men into danger. "Let's live on thrills," a young woman cries in a short story in the *Voice*, taunting her man on to drive recklessly, an adventure which ends with her in the hospital after the car crashes. "Freddy sustained only a broken collar bone. It was Barbara who paid the severe penalty with a crushed chest."[49] Young women are defined by their discontent and ambitions.[50]

They are punished for these things: the stories always end with the young women chastened by grief, pain, sickness – which they admit they have brought on themselves – alone in squalid rooms, abandoned by everyone except the saints and the Virgin, resigned to their new lives. Stories that played with this theme were published regularly in the *Voice*, a striking counterpoint to the expressions of suffering and grief in the letters columns. The plot is always the same: a successful young woman abandons the friends of her childhood in her lust for fame and glory, which she achieves very briefly before disaster strikes, after which she learns the true meaning of life. Susan Grayson, in Anne Tansey's "Will-o-the-Wisp," was the pet of her teachers and the darling of a fast crowd of friends. After graduation, she seeks glory on the stage (indeed, she changes her name to "Gloria"), which she finds, although "success went to Susan's head." Suddenly, inexplicably, Susan breaks down and is "confined" to a hospital for three years – "careless and extravagant living exacted its toll." Alone, abandoned by the friends of her days of triumph, humiliated, Susan comes to her senses. She turns to the saints for help, but even here Tansey cannot refrain from ridicule, depicting the sad woman as "rushing" frantically "from saint to saint for succor." Susan finally finds Jude and accepts her lot in life: at the end she is living in a "shabby house in a poor section" but she is "placidly happy" and content with the "companionship of no one" other than Jude.[51] Not even young nuns are exempt from this treatment: in another story, when a novice's mother objects to the harsh discipline her daughter is undergoing at the hands of her novice mistress, the young religious replies, "Mother darling! It is only what I deserve, and you know it!"[52]

Women were warned in devotional culture that to make choices for themselves was to risk the certain destruction of their families. Their desires are always corrosive.[53] So dangerous were these women that at times their ambitions are treated as capital offenses: one young woman's murder in a story published in the *Voice* is called "retributive justice" for her having abandoned the "simple shepherd" who loved her as a girl.[54]

But the favorite gender trope of devotional culture was the woman in pain: suffering was understood to be women's true destiny and vocation, and the source of their access to power in the sacred world.[55] Suffering defined the vocation of motherhood. "We are 'two in one flesh,' with [mother] by a far more intimate physical union than she can possibly achieve with her husband," according to a priest writing in *Sign*, allowing the oedipal subtext of official devotionalism periously close to the surface. This is because "she suffers for us as she suffers for no other."

> In a sense, she dies for us that we might live, for it is of her substance, by the destruction of part of her, that our physical substance grows, differentiates, matures, and is delivered. Of all this, father is a silent spectator, quite helpless to do anything for his child.[56]

Mothers, who are always contrasted in devotional culture with wild young women, suffer with and for their children, and in this way redeem them.

The Christological undercurrents in this portrayal of mothers dying, children (sons) rising, is made explicit in the devotional treatment of Mary, who is described as "co-operatrix" in Jesus' work.[57] Mary alone can avert the disaster that God intends for humankind, becoming in this way the model woman standing loyally beside her fallen, depraved children. In a favorite imaginative exercise of devotional literature, a clerical writer asks, "How would your mother feel if she were to meet you on the way to the electric chair or the gallows?" Any good mother would behave in this situation like Mary. "She approaches Him and kneels, wipes the sweat and blood and spit from His face, throws her arms about Him. True mother even in this anguish, she seeks to console, rather than be consoled, to lift Him up rather than be lifted up, to encourage Him rather than be encouraged."[58]

Women are not just called to suffering in devotional culture, however; they are also taught how to suffer as women: cheerfully, resignedly, and above all, silently. A young, very sick female character in a story published in the *Voice* silences herself so as not to ruin "the little haven to which Jimmy [her brother] might come to the rest he had earned by honest toil."[59] When women complain, they bring down spiritual and physical disaster on their families.[60] Instead, they are called upon to imitate Mary, who is held up as the model of silent and resigned suffering. "Be brave then," a priest writing in *St. Anthony's Messenger* urges his women readers, "whoever you are, be silent, in imitation of her whose heart held the sorrows of the world."[61] "Why were you silent?"

a character asks Mary in a poem published in *Ave Maria;* the Virgin modestly replies, "Why should a voice like mine be heard?"[62] Injunctions to silence seem particularly perverse in the devotional press because it was precisely here, in their letters of thanksgiving and request, that women broke their silence.

On May 30, 1920, a poor Roman matron, Anna Maria Taigi, was beatified by Benedict XV. She was quickly taken up by American Catholic devotional writers and offered as a model to mothers and wives. Taigi had been a "gay bride," according to Florence Gilmore in a sketch published in *Ave Maria,* until "the grace of God touched her soul." Seeing her "frivolity" now in a new light, Taigi began to wear "the commonest and coarsest clothes," under which she hid a hairshirt. She endured a life of terrible sufferings, which included a violently abusive husband, "cheerfully and smilingly" and sought ways to increase her discomforts. "Hot as Rome often is and hard as she worked, Anna Maria often passed several days without a drink of water." She was "unfailingly patient" with her abusive husband, "silent when he was angry, eager to please him in every way." God rewarded Taigi for her silent and willing suffering with the grace of healing: "the mere touch of her toil-roughened hands cured the sick."[63]

Women's pain/women's power; women in pain/women healers; female silence/male violence—this is the grammar of gender in American Catholic devotionalism in the crucial years after the end of immigration. The path marked out for women was clear: rebellion yielded crushing pain, while suffering and sickness made women powerful matrons, able to heal. All women had to do was keep silent. Broken, they were strong; through their own pain they secured the power to heal others.

This seems to be the logic of Jude's devotion as well. Women assumed all the responsibilities for their families in times of distress. They called on the saint, often in grueling prayer marathons that lasted all night or for days; as one woman put it, she prayed "until my throat ached" for a cure for a relative.[64] When a couple was in trouble, for example, or a man's business failing, it was always the responsibility of the women involved to pray and to make whatever sacrifices were thought necessary to propitiate the sacred. The devout believed that to some extent Jude's response to them was dependent on the quality of their prayer: it must be strong, intense, self-sacrificial.[65] It was women's task to negotiate with the sacred, bartering their own sacrifice and devotion for the welfare of their families. Women also assumed the duty of acknowledging and remembering the saint's intervention: years after a crisis, the women of a family continued to write to the shrine, recalling the moment of Jude's intervention.[66]

Women acted as the centers of prayer, domestic unity and order, success, and health, through their special alliance with Saint Jude: they prayed to Jude constantly, monitored his responses, assumed all responsibilities toward the sacred, wrote the narratives of distress and gratitude, and served as their families' memories. True to the warning against complaint in the devotional image of woman, the devout never expressed anger or resentment in their narratives at the husbands who left them, the doctors who failed to comfort them, or the children who rejected them. Participation in the devotion sealed women's sense of obligation: they were responsible for everything. They were also uniquely positioned to suffering—in some sense, identified with it, responsible for it. Like Mary in the devotional literature, they had assumed responsibility for averting disaster and had devoted themselves to others in need. A new generation of Catholic women seemed trapped in the consequences of devotional fantasies: they have been cast as the hidden figures responsible for holding up the world by the powers that are theirs through suffering, brokenness, and self-sacrifice.

Whose Voice? The Dialectics of Popular Religion

This is as far as a historian can go with the structural study of culture, which fails the social historian when he or she comes to the question of how people live in, with, and against, the discourses which they inherit. Göran Therborn has pointed out that ideology is always dialectical: people are both located in and empowered by particular arrangements of reality.[67] Gianna Pomata has criticized Donzelot's *The Policing of Families* in a way that is useful here. She writes,

> The tutelary 'police' is here reconstructed and analyzed through its 'knowledge,' that is to say, the texts of doctors and philanthropists; but the book lacks, by contrast, a reconstruction of the other 'knowledges' which this police encountered and with which it came into conflict, above all the knowledge of popular traditions. In this manner the book privileges the image of social processes and relations of power which emerges from texts linked to the 'police,' in relation to other possible images, other points of view.[68]

I would prefer to focus not on other knowledges but on the seams, disjunctures, and alternative possibilities within popular Catholicism itself. "The point of the new historical investigation," Joan Scott argues, "is to disrupt the notion of fixity, to discover the nature of the debate or repression that leads to the appearance of timeless permanence in binary gender representation."[69] Our task now is to uncover the polysemy of devotional culture, ritual, and belief.

Consider, as a way of beginning this discussion, whose "voice" was heard at the shrine. According to the official understanding, by narrating his intervention in their lives, women were giving Jude back his voice, which had been muted in history because of his identification with Judas. But the "voice" heard at the shrine was always double: by talking about Jude's actions in their lives, women were also speaking their own experience, finding a voice for themselves. Jude could not speak apart from the devout; his voice could be heard only in theirs. Indeed, the devout treated this as a bond of reciprocity or mutuality between heaven and earth: Jude needed them as much as they needed him. Women were thus enabled through this devotional ventriloquism to articulate aspects of their experience which they might otherwise have been unable to speak. The reciprocity between heaven and earth found its ultimate expression in this identity of voices.

Women did not only inherit Jude; they also invented him out of their needs and desires, and continued to invent him throughout their lives as they faced the successive crises and dilemmas of their experience. Jude's followers believed that when they wrote about the saint they were presenting him to the world for the first time. In this way Jude resembles the nameless spirits Gananath Obeyesekere has studied in the religious imaginations of Sri Lankan Buddhists. Obeyesekere writes that in distinction to the formalized, highly delineated dieties of the official pantheon,

> Spirits, by contrast, are a known *category*, but they are not known beings. . . . [T]he individual exercises an option or choice in selecting a spirit from a known cultural category; and he manipulates the spirit. When these conditions obtain . . . the symbol or ideational set is used by the individual to express his personal needs.[70]

Although Jude was certainly in the recognizable and highly valued category of saint, he had had only the most modest prior tradition of popular devotion and the Chicago shrine claimed with some justice to have discovered this hidden figure. Like the spirits Obeyesekere studied, Jude was available for psycho-social improvisation: the blankness of Jude in the tradition became the space for the imaginative work of the devout.

Women imagined Jude as a sympathetic, caring, engaged man, who understood their needs and desires, a figure bound to them by various ties of reciprocity and mutual need and so both constrained and inclined to act on their behalf. Women claimed Jude by imagining him looking at them—in this way they took him away from the shrine and brought him into the centers of their experience. When I asked one woman what Jude looked like, she began by saying that of course he resembled the statue at the shrine, and then went on to offer a powerful, personal, alternative imagining of him.[71] Another woman pointed out that "in enjoying friendship with Saint Jude you feel an intimate personal feeling, almost like you are the only one praying to him."[72]

I have argued that it was a new generation of women who turned to Jude, imagining him into being as much as encountering him in the official cult, when the saints of their various immigrant communities no longer seemed adequate to their needs. The saint that was invented between Chicago and the personal experience of the devout was imagined to have a particular understanding of the special problems of women. He is compassionate and sympathetic, one woman wrote me, and has an "awareness of how we feel when we are going through a desperate situation."[73] Saint Jude, another woman told me simply, "sees us for what we are."[74]

The intensity with which Jude was imagined, of course, reflected the dire circumstances of need and distress that motivated this imagining. "I was twenty years old, single, and very ill, and scared," a woman described the time of her first meeting with the saint, and went on to picture him as "kind, personable, and loving. I always relate to the picture on my prayercard."[75] Jude appeared then as the object of desire, his image constructed of many different sources, and the intensity of this desire threatened the closure of the discourse of woman and gender in devotional culture.

The initial deep connection between Jude and the devout was most often established through an imagining of his eyes, which one woman described as "penetrating," and more generally of his smiling, attentive, and compassionate face. His eyes are "compassionate and loving," "kind and sad," "soft and pleasing."[76] Jude's face is always turned toward his followers in gentle consideration. The devout say that Jude is: "a gentle, kind, loving person who you would like to embrace"; "kind, generous, and helpful"; and "someone to lean on."[77] Above all, Jude is a powerful friend who is sincerely interested in helping and understanding his devout. The saint, according to one woman, is "a compassionate person that would listen to your problems and intercede for you." Jude is "capable of handling the most serious problems in life." Unlike the living persons in their lives, finally, Jude never "turn[s] his head when I ask him for help."[78]

The conversations women had with this figure, whom they imagined in this way, were private and complex, often kept secret from husbands and children, and understood to be distinct from saying the official prayers published at the shrine.[79] "Oftentimes I carry on a full conversation" with Jude, one woman explained, and added that "periodically I plead and become angry." Women say that they came away from these conversations "full of hope."[80]

The material culture of devotionalism facilitated this process of personal appropriation. Women could send away to the shrine for various objects—statues, medals, prayer cards, oils, car ornaments—which they could then use and manipulate as they wanted, often to the consternation of the shrine clergy. This extensive or detachable quality of shrine culture was an important source both of women's power and improvisatory creativity in the practice of the cult. Women painted Jude's statue in bright colors, hid it in secret places in their homes or displayed it in elaborate home shrines; they sewed his medals into their husbands' and children's clothing and wore them on their underclothes when they went for radiation therapy. Until the early 1960s, when it was discontinued at the shrine, women used holy oil blessed with Jude's relic to heal themselves and their families and friends. The oil became the instrument of their power: they administered it on the bodies of sick kin and passed it on to friends with careful instructions about its proper use. When healings occurred, these women expected to be included in the thanksgiving for Jude's intervention.[81] (Older devout still manage to obtain oil for themselves, mainly from a rival shrine of Saint Jude in Baltimore.)

Women used the objects available at the shrine to create networks of support and assistance among their female relatives and friends similar to those their mothers and grandmothers had relied on in the transition from the old world to the new.[82] As they exchanged prayer cards of Saint Jude with each other in times of trouble, women also shared their stories, perceptions, and problems, and the saint became the privileged medium of communication between mothers and daughters, sisters, and friends. As one woman described this interweaving of voices, "A young lady friend of mine sent me the picture of Saint Jude with [the] prayer on the back. When we write to each other she would tell me her troubles, and I mine."[83] The exchange between women involving Jude was always an exchange of feelings, confidence, trust; it was also an exchange of information, one piece of which was about Jude, but included folk remedies, self-healing practices, advice on dealing with troubled husbands and children, recommendations of doctors, and life stories.

Acting within this network and in relationship with the gentle, powerful, attentive companion saint, women felt themselves to be empowered in new ways. They broke off relationships with "mean" boyfriends, rejected unwanted medical treatments, passed difficult qualifying exams of different sorts, and confronted family crises with newfound confidence.[84] Throughout the 1940s and 1950s, for example, when the official voices of devotional culture were decrying women's return to work, the devout found in their relationship with Jude the strength and confidence to look for, secure, and keep their new jobs.[85] Women have always written to describe problems they are having at work, their hopes of finding better employment, and their struggles with management. They have used prayer cards and medals to create networks of support with other women at work.[86] So central has Jude been to the working lives of women in these years that a contemporary devout has come to believe that the saint is particularly interested in the concerns of working women: "it has been my experience . . . that [Saint Jude] is especially good with finding employment and in solving problems related to employment."[87]

Finally, women resisted through various devotional practices, especially the construction of narratives of crisis, the silence imposed by Catholic devotional culture on women in the "Catholic home." The contrast between the male-articulated culture of innocence, as this has been well described by William Halsey in *The Survival of American Innocence*,[88] and the picture that takes shape in the letters pages is striking: the narratives written to the shrine recount tales of alcoholic husbands, financial struggles that are not glossed by sentimental celebrations of Christian poverty, women's fears of having more babies, and so on. Women found their own sources of power and support and their own ways of speaking amid the complex possibilities of devotional culture.

"Devotional Life Can Become Exuberant"

In 1943, Joseph Donovan reflected on one of his colleague's scruples about a new devotional practice in his monthly column of advice for parish clergy in *The Homiletic and Pastoral Review*. Some Irish-American women had taken to eating prayer cards of the Virgin Mary in the hope that this would secure their petitions. Donovan warned his clerical colleague not to be too fussy about such practices. After all, he points out, "devotional life can become exuberant."[89]

Although the clergy were often uneasy with this exuberance, as Donovan's comments suggest they also contributed in these years to an atmosphere of devotional experimentation and creativity. Many voices could be heard in the devotional world, speaking often against each other or from different perspectives, for different audiences. As one woman put it, writing to the shrine in 1949 about her trouble in finding adequate day care for her daughter while she worked, "This may not sound like a difficult problem to you, but. . . ."[90] She seems to be writing past the shrine clergy here to the other women who read and wrote for these pages.

This leads to a new understanding of devotionalism, not only as the place of gender construction, but as the privileged site of gender contestation in American Catholic culture. Devotional culture was polysemous and polyvalent. Women not only "discovered" who they were in the dense devotional world that developed through much of this century in the United States, but created and imagined themselves, manipulating and altering the available grammar of gender. Religious traditions must be understood as zones of improvisation and conflict. The idea of a "tradition" itself is the site of struggle, and historically situated men and women build the traditions and counter-traditions they need or want as they live. Finding meaning in a tradition is a dialectical process: women worked with the forms and structures available to them, and their imaginings were inevitably constrained by the materials they were working with. Still, through the power of their desire and need, and within the flexible perimeters of devotional practice, they were able to do much with what they inherited.

Women believed that they became agents in a new way with Jude's help. Their prayers made things happen in their lives. Then they sat down and wrote out accounts of their experience for publication at the shrine. These narratives must not be understood to provide "closure" to painful experiences in any simple sense. Rather, the narrative process, occurring within the complex world of devotional culture, was a zone of reimagination, a privileged exercise in which frightening experiences were engaged, struggled with, shared, endured, remembered, and in some sense healed. Women used the resources of devotional culture to recreate their world.

Again, the analysis here must always be dialectical. Women did not directly challenge the family arrangements which they experienced as oppressive, more often finding new ways of coordinating their lives within these structures with Jude's help; and I have discussed in this essay some of the ways that Jude's devotion recreated normative structures of gender relations. But these dimensions of the devotion must be read from the perspective of women's own appropriations, manipulations, and recreations of the forms and structures of devotionalism.

Finally, popular religion can now be seen as one of the central intersections of "public" events and "private" experience. Jude appeared as a figure in the space between prayer, desire, and need, on the one hand, and social and cultural structures, authorities, and norms, on the other. Although the devout do not recognize the disciplinary distinction between inner and outer, Jude was both a "public" symbol encountered by women in the language and structures of a particular religious tradition at a particular moment in their social experiences and the creation of private desire and imagination. The saint is a kind of boundary-crossing figure for the devout, serving as a special kind of emissary between levels of their experience. History is always the story of this conjuncture of inner and outer.

The Story of the Switched Statues Again

Why did the daughters of immigrants turn to Saint Jude in the difficult days of 1929? We know how they went on to imagine Jude, and what their lives with this saint looked like. Perhaps they were dissatisfied with the holy figures that their parents prayed to, suspecting that these saints could not understand their new experiences and feelings. Perhaps they were frightened by their fathers' and husbands' difficulties at finding and keeping work, and in response they created a powerful, sympathetic man for themselves who could help them but who was also dependent on them for his own voice.

But I have begun to wonder whether this generation of Catholic women may also have been turning away, perhaps unconsciously, from the model of the Christian woman offered in Thérèse—the saint of "suffering" and "self-abnegation"—in favor of a saint whose existence was rooted in their needs and who would not only understand and comfort them, but empower them as well.

Power in what sense though? Freedom, Sartre said in an interview late in his life, is what a person can make of what has been made of him or herself. This is the dialectic of devotionalism.

NOTES

1. This paper has benefitted from the close scrutiny and generous criticism of two of my friends and colleagues at Indiana University, Jeff Isaac and Rich Miller. I am grateful to both of them for their help.

The history of the founding of the Church of Our Lady of Guadalupe is based on *Dedication of Our Lady of Guadalupe Church*, September 30, 1928. Chicago: John H. Hannigan Publisher; "Necrology: Father James Tort, C.M.F.," a privately printed biographical sketch, 1955; *Our Lady of Guadalupe Church: 50th Anniversary Bulletin, 1924–1974*, privately printed by the Claretian Fathers, 1974; Joachim DePrada, C.M.F., "Our Founder Is Dead," *Voice of Saint Jude* (hereafter cited as *Voice*), June 1955, p. 34; Frank Smith, "Load of Bricks Stumps Priest Who Fled Bullets," *Voice*, February 1935, p. 18; James Tort, C.M.F., ".Dedication Anniversary of the National Shrine of Saint Jude," *Voice*, February 1935, pp. 12–13; George Hull, "Life Begins at Forty," *Voice*, June 1935, pp. 7–10; John Schneider, C.M.F., "Tenth Anniversary," *Voice*, April 1942, pp. 12–17. The history of the shrine is told in comic-book form in "Jude the Forgotten Saint," published in 1954 by the Catechetical Guild Educational Society.

2. Mary Lee Nolan and Sidney Nolan, in their comprehensive survey of contemporary shrine culture in Western Europe, note that Jude ranked third among the Apostles as a "pilgrimage saint," with at least nine European shrines dedicated to him. They go on to say, however, that "the cult of this apostle, who replaced Judas Iscariot among the original group, developed slowly and became important only in the Twentieth Century." Nolan and Nolan, *Christian Pilgrimage in Modern Western Europe* (Chapel Hill, N.C., and London: 1989), p. 137.

3. For women's central place in nineteenth-century popular piety see Ann Taves, *The Household of Faith* (Notre Dame, Ind., 1986).

4. Interview with Frank K, sixty-six years old, Los Angeles, California.

5. J. P. Donovan, C.M., takes up the question of clerical scruples on this matter in "Is the Perpetual Novena a Parish Need?" *Homiletic and Pastoral Review* 56, no. 4 (January 1946): 252–57. Donovan, who wrote a regular advice column for his clerical colleagues, says that some clergy had concluded that devotional practices like the perpetual novena were either "rackets" or "sen-

timentality." For a rather bitter clerical admission of the predominance of women in devotional culture see Francis W. Grey, "The Devout Female Sex," *Ave Maria* 26, no. 20 (November 12, 1927): 609–12.

6. John M. Huels, O.S.M., "The Friday Night Novena: The Growth and Decline of the Sorrowful Mother Novena," privately printed by the Eastern Province of Servites, Berwyn, Illinois, 1977, pp. 21–23; and Joachim De-Prada, C.M.F., "To Whom Shall We Turn?" *Voice*, December 1958. In several different gatherings of clergy I have heard it dryly observed that the problem with the ordination of women is that if women take over clerical duties there would be no one left in the pews.

7. "We Visit a Solemn Novena," *Voice*, October 1954, pp. 14–17.

8. Monica Furlong, *Thérèse of Lisieux* (New York, 1987), p. 1. For an excellent review of the "posthumous history" of the Little Flower, her changing image over time, see Barbara Corrado Pope, "A Heroine without Heroics: The Little Flower of Jesus and Her Times," *Church History* 57 (March 1986): 46–60.

9. Personal communications: FG-F-49-Chicago-M; AC-F-70-Chicago-W; MPD-F-75-So. Chicago-W; MTD-F-27-Haiti-M; AI-F-55-Chicago-D; AG-F-55-Chicago-S; DD-F-62-Whiting, Ind.-M; FA-F-68-Indiana-S. I distinguish in the notes between two kinds of direct communications to me. "Personal communication" refers to women's written responses to twenty very general questions about their devotions to Saint Jude which I distributed at the shrine in Chicago during a novena in the summer of 1987. Seventy women responded. (I did not ask that only women participate, nor do the questions imply that I think men would not pray to Saint Jude, but only five men wrote to me.) Most of the women who responded to my questions did so at length, adding sheets of paper to the form I had distributed. "Personal correspondence" refers to letters sent me about Saint Jude; I received forty of these. I also conducted about thirty-five interviews with the devout, and these are cited in the text as well. These three sources are intended to supplement the letters written to the shrine over the last fifty years.

I will identify my sources by a consistent designation, beginning with fictitious initials, followed by gender, age, residence, and marital status. In the latter category, M=married, S=single, W=widowed, D=divorced.

10. Personal correspondence: MMc-F-89-LaCrosse, Wisc.-W.

11. George Hull, "Life Begins at Forty," *Voice*, June 1935, pp. 8–9.

12. On Mundelein, see Edward R. Kantowicz, *Corporation Sole: Cardinal Mundelein and Chicago Catholicism* (Notre Dame, Ind., 1983), and Charles Shanabruch, *Chicago's Catholics: The Evolution of an American Identity* (Notre Dame, Ind., 1981). According to shrine accounts, Mundelein was an enthusiastic supporter of the cult in its early years, Hull, "Life," p. 8.

13. Information on this important popular devotion is in *Little Flower Magazine*, published monthly until the mid-1970s by the Carmelite Fathers

of Oklahoma City. There is a historical sketch of the origins of the devotion to the Little Flower in Chicago in *The Sword,* May 1948, pp. 106–16.

14. *Voice,* February 1941, p. 18, Mrs. EF, Detroit.

15. Personal correspondence: MCM-F-89-LaCrosse, Wisc.-W.

16. Personal correspondence: RA-F-62-Dracut, Mass.-M.

17. Personal correspondence: AM-F-65+-Carol Stream, Ill.-M.

18. Personal communication: JF-F-49-Chicago-M; BE-F-66-Chicago-M; CD-F-75-Milwaukee-M.

19. There is unfortunately no comprehensive history of this period. Jay Dolan has a short and helpful chapter on the subject in *The American Catholic Experience: A History from Colonial Times to the Present* (Garden City, N.Y., 1985), "The Catholic Ethos," pp. 221–41. The best study of American Catholic popular religion in the nineteenth century is Ann Taves's *Household,* cited earlier. Joseph Chinnici's recent history of piety in the United States, *Living Stones: The History and Structure of Catholic Spiritual Life in the United States* (New York, 1988), is unfortunately not concerned with popular religion.

20. Personal communication: CD-F-75-Milwaukee-M. Another woman wrote me: "I give these prayer cards out all over the U.S. My friends and people are scattered from Cleveland, Ohio, Minnesota, Illinois, Louisiana, Kentucky, Florida, Nevada, Newportnews, Taft, Scranton. I sent for 1000 [prayer cards]. All I can say Where I go my Patron Saint Jude goes with me." Personal correspondence: CG-F-75-Richmond, Va.-W.

21. This sketch of the changing history of immigrant communities is based on a number of studies both of particular ethnic communities as well as of immigration more generally. I owe a great deal to John Bodnar's *Workers' World: Kinship, Community, and Protest in an Industrial Society, 1900–1940* (Baltimore and London, 1982), and *The Transplanted: A History of Immigrants in Urban America* (Bloomington, Ind., 1985). These transitions are helpfully discussed in Shanabruch, *Chicago's Catholics,* pp. 155–87. For studies of particular communities see Judith E. Smith, *Family Connections: A History of Italian and Jewish Immigrant Lives in Providence, Rhode Island, 1900–1940* (Albany, N.Y., 1985); Humbert Nelli, *Italians in Chicago, 1880–1930: A Study in Ethnic Mobility* (Oxford, 1970); Dino Cinel, *From Italy to San Francisco: The Immigrant Experience* (Stanford, Calif., 1982); Virginia Yans-McLaughlin, *Family and Community: Italian Immigrants in Buffalo, 1880–1930* (Ithaca and London, 1971); Samuel L. Baily, "The Adjustment of Italian Immigrants in Buenos Aires and New York, 1870–1914," *American Historical Review* 88 (April 1983); Joseph John Parot, *Polish Catholics in Chicago, 1850–1920: A Religious History* (DeKalb, Ill., 1981); Paul Wrobel, *Our Way: Family, Parish, and Neighborhood in a Polish American Community* (Notre Dame, Ind., 1979); Dennis Clark, *The Irish in Philadelphia: Ten Generations of Urban Experience* (Philadelphia, 1973); Lawrence McCaffrey, Ellen Skerret, Michael F. Funchion, and Charles Fanning, *The Irish in Chicago* (Urbana and Chicago, 1987); Peter d'A. Jones and

Melvin G. Holli, *Ethnic Chicago* (Grand Rapids, Mich., 1981); Audrey S. Olson, *St. Louis Germans: The Nature of an Immigrant Community and Its Relation to the Assimilation Process* (New York, 1980); Josef J. Barton, "Religion and Cultural Change in Czech Immigrant Communities, 1850–1920," pp. 3–24, in Randall M. Miller and Thomas D. Marzik, eds., *Immigrants and Religion in Urban America* (Philadelphia, 1977); William J. Galush, "Faith and Fatherland: Dimensions of Polish-American Ethnoreligion, 1875–1975," pp. 84–102, in Miller and Marzik, *Immigrants and Religion;* and M. Mark Stolarik, "Immigration, Education, and the Social Mobility of Slovaks, 1870–1930," pp. 103–16 in Miller and Marzik, *Immigrants and Religion.*

22. As Linda Gordon has observed of this period in her study of family violence in Boston, although "parental violence against adolescents of both sexes" in immigrant communities which were just experiencing the loss of the "family economy," was "particularly intense," it was "more so with girls." Linda Gordon, *Heroes of Their Own Lives: The Politics and History of Family Violence, Boston, 1880–1960* (New York, 1988), p. 188.

23. *Catholic Women's World*, a "new type of Catholic magazine," according to its editors, "designed for the modern woman," began publication in June 1939. Although intended for a college-educated, middle-class audience, the magazine is a useful guide to the changing concerns and needs of young Catholic women in these years. Of particular interest here is the treatment of married life in the magazine: the women in *Catholic Women's World*'s fiction, advice columns, and true stories all seem to feel that they must work carefully and conscientiously to make their marriages successful, to the extent even of taking classes to learn how to do special things in the kitchen and around the house. (Adele de Leeuw, "Bookcases and Broccoli," *Catholic Women's World* 1, no. 5, [November 1939].) There are beauty hints each month and pages of recipes, as well as highly ambivalent advice about love and work from Jane Frances Downey. Although Jude's devout came from all social classes, *Catholic Women's World* points to a broader shift in social mores among younger Catholic women. The entry of these women into the culture of expertise, their need for advice on everything from buying towels to changing diapers, suggests that they had begun to feel that their mothers' counsel was of limited usefulness to them.

24. "My husband and I were married less than two months," a woman wrote the shrine in October 1936, "when he lost his position. Needless to say, it brought about a great deal of worry and shattered our dreams for the future." *Voice*, October 1936, Mr. and Mrs. MJB, Chicago.

25. *Voice*, September 1936, p. 15, Mrs. MCG, Chicago. For relations between men and women in this period see Susan Ware, *Holding Their Own: American Women in the 1930s* (Boston, 1982), pp. 8–18, and William Chafe, *The American Woman: Her Changing Social, Economic, and Political Roles* (Oxford, 1972), pp. 135f.

26. *Voice,* April 1952, p. 32, DD, Detroit.

27. *Voice,* July 1950, p. 7, PR, Saint Louis.

28. Personal communication: ER-F-74-Chicago-M.

29. *Voice,* July 1953, Mrs. GH, Chicago.

30. *Saint Jude's Journal,* January 1967, p. 4, Miss JF, Baltimore. The *Journal,* a small, four-page, simply printed devotional newsletter, began publication in 1960. At the same time, the *Voice of Saint Jude* was renamed *U.S. Catholic,* and all devotional material was shifted out of that periodical and into the newsletter. The *Voice* had been evolving over the years into a more general Catholic family magazine, which had long been the ambition of its clerical and lay editors and publishers. But the devotional material had fit quite well into this evolving format through the 1940s and 1950s, and indeed there were important connections between the devotional features of the periodical and the more sophisticated political and social commentary that had begun to appear: Jude, for example, was as stalwart an anti-Communist as any Catholic editor. Something else was happening, though, in Chicago and elsewhere at the end of the fifties: devotionalism, which had flourished in the postwar years, had come under sharp criticism from liturgical reformers, parish clergy, and a new generation of Catholic laity. The repositioning of the devotional material at the shrine reflects this new sensibility.

31. *Voice,* April 1958, DSS, Rosindale, Mass.

32. I discuss this aspect of the devouts' understanding of themselves in "What Did Women Think They Were Doing When They Prayed to Saint Jude," *U.S. Catholic Historian* 8, nos. 1–2, (Winter/Spring 1989): 67–79.

33. Personal correspondence: AS-F-65+-Carol Stream, Ill.-M.

34. Joan Scott, *Gender and the Politics of History* (New York, 1988) p. 24.

35. Ware, *Holding Their Own,* pp. 2–24.

36. Chafe, *The American Woman,* p. 135.

37. Bodnar, *Workers' World,* p. 116.

38. *Voice,* June 1935, p. 16, SMT, Chicago.

39. *Voice,* January 1935, p. 16, Mrs. ME, Chicago.

40. On the Police Branch of the Saint Jude's League see: Frank Smith, "Load of Bricks Stumps Priest Who Fled Bullets," *Voice,* February 1935, p. 18; Father Anthony, C.M.F., "The St. Jude Novena," *Voice,* March 1938, p. 10; John Schneider, C.M.F., "Tenth Anniversary," *Voice,* April 1942, pp. 12–18; Joseph M. Puigvi, C.M.F., "Jottings on Devotion to Saint Jude," *Voice,* December 1946, p. 7; "Police Overflow Church for Annual Communion," *Voice,* June 1948, p. 7; "19th Annual Police Mass," *Voice,* June 1951, p. 19; Joachim DePrada, "Our Founder Is Dead," *Voice,* June 1955, p. 34; "Guns and Missals," *Voice,* October 1954, pp. 28–29.

41. A recent shrine director suggested to a reporter from a local Chicago paper that, in the reporter's words, "policemen are logically clients of Saint

Jude . . . in that they carry clubs." Peter Schwendener, "The Patron Saint of Hopeless Cases," *Reader,* May 27, 1983, p. 34. Jude is usually shown holding a thick wooden shaft, the implement of his martyrdom.

42. BC-M-55-Queens, N.Y.-M.

43. As John Bodnar writes, "in nearly every immigrant household economy, the central manager of financial resources, children's socialization, and the entire operation, was the married female." *Transplanted,* pp. 81–82.

44. Father Marrison, O.C.D., "The Woman in Social Life," *Little Flower Magazine* 15, no. 9 (December 1934): 5.

45. "The Discipline of Girls," *Ave Maria* 25, no. 26 (June 25, 1927): 821.

46. Joseph McClellan, "Everyman's Nagging Wife," *Ave Maria* 90, no. 13 (September 26, 1959): 5–9.

47. Nellie R. Ivancovich, "Motherhood," *Ave Maria* 35, no. 11 (March 12, 1932): 338–40.

48. Helen Moriarity, "Jim Graney's Wife," *Ave Maria* 12, no. 15 (October 9, 1920): 463–66, and 12, no. 16 (October 16, 1920): 494–98. See also: E. M. Walker, "East End Granny," *Ave Maria* 25, no. 25 (June 18, 1927): 781–83; James A. Dunn, "The Picture," *Sign* 28, no. 8 (March 1949): 20–23; Constance Edgerton, "Desert Love," *Voice,* April 1938, pp. 17–18; Anne Tansey, "Receive This Word," *Voice,* June 1944, pp. 14, 16–17; Pauline Marie Cloton, "Larry's Wife," *Sacred Heart Messenger,* 56, no. 6 (June 1921): 325–32.

49. Tansey, "Receive This Word," p. 14.

50. P.J.C., "Contentment," *Ave Maria* 35, no. 14 (April 2, 1932): 437.

51. Anne Tansey, "Will-o-the-Wisp," *Voice,* July 1944, pp. 10, 17.

52. Sister M. Marguerite, R.S.M., "Barter and Exchange: For Fathers Only," *Voice,* May 1947, pp. 4, 19, 24.

53. Ben Hurst, "Sibyl's Awakening," *Ave Maria* 26, no. 22 (November 26, 1927): 688–91; Ann Tansey, "Going Home," *Voice,* September 1944, pp. 10, 16.

54. Edgerton, "Desert Love," p. 18.

55. For a good discussion of the history of women's identification with suffering in the Catholic tradition, and the special place in this story of Augustine's suffering mother, Monica, see Clarissa W. Atkinson, "'Your Servant, My Mother': The Figure of Saint Monica in the Ideology of Christian Motherhood," pp. 139–72 in Atkinson, Constance H. Buchanan, and Margaret R. Miles, eds., *Immaculate and Powerful: The Female in Sacred Image and Social Reality* (Boston, 1985).

56. Hilary Sweeney, C.P., "When Ignorance is Bliss," *Sign* 28, no. 11 (June 1949): 39–40.

57. "The Union of Jesus and Mary," *Ave Maria* 12, no. 26 (December 25, 1920): 820–21. This theme is most strongly articulated in the widely read work of Don Sharkey. See for example *The Woman Shall Conquer* (New York, 1954), which is a celebration both of Mary's (and in general, women's) powers and of women's suffering.

58. Arthur Tonne, O.F.M., "Swords of Sorrow," *St. Anthony's Messenger* 48, no. 8 (January 1941): 25, 47.

59. Maude Gardner, "The Undaunted Christmas Spirit," *Voice*, December 1937, pp. 15–17.

60. Sister M. Adelaide, R.S.M., "Short Wave to Saint Jude," *Voice*, April 1950, p. 4.

61. Tonne, "Swords," p. 31.

62. Alice Pauline Clark, "The Silent Saint," *Ave Maria* 35, no. 12 (March 19, 1932): 353.

63. Florence Gilmore, "Wife, Mother, and Saint," *Ave Maria* 35, no. 8 (February 20, 1932): 240–43; also Countess de Courson, "A New Beata. Anna Maria Taigi," *Ave Maria* 11, no. 25 (June 19, 1920): 782–87.

64. *Voice*, December 1950, p. 5, MC, Chicago. One female correspondent reports that she made a fifty-four day "rosary novena" while she and her husband were looking for a home. *Voice*, September 1958, ARS, Chicago.

65. *Voice*, May 1955, p. 34, Mrs. CEN, Bay City, Michigan; ibid., June 1951, p. 32, RM, St. Louis; personal communication: DH-F-67-Indiana-M.

66. *Voice*, January 1935, Mrs. MB, Chicago; ibid., March 1935, p. 15, Mrs. EH, Hasbrouck Heights, N.J.; ibid., December 1950, p. 5, IB, Kent, Conn.; ibid., April 1955, p. 34, Miss CM, Chicago.

67. Göran Therborn, *The Ideology of Power and the Power of Ideology* (London, 1980), pp. 16–18.

68. Quoted in Peter Dews, *Logics of Disintegration: Post-Structuralist Thought and the Claims of Critical Theory* (London and New York, 1987), p. 188.

69. Scott, *Gender*, p. 43.

70. Gananath Obeyesekere, *Medusa's Hair: An Essay on Personal Symbols and Religious Experience* (Chicago, 1984), pp. 115–22.

71. Personal communication: DA-F-54-Chicago-W.

72. Personal communication: EA-F-59-Chicago-M.

73. Personal communication: BC-F-36-Joliet, Ill.-S.

74. Personal communication: BF-F-75-So. Chicago-W.

75. Personal communication: GG-F-55-Chicago-M.

76. Personal communications: BB-F-48-Chicago-S; HH-F-33-Chicago-M; CD-F-75-Milwaukee-M; CH-F-69-Chicago-W.

77. Personal communications: DG-F-76-Chicago-M; AH-F-58-Chicago-M; BE-F-66-Chicago-M.

78. Personal communications: CD-F-67-Chicago-M; EF-F-63-Chicago-W; *Journal*, April 1967, p. 4, OJB, Forest Park, Ga.

79. Personal communication: BG-F-63-Chicago-M. She writes, "Somehow I would much rather talk [to] him than say the Journal prayers."

80. Personal communications: BD-F-46-Chicago-M; AH-F-58-Chicago-M.

81. See, for example, *Voice*, January 1935, p. 17, Mrs. CGF, Chicago;

ibid., May 1935, p. 16, Mrs. MHF, Chicago, and Mrs. MK, Chicago; ibid., March 1950, p. 6, AS, Wyoming, Ohio; ibid., April 1950, p. 5, LW, Malden, Mass.; ibid., March 1951, p. 29, DR, Santa Clara, Calif.; ibid., March 1958, Mrs. ERP, Lawrence, Mass.; *Journal,* August 1966, p. 4, Mrs. PS; ibid., April/May 1964, p. 4, Mrs. MS.

82. See Bodnar, *Workers' World,* p. 173.

83. Personal communication: US-F-65+-Michigan-M. On the importance of women's networks see Ellen Ross, "Survival Networks: Women's Neighborhood Sharing in London Before World War I," *History Workshop* 15 (Spring 1983): 4–27; Mary P. Ryan, "The Power of Women's Networks: A Case Study of Female Moral Reform in Antebellum America," *Feminist Studies* 5, no. 1 (Spring 1979): 66–86; and Temma Kaplan, "Female Consciousness and Collective Action: The Case of Barcelona, 1910–1918," *Signs* 7 (1982): 545–66.

84. Personal correspondence: MF-F-60(?)-Yarmouth, England-S; *Voice,* April 1941, p. 18, Mrs. AG, Chicago; ibid., May 1953, p. 33, Mrs. PK, Louisville, Ky. "When I have a problem," a correspondent wrote in 1967, "I always say a prayer to Saint Jude and it seems I can face that problem with more courage." *Journal,* August 1967, Miss MP, no location cited.

85. On the consensus in the devotional press against women's working see Joseph McShane, S.J., "And They Lived Catholicly Ever After: A Study of Catholic Periodical Fiction between 1930 and 1950," unpublished paper; on the general social disapproval of this, see Chafe, *American Woman,* pp. 174–89.

86. *Voice,* July 1955, Mrs. MF, Cincinnati.

87. Personal communication: BC-F-36-Joliet, Ill.-S.

88. William Halsey, *The Survival of American Innocence* (Notre Dame, Ind., 1980).

89. Joseph P. Donovan, C.M., "Novenas and Devotional Tastes," *Homiletic and Pastoral Review* 43, no. 7 (April 1943): 643–44.

90. *Voice,* June 1949, p. 4, MC, Providence, R.I.

PART II
Religion and Politics

5

The Religious Origins of the Patriot and Ministerial Parties in Pre-Revolutionary France

Dale K. Van Kley

This Jansenism, having expended most of its capital and made its most valuable contribution in the suppression of the Jesuits in France, has transformed itself into the party of patriotism. One should give [Jansenism] its due, for it has always been greatly inclined toward independence, and did battle against papal despotism with invincible courage. But political despotism is a hydra no less formidable to fear, and it is against that enemy that we must now direct all the forces no longer needed on the other battlefront.

Pidansat de Mairobert,
*Journal historique sur la révolution operée
dans la constitution de la monarchie françoise,
par M. de Maupeou, chancelier de France,* 1772[1]

1. Introduction

Hardly had they returned from their annual autumnal recess (*vacances*) in December 1770, than the magistrates of the French monarchy's chief law court, the *Parlement* of Paris, received from their chancellor a royal edict which, had they accepted or "registered" it, would have been tantamount to a disavowal of all the "constitutional" gains that they had made at the expense of royal absolutism during the preceding twenty years. Defending the king's undivided and divinely ordained sovereignty against his disobedient magistrates' "systematizing mindset" (*esprit de systeme*), this so-called Edict of December explicitly condemned such theses as that the Parlement of Paris together with France's thirteen provincial parlements constituted the various "classes" of a single national parlement, that these parlements whether singly or together legitimately "represented" the French "nation" vis-à-vis the king, or again that this "representative" capacity entitled them to refuse their consent or "registration" to royal declarations and edicts—including of course the Edict of December. The same edict also outlawed the practice of the judicial "strike"—that is, suspension of the administration of routine justice—by means of which the Parisian magistrates had been able to make good their now proscribed constitutional claims.[2]

The presumed author of this provocative edict was the new chief of justice or chancellor, René-Nicolas-Charles-Augustin de Maupeou, himself a former councillor and president in the Parlement of Paris. And if by means of this edict Maupeou or King Louis XV had hoped, for whatever reason, to goad the Parlement into a punishable act of disobedience, he probably succeeded well beyond his own expectations. Faced with the unattractive alternatives of signing their own constitutional death warrant or inviting it by defying the edict's express provisions, the Parlement chose the latter course, refusing either to "register" the offending edict or to administer routine justice after the king forcibly registered the contested edict in a royal "bed of justice" (*lit de justice*) on December 7. The magistrates' unanimous resistance initially obliged Maupeou to exile each and every one of them, the more moderate ones to their country estates and notorious "troublemakers" to sundry remote and inhospitable locations in the midst of an inclement winter, and eventually to replace the Parlement's entire judicial personnel with hastily impressed recruits. The continued defiance of other Parisian courts, particularly the *Cour des aides,* as well as the provincial parlements, further challenged the chancellor's improvisational prowess, forcing him either to abolish or to purge these courts as each in turn, acting on the condemned theory of parliamentary "classes," refused to register the new edicts legalizing the previous improvisations. In this way one expedient led to another, all of them eventually adding up to the reconstitution of France's entire judicial system and the replacement of much of its personnel.[3]

"The revolution perpetrated on the constitution of the French monarchy by M. de Maupeou," as the Parisian "publicist" Pidansat de Mairobert's *Historical Journal* called it, did not ultimately escape the fate traditionally assigned to "revolutions," coming as it did full circle with the restoration of the old parlements by the new King Louis XVI in 1774. And the event's sometime reputation as one of the Bourbon monarchy's last chances for salvific reform has no more successfully survived the historiography of the 1980s than the Bourbon monarchy itself survived the "real" revolution of 1789. To be sure, Maupeou abolished privately purchased or "venal" offices in all the parlements, replacing them with royal appointees, and tried to make justice cheaper and more accessible by parceling out much of the parlements' former jurisdiction among "superior courts," especially within the huge and unwieldy jurisdiction of the Parlement of Paris. But as reform, none of this was very serious. The reformist aspects of Maupeou's constitutional *coup*, it now seems clear, were at best justificatory afterthoughts, the original intent having had more to do with obscure maneuvering among court factions led by Maupoeu himself and the new minister of foreign affairs, Emmanuel-Armand de Vignerot, the Duc d'Aiguillon.[4] And despite the plaudits of Voltaire, the reforms themselves remained unconvincing, resulting in neither cheaper nor better justice nor in any sustained attack on the luxuriant undergrowth of purchasable offices and the privileges they conferred. Nor for that matter do the eventually restored parlements now appear to have been the obstacles to subsequent reform that they were once thought to be. The chastened Parlement of Paris in particular rubberstamped just about all of the crown's fiscal exigencies after its restoration in 1774 until the combination of an Assembly of Notables and an aroused "public opinion" galvanized it into a last-ditch resistance to an insolvent government in 1787.[5]

But if Maupeou's constitutional "revolution" effected no lasting changes in the institutional landscape, it was otherwise in the more pliable domain of political culture. For parallel to the contemporaneous body of support for John Wilkes and parliamentary reform in England as well as to the "patriots" who organized against the Stamp Act in the American colonies, a "party of patriotism" rapidly took shape in support of the suppressed parlements in France. By "patriot party" Mairobert and other sympathetic journalists or "publicists" meant to designate, not a modern political organization—unthinkable in any case under Bourbon absolutism—but rather an informal coalition of groups and individuals associated in defense of the parlements and against Maupeou. However loose, this coalition effectively harnessed for a while the corporate discipline of the Parisian lawyers or *avocats;* it also enjoyed the support of an overlapping and clandestinely organized group of disaffected French Catholics known as appellants or Jansenists. Together these allies managed to orchestrate the publication and distribution of over five hundred books and pamphlets in the course of two or three years in defiance of perhaps the Old Regime's most strenuous censorship effort. Although this number may not seem impressive in comparison to the seventeenth-century Fronde's thousands of *mazarinades,* or pamphlets against Cardinal-Minister Jules Mazarin, the patriot party's *maupeouana*, or pamphlets against Maupeou, are more modern and proto-revolutionary in their explicit appeal to both "public opinion" and to the "fatherland" or "nation" against the chancellor's "despotism."[6]

In response to the patriot party's constitutional and antidespotic rhetoric, Maupeou and some of his fellow maligned ministers had recourse not only to the censorship efforts of the Paris police but also to a propagandistic counterattack of their own, eventually subsidizing the publication of a hundred or so pamphlets in defense of "reform" and the absolute monarchy. On behalf of "reform," Maupeou was of course able to count upon the support of his enemies' enemies: some peers and other rank-conscious nobles long fed up with the "bourgeois" *parlementaires'* pretensions, and pro-papal or ultramontanist Catholic clergymen and pious courtiers—together known as the "devout party" (*parti dévôt*)— long opposed to Jansenist "heretics" and the parlements that defended them. But the label of "devout party" would seem only imperfectly to describe a coalition of the ministry's partisans that included the king's infamous mistress Madame Dubarry, the arch-*philosophe* Voltaire, and an unlikely assortment of "publicists," the best known of which was Simon-Henri Linguet. Although unsanctioned by contemporary usage, the term "ministerial party" seems less misleading and will therefore be used here. To defend royal ministers, however, was to defend the monarchy which employed them, and in thus pleading the monarchy's case in pamphlet form and implicitly accepting "public opinion" as judge, this "ministerial party's" propaganda may well have undermined divine-right monarchy more effectively than it defended it. By accusing the magistrates of egotistical "aristocracy" it may also have dealt as severe a blow to the Old Regime's social structure as did the patriot party's charge of "despotism" to its political structure.[7]

As it happens, the three most maligned partisans of Maupeou's *coup* in the patriot party's most successful pamphlet—namely Jacques de Flesselles, Foulon de Doué, and Berthier de Sauvigny, who figure ignominiously in the anonymous *Personal and Confidential Correspondence*—were among the very first victims of the triumphant stormers of the Bastille in 1789.[8] But such anecdotal and melodramatic material is not really needed to underscore the long-term significance of the changes in political culture wrought by the Maupeou episode. For it was the faithful remnants of the patriot party who, still under that banner, led the pre-revolutionary charge in 1787–1788 against the "despotism" of the royal ministers Alexandre de Calonne and Loménie de Brienne, who in turn followed Maupeou's example in subsidizing pamphlets which renewed the charge of "aristocracy" against the parlements and their partisans.

The patriot-ministerial pamphletary debate of the Maupeou era also played a certain if unsung role in politicizing the French Enlightenment. On the patriot side, sometime *Encyclopedia* editor Denis Diderot, for example, whose political thought underwent a sharp radicalization around 1770, wrote hauntingly of confronting the "hideous head of despotism" which Maupeou's unceremonious rending of the web of constitutionality had exposed to plain view; while from the safety of the Genevan border the "king of Ferney" himself, Voltaire, threw in his lot with Maupeou and the monarchy, arguing the case of Maupeou's "enlightened" reforms against the benighted opponents of smallpox inoculation and the fanatical "butchers of [Jean] Calas."[9]

Such evidence, of course, points up the knotty problem of the relationship between the French Enlightenment and the political thought and rhetoric of the late eighteenth century, and of these in turn to the French Revolution. Were philosophes such as Diderot and Voltaire just incidentally politicized by Maupeou's *coup* and its rhetorical fallout, or did the "influence" really run in the other direction, with both patriotic and ministerial "discourses" drawing out the diverse political implications of the French Enlightenment and selectively equipping themselves with its concepts? It was not long before many Frenchmen thought the former, at least where the patriot movement was concerned. Indeed, the same Pidansat de Mairobert who in the heat of battle celebrated "Jansenism's" transformation into the "party of patriotism" had apparently already changed his mind when, writing just a few years later, he virtually identified the anti-Maupeou "patriots" with the third and political stage of what he then called the "philosophical movement."[10]

What the following pages will argue, on the contrary, is that however close to the event Mairobert's attempt at historical reconstruction in 1777, it is less reliable than his ground-level observations in 1772; and that however numerous its "philosophical" and "enlightened" allies, the patriot movement of the early 1770s was quite literally a transformation of what had been known as the Jansenist party (*parti janséniste*) in the 1750s and 1760s. In view of this religious ancestry, it should hardly be surprising that when Maupeou sought allies against these rechristened "patriots" he should have found them in part among Jansenism's traditional enemies, namely ex-Jesuits (their society had been disbanded in France in 1762) and their partisans among the bishops and courtiers, or what was still known as the *parti dévôt*. At the origin of the late eighteenth-century ministerial party and its rhetorical tactics, it will therefore also be argued, stands the Jesuitical and pro-papal or ultramontanist *parti dévôt*. The argument in favor of the religious and specifically Catholic origins of both the patriot and ministerial parties and ideologies in prerevolutionary France, while it undoubtedly challenges the pride of place generally accorded the Enlightenment among the ideological progenitors of the French Revolution, is not meant to suggest that either of these parties escaped ideological contamination by that Enlightenment, or that the Enlightenment should not figure significantly in an account of the Revolution's origins. To the contrary, reciprocal interaction between the French Enlightenment and these religious-political "parties" is but another facet of the political and ideological fecundity of the Maupeou episode.

2. The Themes of "Patriotic" Pamphlets

When late eighteenth-century observers such as Mairobert used the term "Jansenism," they no longer uniquely designated an austere group of theological and moral disciples of the movement's seventeenth-century founders, namely Cornelius Jansen, bishop of Ypres, and the illustrious sisters and "solitaires" gathered in and around the convent of Port-Royal des Champs, or even disciples of Saint Augustine, the mentor that Jansenists themselves most readily acknowledged. Such authentic disciples there were, to be sure—although probably in diminishing numbers as the century progressed—who steadfastly maintained the Augustinian doctrinal emphases on (1) a human nature radically vitiated by "concupiscence" or sin as opposed to one merely deprived of "supernatural" gifts; (2) the consequent need for God's sovereign "predestination" of some to "salvation" as opposed to a mere foreknowledge of their future merits; (3) the salvific agency of an all-powerful or "efficacious grace" as opposed to a merely "sufficient" one dependent on the penitent's free will; and (4) the penitential requirement of "charity" or pure love (*amour*) for God, the chief fruit of efficacious grace, as opposed to mere fear (*crainte*) of punishment for sin. For such "friends of the Truth," as the Jansenists christened themselves, these "truths" made up the core of a "continuous tradition" as enunciated by the inspired authors of the Holy Scriptures and the early church fathers, especially saints Cyprian and Augustine, while the opposing doctrinal tendencies represented recent "Molinistic" or neo-Pelagian "innovations" introduced by the Jesuits, in particular the sixteenth-century Spanish Jesuit philosopher and theologian Luis Molina, in an attempt to denature divine revelation the better to accommodate unregenerate human nature.[11]

Under constant attack themselves, however, as heretical crypto-Calvinists, eighteenth-century Jansenists had shed the rough edges of their Augustinianism by bringing that North African father's doctrine of grace into contact with that of Thomas Aquinas.[12] (The doctrine of grace they defended was always said to be the doctrine of saints Augustine *and* Thomas.) Intense persecution of Jansenists during the first half of the century had moreover spawned not only the notorious miracles and convulsions around the tomb of the saintly deacon François de Pâris in the Parisian cemetery of Saint-Médard, but also a dubious hermeneutic called "figurism" whereby biblical passages might be read as prefiguring contemporary events such as the papal bull *Unigenitus* as well as events yet to come such as the Jews' conversion to Christianity.[13] This eschatological hermeneutic reinforced the Jansenists' long-standing insistence on translating the Scriptures into the vernacular so that they could be read by the lay "faithful." It also transformed Jansenists into the century's most assiduous observers of and commentators on contemporary events—what were called *les affaires du temps* or *les affaires présentes*—and thereby ironically contributed to a certain secularization or at least politicization of the movement.[14]

The primary catalyst in eighteenth-century Jansenism's secularization and politicization was persecution, especially in the form of Pope Clement XI's bull *Unigenitus* which condemned Jansenist doctrinal tenets in 1713, prompting French Jansenists to appeal to a future ecumenical council and henceforth committing them to an anti-papal conciliarism. The fact that conciliarism, or the doctrine of the ecumenical council's superiority over the pope, was one of the chief tenets of the French ecclesiological tradition known as Gallicanism, parts of which also sustained condemnation by *Unigenitus,* made French Gallicans sympathetic to Jansenists and further elided these hitherto distinguishable movements. Although Mairobert may have been right about Jansenism's perennial penchant toward "independence," the movement's conversion to Gallicanism and consequent battle against papal "despotism" was more recent than he remembered.[15]

In contrast, Jansenists had hardly waited for the "patriot party" or Mairobert's journal to become "patriots" in a pro-parliamentary and constitutional sense, since that development too came largely in response to *Unigenitus.* Solicited by the aging Louis XIV and rigorously enforced by his successor, *Unigenitus* indeed became a symbol of "political" as well as of "papal despotism," thereby throwing Jansenists into close association with the Parlement's magistrates, who for their part opposed the bull as good Gallicans and whose constitutional rights of remonstrance and registration alone stood in the way of its being fully enforced as a law of the state. The parlements, especially the Parlement of Paris, soon numbered some *bona fide* Jansenists in their midst — indeed, as contemporaries used it, the term *parti janséniste* referred above all to a group within and around the Parlement of Paris — while, aside from Montesquieu, the Jansenists became the century's foremost apologists of parliamentary constitutionalism.[16] As Mairobert well knew, the authority and status of the bull *Unigenitus* and the attempts by Archbishop of Paris Christophe de Beaumont, among other bishops, to refuse Jansenists the last sacraments in the 1750s were among the chief bones of contention dividing monarchy from parlements until 1770; the 1760s suppression of the Jesuits, who had by that time become the symbols of both political and papal "despotism" as well as of theological "Molinism," represented the triumph of the parlements as well as of Jansenism. These same mixed religious and political confrontations had moreover led directly to the escalation of the parlements' constitutional pretensions during the 1750s and 1760s, and therefore also to Maupeou's constitutional counterattack in 1770.[17]

It was this loose alliance between parliamentary lawyers and magistrates, disaffected Jansenist clergy members as well as politicized bourgeois and even some Parisian "little people" (*menu peuple*) that eighteenth-century observers such as the lawyer Barbier referred to by a *parti janséniste,* just as it was this ideology composed of elements of Jansenism, Gallicanism, and parliamentary constitutionalism that they most often referred to by the shorthand term of "Jansenism."[18] In its anti-Jesuitical and papal proto-nationalism and its defense of a putatively ancient constitution against "despotism," as well as in its continued close association with a "puritanical" religious "conscience" against all forms of "domination," the ideology was in many respects the Gallic counterpart to the "real Whiggism" or "commonwealth-man" ideology then current in England and the American colonies. In looking for a "Jansenist" presence in the pamphlet literature of the patriot movement, therefore, it is imperative to bring to bear the wider meanings that this term had acquired, especially those having to do with the varieties of parliamentary constitutionalism in whose articulation Jansenists had been so very influential.

By far the most prevalent form of parliamentary or magisterial constitutionalism in the patriot pamphlet literature of the period 1771–1775 rooted the Parlement of Paris's rights of remonstrance and registration in its supposedly lineal descent from the medieval court of peers (*Cour des pairs*) and ultimately from the much earlier Merovingian royal court (*Cour royal*) and general assemblies (*parlements généraux*) of all Frankish warriors. Since in this reconstruction of French institutional history these primitive *parlements généraux* had consisted of the entire Frankish nation which, when assembled, possessed the right to accept or annul all of the Merovingian kings' legislative initiatives, it followed that the Parlement of Paris as its legitimate institutional descendant was also "in its own manner possessed of a role in legislation," in the words of the anonymous *Letter from Monsieur Xxx, a Councillor in the Parlement to Monsieur the Count of Xxx,* and therefore also entitled to the quality of "representative of the Nation, for stipulating its interests. . . ." Yet this capacity as representative of the nation did not prevent the Parlement from also being the successor of both the Merovingian royal court and the medieval court of peers and, as the offspring of those royal institutions, from being the king's only legitimate "mouthpiece vis-à-vis the Nation," according to the same pamphlet.[19] From these historical and constitutional premises pamphleteers such as the anonymous author of a *Letter from a Bourgeois of Paris* also frequently drew the corollary that the royal "bed of justice" (*lit de justice*) whereby the king now high-handedly imposed his legislative will on the parlements had once been a genuine consultation between the king and his trusted magisterial councillors which had only recently degenerated into a display of arbitrary force—that "this solemn assembly," in that pamphlet's words, "once intended to *enlighten* the king and *show him the truth,* had become instead a dumb scene just as distressing for its members as it is useless for the instruction of the king."[20]

Although examples of this kind of magisterial constitutionalism abound in patriot pamphlets, a single one must suffice, illustrating as it does the intertwined theses of the Parlement of Paris's descent from the Merovingian representative institutions and the recent degeneration of the *lit de justice.* "Long ago the Nation had the good fortune of assembling frequently under the eyes and in virtue of the orders of its Sovereign, who deigned to consult that Nation directly, to listen to her respectful entreaties, and to propose laws for her approval," recalled the anonymous *Petition for the King by the Estates General of France.* For "in these assemblies known indifferently under the names of the fields of Mars, general petitions (*placites généraux*), plenary courts, parlements, and finally of *lits de justice*, [the nation] deliberated out loud concerning the matters presented to her by the king . . . and then decided by voting." But alas, bewailed this pamphlet, "these happy moments for the monarchy, times of its glory and splendor," had declined to the point that "for a century and a half or so we have been relegated far from our Prince and experience his authority by its rigors alone." Although in the absence of the more recent Estates General the nation's "interests had not remained without defenders," namely the parlements "commissioned with the duty of conserving them," the salutary forms of parliamentary remonstrance and registration had—alas again—fallen in turn upon hard times, "now serving only to kindle our regrets," seeing that "the ceremony of kindness had given way to the terror of a *lit de justice* of an unprecedented kind. . . ." This despotic trend had of course come definitively to roost with Maupeou's Edict of December, "come [in fact] to consummate our slavery."[21]

However ancient this and a score of other pamphlets thought the origins of the Parlement of Paris to be—they were not nearly so ancient, we now know—the thesis of those ancient origins was quite recent, at least in that precise form, having found expression less than twenty years earlier in a two-volume book entitled *Historical Letters on the Essential Functions of the Parlement of Paris, on the Right of the Peers, and on the Fundamental Laws of the Realm.*[22] And however recent the deformation of the *lit de justice* (it was the *lit de justice*, we now know, and not its deformation that was recent) the thesis of that degeneration was more recent still, having appeared almost simultaneously in books entitled *Manual for Sovereigns* and *Discourse on the Origins of the Present Troubles in France,* published in 1754 and 1756 respectively, as well as in a pamphlet entitled *Letter on* Lits de Justice, which also appeared in 1756.[23] As it happens, moreover, the author of the two *Letters* was a certain Louis-Adrien Le Paige or Lepaige, a lawyer and political *éminence grise* in the Parlement of Paris, as well as the personal librarian and legal consultant to the king's cousin the Prince de Conti, who as secular head of the Order of Malta also employed Le Paige as his judicial bailiff over the order's privileged Parisian domain called the Temple. A temperamental *frondeur,* Conti had for his part thrown himself heart and soul into the "patriot" protest against Maupeou's *coup,* sponsoring a quasi-official *Protestation by the Princes* against the Edict of December—and retrospectively making a strong case for the "influence" of Le Paige on the contents of this and other documents in the "patriots'" protest literature.[24] And as it also happens, Le Paige was a Jansenist in just about every sense of that term – figurist, convulsionary, Augustinian, Gallican, conciliarist, *parlementaire*.

Le Paige's Jansenism may of course have been incidental to his constitutionalism, which consisted in turn of a reworking by him of materials dating from the seventeenth-century Fronde and the sixteenth-century wars of religion. Yet Le Paige was able to give that material a singularly Jansenist form. For his *Historical Letters* had subtly cast the parliamentary magistrates as a faithful constitutional remnant within a woebegone nation, steadfastly committed, like the Jansenist minority within the post-*Unigenitus* church, to witnessing to truth amidst the apostasy of despotism in post-Frondish France. The magistrates' truth was of course constitutional truth, attested to by history – or at least Le Paige's history – rather than by divine revelation, yet hardly less hoary and definitive than the Jansenists' parallel conception of patristic and especially Augustinian truth. And just as the Jansenists had suffered persecution throughout the century, contributing more recruits to the Bastille than any other identifiable religious or ideological group, so the magistrates' unenviable lot was passively to sustain intermittent persecution in the form of "sealed letters" (*lettres de cachet*) exiling them to various parts of France, such as the places inflicted upon them by Maupeou in 1771.

As it happens, a Jansenistic tone pervades much of the anonymous patriot pamphlet literature of 1771–1775. What was the parliamentary magistracy, asked the *Letter by a Frenchman to the Victims of Ebrouin,* if not a "civil priesthood which imprints on those who receive it an ineffacable character which can never be destroyed . . . ?" Hence the usurping and tyrannical seventh-century Frankish mayor of the palace named Ebrouin, that is to say Maupeou, could not have "defrocked" the magistrates by either abolishing their offices or reimbursing what they had paid for them.[25] The magistrates had only done their "solemn duty to refuse until death" any assaults such as Maupeou's against the "dogma of our national constitution," according to the *Petition for the King by the Estates General of France.* Far from having seditiously challenged the king's rightful authority, added the *Letter from Monsieur Xxx, a Councillor in the Parlement,* they had only uttered a "cry of conscience" and defended the "always subsistent [fundamental] laws" by "passively" refusing to "lend their ministry" to Maupeou's projected transformation of France into a despotism. The *Letter from a Bourgeois of Paris* maintained that Maupeou had replaced the "love" hitherto characteristic of relations between the French monarchy and its subjects with a reign of "fear," in the teeth of which the magistrates had dutifully persisted in "presenting the truth to the king." In doing so these magistrates had performed a "most difficult and perilous duty," opined the *Letter from a Former Magistrate,* because they had willingly run the risk of "exposing themselves to everything" and "sacrificing everything."[26] And so on.

But coexisting uneasily with this Le Paige-like magisterial constitutionalism in the pamphlet literature of the patriot movement is another strain that, however respectful of the parlements and grateful for their stand against Maupeou, clearly questioned their claim of being direct descendants of the Frankish national assemblies and the "representatives" of the French nation. It touted instead the candidacy of the defunct Estates General. These two somewhat competitive constitutionalisms were not of course mutually exclusive. Witness the anonymous *Petition for the King by the Estates General of France,* or the equally pro-parliamentary *Conversation between a Lawyer and Monsieur the Chancellor* which conceded that, where consenting to taxes was concerned, the Parlement had at best acted in virtue of a mandate given to it by the Estates General of Blois in 1577—and only provisionally at that.[27] Also very respectful of the parlements, the anonymous and widely read *Inauguration of Pharamond* went further, calling for the restoration of a supposedly original National Diet for the purpose of constitutional legislation and explicitly arguing that "even the Parlements . . . are never more competent to deliberate concerning a new law than they are concerning the establishment or prorogation of a tax, for the reason that no tax can be established or continued except in virtue of a law whose rationale is the public utility recognized as such by the nation."[28]

One of the defining features of the patriot party's more radical fringe is arguably the peremptoriness of this anti-parliamentary bias. The much commented upon *Letters from One Man to Another,* for example, laid it down in no uncertain terms that "the parlements do not compensate for the loss of the Estates General, which they certainly do not represent: in no way where taxes are at issue can the Estates General be supplanted by the parlements, which have acquired I know not how the right of registration." This supposed right the immensely successful and satirical *Personal and Confidential Correspondence of Monsieur de Maupeou, with Monsieur de Sorhouet, a Councillor in the New Parlement* would call boldly a "felony" and a "usurpation."[29] The same radical fringe in the person of the *nouvelliste* Pidansat de Mairobert, author of the *Historical Journal,* frequently faulted the patriot pamphlets that came to his attention for being "very *parlementaire*" and blamed the parlements themselves for the "weakness of repeating [in their remonstrances] that the king holds his crown from God alone," a "proposition," according to Mairobert, "which should never have been advanced in a century as enlightened and philosophical as our own."[30]

A century distinguished by its enlightenment and philosophy? Has Pidansat de Mairobert's *Historical Journal* taken us across a line separating not only moderate from radical "patriotism," but vaguely "Jansenistic" from "enlightened" patriotism as well? This impression is reinforced by the fact that Pidansat de Mairobert faulted other anonymous patriot publications for being both too "Jansenist" and "*parlementaire*," and derived special encouragement from such "enlightened" adhesions to the patriot cause as those of the philosophes Claude-Adrien Helvétius and the Baron d'Holbach.[31] The same *Letters from One Man to Another* that so peremptorily challenged the Parlement's right to register taxes emits a similar if more subdued philosophical glow. Written, according to Mairobert, in the "lively style of a man about town," a veritable "Fontenelle of politics," this pamphlet characteristically celebrated the "few lights" bestowed on France by Louis IX and the thirteenth century, lights which began to "dissipate the darkness of barbarism" and medieval "trouble and ignorance."[32] The Comte de Lauraguais's *Tableau of the French Constitution*, although still significantly dependent upon a Le Paige-like version of France's institutional past, obviously chafed at this dependence and sought to rehabilitate the Estates General.[33] Fifteen years later the same Lauraguais would develop a constitutionalism which, however historical and "gothic" by revolutionary standards, espoused a very different notion of national representation that drew liberally from the political thought of Jean-Jacques Rousseau.[34]

Yet the "influence of the Enlightenment" in a given patriot pamphlet is by no means measurable in terms of its announced preference for the Estates General over the parlements. For example, despite Mairobert's objection that the two-volume *Maxims of French Public Law* revealed "too marked an interest in the Company [the Parlement]," that massive *summa* of patriot constitutionalism contained one of the movement's most radical statements of the Estates General's constitutional powers and of the need for its immediate convocation. At the same time it argued for these theses by means of the ecclesiastical analogy of the ecumenical council's superiority over the papacy in the governance of the Catholic Church—hardly a likely argument for an anti-Catholic Enlightenment.[35] On the contrary, it is altogether Gallican and therefore

also Jansenist to the extent that Jansenists had made conciliar Gallicanism one of the hallmarks of their ecclesiology. And although this secular and political use of Gallican concilarism to transfer sovereignty from
monarchy to nation as represented in the Estates General is not explicitly found in Jansenist literature dating before 1770, it is unmistakably
foreshadowed there in some treatises published earlier in the century,
the latest being Abbé Claude Mey's and Gabriel-Nicolas Maultrot's *Defense of All the Sentences Delivered by the Secular Courts Against the
Schism,* which appeared in 1752.[36] During the patriot protest itself the
conciliarist argument stood out conspicuously in the anonymous and
incendiary *Manifesto to the Normans* (1772) as well as in Guillaume
Saige's *The Citizen's Catechism* (1775).[37]

Such a Jansenist textual "presence" beneath patriot constitutionalisms may seem real enough to the already converted, but it will probably strike the more empirical-minded as less than substantial. Perhaps
those Jansenist elements would seem to be more sensibly apparent in
the case of patriot literature's many expressions of anti-Jesuitism. After
all, the dissolution of the Society of Jesus in France had by no means
satiated the Jansenists' animus against their century-old theological enemies and persecutors, while the corpus of polemical patriot literature
is nothing if not awash in insults to Jesuits, Jesuitism, and things Jesuitical. Yet even this sort of evidence is difficult to interpret because
the nature of Jansenist anti-Jesuitism had kept pace with the development of Jansenism as a whole. That is to say that as Jansenism had pro-
gressively embraced Gallicanism and parliamentary constitutionalism,
it again encountered the Company of Jesus, but this time as the defender of ultramontanism or papal infallibility as well as of Bourbon
absolutism, all by way of defending *Unigenitus.*[38] To the extent that the
Jesuits had become, in Mairobert's words, symbols of papal and political "despotism" as well as of theological and ethical "Molinism," they
conveniently functioned as rhetorical scapegoats not only for Jansenists
narrowly defined but for "patriots" of the most diverse ideological per-
suasions—including the likes of Pidansat de Mairobert. And that ex-
Jesuits should have been suspected as implicated in Maupeou's *coup*
against the parlements and excoriated accordingly is natural enough,
given the parlements' role in the formal dissolution of their company
just a few years earlier. In a word, expressions of anti-Jesuitism cannot
be taken as *prima facie* evidence of Jansenism except in the synthetically
broadest—and analytically most useless—sense of that term.

By no means all expressions of anti-Jesuitism are so ambiguous as these cautionary comments would suggest. When, for example, the anonymous *The Parlement Vindicated by the Empress-Queen of Hungary* detected a "Jesuitical touch" on the part of "those who had been forced by the wise and prudent firmness of our Corps [parlements] to cease troubling peoples' consciences by means of indiscreet and useless questions," it clearly referred to priests who had refused the last sacraments to deathbed opponents of the bull *Unigenitus* – and also sided with those opponents or appellants in the still recent controversy over that issue.[39] The evidence is similarly suggestive when, as in the previously encountered *Petition for the King by the Estates General of France*, the Jesuits' society was faulted for being "criminally guilty in regard to Religion in virtue of its perverse moral theology."[40] And the evidence for Jansenism would seem altogether conclusive in the case of two anonymous pamphlets entitled *The Point of View* and *The Fulfillment of Prophecies*, which, aspiring to put the Maupeou *coup* into a larger historical perspective, not only defined the "phantom of Jansenism" as "everybody of any worth in both Church and State," but also paranoiacally attributed everything that had gone "wrong" in the political and ecclesiastical history of France from 1750, including of course the Maupeou *coup* itself, exclusively to the machinations of the Jesuits.[41]

The identity of both *The Point of View* and *The Fulfillment of Prophecies* as Jansenist pamphlets receives further corroboration from Pidansat de Mairobert's trusty *Historical Journal*, which noted that their publication had caused "a considerable sensation in the party of the Jansenists, which is growing remarkably stronger day by day," and that the *The Fulfillment of Prophecies* had obviously come from the pen of "a very ardent Jansenist, [who] persists in seeing the Jesuits everywhere."[42] In contrast to the *Historical Journal*'s less than reverent reviews, these same pamphlets elicited altogether humorless ones from another of the patriot movement's anonymous periodicals, the short-lived *Supplement to the Gazette of France*, which ran through thirteen numbers between late 1771 and 1773. Indeed, having respectfully reviewed *The Point of View*, the *Supplement* positively anticipated the publication of *The Fulfillment of Prophecies* by suggesting that the Jesuits had not only plotted Maupeou's *coup* but had successfully prophecied it as well.[43] Does this mean that the *Supplement*, too, was a Jansenist publication? That, apparently, was the opinion of Pidansat de Mairobert, whose remarks about Jansenism's metamorphosis into "patriotism" occurred in the context of his review of the *Supplement*'s third number. The *Supplement*'s Jansenist identity is further suggested by its particular interest in the fate of identifiably Jansenist councillors in the Parlement of Paris such as Clément de Feillet, to say nothing of its occasional swipes in the direction of the Archbishop of Paris Christophe de Beaumont and his beloved bull *Unigenitus*.[44]

If in spite of these few firm conclusions anti-Jesuitism remains imperfect as evidence of Jansenism, it would seem otherwise for specifically theological references, including ones to the bull *Unigenitus*. In the course of defending the Parlement of Paris's right to have suspended the administration of routine justice, *Letters from Monsieur Xxx, a Councillor in the Parlement, to Monsieur the Count of Xxx* appealed to the authority of Hincmar, the ninth-century bishop of Reims, describing him as "more competent in political matters than in theological science," obviously referring to the bishop's role in the condemnation of the monk Gottschalk—and the doctrine of predestination, a Jansenist doctrinal stigmatum.[45] Both the *Petition for the King by the Estates General of France* and the *Letter from a Former Magistrate to a Duke and Peer* devote pages to the conduct of the Parlement of Paris in the long controversies over *Unigenitus* and the refusal of sacraments to Jansenists, praising the Parlement for "that inflexible firmness, to which its conscience and oath obliged it," thus likewise revealing their Jansenist coloring and confirming previously noted suspicions to that effect based on their particular brands of anti-Jesuitism and parliamentary constitutionalism.[46]

On only one occasion, however, did Jansenism come out into the open to confront Maupeou's Edict of December with its unique armor of faith. Divulging his figuratist *Reflections on Present Events*, the anonymous author explained France's fall into despotism as a long-suffering Jehovah's delayed punishment for the eighteenth century's "flood of corruption, injustice, irreligion, and impiety which have inundated all estates and professions." Standard sermon fare, this, and just as probably Jesuitical? Perhaps. But look again, because France's paradigmatic sin, in this pamphleteer's estimation, turns out to have been especially subtle, "of a sort to wound the heart of God more directly, and therefore also to merit a severer vengeance than even the grossest of crimes." That subtle sin was none other than an "insulting disdain for the truth" in the form of the theological Molinism of the bull *Unigenitus,* which replaced love or contrition with fear or attrition as the principle governing relations between God and men. Molinism had now given birth to the fearful and despotic Edict of December, henceforth governing relations between king and subjects. "In a word, State Molinism is now trying to follow in the footsteps of Religious Molinism. We are punished exactly as we have sinned. . . ." There followed a long list of "parallels:" "the bull *Unigenitus* and the Edict of December 1770;" "Molinism introduced by the Jesuits" and "despotic authority introduced by Maupeou;" just as "the Chancellor . . . is now accusing the parlements of constitutional innovations;" and so on.[47]

3. The Authorship of Anonymous Pamphlets

Buried in the middle of one of the bulkier *recueils*, or bound collections, consisting of contemporary publications and personal notes and letters of the Jansenist lawyer Louis-Adrien Le Paige is a one-page manuscript entitled "outline for a *State Molinism*, a small writing in manuscript." Written in Le Paige's neat but miniscule hand, the manuscript contains the parallelisms which conclude the published *Reflections on Present Events*. This rather conclusive evidence for Le Paige's authorship of this pamphlet is further buttressed by his handwritten additions and corrections in his personal copy, including the date of its publication, May 14, 1771.[48] That Le Paige wrote the pamphlet should come as no surprise, combining as it does his twin fortes as theologian and political *éminence grise*. An exercise in political commentary in the Jansenist or "figurist" mode, it attempted to spell out the political implications of the prophecies of general defection or apostasy which he and his co-religionists thought they discerned in the Old and New Testaments and whose fulfillments they were witnessing in post-*Unigenitus* France.

Is it possible to go beyond this single identification and connect Le Paige to other anonymous patriot pamphlets? It would surely seem so. Another of the *recueils* contains a long letter dated March 20, 1772, from Le Paige to the exiled magistrate Jean-François Alexandre de Murard in which the Jansenist lawyer eloquently defended the parliamentary principle of unforced registration, called for the monarchy's reconversion to the penance of "good laws" and the constitution, and suggested such specific reforms as the restoration of French royal taxes on the foundation of national consent, the virtual elimination of the use of *lettres de cachet*, the abolition of the "tyranny" of the intendants and provincial governors, and finally the purging of morals and the nation's excessive taste for "luxury" along with the "restoration of the national spirit, honor, disinterest, and the love of truth and candor." All of this was to be effected, if not by the Estates General, at least by an assembly of notables in which those distinguished by "merit" would play their deserved role.[49]

Le Paige did not usually retain copies of his own letters, so why did he make a copy of this one? Was it perhaps to serve as an outline for a pamphlet entitled *A Petition for the King by the Estates General of France*, which appeared some three or so months later and bears an uncanny resemblance to Le Paige's epistolary agenda, including the call for a sort of permanent assembly of notables or what the pamphlet called an Order of the Fatherland (*Ordre de la patrie*) to advise the king in all of the areas of suggested reform?[50] Unlike the letter, the pamphlet only hinted at the necessity of convoking the Estates General to consent to royal taxes, but it compensated for this measure of moderation with the audacity, in the words of Mairobert, of a "vigorous and terrible" portrait of the Sun King Louis XIV and the advice to his successor to "leave your palaces inhabited by high society and pleasure once in awhile and get acquainted with the vast reaches of your State."[51] Le Paige's handwritten corrections in his own published copy of the pamphlet further implicate him in its composition, an authorship already strongly suggested by the pamphlet's theological anti-Jesuitism and version of French institutional history.

But it would be tedious to review here each and every scrap of evidence linking Le Paige to particular patriot pamphlets. Suffice it to say that that evidence—handwritten corrections in his personal published copies, similarity between these pamphlets and yet other manuscripts, the presence in some of these pamphlets of telltale language—point rather surely to Le Paige as author of about twenty pamphlets, including several mentioned earlier, such as the many *Letters*, one from a *Frenchman to the Victims of Ebrouin*, another from *A Former Magistrate to a Duke and Peer*, two more from a *Bourgeois of Paris to a Provincial, on the Occasion of the Edict of December 1770*, and yet another from a *Monsieur Xxx, a Councillor in the Parlement, to Monsieur the Count of Xxx*, as well as the figuristic and anti-Jesuitical *Point of View* and *Fulfillment of Prophecies*. This number is moreover a conservative one. It does not include those pamphlets of which manuscript copies exist in his handwriting but which he may have simply copied—a practice not uncommon at the time—because he had borrowed the rare originals from someone else. Nor does it include his undoubtedly numerous contributions to the official protestations of the Parlement of Paris and its provincial "classes," to say nothing of the many subaltern bailiwick and seneschal courts, many of which protested in their turn. In sum, Le Paige's "influence" on the literature of the patriot movement turns out to be influence indeed, having been exercised directly by himself on much of its content and form.

If this torrid output seems beyond the energy and resources of even a very industrious lawyer, it is well to remember that, along with many of his colleagues in the Parisian bar, Le Paige remained "on strike" in protest against Maupeou's edicts and his "scab" parlements, and hence had nothing better to do with his time. Moreover, he enjoyed the protection of the Prince de Conti and the enclosure of the Temple which, as a juridically immune enclave, was off-limits to both Maupeou's parlement and to the Paris lieutenant of police. All the same, Le Paige's pamphleteering activities and the Temple's secret printing presses eventually provoked enough suspicion so that in early September 1772 the Maupeou parlement ordered Le Paige's arrest after he failed to appear for interrogation. Le Paige himself fled for parts unknown while Conti ostentatiously arranged for a formal inspection of the Temple.[52] Le Paige did not return to the Temple until January 1774, and the dramatic trailing off of patriot publications in late 1772 and 1773 may be attributable in part to his absence.[53]

Sixteen years later, as "pre-revolutionary" pamphlets grew ever more revolutionary, the nearly blind octogenarian Le Paige grumbled in the margins of one of those pamphlets that "we [should] be doing what was done in 1771, and have everything [to be published] reviewed by the same pair of eyes" – clearly implying that those eyes had been his.[54] Perhaps, then, Le Paige's obituary in the Jansenist weekly *Ecclesiastical News* in 1803 was only slightly exaggerating in attributing "most of the letters and small writings that afflicted the Chancellor Maupeou" to this tireless Jansenist *avocat*.[55]

That patriot pamphleteering was sometimes collaborative, with Le Paige acting as informal editor and censor, is illustrated by the story of the composition of the *Inauguration of Pharamond,* a pamphlet universally respected in patriot circles and regarded by the *Supplement to the Gazette of France* as "the most learned and profound of all those [works] which have yet appeared on the subject."[56] Was its author really the Martin de Morizot named by the secret Bachaumont memoirs?[57] Not if the Parisian police were right, who got a very different story from Dom Isidore Mirasson, a Jansenist Barnabite monk whom the police arrested on August 6, 1771, because they suspected him of being the author. Strolling in the Tuilleries gardens one day, according to Mirasson, he was accosted by "someone unknown to him carrying a small dog" and who, as the conversation thickened, asked him if the Barnabite residence had a library. Upon learning that it did, this somebody called Vialdome came to use it repeatedly, consulting different histories, including Mézerai's big *History of France,* and eventually producing a collection of extracts of his researches. Later, Mirasson repeatedly visited Vialdome at the latter's invitation in the enclosure of the Temple. Finding Vialdome working in poverty on a manuscript which later became the *Inauguration,* Mirasson helped him financially and admitted to having read – and "made some corrections on" – sections of the book as Vialdome transcribed them.[58]

Vialdome disappeared after the book appeared, apparently leaving no trace of himself behind, but it is hard to believe that while at the Temple he had not received a little editorial assistance from Le Paige, whose own copy of the book contains a few handwritten additions and corrections. In a letter written to his brother while in hiding a few months later, Le Paige acknowledged that he was suspected for his complicity in the work and did not exactly deny it.[59]

That Le Paige could not have been the principal author of the *Inauguration* is evident from its constitutionalism which, as earlier noted, was less favorable to the parlements than his. Vesting both fiscal and legislative sovereignty in a national diet – an institution more faithful to the structure of the original Frankish assemblies, in the author's opinion, than the more recent Estates General – the pamphlet demoted the parlements to the status of mere "verifiers" of the conformity of the monarchy's administrative acts with constitutional law.[60] The constitutionalism of the *Inauguration* therefore had more in common with that of the monumental *Maxims of French Public Law,* which, though very respectful of the parlements, still clearly subordinated them to the nation as better represented in the Estates General. Like the *Inauguration*'s national diet, the *Maxims'* Estates General possessed full legislative sovereignty, explicitly including the right to change the French monarchy into an aristocracy or democracy if it chose.[61]

But the *Maxims* do not really take leave of Jansenist turf. Wrongly attributed by Mairobert to the parliamentary magistrate Michau de Montblin, who in fact did not survive his exile during the Maupeou "revolution," the treatise was the product of collaborative effort by parliamentary lawyers who, like Le Paige, were chafing at the bit of their self-imposed regime of legal inactivity. Although the total number of contributors to this enterprise is uncertain, the most important was the Abbé Claude Mey, who, his clerical title notwithstanding, had never advanced beyond minor orders but had become a specialist in canon law and an influential consultant in that capacity to the Parlement of Paris. Next in importance was one Gabriel-Nicolas Maultrot, apparently the author of a pungent little *Dissertation on the Right to Convoke the Estates General* that was appended to the *Maxims'* second edition. Like

Mey he was also a canonist and one of the old Parlement's most influential legal consultants. The similarity noted earlier, then, between the Gallican and specifically conciliar argumentation of the *Maxims* and that of the *Defense of All the Sentences* published in 1752 is hardly coincidental, since the two were in part the authors of both treatises.[62]

Rounding out this list of the *Maxims'* known contributors are the lawyers Aubri, noted by the Bachaumont memoirs at the time of his death as a "lawyer renowned above all in the Jansenist party," and André Blonde, another canonist and known chiefly in the 1770s for his Jansenistic refutation of the Abbé Bergier's somewhat "Molinistic" apologetical writings against Rousseauian deism and Holbachian atheism.[63] Besides being lawyers loyal to the exiled parlements and specialists in canon law — and well acquainted in both capacities with the conciliar tradition — all were well-known Jansenists in the religious as well as more secular senses of that term. Much later, in 1790, André Blonde would recall that he too had had to go into exile to escape the "tyrant Maupeou," whether in connection with the Maupeou parlement's search for the authors of the *Maxims* or apropos of other writings he did not say.[64] For Blonde was also the author of two other widely noted anti-Maupeou pamphlets, namely *The Parlement Vindicated by the Empress of Russia* and *The Parlement Vindicated by the Empress-Queen of Hungary and by the King of Prussia.*[65] The Jansenist tone of this latter pamphlet's anti-Jesuitism is therefore hardly accidental.

Anathase-Alexandre Clément de Boissy, a councillor in the Paris *Chambre des comptes*, is usually credited with the authorship of the highly successful *Mayor of the Palace*, suffused though that pamphlet is with Le Paigian parliamentary constitutionalism. But whether Boissy or Le Paige wrote it makes no difference for this tally of Jansenist pamphleteers, since Clément de Boissy was a member of an integrally Jansenist family that included Clément de Barville, solicitor general (*avocat général*) of the Paris *Cour des aides;* Clément de Feillet, councillor in the Parlement of Paris; and the Abbé Clement Du Tremblay, treasurer of the cathedral church of Auxerre and future constitutional bishop of Versailles. Finally, the Parisian police's search of the premises of one Zacarie-Mathieu de Ponchon, Chevalier de Montfort, turned up evidence of his authorship of a small pamphlet entitled *Frank and Loyal Remonstrance by the Nobility.* If not himself a Jansenist, he was in the police informer's estimation "connected to many Jansenists" — principally the Le Nain and d'Asfeld families — and had loudly blamed Maupeou's *coup* on the Jesuits in some of his impromptu café commentaries.[66]

It is surely time to take inventory and see what all these pamphlets and books amount to in relation to the patriots' polemical production as a whole. Now of about eighty pamphlets carefully perused in the course of this study, nearly half, or thirty-eight of that number, can safely be labeled as "Jansenist" by reason of textual or authorial considerations. These raw figures call for several refinements. First, the total of eighty refers to the unofficial and anonymous publications that bear the personal stamp of one or several authors and, with the exception of President Lamoignon de Malesherbes's highly individual remonstrances for the Paris *Cour des aides* and the playwright Caron de Beaumarchais's equally eccentric judicial memoirs in 1773, does not include the much more numerous official pronouncements – remonstrances, judgments, entreaties, etc. – of the various parlements and other judicial bodies which usually assumed the form of pamphlets. Second, this figure includes only whole works and does not count either multiple editions of a single work or the several parts of works that appeared in installments, such as the famous *Personal and Confidential Correspondence* and the *Letters from One Man to Another,* or the successive numbers of a periodical such as the thirteen odd numbers of the *Supplement to the Gazette of France.* The eighty are hence a significant percentage of the patriots' total literary production from 1770 to 1775; Durand Echeverria's exhaustive bibliography includes less than a hundred and twenty such "individual" publications, including the many quasi-official *Recitals* or *Renditions of What Transpired* in this or that parlement.[67] Finally, thirty-eight is a conservative figure, and does not exclude the possibility that other less clearly identifiable pamphlets may have been written by Jansenists as well.

Not only is the figure thirty-eight numerically significant, but it includes most of the major pamphlets of the protest – the ones that apparently made the biggest impression and gave rise to the most comment. The most glaring exceptions to this rule are of course Lamoignon de Malesherbes's memorable remonstrances as president of the *Cour des aides;* the spectacularly successful *Personal and Confidential Correspondence,* which the Parisian lawyer Jacques-Mathieu Augéard admitted to having written in his subsequently published memoirs; and the *Letters from one Man to Another* written by Jean-Baptiste Target, yet another Parisian lawyer who went on to play an important role in the early phases of the Revolution.[68] Constituting as it were a separate wing or flank of the patriot front, Augéard, Malesherbes, and Target had found their own paths to the thesis of national sovereignty, and it may readily be granted that these paths were illuminated in part by the French Enlightenment. Indeed, Target, whose *Letters* bear textual evidence of enlightenment, was at that moment moving out of the parliamentary and Jansenist circles in which he had been formed and into the "philosophical" salon of Madame Géoffrin; while Malesherbes could lay claim to being at least a lesser luminary in the century's firmament of lights.[69]

That said, it would be misleading to draw too sharp a line between the "enlightened" and "Jansenistical" flanks of the patriot movement. However enlightened he was in his attitudes toward religious toleration and the freedom of the press, Lamoignon de Malesherbes had learned his constitutionalism at the feet of Abbé Pucelle, the great Jansenist magistrate of the century's first decades; while both Augéard's and Target's constitutionalism remained very historical and heavily indebted to that of Le Paige.[70] Even the self-consciously "enlightened" Pidansat de Mairobert could rail against the Jesuits in accents barely distinguishable from those of Jansenists.[71] And on the Jansenist and parliamentary flanks of the patriot front, the forensic necessity of appealing to the broadest possible constituency forced it further to secularize its sectarian constitutionalism: to reconceptualize, for example, the magistrates' venal offices in terms of the "natural right" of property and their "representative" role in the language of "natural law." This was especially true of Mey's and Maultrot's *Maxims of French Public Law*, which drew heavily from such seventeenth-century natural-law theoreticians as Samuel Pufendorf and Hugo Grotius as well as such Anglo-Saxon "commonwealth-man" ideologists as John Locke and Algernon Sidney.[72] In one of his pamphlets the Jansenist André Blonde even quoted from that boldest of the century's atheistic statements, Baron d'Holbach's *System of Nature*![73]

Pidansat de Mairobert, then, had it about right: in rebaptising itself as the patriot party, the Jansenist party became at once more and less than it had been. It remains the case, however, that until less than twenty years before the Revolution the century's most frontal protest against Bourbon absolutism was organized largely if not exclusively by Jansenists.

4. The Printing and Distribution of Patriot Pamphlets

These "anti-chancellor writings," as the Parisian bookseller Siméon-Prosper Hardy called them, were the objects of eighteenth-century France's most massive censorial crackdown. By the time it was over, all branches of the printing industry had been affected, including the content of French-language newspapers printed outside of France.[74] The initial phase of this governmental effort was "extrajudicial," its principal agent being the police inspector – and "literary specialist" – Joseph d'Hémery made familiar to us by the work of Robert Darnton.[75] With the help of commissioners Hubert Mutel and Miché de Rochebrune, d'Hémery acted under the authority of the Parisian lieutenant of police Gabriel de Sartine. But in March 1772 the Maupeou Parlement also got into the act with its own noisy "judicial" investigation under the direction of the court reporter Valentin Goezman, who was later subject to a spectacular literary drubbing at the hands of playwright Caron de Beaumarchais. Rather than reinforcing each other, the extrajudicial and judicial investigations got in each other's way. His police investigation was "a simple matter of time and patience," grumbled d'Hémery on May 27, 1772, at the conclusion of one of his reports, "and it would have entirely succeeded if the *arrêt* of [Maupeou's] Parlement of Paris had not given to these matters a celebrity instead of the scorn which at bottom is all they are worth."[76]

As the title of d'Hémery's report makes clear, the targets of this censorial effort were at once the "authors, printers, booksellers, and peddlers of scurrilous pamphlets (*libelles*) published since the Edict of December 1770." Unless the flights of Blonde and Le Paige can be counted as successes – they were of sorts – and apart from the case of Dom Isidore Mirasson, the only writers that this vast repressive effort turned up were the Chevallier de Montfort, author, as we have noted, of the *Frank and Loyal Remonstrance by the Nobility,* and one Claude-Antoine Boulemier, the author of a small ode against the chancellor. Nor was the investigation much more successful where printers were concerned.[77] The brunt of d'Hémery and company's crackdown therefore fell on the booksellers, street peddlers, and the much more numerous individuals guilty of selling, copying, distributing, or procuring some "anti-chancellor writings" – or occasionally only of uttering some "anti-chancellor" remarks.

However unlucky for them, the resultant collection of "embastilled" unfortunates makes it possible to measure the presence of Jansenism at the lower levels of the patriot movement's constituency and distributional infrastructure. Owing to the fragmentary state of both the Bastille's archives and the trial records of the Maupeou Parlement, the collection of names is incomplete. Yet a list of eighty-four individuals subjected to intense surveillance, attempted arrest, arrest and imprisonment, or sometimes to trial, probably represents at least three-fourths of the total, and hence provides an adequate sampling. Of this number, twenty-eight and possibly thirty, or about one-third of the total, were Jansenists or *jansénisants* in rigorous senses of these terms. The figure is again a conservative one, since it cannot include Jansenists whose identity is unapparent on the basis of the often sketchy information available.

What constitutes evidence of Jansenism? Consider a case that falls somewhere near the center of spectrum of probabilities, that of one Pierre-Athanase-Nicolas de Desgrouhette, a twenty-two-year-old apprentice living with his widowed mother at the time of his arrest in March 1771. Accused by a police spy of being the author of a "play of words on Terray, d'Aiguillon, and Maupeou" (the three chief ministers or "triumvirs" in 1771) and an "infinity of other writings against the chancellor," he denied having written anything "on the present affairs," but owned up to writing a comic opera, some three-act comedies, and a novel. Hardly very promising Jansenist material, it would seem, unless it be in the titles: "The Pacified Quarrel, or the Happy Celebration;" "Colin and Colette, or Virtue Triumphant;" and so forth. But the interrogatory plot thickened a little when, pressed on the subject of his political views, he admitted "to having taken the side of the Parlement of Paris in several encounters," which he had done "as both Christian and citizen" because "the destruction of the Parlement was contrary to the Sovereign's true interests" and he "could not see innocent magistrates treated like animals without feeling heartbroken." A purely pro-parliamentary profession of faith? Perhaps, but not his identity as "friend of the Truth as well as of justice" in which twin capacities he "raised his voice like an eagle to demand justice for the magistrates," seeing that "the ruin of the Parlement would spell the triumph of the enemies of Religion, that is, the Jesuits." Announcing himself prepared "to suffer for such a cause," he demanded "his books, some paper, a New Testament [undoubtedly in the vernacular] and a missal."[78]

While a phrase such as "friend of the Truth" may ring efficaciously only in the ears of initiates, the evidence of Jansenism in the case of four unmarried women arrested on September 5, 1771, would seem sufficient for everyone. Forced by suspicious commissioners to dismount from their carriage at the Paris "hell's gate" upon returning from an outing in Arcueil, these women displayed a suspicious waddle in their movements which turned out, upon inspection, to be caused by copies of an anti-Maupeou pamphlet somehow attached to the undersides of their petticoats. The obligatory arrests were almost as embarrassing to the police as to the women and their families, because the four in question were hardly nobodies: Françoise-Julie Danjean, daughter of a well-known Parisian architect; Dlle Gerbier de La Massilaye, sister of the famous parliamentary lawyer by the same name; Dlle Heuvrard, the trusted chambermaid of the master of requests (*maîtres des requetes*) Guillaume Lambert; and Anne-Madeleine Morin, the first cousin of the bookseller Butard, long established "at the ensign of Truth" on the rue Saint-Jacques—all of them notoriously Jansenist as well as prominent Parisian families. They are "the most outrageous Jansenists," was all a police spy could find to report to Sartine concerning Gerbier mother and daughter after the police had allowed the latter to return home.[79]

But the police learned little from the less fortunate Danjean and Morin, who endured a four-month stay in the Bastille, not in this case because the prisoners knew nothing but because in the purest tradition of Port-Royal they insisted upon keeping their biblical "yea's" to a tight-lipped minimum. Typical of their indomitable "nay's" under interrogation are those of Julie Danjean, who, when asked by Commissioner Mutel if she knew the author of the pamphlet *General Reflections on the Mayor of the Palace's Systematic Design of Changing the Constitution of the State,* which they had been carrying, responded that "she had nothing to respond" seeing that "neither the law of God nor that of honor obliged her to inform on her brothers."[80]

But the Jansenist presence at the lower reaches of the patriot movement looms even larger when subjected to a more qualitative analysis. Many—even most—of those arrested, investigated, or harassed by the police or the Maupeou Parlement were in fact related to one another as strands of small distribution webs which, in five of six cases, led to a Jansenist center. At or near the center of the one involving the four Jansenist women, for example, was a certain Vion, alias Jean-Pierre Dumont, a sometime Dominican monk who, having been obliged to leave his order in 1741 after running afoul of the Archbishop of Embrun "over matters relating to the constitution [*Unigenitus*]," had since lived in Paris above Butard's Jansenist bookstore and in contact with "the most important Jansenists and especially with the Gerbiers, the Butards, the Danjeans, etc., etc."[81] The police finally did get Anne-Madeleine Morin to confess by means of indisputable evidence that it was this Dumont, or Vion, who had engaged her to write to a certain Abbé Le Chanteux at Arcueil asking him to accept and store cases of pamphlets which she and her sister "pilgrims" then picked up, not only on September 5, but also on previous and more successful occasions. But that is about as much as the police ever learned. The Abbé Le Chanteux convinced the police that he had been an unwitting accomplice of Morin and Dumont, while Dumont or Vion, spectacularly arrested by d'Hémery on September 19, stubbornly refused to divulge the identity of the pamphlet's printer or distributor in Arcueil. And as for the Parisian direction, Morin revealed that she and her companions had deposited their previous stock at the *hôtel* of the chambermaid's master, Guillaume Lambert, whose Jansenist zeal had not been dampened by his recent promotion from the Parlement of Paris to the royal council. The police apparently did not think it appropriate to importune Lambert himself.[82]

D'Hémery and Mutel stumbled onto another such distributional network on June 10, 1772, when, tipped off by a police spy or a neighbor, they arrested an out-of-work tailor and his family named Prestrelle, whom they caught in the act of recopying patriot pamphlets and found in their possession a sizable collection. Recently immigrated from Noyon, the indigent Prestrelle family was selling their copies to one François-Amadée Kaufmann, an interpreter and secret agent of the French diplomatic service, who on orders from his superiors was busily ingratiating himself with the Saxon and Prussian ambassadors by procuring the pamphlets they desired. Unable to go further in the direction of demand, the police then tracked down the Prestrelles' source of supply, which led them to a minor employee of the indirect tax farmers, or General Farm, named De La Roche, whom the police arrested the following day. Also caught *en flagrant délit,* La Roche for his part pointed to a fellow employee of the General Farm, who in turn had been getting the pamphlets from his brother, an out-of-work procurator at the Paris Châtelet who, in d'Hémery's words, was a "young man entirely devoted to the Jansenist party" and bent upon "imitating one of his uncles named the Abbé de François, a former inmate of the Bastille and prominent Jansenist canon in Troyes."[83]

This Jansenist brother, François de Quiney by name, concocted a cock-and-bull story about his own source of supply until the Jansenist colporteur La Gueyrie, who had been arrested earlier that June, indicated the widow Mecquignon and sons, booksellers established on the rue de la Juiverie, as his own principal source. At that point François de Quiney confessed that he too had gotten his pamphlets from Mecquignon, but from Mecquignon herself the police learned nothing except that she sometimes went with her servant Jeanneton to the enclosure of the Temple "to consult Monsieur Le Paige."[84] Invoking her "honor

and conscience" and the "commandment of charity," and refusing repeatedly to take the oath because her first one was "irrevocable," this
Jansenist widow remained steadfastly silent throughout her stay in the
Bastille and her trial by the Maupeou Parlement, which sentenced her
to a nine-year exile from the environs of Paris. Fortunately for her, the
dauphine Marie-Antoinette took a benevolent interest in the widow's
plight, obtained the king's pardon, and invited her whole family to din-
ner at Versailles— all this over the protests of the Archbishop of Paris,
who objected that "that widow is Jansenist, receives no one but Jansenists, and sells no books except Jansenist ones."[85]

The two cases considered thus far overlapped a little in that the
Jansenist book peddler Jean La Gueyrie began purchasing his "patriotic"
pamphlets from the widow Mecquignon only after the arrest of Julie
Danjean, one of the female Jansenist foursome, from whom he had obtained them earlier. And the two cases intersected a third distributional
network in that the same La Gueyrie frequented the residence of an out-
of-work lawyer named Convers Desormeaux, who like La Gueyrie may
once have purchased his pamphlets from Danjean and Gerbier. Nonetheless this third network seems to have existed largely independently
of the others and began to unravel with the arrest of Elisabeth Fleury,
known as Babet, a countergirl employed in the printshop of Simon, who
in turn sold them to—as well as bought them from—Convers Desormeaux,
who was finally arrested on September 16. Fleury herself, however, had
purchased her pamphlets from one Michel Sorin, an apprentice in Bou-
det's bookstore-printshop in the rue Saint-Jean-de-Beauvais, who had
in turn obtained them from the seventy-year-old Abbé Bruey Duclos
assisted by his housekeeper Louise Mercier.[86]

Meanwhile the arrest on August 27 of one De La Brande, who
had been legal secretary for a now exiled parliamentary magistrate and
had sold pamphlets to La Marche and Amaury, likewise led to Mercier
and Duclos. An interdicted priest from the diocese of Sens—probably
one of the many victims of the anti-Jansenist Bishop Languet de Gergy—
Duclos was no stranger to the Bastille, having spent some time there
for distributing pro-parliamentary pamphlets during the refusal of sacraments controversy in 1753. "Too respectful of oaths to swear one in
such a case," Duclos's "conscience" forbade him to divulge anything,
"believing himself conformed in that resolve to the Gospel which for-
bids us from compromising anyone."[87]

Two additional series of arrests beginning or centering in the province of Normandy completes this portrait of Jansenist involvement in

the printing and distribution of patriot literature. The first began with the arrest of a stagehand (*metteur en scène*) named Moret in Rouen on June 13, 1772, for having spoken too freely about establishing some sort of "academy" (*académie de gens permis en société*) which would among other things read all the brochures about Maupeou's *coup*. Moret was no Jansenist, nor apparently were any of the other unemployed lawyers, attorneys, and attorneys' clerks who had directly or indirectly furnished him with pamphlets and found themselves arrested in his train. But these arrests eventually took the police back to the enclosure of the Temple – where Moret had been temporarily living and occasionally giving impromptu public readings of anti-Maupeou pamphlets – as well as to mysterious and suggestive talk by Moret and others about "pamphets which were still moist and uncut," about "the towers of the Temple and everything that went on in them," and about "M. le Pege [sic], bailiff of the Temple, who was a man of singular merit, an excellent head, and much opposed to the present administration of justice."[88]

In contrast to this ambiguous case, the second series of Norman arrests – or attempted arrests – remained confined to Normandy, and those involved were almost all Jansenists. Those arrested were the probable authors and undoubted distributors of the *Petition by the Nobility of Normandy in October 1772 Against the Suppression of the Parlement and the Estates of the Province*: the young lawyer Pierre-Jacques Le Maître, the nobleman Pierre de Manneville, the Père Brunier of the Genovefain priory at Saint-Lô, and Antoine-Augustin Thomas du Fossé, councillor in the Parlement of Normandy and grand nephew of the famous Jansenist solitary and author of the memoirs of Port-Royal. These arrests culminated with that of Antoine-Augustin's eighteen-year-old daughter Perpétue on November 29 while trying to enter Paris in possession of 179 copies of the incriminating *Petition*.[89]

The conspicuous role of Jansenists at all levels of the patriot movement strongly suggests that that movement sought out and spread by means of the same clandestine channels of communication originally set up for the dissemination of Jansenist ephemeral literature, in particular the weekly *Ecclesiastical News*. The fact that, when arrested, the Jansenist colporteur La Gueyrie was carrying fifty numbers of the *Ecclesiastical News* as well as such anti-Maupeou pamphlets as the satirical *Mandemus by the Archbishop of Paris Proscribing the Use of Red Eggs* lends additional credence to this possibility. La Gueyrie's interrogation and his confiscated account book amply confirm Pidansat de Mairobert's assertion that he was a regular distributor of the *News*, both in Paris and in the provinces. Hardly different is the case of Le Sage: according to Mairobert a "big Jansenist and a big distributor of Ecclesiastical Gazettes." Denounced as a colporteur of anti-Maupeou pamphlets and arrested on October 27, 1772, Le Sage was found in possession of another fifty numbers of the *News* and letters from the provinces requesting more.[90]

Le Sage's footsteps led in some very strange directions, however, among them one of the patriot movement's incontestably "philosophical" or "encyclopedic" distributional nexus uncovered by the police. Le Sage, as it happened, worked as a shopboy (*garçon*) for a certain bookseller named Etienne Devaux, who had served time in the Bastille for selling anti-religious and pornographic books and who, far from mending his ways after his release, only added anti-Maupeou pamphlets to his prohibited stock until death closed down his business in 1772. What his death and the necessary inventory of his effects eventually revealed was that Devaux had plied his prohibited commerce in close cooperation with a policeman (*exempte de police*) named Joseph Archier, who was able to provide the ailing Devaux with the indispensable legal protection as well as to procure the "philosophical" and pornographic books from somewhere outside Paris. And indeed the perquisition of Devaux's stock turned up mainly pornographic and "philosophical" books ranging from *Celebrated Girls of the Eighteenth-Century* to Voltaire's *The Century of Louis XV*.[91]

For anti-Maupeou pamphlets, however, Archier had had recourse to Le Sage, who of course enjoyed access to the Jansenist distributional underground. But Archier had also exploited others, including a defrocked Benedictine monk named Guillaume Imbert. Denounced by Archier and arrested in turn, this former monk confessed to having indeed sent a couple of hawkers of anti-Maupeou pamphletary wares in Archier's direction because Archier had told him that he needed the pamphlets for an important parliamentary magistrate, who turned out to be none other than the pious Jansenist Rolland de Challerange. But the unfortunate Imbert himself was found in possession of all manner of anti-religious "philosophical" books which, he apologetically explained, he had borrowed or bought from Archier for the express purpose of writing a "systematic refutation." A self-proclaimed acquaintance of the philosophes d'Alembert and Madame Géoffrin, Imbert boasted a collection of books and pamphlets in which Diderot's *Thoughts on Nature*, d'Holbach's *System of Nature*, and Voltaire's *Sermon by the Fifty* sat uneasily next to Le Paige's *Letters on the* Lits de Justice, La Chalotais's judicial *Account Rendered* against the Jesuits, and some numbers of the Jansenist *Supplement to the Gazette of France.*[92]

Nothing better illustrates the ideological promiscuity of the patriot movement, at least at its fringes, than this juxtaposition of "encyclopedic" and Jansenist literary undergrounds, persons, and books in the Devaux-Archier case, unless it is the case of François de Quiney, the "entirely Jansenist young man" whom d'Hémery arrested earlier for buying anti-Maupeou pamphlets from the widow Mecquignon and then giving them to his brother for distribution elsewhere. "I suppose I had better be prepared for the worst, since brother has already been pitted against brother, a mother against her children, . . . relatives against relatives, and friends against friends," he wrote resignedly to the lieutenant of police Sartine after "confrontations" with his mother, brother, and Mecquignon as well as spending three months in the Bastille. "And thus," he continued more bitterly, "have I witnessed the overthrow, if not of divine laws, at least the laws of nature which even the most barbarous nations respect—and that by means of this very imposing display of justice that ought to be used to uphold these same laws. Ah," he concluded, "how Monsieur Rousseau is right to say that we have only the appearance of humanity. And thus, moreover, I am content so long as I enjoy the good fortune of not thinking." Misery loves company. For thus did persecution convert a disciple of Saint Augustine into a disciple of that self-anointed spokesman for the persecuted of even an "enlightened" century: Jean-Jacques Rousseau.[93]

5. "Acts of Schism"

Evidence of Jansenist participation in the patriot movement calls for some explanation. Why would Jansenists have run the risk of compromising their religious identity by throwing themselves body and soul into a movement so apparently devoid of religious meaning as a political protest against Maupeou's constitutional *coup?* Was it just in repayment for past services rendered by the parlements to the Jansenist cause, notably judicial protection from public refusals of the sacraments in the 1750s and the dissolution of the Jesuits in the 1760s? Or did the Maupeou *coup* itself have a religious agenda which has hitherto eluded the attention of the event's many historians?

The event's possible religious dimension is indeed likely to be elusive. Consider, for example, the possibility that Maupeou's anti-parliamentary "revolution" meant that the Archbishop of Paris and other like-minded prelates found themselves able to resume their policy of depriving suspected Jansenists of the sacraments of viaticum and extreme unction. But if they did so, how would we know in the absence of any judicial actions on behalf of the Jansenists, which would be unlikely in Maupeou's courts? To be sure, the Jansenists' vigilant *Ecclesiastical News* might have been trusted to bring every last such incident to the attention of its outraged readers, as it had certainly done during the 1750s and 1760s. But in 1770 this hitherto feisty journal began to retreat from the politically controversial and to restrict its coverage to "ecclesiastical news" more narrowly defined. The reason, hinted the anonymous *Supplement to the Gazette of France,* was that "after thirty or more years of fuss and bother, thirty-million [livres] and thirty-thousand spies," the police had finally penetrated the anonymity of the Jansenist weekly.[94] In short, the periodical was pretty definitely on probation, which may be why it had little to say about Maupeou's "revolution." Nor did the *Supplement* itself pick up the slack in the reporting of mixed political-ecclesiastical events.

Fortunately another source comes to the rescue, namely the manuscript diary of the Parisian bookseller Siméon-Prosper Hardy. Hardy has suffered no neglect at the hands of historians; along with Arthur Young's *Travels,* his diary is among the most cited sources on France on the eve of the Revolution, particularly on the subject of pamphlets and popular disturbances. But what seems largely to have escaped historiographical attention is Hardy's Jansenism—a Jansenism brazen enough to have accepted as authentic all the miracles attributed to the Deacon Pâris and persistent enough to have seized every occasion to extol the memory of Port-Royal. What makes Hardy's Jansenist testimony especially interesting is that it is that of a lay, and somewhat anti-clerical, Parisian bourgeois, strategically located in the largely Jansenist quarter of Saint-Jacques, next to another Jansenist bookseller, Jacques Butard, "at the ensign of the Truth." So it is Hardy who indignantly informs us that most of the clerical councillors for Maupeou's new Parlement of Paris had been recruited by none other than the anti-Jansenist Archbishop of Paris, Christophe de Beaumont, who raided his cathedral clergy for that purpose.[95] But what particularly outraged Hardy, aside from the persecution of his beloved parlements, was the Maupeou *coup*'s green light for ecclesiastics to resume the sacramental harassment of suspected Jansenists and appellants of the bull *Unigenitus.*

The first recorded victim of this renewed anti-Jansenist offensive was a sort of lay saint, one Claude Boucherette Du Roule who, son of a well-known Parisian lawyer, "had been living for a long while as a simple individual in the profoundest retreat while devoting himself to penitence and other good works" in the Saint-Antoine quarter of Paris. Finding himself at extremities in April 1772, he requested viaticum and extreme unction, only to be refused by the entire resident clergy of the Sainte-Marguérite parish. They acted apparently on the instructions of the Archbishop of Paris who insisted that Du Roule name his confessor. In the absence of the exiled Parlement of Paris, the ultimate "public scandal" of death without the sacraments was avoided only by the quick action of the lieutenant of police, who had Du Roule transferred to the rue de la Mortellerie, where he was ministered to by the more irenic curé of Saint-Gervais.[96]

Du Roule's case was followed in October 1772 by several others: Abbé Jacques-Martin Bouillerot, the curé of Saint-Jacques de Corbeille outside Paris, narrowly escaped being denied the last sacraments by his own curate; the "venerable" and "esteemed" Abbé Augustin Gardane, importuned with questions about his insubmissive stance toward *Unigenitus* by the curé of Saint-Sévérin, barely managed to take communion by having himself carried to a chapel before expiring; the "respectable" Abbé Dumoulin, having responded with "characteristic candor" to the curé of Saint-Germain's questions about his sentiments in regard to *Unigenitus,* made no judicial effort to obtain the refused sacraments because he was "of a pacific disposition;" and the octogenarian Abbé Armand Colas, "a respectable and edifying priest," was denied the last sacraments by the curé of Saint-André-des-Arts.[97] The Archbishop of Paris's anti-Jansenist sacramental offensive finally broke the patience of even the newly restrained *Ecclesiastical News,* which on March 7, 1774, ran the risk of a belated and understated issue devoted to these renewed "acts of schism."[98]

None of these incidents warrants the conclusion that the king himself stood behind this sacramental offensive against Jansenists; on the contrary, in at least one case where an "unpurged" suburban bailiwick dared to institute a judicial procedure against a sacrament-refusing curé, the king indirectly resolved the issue by having the archbishop arrange for the curé's early retirement. What the evidence suggests is that Christophe de Beaumont profited from the dispersal or purging of the old parlements in that he was now able "to commit," as the *Ecclesiastical News* put it, "these new acts of schism after which his heart has pined for so many years."[99]

Perhaps the most provocative "act of schism" to come to Hardy's outraged attention involved an unfortunate schoolmistress who absent-mindedly left her book of liturgical offices on her chair in the parish church of Saint-Sulpice after attending mass there one Sunday morning in 1774. Turned in to the church sacristan, the book fell into the hands of one of the church's curates who, finding in its pages a portrait of the deceased Jansenist "saint," the Deacon Pâris, brought this incriminating evidence to the attention of the curé, who sent it to the *grand chantre* of the cathedral church. This prelate in turn informed the Archbishop Christophe de Beaumont, who finally delegated the task of investigating "such an important fact" to one of his principal curates, the Abbé de L'Ecluse or Delescluse. The terrified schoolmistress confessed to seeing nothing amiss in using the "venerable deacon's" portrait as a bookmark, and her catechism pupils, who were each interrogated separately, had apparently learned nothing from their teacher about the bull *Unigenitus*. Nonetheless de L'Ecluse dismissed the schoolmistress, allowing her only enough time to collect some of her tuition – and "to which he added the injustice of refusing to return her book of offices." "Thus," commented Hardy indignantly, "have these turbulent and fanatical ecclesiastics profited . . . from present circumstances to exercise with tranquility their false and indiscreet zeal, in tormenting simple laypeople with ridiculous gestures which are an affront to common sense."[100]

Who, it might be asked, was Jacques de L'Ecluse? He had long been one of the archbishop's principal curates, but he had also once been the curé of the parish church of Saint-Nicolas-des-Champs – until 1759, when the old Parlement of Paris had banished him from the realm for life for having refused the viaticum and extreme unction to one of his appellant parishioners.[101] So his renewed presence and "schismatic" activity in Paris in the 1770s calls for explanation, and is part of a wider pattern also assiduously noted by Hardy. Availing himself of a royal declaration of amnesty promulgated on June 15, 1771, for precisely such exiled priests (and docilely registered by the Maupeou Parlement four days later), Christophe de Beaumont systematically brought such exiled priests as well as ex-Jesuits back to the archdiocese of Paris and found benefices for them wherever he could. Besides finding a place for de L'Ecluse as canon in the cathedral clergy, for example, the archbishop appointed him superior to the Ursuline convent in Saint-Cloud.[102]

A few of the other priests and ex-Jesuits to benefit the archbishop's solicitude were the Abbé Roche-Damien Dubertrand, formerly one of de L'Ecluse's curates in Saint-Nicolas-des-Champs and in 1772 appointed to the cure of Saint-Hilaire; the Abbé Claude-Jacques Perin, chased from the cure of Saint-Leu-Saint-Gilles by the Châtelet of Paris in 1755 only to be imposed on the parish of Saint-Paul in 1774; and the Abbé—and ex-Jesuit—Madier, driven from the parish of Saint-Séverin in 1756 and restored to the same cure in 1771 (besides also being named confessor to the sisters of the king with a pension of ten-thousand livres a year). It was this same unrepentant Madier who again denied the last sacraments both to the eighty-eight-year-old Abbé Augustin Gardane in 1773 and to the octogenarian Abbé Armand Colas in 1774.[103]

Madier was not the only ex-Jesuit to benefit from the archbishop's largesse. Witness one Reverend Père Garnier, in 1772 reincarnated as Abbé Garnier and newly installed as chaplain of the convent of the Holy Sacrament; or another ex-Jesuit promoted as curé over the head of the long-resident curate of the village church of Ivry in 1774.[104] The curé in question had apparently obtained this position on the recommendation of the king's sister, Madame Louise de France, who had undergone a highly publicized "devout" or Jesuit-oriented religious conversion in September 1771 and then took up residence as a novice in the Carmelite convent of Saint-Denis. Saint-Denis thereafter functioned as the spiritual Jerusalem of the ministerial and episcopal *parti dévôt,* attracting weekly visits from the Archbishop of Paris accompanied by Louise's confessor, Madier, as well as an occasional visit by Maupeou himself, who deemed it politically prudent, according to Mairobert's *Historical Journal,* occasionally "to play the *dévôt.*"[105]

From Saint-Denis emanated the project not only of persuading other French bishops to employ ex-Jesuits in their dioceses, but of reestablishing the society itself on a legal footing in France. This latter project survived even the papal dissolution of the society in the brief *Dominus ac redemptor,* fulminated by Clement XIV in 1773 under pressure from the Bourbon courts of Naples and Madrid, after which it assumed the form of a proposal to regroup the disbanded Jesuits as a congregation of secular priests. Hostile reaction to *Dominus ac redemptor* briefly cast the ultramontanist *parti dévôt* into the role of an opposition more papal than the pope—indeed threatened, as Hardy ironically noted, "to produce a new genre of appellants very different from those whom the Jesuits have persecuted for so long." This opposition struck the secretary of foreign affairs, d'Aiguillon, as sufficiently "violent" and "fanatical" as to give him pause, prompting him to solicit from Clement XIV an additional brief reaffirming the authority of *Dominus ac redemptor.*[106]

If the Maupeou *coup* did not finally produce the triumphal restoration of the Company of Jesus in France, it witnessed many mini-triumphs of Jesuit-sponsored devotions, at least in Paris. On January 10, 1772, it was the celebration in the church of Saint-Roch of the first annual mass patronized by the archbishop of Paris and christened "the triumph of the faith." The "faith" in question, according to Hardy, was that of the "turbulent ecclesiastics and disturbers of the public peace" because the "triumph" referred to the "destruction of the parlements." "Everyone murmured against this novelty," he further reported, "especially at a time when the faith, far from growing stronger and achieving any triumphs, . . . has on the contrary been weakening day by day. . . ." On May 1, 1772, it was the veneration of a relic of the newly canonized (1767) but "Molinist" Saint Jeanne-Françoise-Fremyot de Chantal, cofounder with François de Sales of the order of the Visitation of Holy Mary, in the church of Saint-Médard at the instigation of its curé, Hardy de Levaré, another of the many exiled priests who had recently returned to Paris. The date of May 1 had not been randomly chosen, for it was calculated to compete with the anniversary of the death of the "uncanonized" Jansenist Deacon Pâris, whose tomb was still located in the graveyard of that church and whose devotees were still wont to congregate in some numbers on that day, "as though," commented Hardy, "the voice of the people, recognized by all ages as the voice of God himself, had not sufficiently canonized the virtues and miracles of this holy personage, whose glory and merit certain people have made it their business to obscure." And on the following June 28 it was the celebration of the feast of the Sacred Heart of Jesus—perhaps the Jesuits' favorite devotion—imposed on the parish church of Saint-André-des-Arts by its first curate against the express wishes of the parish churchwardens or *marguillers*. For Hardy this was another "occasion to observe how, under the cover of the present troubles and all the chancellor's operations, the ecclesiastics are growing ever bolder and more enterprising, imagining that they can now do anything with impunity."[107]

If the political implications of these devotions were not obvious enough, Hardy had repeatedly to hear them spelled out *en toutes lettres* on the occasion of the many processions which he was obliged to attend as adjunct syndic of the Parisian booksellers guild. On one such occasion, on October 7, 1771, the procession headed ominously toward the Carmelite convent in the faubourg Saint-Jacques where the chagrined bookseller had to listen to one Abbé Rétard extol Madame Louise's recent profession of monastic vows and explain how, although France had had reason enough to fear the wrath of God until then, everything had forthwith changed for the better—"by which he undoubtedly referred,"

Hardy was sure, "to the recently destroyed parlements and the ecclesiastics thereby put into possession of the right to disturb the public peace by their harassments so opposed to the spirit of the Gospel and the good of religion." In another procession which wound up at the Collège Mazarin, Hardy endured the under-principal's pointed eulogy of Mazarin, the seventeenth-century cardinal-minister for whom the college was named, joined to the observation that the effect of calumny was always short-lived – a phrase obviously intended, Hardy noted, "at once to canonize and exculpate the great personage [Maupeou] who at the present moment is no less odious to the nation than was his celebrated eminence [Mazarin] in his own time and who, according to his zealous partisans, is [like the cardinal] a victim of the blackest calumny."[108]

The Sorbonne's sounding of Maupeou's virtues meant another open season on Jansenists or excessively Augustinian doctors within its precincts. One Jacques-Albert Hazon, a regent-doctor of the faculty of medicine, found himself forbidden to preside over any public functions for ten years for having found a kind word for such skeletons in the Sorbonne's closet as Antoine Arnauld, Jacques Boursier, and Nicolas Petipied in a "Historical Eulogy of the University of Paris" delivered on October 11, 1770. Since Hazon was already seventy, he was not likely to outlive this interdiction. And another *lettre de cachet* felled Doctor Xaupi, the theological faculty's eighty-eight-year-old dean, prohibiting him from exercising his functions or even attending the faculty's monthly assemblies until he could prove that a benefice he possessed in the cathedral church of Perpignan did not require his residence there. But his real fault was to have signed a legal consultation written by the inevitable Jansenist duo, Abbé Claude Mey and Gabriel-Nicolas Maultrot, on behalf of some "second-order" curés against the cathedral chapter in the neighboring diocese of Cahors.[109]

But the case that best illuminates the religious underside of Maupeou's "constitutional" revolution is another miscarriage of academic justice, this one involving the College of Auxerre where numbers of Jansenist professors had evidently congregated under the long and protective episcopacy of Charles de Caylus. Things had changed drastically under Caylus's militantly anti-Jansenist successors Caritat de Condorcet and Champion de Cicé, who spent much of their pastoral energy purging their largely Jansenist cathedral and parish clergies. In 1773 attention was turned against the college. Champion de Cicé somehow obtained a sentence from the local bailiwick court condemning two professors to perpetual galley labor and confiscation of property, two more

professors to perpetual banishment from Auxerre as well as confiscation
of property, and three others to somewhat lesser penalties. Among their
stated crimes were not only "having raised the youth in a spirit of con-
tentiousness and disobedience toward the Laws of the Realm concerning matters debated in the Church" – against *Unigenitus*, in other words –
but also for having "explained and commented on seditious, injurious,
and calumnious *libelles* against the Government and the honor of its
Ministers and Magistrates" – that is, for having directed the students'
attention to pamphlets against Maupeou and his replacement parlements.
It was the chief of these parlements, that of Paris, which on February 25,
1774, appropriately upheld this sentence by the *"bailliage Cicé,"* as it
was derisively christened.[110]

6. The Ministry's Pamphlets and the *Parti Dévôt*

That Maupeou's constitutional *coup* possessed a *dévôt* religious dimension is just as certain, then, as that the patriot protest possessed
a Jansenist one. That dimension is most apparent in new "acts of schism,"
that is to say the upper clergy's renewed sacramental persecution of Jansenists as heretics, as well as in the reappearance of the *dévôt* party's
chief constituents, namely the ex-members of the recently dissolved Company of Jesus. At the same time *dévôt* religiosity asserted itself more
positively by means of the imposition of certain devotions, such as that
of the Sacred Heart of Jesus, which – in sharp contrast to austere Jansenist spirituality – affectively fastened themselves onto palpable objects as
conduits of grace and symbols of sanctity. The Parisian archepiscopal
palace and the Carmelite convent at Saint-Denis functioned as *dévôt*
spiritual outposts – the party's Antioch and Jerusalem, as it were – the
former as long as the aging Christophe de Beaumont remained there,
the latter since Louise de France had taken up residence as a Carmelite
novice. But Versailles remained the party's spiritual Rome, with or without Jesuit confessors and preachers, what with such illustrious lay sponsors as the king's other sisters, *Mesdames de France;* the minister of state
Henri-Leonard Bertin; and the seemingly indestructible governor of the
royal children, the Duc de La Vauguyon, who finally died in 1771 "re-
gretted by no one," to believe Hardy, "except for the archbishop of Paris
and the Jesuits."[111]

The notion of the king's person as a palpable intermediate embodiment of divinity – the religious basis, in short, of the doctrine of
the divine right of kings – may have sat more easily with *parti dévôt's*

"baroque" religious sensibility than with Jansenist sacral parsimony from the outset. Then, too, the royal court and its Jesuit confessors and preachers had served as the spiritual home of the French *parti dévôt* since the early seventeenth century. All the same there was a time when the *parti dévôt*'s loyalty to a "national" and temporal monarchy was tempered by its prior commitment to the international and spiritual authority of the Catholic Church under the militant leadership of the post-tridentine popes, a commitment that had embroiled it in subversive political activity and had stigmatized it with a reputation for assassinating kings. There was also a time when a sworn loyalty to a "Roman" papacy combined with papal exemptions from episcopal jurisdiction had made the Jesuits anathema to many if not most of the French or Gallican bishops. Enough of this conspiratorial reputation still clung to eighteenth-century French Jesuits in particular that when, in 1757, an unemployed domestic servant named Damiens stuck a knife blade between Louis XV's ribs and articulated his motivation in the language of Jansenist-parliamentary constitutionalism, the *parti janséniste* contrived to redirect suspicion in the direction of the *parti dévôt*.

Thanks to the bull *Unigenitus,* however, the *parti dévôt*'s competitive commitments to papacy and monarchy had become at least temporarily compatible. For on the one hand, the bull transformed many "Gallican" bishops into ecclesiastical ultramontanists, inasmuch as defending the bull entailed defending the papal authority which had fulminated it. And on the other hand, the same bull made ultramontanist Jesuits into temporal Gallicans—into defenders, that is, of the divine right of kings—since it was the French monarchy of Louis XIV and Louis XV which had both solicited this bull and, until 1757, tried steadfastly to enforce it. So to the *parti dévôt*'s natural inertia in the direction of divine-right monarchy, *Unigenitus* added the impetus of reconciled interests, thus politicizing that party to a degree equal though opposite to that of the *parti janséniste*.[112]

But how if at all did the *dévôt* party's characteristic political and religious sensibility make itself felt in the hundred or so pamphlets subsidized by Maupeou in an effort to plead the monarchy's case in the public forum? Unfortunately, no *dévôt* counterpart to Le Paige is at hand to help crack the anonymity of these pamphlets, nor did Le Paige himself seem to know the authors of very many of them. Very few of these pamphlets can therefore be connected to card-carrying members of the Jesuitical *parti dévôt*—among Catholic clergymen, probably a certain Abbé Joseph-François Marie, one of the chancellor's clerical councillors in his makeshift Parlement of Paris and the author, according to Le Paige, of some apologetical *Considerations Concerning the Edict of December 1770* as well as the critical *Observations on a Writing Entitled: Protestations of the Princes;* probably also the lawyer and abbé Pierre Bouquet, a "kind of erudite" on good terms with the Duc de La Vauguyon and the arch-*dévôt* La Motte, bishop of Orléans. Bouquet was also the author of some *Provincial Letters* critical of patriot constitutionalism.[113]

Among laymen, the cases of the lawyers Jacob-Nicolas Moreau and Simon-Henri Linguet are even more ambiguous. Both were sons of persecuted Jansenist professors of philosophy but revolted against their upbringing. Moreau first distanced himself from the Parlement of Paris's pro-Jansenist stand in the controversy over the refusal of sacraments in the 1750s and thereafter defended the monarchy against the parlements until neither monarchy nor parlements remained standing; while Linguet raised his voice in public defense of the Jesuits in the pamphletary debate accompanying their trial in the 1760s, and later he assumed the mantle of an apostle of "despotism," until that term fell once and for all from favor in 1789. Although Moreau acknowledged only his monumental *Lessons in Ethics, Politics, and Public Law* during this period and claimed to have put youthful pamphleteering behind him, it is hard to believe that this sinecured "royal historiographer" did not write one or two of the pamphlets; while Linguet was most certainly the author of at least three or four.[114] If nothing else, the two careers illustrate the close connection in eighteenth-century France between the defense of the Jesuits and integral absolutism on the one hand, and between Jansenism and parliamentary constitutionalism on the other.

A thematic dredging of the same pamphlets yields little more in the way of an obvious *dévôt* Catholic religious presence, unless accusations of "Jansenism" may count as such. For accusations of "Jansenism" against both the old parlements and the patriot opposition appear rather frequently in the pro-Maupeou pamphlets, in part corroborating our own anlaysis of that opposition. Conjuring up the ghosts of the Abbé Pucelle and the "blessed" Deacon Pâris, for example, the sometime magistrate in the anonymous *Visions and Revelations* invoked Pâris's help, lest the anti-monarchical labor of his parliamentary "faithful servants . . . , defenders of the so-called good cause [Jansenism] . . . , be destroyed by a single person [Maupeou]." Again, the abbé in the anonymous *Conversation between a Former Magistrate and an Abbé* accused his magisterial conversant of having invoked the authority of the Estates General "with no better faith than the Sectaries [Jansenists] have called for an Ecumenical

Council," clearly implying the close proximity of the two sets of appellants. And Linguet's *A Citizen's Remonstrance to the Parlements* did not hesitate to attribute the origins of parliamentary audacity in the early 1750s to the "expiring [Jansenist] sect: ambitious, enterprising, enemy of every yoke and subordination, and [hence the parlements'] natural ally."[115]

By itself, it is true, anti-Jansenism is no more evidence for a "devout" religious presence than anti-Jesuitism is of a Jansenist one. Pamphlets which mentioned this controversy most often did so in order to explain the cause or occasion of the parlements' recent constitutional audacity, as in Linguet's *A Citizen's Remonstrance,* or to illustrate the robe's intention of lording it over all the realm's other corps, in this instance the clergy, as in *The Final Word in the Affair.*[116] Yet what qualifiedly makes such accusations of Jansenism into plausible indications of "devout" religiosity is that they often come paired with accusations of "philosophical" or "encyclopedic" unbelief. For the pejorative coupling of Jansenism with *philosophisme* was part and parcel of the *parti dévôt*'s rhetorical stock-in-trade during the eighteenth century—the anti-Jansenist Moreau, for example, was also the author of the well-known anti-"philosophical" *History of the Cacouacs*—just as the linking of Jesuitism with *philosophisme* was routine rhetorical fare for the *parti janséniste.* The anonymous *Their Heads Are Spinning,* for example (which was reprinted in 1788 *without* the reference to Jansenism), facetiously fingered the Jansenist who "wants everything to be efficacious, including the Gazette [the *Ecclesiastical News*]," the philosophe, who "wants everything to be free," as well as the *parlementaire,* who "wants twelve [parlements] to make no more than one." More explicit was the anonymous *The Final Word in the Affair,* which blamed the patriot opposition's "republican spirit" and rhetorical anti-despotism on "self-styled Philosophy" that had been joined by a "Sect, the most dangerous perhaps that might ever have existed in a State, and which would destroy in a day our own if it were ever able to deprive it of its resources. This Sect," this pamphleteer continued, "enemy of Kings as well as of Pontiffs, because it is the enemy of every kind of authority, believes itself to have the greatest obligations to the former magistrates, and therefore the greatest interest in their preservation."[117]

It is surely ironic, then, in view of these "devoutly" oriented accusations of "philosophy," that "ministerial" or pro-Maupeou propaganda availed itself as liberally of "enlightened" rhetorical help as did patriot propaganda. The opening charge in its anti-parliamentary offensive, the preamble to the Edict of December, had the magistrates falling prey to an oppositional *"esprit de système"* – the accusation that the French philosophes routinely leveled at their seventeenth-century Cartesian predecessors. Voltaire was the only *bona fide* philosophe to have entered the fray as a pamphleteer – wielding his formidable rhetorical cudgels in the form of six or seven pamphlets on Maupeou's side. Hard on his heels came an anonymous "master wigmaker" (*maître perruquier*) who, in the person of Voltaire's self-proclaimed acolyte Charles, Marquis de Villette, added another three or four.[118] Yet Villette's anonymous pamphlets curiously testify to the ideological promiscuity of the ministerial party inasmuch as one of them explicitly defended "our good Archbishop" (of Paris), of all people, in the recent refusal of sacraments controversy, while another accused the patriot party of allying those "who do not believe in the church" (probably Jansenists) with "those who do not believe in God" (presumably philosophes).[119]

Perhaps this enlightened rhetoric was most telling in the incendiary charge that the old parliamentary magistrates had constituted a "monstrous hereditary aristocracy," a sort of throwback to medieval feudal aristocracy. Their selfish and particularistic "corporate spirit" (*esprit de corps*) and "particular interest" (*intérêt particulier*) was only imperfectly obscured by the "gothic" style of its constitutionalism. This charge together with its vaguely "enlightened" vocabulary were in turn embedded in a royalist version of French history most immediately indebted to the works of such early eighteenth-century proto-philosophes as the Marquis d'Argenson and the Abbé de Saint Pierre, which featured the king as civil liberator of the people from the yoke of "feudal" oppression and the "barbarous" Middle Ages.[120] In the words of one pamphleteer, the moral of this story was that "the absolute independence of the Master is the rampart of the liberties of the subjects, and the surest guarantee of their welfare;" or again, in the words of another, that "France was never happier or more tranquil than when her kings were most absolute."[121]

The association of anti-"aristocratic" and anti-"feudal" rhetoric with the French Enlightenment (however that elusive term be defined), is suggested by its greater concentrations in Enlightenment literature (especially if Rousseau and his disciples qualify as "enlightened") than in the century's competitive political discourses. As educators of the realm's nobility until their dissolution in 1762, the Jesuits could no more have been expected to perpetrate anti-elitist rhetoric than their many courtly and episcopal partisans, while the Jansenists' occasional indulgence in it occurred in an ecclesiastical more than in a political context. The charges of neo-"feudalism" and "aristocracy" also tend to figure disproportionately in pamphlets written by Linguet, who, though a self-proclaimed critic of Voltaire and the philosophes, was more open to influences from those ideological quarters than most of the other partisans of the ministry.[122] Yet Voltaire, surely the Enlightenment incarnate, did not rebuke the *parlementaires* as "feudal" or "aristocratic" in the pamphlets he wrote. And what further undermines the association between "enlightened" and "anti-aristocratic" is the fact that charges of "feudal anarchy" and "aristocratic usurpation" were already commonplace complaints against the Middle Ages in such seventeenth-century royalist histories of France as those by Père Gabriel Daniel and Eudes de Mézeray.[123] Perhaps "royalist" historiography of the late sixteenth and seventeenth centuries is then a likelier orgin of anti-aristocratic rhetoric in eighteenth-century France.

Whether of enlightened or simply royalist origin, the anti-aristocratic or feudal language of ministerial pamphleteering is in any event not the rhetorical doing of the *parti dévôt*. For when, during the 1750s and 1760s, it was they who had been the monarchy's principal defenders, *dévôt* spokesmen such as the Abbé Capmartin de Chaupy or Lafiteau, Bishop of Sisteron, had on the contrary reproached the magistrates for being uppity bourgeois, fraudulent claimants to being the true Court of Peers and the social equals of the realm's nobility.[124] Indeed, the same reproaches that the magistrates were only "a few hundred bourgeois," mere "legists" or, worse still, "villains and commoners," lingered on in ministerial propaganda, the ones in vaguely *dévôt* pamphlets curiously juxtaposed to similar ones in Voltaire's pro-Maupeou pamphlets![125] What is new in the early 1770s—and also pregnant with a revolutionary future—is the application of the charges of "aristocracy" and "feudalism" against the parliamentary magistracy, as opposed to, say, the dukes and peers of the realm or the medieval feudal nobility itself.

But if ministerial propaganda's anti-aristocratic rhetoric is of enlightened or royalist rather than of *dévôt* extraction, it is otherwise with another component of its royalist reading of the French past, namely its very exalted view of monarchical sovereignty. Indeed, some of the formulations of monarchical sovereignty in that literature were as unguarded as anything that had been said at the height of the Bourbon dynasty's prestige under Henry IV or Louis XIV and seemed designed to substantiate the patriot opposition's worst "despotic" nightmares. In depaternalized monarchical "master" (*maître*) in ministerial pamphlets, who lorded it over mere valets instead of lovingly governing children and servants, belligerently confronted a benign "chief" (*chef*) in patriot pamphlets, who was a sort of constitutional *primus inter pares*. Similarly, ministerial propagandists vested the "property" (*propriété*) of the state in this "master," defying the patriot tendency to vest it in the "nation" and to confide only the "administration" to its "chief."[126]

For a certain number of Maupeou's pamphleteers, including the anonymous author of *Their Heads Are Spinning*, the "power" of their royal "master" effectively "raised him above the laws, so that he might change [the laws], abrogate them, reestablish them, make new ones—a power, in fine, which only he himself can limit, and whose cause may not be obstructed by any [other] will whether particular or general. Such is the French constitution."[127] Principles such as these both justified and found justification in the supposedly ancient summary of the French constitution in the lapidary phrase, "*Si veut le Roi, si veut la Loi*" (as the king wills, so wills the law), as reported by the seventeenth-century jurist Charles de Loyseau.[128]

This almost anti-constitutional view of the French monarchy can be regarded as a *dévôt* legacy not only in that it is indebted to a "devout" counter-reformational exaltation of the monarchy going back to the late sixteenth and early seventeenth centuries, but that it stands in direct succession to an almost identical view of the monarchy as articulated by such mid-century episcopal and Jesuitical apologists as André-Christophe Balbani; Abbé Capmartin de Chaupi; Lafiteau, bishop of Sisteron; and Jean-Georges Lefranc de Pompignan, bishop of Le Puy. These apologists—they were not quite publicists—had articulated this view against the "Jansenist" parlements and in defense of the bull *Unigenitus*, which had become a symbol of royal authority, as well as on the model of their very anti-Gallican conception of the papacy's authority over the church.[129] Yet while they had exalted the king's power over his lay subjects, the better to restrain him by divine law in relation to the "spiritual" power of the church, their more journalistic and "ministerial" successors of the Maupeou era contented themselves with only the fewest and most perfunctory references to things divine—even to divine right—and argued the monarchy's case on the grounds of either natural law or, more often, historically demonstrated utility.[130] But what the king lost in divine wisdom he gained in human will. For the consequent secularization—and humanization—of the *dévôt* rhetorical tradition's representation of the monarchy, combined with the same tradition's long-standing defense of the freedom of the human will against

Jansenist predestinarianism, produced a conception of royal power as an exercise in will so unrestrained as all but to obliterate Bishop Bossuet's hallowed distinction between "arbitrary" and "absolute" power. In thus distilling the essence of monarchy into will, however, this rhetorical tactic ran the obvious risk of making the monarchy more vulnerable to patriot opposition if and when, as eventually happened, that discursive tradition came to express itself in similarly willful terms.[131]

More frontally than in the 1750s and 1760s—and in a manner to make even Bossuet stir uneasily in his grave—the Maupeou period's defenders of the monarchy also questioned the very existence of constitutional or "fundamental" law. "These *fundamental laws,* about which so much noise is made . . . and which are nowhere to be found, are they any better known and spelled out" for all that, asked an irate Linguet, obviously out of patience with the parlements' "faithful archives, where its corporate spirit blends so happily with the spirit of the law."[132] Reminding the *parlementaires* that there were kings such as Frederick the Great who would teach them to "find out about affairs of state from the Gazettes," the anonymous *Henry the Great's Response to the Parlements' Remonstrances* warned them also that they "could appeal all they wanted to their fundamental laws (of which God alone knows the originals). He [the king] will simply make some new ones to suit his convenience, to which they will be obliged to submit."[133] The anonymous author of a *Letter from M.D.L.V., a Lawyer in the Parlement* went further, denying not only the historical existence of fundamental laws but their very possibility, "diametrically opposed as these were to good sense as well as to right reason." No more than his predecessors could Louis XV legally bind his successors, who would be free to legislate "apropos of the welfare of our descendants."[134]

Combining *dévôt* moralism with some Montesquieuian relativism, the Abbé J.-F. Marie's skeptical and royalist assault on fundamental law went so far as to come full circle and paradoxically resubjected the monarchy to a kind of national will. In imprudently disseminating *parlementaire* palaver, Marie charged, the princes' *Protestations* had confounded "the civil order with the moral order, or rather it assimilated the mobile and variable laws of the former with the constant laws of the latter. In morality," he explained, "all is immutably true, while in politics what is true for one time can become error in another," with the result that "the antiquity of laws gives them no title to irrevocability." Abbé Marie's audacious line of reasoning produced the startling conclusion that not even absolute monarchies had any "*absolute* consistency, because the same laws do not always produce the same effects, because alterations in the principles and character of a nation necessarily entail new needs and precautions. If authority does not adjust to popular changes, the diverse pieces of that immobile monarchy will lose flexibility and eventually fall apart."[135] The royal will was similarly indistinguishable from a changing "national spirit" for the author of a *Letter From a Parisian Lawyer to the Magistrates of the Parliament of Rouen*—a national spirit "to which laws and ordinances cannot give orders and to which political institutions must themselves give way."[136]

A radical, potentially subversive strand of ministerial pamphleteering therefore stands out in contrast to a moderate one. And what distinguishes this radical strand is in part its skepticism about the relevance or even accessibility of the past. While a moderate defender of the monarchy like Moreau attempted to fashion a royalist version of French history and even constitutional archives in order better to compete with the parliamentary and patriot versions, the likes of Linguet and Marie turned their backs on history altogether and argued the case of the royal will in utilitarian terms.[137] Even sharper, then, was the contrast with patriot pamphleteering. For where patriot pamphleteering—especially the more Jansenist versions of it—all but eliminated the flesh and blood monarch in favor of immutable "fundamental laws" as they supposedly existed by national consent during the French monarchy's earliest centuries, this more radical wing of the ministerial front strove to free the monarchical will from the constraints of the past however construed. But these radical and moderate wings of the ministerial front were no more manned by enlightened and *dévôt* recruits respectively than were the patriot party's radical and moderate flanks composed of enlightened and Jansenist ones in that order. For just as some of the most radical patriot constitutionalism had roots in Jansenist conciliarism and its vision of a pristine patristic revelation—for the Jansenists the touchstone of all ulterior theologizing—so some of this radical ministerial anticonstitutionalism arguably had roots or at least a counterpart in a *dévôt* apologetical tactic developed during the eighteenth century's earlier decades.

That apologetical effort, undertaken by the Jesuits Jean Hardouin and his disciple Isaac Berruyer, had audaciously challenged the authenticity or at least accessibility of much of the historical and documentary evidence of Christian revelation, such as the writings of the church fathers and the pronouncements of church councils. Thereby freed from the constraints of both ecclesiastical and dogmatic history—so ran the strategy of this apologetic – the papal magisterium would be free to define what the church had presumably always believed as it infallibly saw fit. In the works of Jean Hardouin, who wrote during the earlier decades of the century, this apologetic took the crude form of challenging the authenticity of all the church's documentary evidence except for the Vulgate before the fourteenth century, at which time some atheistical monks forged all of the patristic and conciliar evidence in an attempt to undermine papal authority.

Hardouin's disciple Isaac Berruyer took a subtler tack, holding that the meanings of terms and the systems of reference of such ancient documents were so time-bound as to render their meaning all but impenetrable to the eighteenth-century understanding. Berruyer therefore felt free to interpret even Holy Scripture in ways he felt would be intelligible to his own generation, which he did with scandalous effect in his multi-volume and novelistic *History of the People of God*. But the intended effect, as in Hardouin's work, was to emancipate the papacy from documentary evidence of just about any kind, allowing it to define or redefine the Catholic dogmatic tradition in the sense of the bull *Unigenitus*. Hardouin and Berruyer were hence predictably outspoken "Molinists" and anti-Jansenists, defending not only the authority of the papal present against the patristic past but an essentially benign view of "fallen" humanity against the Jansenist insistence upon the fall's tragic consequences. Intoned as one word in the pages of the *Ecclesiastical News*, Hardouin-Berruyer and Company figured as the Jansenist weekly's chief *bêtes noires* during the century's central decades.[138]

The distance between the epistemological liberation of the papacy from its patristic and especially Augustinian past and the liberation of the monarchy from its Frankish and putatively constitutional past is not a great one, especially in view of the role that eighteenth-century Jesuits had played in the defense of the French monarchy. The most visible bridge between the two is perhaps the *avocat*-abbé Pierre Bouquet's *Provincial Letters, or an Impartial Examination of the Origins of the Constitution and the Revolutions of the Monarchy*, a stout book published in late 1772.[139] Although "very royalist" and a self-anointed defender of the monarchy, Bouquet apparently wrote at the behest of the ministry's *dévôt* stalwart Henri-Léonard Bertin rather than the sometime *parlementaire* Maupeou.[140] This difference in ministerial sponsorship symbolizes if it does not explain Bouquet's Berruyer-style epistemological assault upon the documentary bases of Le Paige's historical constitutionalism, underscoring as it did the relative paucity and dubious authenticity of these documents as well as the formidable semantic barriers to their proper interpretation. Bouquet did not go so far as to deny the possibility of any reliable knowledge about the French constitutional past. But he came pretty close, going so far as to raise doubts about the Salic Law which regulated the succession to the French throne – the one "fundamental" law that just about all defenders of the monarchy accepted.[141] In any case he went too far for Maupeou, who had the book condemned by a decree in council for "containing dubious assertions and inexact notions about the history of the monarchy" – and thereby procuring for the book a brief *succès de scandale*. With friends like that, the French monarchy hardly needed any "patriot" enemies.[142]

7. Conclusions

At least one of the immediate antecedents of late-eighteenth-century France's ministerial alliance is therefore the Jesuitical and ultramontanist *parti dévôt* just as the patriot party's main predecessor in the preceeding decades is what had been called the *parti janséniste*. These parallel political and ideological metamorphoses, admittedly better documented on the Jansenist than on the *dévôt* side, took place during the years 1771–1775, the long season of Chancellor Maupeou's constitutional "revolution" and its many discontents.

To say this much is of course not to say that either the ministerial or the patriot party was simply a linear extension of its religious antecedent, reflecting nothing more than a change of terminology, or that either again was impervious to the wider context of the eighteenth-century French Enlightenment. Both political alliances emerged significantly transformed in relation to their respective religious chrysalises; both took on a somewhat more "enlightened" coloration. Most striking is the gradual but steady secularization of both discursive traditions, emboldening each in its own way to soar confidently in spaces that its more confessionally bound predecessor had only timidly probed. Contact with a certain enlightenment, more specifically the natural law tradition, perhaps enabled the "patriots" to state the thesis of national sovereignty in more unmistakable terms than had Jansenists in the preceeding decades; it more certainly taught them to couch their defense of the magistrates' venal offices and representative pretensions in the language of natural right. Exposure to the same enlightenment all but dried up *dévôt*-style references to divine right in ministerial pamphlets, which substituted legitimizations of absolutism in a utilitarian and secular guise. It may also in part have furnished ministerial pamphleteers with new pejorative categories such as "aristocracy" and "feudalism." That much said, the additional point seems worth making that the Enlightenment provided basic ideological and political direction to neither of these two parties, pointed as each had long been toward its subsequent course.

Modest enough by itself, this set of conclusions takes on added significance in the light of the revolutionary drama to come. For the *dramatis personae* of this Maupeou prologue was also to be that of the Revolution's opening scene in the years 1787–1788. It was the ragged remnants of the anti-Maupeou "patriot party"—Augéard, Target, the inevitable Le Paige—who commenced pamphletary action against the Calonne and Brienne ministries in 1787–1788. And it was the remains of the Maupeou-engendered ministerial party, reinforced by remnants of the former controller-general Turgot's physiocratic *équipe* of the mid-1770s, that initially returned the rhetorical fire. Maultrot's pungent little *Dissertation on the Right to Convoke the Estates General* (appended to the second or 1775 edition of the *Maxims of French Public Law*) and the anonymous (but probably Linguet's) *Their Heads Are Spinning* are only the most conspicuous of the many pamphlets originally written and published during the Maupeou era which the French public still found current enough to reread in republished form some fifteen or so years later. They thereby testified to the remarkable rhetorical continuity from the Maupeou-patriot confrontation of the early 1770s to the "pre-revolution" of 1787–1788. To a considerable extent, the actors of the French pre-revolution began with roles assigned to them by the script of the Maupeou episode.[143]

Or nearly. One change has to do with patriot propaganda's appeal to the principle of national sovereignty as represented in the Estates General, which was possibly more dominant in 1787–1788 than in the early 1770s. In other words, Le Paige's version of parliamentary constitutionalism ceded dominance to Mey's and Maultrot's, which recast the parlements as mere mandatories of the temporarily defunct Estates General. A constitutionalism which featured the parlements as lineal descendants of Frankish legislative assemblies—and therefore as the nation's chief "representatives"—was among the casualties of Maupeou's *coup*, which had revealed the vulnerability of the these institutions as representatives of the nation. More pronounced as well in 1787–1788 was ministerial rhetoric's tactic of denouncing the parliamentary opposition as selfishly corporate and hence "aristocratic." What made this accusation not only more pronounced but also more effective in 1788 than in 1771 was the Parlement of Paris's ostentatious courting of the alliance of the upper clergy and court nobility after 1774—another product of the parlements' weakened position in the wake of the Maupeou *coup*— which lent substance to ministerial rhetoric's denunciation of a new "feudalism" about to be perpetrated by an unholy "aristocratic" alliance of magistracy, episcopacy, and nobility. As in 1771, this rhetoric drew in part on the Enlightenment, which, in the persons of the Marquis de Condorcet and the Abbé Morellet, more decisively aligned itself on the ministry's side in 1788 than in 1771. Yet none of this prevented ministerial propaganda from defending the king's undivided sovereignty in language at least as brittle as that used in defense of Maupeou.

Largely continuous, then, with the configuration of ideological and political forces as it emerged from the Maupeou era, this pre-revolutionary scenario is in turn significant because much of revolutionary rhetoric can be dialectically accounted for in terms of this patriotic-ministerial standoff. At the most superficial level, the Revolution's synthesis of these opposing discursive traditions shows up in revolutionary ideology's twin hydras of "despotism" and "aristocracy," inherited from patriotic and ministerial language respectively. At a deeper level, revolutionary ideology both directly and indirectly owed its vast disdain for history—or at least French history—to the same patriot-ministerial confrontation: directly inasmuch as this disdain already figured as a "subtext" in ministerial propaganda, indirectly inasmuch as, by mutually eliminating their competitive readings of French history in 1788, that ultimate patriot-ministerial debate cleared the way for revolutionary ideology's appropriation of the political works of the profoundly ahistorical Rousseau.

At an even deeper level revolutionary ideology's dialectical appropriation of these opposing patriot and ministerial languages helps to explain some of its inherent instability. From Jansenist and patriot political discourse, curiously reinforced in this instance by the authority of Rousseau, revolutionary ideology inherited a notion of national sovereignty as evenly diffused throughout the political nation, a profound suspicion of representation, and the exercise of political power generally (and that despite its willingness to see the Parlement or the Estates General as the nation's "representative" or rather "mandatory"), as well as a tendency to see anticonstitutional and "despotic" conspiracies behind each and every event. And from ministerial political discourse reinforced by yet other elements of Rousseau, revolutionary ideology inherited an anticorporate conception of the nation as consisting exclusively in the third estate, together with a notion of undivided national sovereignty which, when transferred from king to nation, tended to free representative assemblies from any real accountability to their constituents. The interplay of these tensions would account in some measure for the endemic instability of the Revolution itself.[144]

It is surely paradoxical, in view of these religious and specifically Catholic ideological origins, that the Revolution came to direct so much of its "terror" against priests and went so far as to undertake the "dechristianization" of France. The most obvious explanation for this paradox suggested by the preceding pages is that the Revolution's religious origins were in fact dual and competitive, even in their late-eighteenth-century politicized form, and that by all but eliminating each other from the field in the Armageddon of 1788–1789 they cleared the way for a radical Enlightenment and its subsequent denial of both French history and Gallican Catholicism. The study of the pamphletary debate surrounding the Maupeou "revolution" would in that case corroborate, albeit in new and unexpected ways, the long-received dictum that the interconfessional conflicts between Jansenists and Jesuits contributed to the triumph of Enlightenment and Revolution in eighteenth-century France. Yet part of the argument of the forgoing pages is that, far from conveniently disappearing in 1788 or 1789, both the "Jansenist-patriot" and "devout-ministerial" political discourses—in combination, to be sure, with various elements of the Enlightenment and Rousseauism—entered dialectically into the making of revolutionary ideology. And in that case the Revolution's ideological and political conflicts must in some measure be construed as the secularized continuation of conflicts which had long divided the French Catholic community. The ultimate paradox would in that case be that the French Revolution played out the drama of terror and dechristianization in terms that remained derivatively Catholic and Christian.[145]

NOTES

1. Mathieu-François Pidansat de Mairobert, *Journal historique de la révolution operée dans la constitution de la monarchie françoise, par M. de Maupeou, chancelier de France*, 7 vols. (London, 1774–1776), "du 20 janvier," 2:351. Unless otherwise specified, the pamphlets and books referred to in these notes were consulted in the Bibliothèque nationale.

2. François-André Isambert et al., eds., *Recueil des anciennes lois françaises depuis l'an 420 jusqu'à la Révolution de 1789* (Paris, 1821–33), 22:501–7.

3. The standard narrative accounts of Chancellor Maupeou's judicial

and constitutional reforms remain Jules Flammermont, *Le Chancelier Maupeou et les parlements,* 2nd ed. (Paris, 1885); and Jean Egret, *Louis XV et l'opposition parlementaire* (Paris, 1970), pp. 133–228.

4. See in particular William Doyle, "The Parlements of France and the Breakdown of the Old Régime," *French Historical Studies* 6 (Fall 1970): 415–58; and Martin Mansergh, "The Revolution of 1771, or the Exile of the Parlement of Paris," Ph.D. diss., Oxford, 1973.

5. See William Doyle, *The Origins of the French Revolution* (Oxford, 1980), and Baily Stone, *The French Parlements and Crisis of Old Régime* (Chapel Hill, N.C., 1986). On the essential role played by venal offices and privilege in royal finance, see David Bien, "Offices, Corps, and a System of State Credit: The Uses of Privilege under the Ancien Régime," and Gail Bossenga, "City and State: An Urban Perspective on the Origins of the French Revolution," in *The Political Culture of the Old Regime,* vol. 1 of the *The French Revolution and the Creation of Modern Political Culture,* ed. Keith M. Baker (Oxford and New York, 1988), 1:89–140.

6. The best and most recent work on the "patriots" and "patriot constitutionalism" is now Durand Echeverria's *The Maupeou Revolution: A Study in the History of Libertarianism* (Baton Rouge, La., and London, 1985), pp. 37–122.

7. Echeverria, *The Maupeou Revolution,* pp. 125–77. Still useful on this subject is David Hudson's "In Defense of Reform: French Government Propaganda during the Maupeou Crisis," *French Historical Studies* 8 (1973): 51–76.

8. [Jacques-Mathieu Augéard], *Correspondance secrète et familière du M. de Maupeou, avec M. de Sorhouet, conseiller au nouveau parlement,* in *Les efforts de la liberté et du patriotisme contre le despotisme du Sr de Maupeou, chancelier de France, ou recueil des écrits patriotiques publiés pour maintenir l'ancien gouvernement françois,* 6 vols. (London, 1775), 2:32, 62–63, 95–96.

9. Denis Diderot, *Observations sur le Nakaz* in *Oeuvres politiques,* ed. Paul Vernière, Classiques Garnier (Paris, 1963), p. 358; Voltaire, *Oeuvres complètes de Voltaire,* ed. Louis Moland, 52 vols. (Paris, 1877–1885), 28:386–424; Peter Gay, *Voltaire's Politics* (Princeton, 1959), pp. 318–51; and Echeverria, *The Maupeou Revolution,* pp. 147–68.

10. Pidansat de Mairobert, "Avertissement des éditeurs," in Louis Petit de Bachaumont, *Mémoires secrets pour servir à l'histoire de la république des lettres en France, depuis MDCCLXII jusqu'à nos jours, ou journal d'un observateur . . . ,* 36 vols. (London, 1784–1788), 1:3–4.

11. Definitions and characterizations of French Jansenism are legion, but among the best and most recent in English are Walter Rex, *Pascal's Provincial Letters: An Introduction* (London and Sydney, 1977); and Alexander Sedgwick, *Jansenism in Seventeenth-Century France: Voices from the Wilderness* (Charlottesville, Va., 1977).

12. Edmond Préclin, *Les jansénistes du dix-huitième siècle et la Constitu-*

tion civile du clergé: le développement du richérisme, sa propagation dans le bas clergé, 1713–1791 (Paris, 1929), p. ii.

13. On the convulsionary movement, see B. Robert Kresier, *Miracles, Convulsions, and Ecclesiastical Politics in Eighteenth-Century Politics* (Princeton, 1978). On figurism in particular, see pp. 243–50. The best introduction to the hermeneutic from the "inside" is Jean-Baptiste-Raymond de Pavie de Fourquevaux's *L'introduction abregée à l'intelligence des prophéties de l'Ecriture, par l'usage qu'en fait Saint Paul dans l'Epitre aux Romains* (n.p., 1731).

14. On the politicization of Jansenism in general, see René Taveneaux, *Jansénisme et politique* (Paris, 1965). Among more recent works on this subject, Monique Cottret's "Aux origines du républicanisme janséniste: Le mythe de l'église primitive et le primitivisme des lumières," in *Revue d'histoire moderne et contemporaine* 31 (January–March 1984): 98–115, is especially suggestive.

15. On Gallicanism, see Victor Martin, *Les origines du gallicanisme*, 2 vols. (Paris, 1939); Albert Le Roy's *Le gallicanisme au dix-huitième siècle: La France et Rome de 1700–1715* (Paris, 1892), remains the only work which intensively covers the period of Gallicanism's juncture with Jansenism.

16. On Montesquieu's place in the articulation of parliamentary constitutionalism, the best work remains Elie Carcassonne's *Montesquieu et le problème de la constitution française au dix-huitième siècle* (Paris, 1926). On the Jansenists' contribution, see D. Carroll Joynes, "Jansenists and Ideologues: Opposition Theory in the Parliament of Paris, 1750–1765" (Ph.D. diss., University of Chicago, 1981); and Dale Van Kley, "The Jansenist Constitutional Legacy in the French Prerevolution," *Historical Reflections/Réflexions historiques* (Summer–Fall 1986): 393–453.

17. See Jean Egret's *Louis XV et l'opposition parlementaire, 1715–1774* (Paris, 1970), for a general overview of these developments.

18. Edmond J.-F. Barbier, *Chronique de la Régence et du règne de Louis XV, ou journal de Barbier, 1718–1763,* ed. Charpentier, 8 vols. (Paris, 1866), 5:221; 6:145. In order to distinguish between the broader and narrower senses of the term, the Marquis d'Argenson had recourse to the expressions "jansénistes de profession" and "ce qu'on appelle aujourd'hui jansénistes." See René-Louis, Marquis d'Argenson, *Journal et mémoires,* ed. E.-J.-B. Rathery, 8 vols. (Paris, 1859–1867), 8:110–11, 181, 202, 204.

19. *Lettre de Monsieur Xxx, conseiller au parlement, a M. le comte de Xxx* (n.p., 1771), pp. 11–12.

20. *Lettre d'un bourgeois de Paris à un provincial, à l'occasion de l'édit de décembre 1770* (n.p., n.d.), p. 8, in Bibliothèque de Port-Royal (henceforth BPR), Le Paige collection (henceforth LP) 800, no. 14. See also *Lettres d'un homme à un autre homme* (n.p., n.d.); and *Le parlement justifié par l'impératrice de Russie, ou lettre à M. Xxx dans laquelle on répond aux différents écrits que M. le Ch[ancelier] fait distribuer dans Paris* (n.p., n.d.), pp. 106–7, 109.

21. *Requête des Etats-généraux de France au roi* (London, 1772), pp. 12–14, in BPR, LP 805, no. 17.

22. [Louis-Adrien Le Paige], *Lettres historiques sur les fonctions essentielles du parlement, sur le droit des pairs, et sur les loix fondamentales du royaume,* 2 vols. (Amsterdam, 1753–1754).

23. [Le Paige], *Lettre sur les lits de justice* (n.p., 1756). On the *lit de justice*'s recent origin, see Sarah Hanley, *The Lit de justice of the Kings of France: Constitutional Ideology in Legend, Ritual, and Discourse* (Princeton, N.J., 1983). See also Abbé Pierre Barral, *Manuel des souverains* (n.p., 1754), pp. 171–73; and *Discours sur l'origine des troubles présens en France, dans lequel on expose les causes, les progrès, et les effets de la bulle* Unigenitus; *et où on traite de la nature de ce decret, et de la fausse apparence de son autorité* (n.p., 1754), pp. 317–18, 324–25. Both Barral and the anonymous author of the *Discours* were clearly Jansenists.

24. *Protestation des princes du sang contre l'édit de décembre 1770, les lettres patentes du 23 février 1771, et contre tout ce qui s'en est ensuivi ou pourroit s'ensuivre; signifiées et déposées au greffe du parlement, et lues en présence de MM. du Conseil siégeant au palais, le 12 avril 1771* (n.p., n.d.), of which Le Paige's handwritten copy is in BPR, LP 569, no. 147. On Conti as Le Paige's patron and would-be *frondeur,* see Dale Van Kley, *The Damiens Affair and the Unraveling of the Old Régime, 1750–1770* (Princeton, 1984), pp. 56–165.

25. *Lettre d'un François aux victimes d'Ebrouin* (n.p., 1771), p. 8, in BPR, LP 817, no. 29.

26. *Requête des Etats-généraux de France au roi,* pp. 18–19; *Lettre de Monsieur Xxx, conseiller au parlement,* pp. 28–29; *Lettre d'un bourgeois de Paris,* pp. 20–21; *Lettre d'un ancien magistrat à un duc et pair, sur le discours de M. le chancelier au lit de justice du vendrédi 7 décembre 1770* (n.p., n.d.), p. 59.

27. *Conversation entre un avocat et M. le chancelier* (n.p., 1771), pp. 31–32.

28. *Inauguration de Pharamond, ou exposition des loix fondamentales de la monarchie françoise; avec les preuves de leur exécution, perpetuées sous les trois races de nos rois,* in *Les efforts,* 4:188–89.

29. *Lettres d'un homme à un autre homme,* pp. 202–3; and *Correspondance secrète et familière,* in *Les efforts,* 2:45, 99.

30. Pidansat de Mairobert, *Journal historique:* on being too *parlementaire,* July 25, 1772, 1:217; on the proposition of holding the crown from God alone, February 13, 1772, 2:309 and on an enlightened and philosophical century, June 17, 1771, 1:364–65.

31. On being too "Jansenist," ibid., December 13, 1772, 3:390–92; on "philosophical" adhesions, see Echeverria, *The Maupeou Revolution,* pp. 56–57.

32. Pidansat de Mairobert, *Journal historique,* August 6, 1771, 2:69–70; and *Lettres d'un homme à un autre homme,* pp. 171–72, 180–81.

33. Louis-Léon-Félicité, duc de Brancas, comte de Lauraguais, *Tableau*

de la constitution françoise, ou autorité des rois de France, dans les différens ages de la monarchie (n.p., 1771), pp. 60, 70–78.

39. Lauraguais, *Receuil de pièces historiques sur la convocation des Etats-généraux et sur l'élection de leurs députés* (Paris, 1788), pp. 101–12; and *Dissertation sur les assemblées nationales, sous les trois races des rois de France* (Paris, 1788), pp. 11–14, 98.

35. *Maximes du droit public françois, tirées des capitulaires, des ordonnances du royaume, et des autres monumens de l'histoire de France*, 2nd ed., 2 vols. (Amsterdam, 1775), especially the "Dissertation sur le droit de convoquer les Etats-généraux" appended to the end of the first volume and paginated separately, pp. 17–18, but also 1:167–69, and 2:154–60.

36. Gabriel-Nicolas Maultrot and Claude Mey, *Apologie de tous les jugemens rendus par les tribunaux séculiers en France contre le schisme*, 2 vols. (France, 1752), esp. 1:481–85.

37. *Manifeste aux Normands* (n.p., n.d.), in *Les efforts*, 6:8, 12–13; and Guillaume Saige, *Catéchisme du citoyen, ou éléments du droit public françois, par demandes et réponses; suivi de fragments politiques; par le même auteur* (en France, 1788, although originally published in 1775), pp. 24–25, 74–76, 96–97, 115.

38. On this development, see Dale Van Kley, *The Jansenists and the Expulsion of the Jesuits from France, 1757–1765* (New Haven, Conn., 1975), pp. 6–36.

39. *Le parlement justifié par l'impératrice reine de Hongrie, et par le roi de Prusse; ou seconde lettre, dans laquelle on continue de répondre aux écrits de M. le chancelier* (n.p., n.d.), in *Les efforts*, 4:209–10.

40. *Requête des Etats-généraux de France au roi*, pp. 88–89.

41. *Le point de vue, ou lettres de M. le prés . . . a M. le duc de N. . . .* (n.p., 1772), p. 6 and *passim*, in BPR, LP 811, no. 5; and *L'accomplissement des prophéties. Pour servir de suite à l'ouvrage intitulé Le point de vue. Ecrit intéressant pour la maison de Bourbon* (n.p., 1772), in BPR, LP 811, no. 6.

42. Pidansat de Mairobert, *Journal historique*, April 24, 1772, 3:83 and 3:391–92 (December 13, 1772).

43. *Supplément à la Gazette de France* (n.p., n.d.), May 1, 1772, on subject of *Le point de vue*, and June 1, 1773, on *L'accomplissement des prophéties*, in *Les efforts*, 5:134, 232.

44. For example, ibid., August 16, 1772, 5:159.

45. *Lettre de Monsieur Xxx, conseiller au parlement*, p. 46.

46. *Lettre d'un ancien magistrat à un duc et pair*, p. 46, and in general pp. 45–47; *Requête des Etats-généraux de France au roi*, pp. 69–73.

47. *Réflexions sur les affaires présentes* (n.p., n.d.), pp. 1–7, in BPR, LP 811, no. 8.

48. BPR, LP 569, no. 173, "plan du *molinisme d'état*, petit écrit en manuscrit;" and LP 811, no. 8, "14 mai 1771."

49. BPR, LP 571, no. 26, "20 mars 1772 à m. le p. de Murard."

50. *Requête des Etats-généraux de France au roi,* pp. 80–87.

51. *Journal historique,* July 25, 1772, 3:216, but see also ibid., May 17, 1772, p. 121 on the subject of the pamphlet's appearance. The quotation about Louis XV's palaces, etc., comes from *Requéte des Etats-généraux de France au roi,* pp. 46–47. For the "terrible portrait" of Louis XIV, see ibid., pp. 34–36.

52. On Le Paige's flight from Paris, see Pidansat de Mairobert, *Journal historique,* September 8, 12, and 14, 1772, 3:271–72, 276, 278; and Le Paige's own letters from his place of hiding to his brother and Conti in BPR, LP 571, nos. 48–63.

53. On Le Paige's return to the Temple, see Prosper-Siméon Hardy, "Mes Loisirs, ou journal d'événemens tels qu'ils parviennent à ma connoissance," in Bibliothèque nationale (henceforth BN), Manuscrits français (henceforth MSS Fr) 6681, p. 280 (January 20, 1774).

54. BPR, LP 928, no. 6, on reading the second part of [Pierre-Jean Agier's] *Le jurisconsulte nationale* (n.p., 1788).

55. The Abbé Rondeau in the *Nouvelles ecclésiastiques, ou mémoires pour servir à l'histoire de la bulle* Unigenitus (1727–1803), May 10, 1803, pp. 37–38.

56. *Supplément à la Gazette de France,* March 6, 1772, in *Les efforts,* 5:114. See also Pidansat de Mairobert, *Journal historique,* March 7, 1772, pp. 5–13.

57. Bachaumont, *Mémoires secrets,* 24:181.

58. Archives de la Bastille (henceforth AB) 12,401, interrogations of Dom Isidoire Mirasson by Miché de Rochebrune on August 27, 28, and 29, 1772, nos. 139–50.

59. Le Paige's corrections and additions are in his personal copy of the *Inauguration* in BPR, LP 815, no. 5, pp. 16, 65, 135. These additions and corrections did not appear in any published edition. For his epistolary remarks about his suspected complicity in the writing and publication of the pamphlet, see BPR, LP 571, Le Paige to his brother, September 14, 1772, no. 50.

60. [Vialdome], *Inauguration de Pharamond,* in *Les efforts,* pp. 188–89.

61. *Maximes du droit public françois,* 1:155, 237–38, 267–69.

62. On attribution by Pidansat de Mairobert, see *Journal historique,* August 23, 1772, 3:252. On authorship of *Maximes,* see Michaud, *Biographie universelle:* on Maultrot (and Blonde), 27:311–14; on Mey, 28:162–63.

63. On Aubri, see Bachaumont, *Mémoires secrets* 34:10; for André Blonde in general, see Michaud, *Biographie universelle,* 4:448–49; and as anti-Molinist, see his *Lettre à M. Bergier, docteur en théologie et principal du collège de Besançon, sur son ouvrage intitulé: Le déisme réfuté par lui-même* (n.p., n.d.).

64. André Blonde, *Réponse de Monsieur Blonde, aux écclaircissemens données par M. Agier, dans l'affaire de M. Augéard* (n.p., [January 29, 1790]), pp. 54–59.

65. Augéard, *Mémoires secrets,* p. 44.

66. AB 12,392, dossier dated February 7, 1771, nos. 202–3; perquisition by Commissioner Hubert Mutel, March 25, 1771, no. 205; and interrogation by Mutel, March 30, 1771, nos. 208–13.

67. Echeverria, *The Maupeou Revolution,* pp. 305–14.

68. Augéard, *Mémoires secrets,* pp. 44–45, 65. Augéard also took credit for the *Oeufs rouges. Première partie. Sorhouet mourant à M. de Maupeou, chancelier de France* (n.p., 1772); and *Mandement de Monseigneur l'archévêque de Paris, qui proscrit l'usage des oeufs rouges, à commencer du vendrédi dans l'octave de l'ascension jusqu'à la résurrection des morts exclusivement* (Paris, 1772). In an anonymous pamphlet written on the eve of the Revolution, however, Augéard hinted that President Chrétien-François de Lamoignon may also have contributed to the composition of the *Correspondance secrète.* See [Augéard], *Les mânes de Madame la présidente Le Mairat à M. de Lamoignon, quatrième président au parlement, et garde des sceaux* (n.p., 1788), pp. 3–4., in Newberry Library (henceforth NL), case French Revolution Collection (henceforth FRC) 5235–39.

69. On Target's early career, see Van Kley, *The Jansenists and the Expulsion of the Jesuits,* pp. 100–101; and Charles O'Brien, "New Light on the Mouton-Natoire Case (1768): Freedom of Conscience and the Role of the Jansenists," *Journal of Church and State* 27 (1985): 65–82.

70. On Malesherbes's constitutionalism, see Pierre Grosclaude, *Malesherbes, témoin et interprète de son temps* (Paris, 1961), pp. 55–60.

71. Pidansat de Mairobert, *Journal historique,* 1:75, 93, 113, 127, 248, 250, 265, 287.

72. Maultrot, Mey, et al., *Maximes du droit public françois,* 1:309–10, 317, 374; 2:84–89.

73. [André Blonde], *Le parlement justifié par l'impératrice de Russie,* pp. 119–20.

74. Robert Darnton, "Reading, Writing, and Publishing in Eighteenth-Century France: A Case Study of the Sociology of Literature," *Daedalus* (Winter 1971): 226–38; and Jeremy Popkin, "The Gazette de Leyde under Louis XVI," in *Press and Politics in Pre-Revolutionary France,* ed. Jack R. Censer and Jeremy Popkin (Berkeley, Los Angeles, and London, 1987), pp. 88–89.

75. Robert Darnton, "A Policeman Sorts His Files: The Anatomy of the Republic of Letters," in *The Great Cat Massacre and Other Episodes in French Cultural History* (New York, 1984), pp. 145–89.

76. BN, Anisson-Duperron Collection (henceforth A-D) 41, MSS Fr 22101, report dated May 27, 1772, folios 180–83.

77. On Boulemier, see AB 12,387, no. 173. Two sweeps through Normandy by d'Emery and Mutel in 1771 netted them a few printers of patriotic literature. But the person who stood behind these printers' activity, a former assistant to the attorney general of Brittany named Du Brossais de Peray, escaped with whatever interesting information he might have divulged. See BN,

A-D 41, MSS Fr 22101, fols. 70–71, 100–105; AB 12,392, nos. 73, 78–81, 93, 111, 140–41, 179.

78. AB 12,393, interrogations by Miché de Rochebrune at Bastille on March 30, 1771, nos. 99–100; summary of another interrogation, no. 101; and perquisition of his effects on March 2, 1771, no. 91.

79. The quotation is from a report by a police spy, or *mouche*, dated February 8, 1772, in AB 12,392, nos. 377–78; for basic information on this case, see ibid., 12,403, no. 221; BN, A-D 41, MSS Fr 22101, report of February 18, 1771, fol. 158; and Pidansat de Mairobert, *Journal historique*, September 15, 1771, 2:140–41.

80. AB 12,392, interrogation of Julie Danjean at Bastille by Hubert Mutel on September 21, 1771, no. 313.

81. BN, A-D 41, MSS Fr 22101, report dated September 19, 1989, fol. 160. On Dumont's or Vion's arrest and previous difficulties apropos of *Unigenitus*, see Hardy, "Mes loisirs," BN, MSS Fr 6680, September 19, 1771, p. 279.

82. BN, A-D 41, MSS Fr 22101, fols. 159–60. See also AB 12,392, d'Hémery to Sartine, September 19, 1772, no. 301; interrogation of Morin by Mutel at Bastille on September 23, 1771, nos. 318–19; and of Dumont or Vion by Mutel on September 24, 1771, nos. 321–22.

83. AB 12,403, d'Hémery to Sartine, June 10, 1772, nos. 48–50; while Kaufmann's declaration is dated July 10, 1772, no. 154. On Prestrelle and De La Roche, see BN, A-D 41, MSS Fr 22101, report of June 10–11, 1772, fols. 178–79; and Archives nationales (henceforth AN) X2b 1400, interrogation of Prestrelle family by Mutel on June 10, 16, 1771, and by Goezman on February 27, 1773; perquisition and interrogation of De La Roche by Mutel and d'Hémery on June 11, 1771; and perquisition and interrogation of Quiney brothers on June 10–11, 1771.

84. Quotation from Mecquignon's interrogation and confrontation with La Gueyrie by Jean Serreau on June 19–22, 1771, in AN X2b 1400. See also confrontation of François de Quiney with Mecquignon at Bastille on June 23, 1771.

85. The quotation from Mecquignon is from her *requête* to Maupeou's *parlement* of Paris in AB 12,403, no. 421. Mecquignon's sentence is in *Arrest de la cour de parlement, qui condamne différens particuliers au bannissement et au blâme, etc., pour avoir colporté et vendu différens libelles contre l'autorité du roi et l'honneur des magistrats. Du 29 janvier 1774* (Paris, 1774), p. 23, in NL, case wing folio oZ 144, .A1, vol. 8, no. 77. On Mecquignon's pardon and Archbishop of Paris, see Hardy, "Mes loisirs," MSS Fr 6682, January 29, February 11, 23, and March 9, 1774, pp. 280, 287, 297, 305 respectively. The archbishop's attitude toward this family as reported by Hardy is confirmed by a letter from that prelate dated June 17, 1772, in AB 12,403, no. 98.

86. On Sorin, see his interrogation at Bastille on August 9, 1771, in AB

12,387, no. 206; and on Desormeaux, AB 12,388, except from his interrogation, no. 42, and d'Hémery's report, September 16, 1771, no. 30. On Fleury, see interrogation by Goezman on February 26, 1773, in AN X2b 1400. See also BN, A-D 41, MSS Fr 22101, fols. 61, 146–47.

87. Quotation from Duclos's interrogation at Bastille on April 10, 1771, in AB 12,387, no. 209. On De La Brande, see ibid., his letter to Sartine and excerpt from his interrogation, nos. 213, 192. See also BN, A-D 41, MSS Fr 22101, fols. 145–46, 148.

88. Quotations from a letter by Moret dated June 23, 1772, in AB 12,403, no. 121, and letter from Receveur, June 17, 1772, nos. 85–86; and Moret's interrogation by Goezman in Conciergerie, February 27, 1773, in AN X2b 1400. Also relevant in AB 12,403 are nos. 41, 43, 46, 73, 88–89, 107, 112.

89. On this affair, see André Doyon, *Un agent royaliste pendant la Révolution: Pierre-Jacques Le Maître, 1790–1795* (Paris, 1969), pp. 1–37, which is in turn based on documents in AB 12,400, 12,402, 12,430, and 12,478. See also Pidansat de Mairobert, *Journal historique,* November 6, 19, 26, and 28, 1772, pp. 333–34, 350–51, 375, 410 respectively; and Hardy, "Mes loisirs," BN, MSS Fr 6681, December 2, 1772, p. 120.

90. La Gueyrie's account book as a colporteur along with the numbers of the *Nouvelles ecclésiastiques* confiscated from both him and the colporteur Le Sage are in AN X2b 1400. The quotation about La Gueyrie as Jansenist is from a letter by Serreau to Sartine dated June 3, 1772, in AB 12,403, no. 39. See also Pidansat de Mairobert, *Journal historique,* October 27, 1772, 2: 319; and Hardy, "Mes loisirs," BN, MSS Fr 6681, October 20, 1772, p. 107.

91. This list of seized books, along with the interrogations of the *garçons* Veille and Lamare by Goezman on February 22–23, 1773, are in AN X2b 1400. See also Hardy, "Mes loisirs," MSS Fr 6681, October 26, 1772, p. 107.

92. The interrogations of Imbert by Rochebrune in Bastille on December 10, 1772, are in AB 12,400, nos. 94–97; and by Goezman in Conciergerie on February 20 and following days, 1773, in AN X2b 1400. For the inventory of Imbert's papers and books, and the letter from Rolland de Challerange to Archier, dated July 29, 1771, at Etampes, see AN X2b 1400.

93. D'Hémery's description of François de Quiney is in BN A-D 41, MSS Fr 22101, report of June 10–11, 1772, fols. 178–79. The prisoner's letter to Sartine, dated September 1772, is in AB 12,403, no. 286.

94. *Supplément à la Gazette de France,* August 16, 1772, in *Les efforts,* p. 152.

95. Hardy, "Mes loisirs," MSS Fr 6680, April 24, 1771, p. 253; and 6681, February 20, 1772, p. 24.

96. Ibid., 6681, May 14, 1772, p. 59.

97. Ibid. For Bouillerot, Oct. 3, 1772, p. 106; February 27, 1773, p. 162; for Gardane, April 7, 16, 1773, pp. 180, 182; for Dumoulin, July 30 and August 12, 1773, pp. 213, 217; and for Colas, February 15, 27, 1773, pp. 291–92.

98. *Nouvelles ecclésiastiques,* March 7, 1774, pp. 37–38; and Hardy, "Mes loisirs," BN, MSS Fr 6681, March 10, 1771, p. 310.

99. On this incident in the small town in Brie-Comte-Robert, see Hardy, "Mes loisirs," BN, MSS Fr 6681, April 10, 1772, p. 46; and BPR, LP 570, no. 262, p. 1. Quotation from *Nouvelles ecclésiastiques,* March 7, 1774, pp. 37.

100. Hardy, "Mes loisirs," BN, MSS Fr 6681, February 22, 1774, pp. 296–97.

101. BN, Collection Joly de Fleury (henceforth JF) 1569, fols. 306–14; and *Arrest de la cour de parlement. Extrait des registres du parlement. Du 17 janvier 1759* (Paris, 1759).

102. *Déclaration du roi, portant rappel des prêtres décrétés ou bannis. Donné à Marly le 15 juin 1771. Registre au parlement le 19 juin 1771,* in BPR, LP 570, no. 262. See also Pidansat de Mairobert, *Journal historique,* June 27, 1771, 1:373. On De L'Ecluse's appointment, see Hardy, "Mes loisirs," BN MSS Fr 6681, September 6, 1772, p. 94.

103. On Madier or Madrier, see Hardy, "Mes souvenirs," BN, MSS Fr 6680, October 3, 1771, p. 281; on Dubertrand, 6681, April 6, 1772, p. 45 and February 15, 1773, p. 291; on Perin or Perrin, January 1, 1774, p. 269. On these ecclesiatics' previous scrapes with the law, see BN, JF 1487, fol. 288 for Madier or Madrier; ibid., 1569, fols. 306–14, for Dubertrand; and *Nouvelles ecclésiastiques,* September 25, 1757, pp. 158–60, for Perin or Perrin.

104. Hardy, "Mes souvenirs," BN, MSS Fr 6681, May 8, 1772, p. 57.

105. Ibid., 6680, July 9, 1771, 262; December 29, p. 299; and 6681, Sept. 13, 1773, pp. 227–28; October 20, 1773, p. 236; and Pidansat de Mairobert, *Journal historique,* February 6 and 10, 1772, 2:369, 373–74.

106. Hardy, "Mes souvenirs," BN MSS Fr 6681, September 8, 1773, p. 226; and Lucien Laugier, *Un ministre réformateur sous Louis XV: le triumvirat, 1770–1774* (Paris, 1975), pp. 485–86.

107. Hardy, "Mes loisirs," BN, MSS Fr 6681: on Saint-Roch, January 10, 1772, p. 141; on Saint-Médard, May 1, 1772, p. 55; and on Saint-André-des-Arts, June 28, 1772, p. 76.

108. Ibid., 6680: on Carmelite convent sermon, October 7, 1771, p. 281; on Collège Mazarin sermon, December 12, 1771, pp. 296–97.

109. Ibid., 6680, September 2, 1771, p. 275, for Hazon affair; and 6681, December 1, 1772, p. 119, and March 14, 1773, pp. 169–70, for Xaupi affair. On Hazon affair, see also the printed *Arrest du Conseil du roi. Du 18 aoust 1771. Extrait des registres du Conseil du roi* (Paris, 1771) in BN, A-D 41, MSS Fr 22101, fol. 151.

110. Hardy, "Mes loisirs," BN, MSS Fr 6681, November 7, 11, 24, and 29, 1773, pp. 243, 244–45, 250, 253 respectively; January 26 and February 25, 1774, pp. 278–79, 298. See also the printed *Arrest de la cour du parlement. . . . Du 25 février 1774* (Paris, 1774), in NL, case wing folio oZ 144, .A1, vol. 8, no. 82.

111. Hardy, "Mes loisirs," BN, MSS Fr 6681, February 4, 1771, p. 65.
112. A good book on the eighteenth-century *parti dévôt* remains to be written. For lack of anything better, see Van Kley, *The Damiens Affair,* pp. 60–65, 196–200, 213–19. See pp. 3–96 for the story of Damiens's attack on Louis XV and the politicization of his trial.
113. On Abbé Marie, see Michaud, *Biographie universelle,* 26:648–49; and on Pierre Bouquet, Jacob-Nicolas Moreau, *Mes souvenirs,* ed. Camille Hermelin, 2 vols. (Paris, 1898), 1:176–77. Le Paige attributed the following pamphlets to Marie: *Considérations sur l'édit de décembre 1770* (BPR, LP 804, no. 7) and *Observations sur l'écrit intitulé: Protestations des princes* (LP 569, no. 190).
114. On Linguet, see Darlene Gay Levy, *The Ideas and Careers of Simon-Nicolas-Henri Linguet: A Study in Eighteenth-Century French Politics* (Urbana, Chicago, and London, 1980), esp. pp. 8–16; and on Moreau, his *Mes souvenirs,* esp. 1:1–12, 286–330; and Dieter Gembicki, *Histoire et politique à la fin de l'ancien régime: Jacob-Nicolas Moreau, 1717–1803* (Paris, n.d.). Le Paige attributed the following pamphlets to Linguet: *Réflexions d'un citoyen sur l'édit de décembre* (BPR, LP 804, no. 8); *Nouvelles réflexions d'un citoyen sur l'édit de décembre* (ibid., no. 9); *Remontrances d'un citoyen aux parlemens de France* (ibid., no. 11); and less certainly the *Réponse d'un citoyen qui a publié ses réflexions* (ibid., no. 10). In addition, it is all but certain that he published a *Recherches sur les Etats-géneraux* (n.p., n.d.), which was republished in 1788. Contemporaries also frequently pointed to the former president of the Parlement of Toulouse, François de Bastard, as the author of pro-Maupeou pamphlets, but unfortunately they pointed to no titles in particular.
115. *Visions et révélations d'un ci-devant* (n.p., n.d.), pp. 1–2, in BPR, LP 810, no. 2; *Entrétien d'un ancien magistrat et d'un abbé, sur le discours de M. Séquier, au lit de justice du 13 avril 1771* (n.p., n.d.), p. 32, in NL, case FRC 3670; and [Simon-Henri Linguet], *Remontrances d'un citoyen aux parlemens de France,* pp. 12–14.
116. [Linguet], *Remontrances d'un citoyen aux parlements de France,* 12–14; and *La fin mot de l'affaire* (n.p., n.d.), pp. 19–20.
117. Ibid., pp. 16–18; and *La tête leur tourne* (n.p., n.d.), pp. 3–4, in BPR, LP 810, no. 8.
118. Charles, marquis de Villette is credited with the authorship of the following pamphlets: *Réflexions du maître perruquier sur les affaires de l'état* (n.p., n.d.); *Lettre d'un maître perruquier à M. le procureur-général, concernant les magistrats de Rouen, et les dames de Paris* (n.p., n.d.); *Le soufflet du maître perruquier à sa femme* (n.p., n.d.); and *Le coup de peigne du maître perruquier, ou nouvel entrétien du maître perruquier avec sa femme* (n.p., n.d.), all in BPR, LP 810, nos. 16–19, On Villette himself and these attributions, see Michaud, *Biographie universelle,* 43:515–16.
119. *Le soufflet du maître perruquier,* pp. 26–27, in BPR, LP 810, no. 19.

120. The "monstrous hereditary aristocracy" comes from [Linguet], *Réflexions d'un citoyen sur l'édit de décembre*, pp. 16–17, while the complaints about a "gothic style" and the magistracy's "particular interest" come respectively from the *Réflexions d'un vieux patriote sur les affaires présentes* (n.p., n.d.), pp. 21–23; and Voltaire's *Sentiments des six conseils établis par le roi et de tous les bons citoyens*, in *Oeuvres complètes*, 28:399. On d'Argenson and Saint-Pierre, see Nannerl O. Keohane, *Philosophy and the State in France: The Renaissance to the Enlightenment* (Princeton, N.J., 1980), pp. 361–391.

121. *La tête leur tourne*, pp. 17–18; and *Réflexions d'un maître perruquier sur les affaires de l'état*, p. 14.

122. See for example [Linguet], *Réflexions d'un citoyen sur l'édit de décembre 1770*, pp. 6–7; and *Remontrances d'un citoyen aux parlemens*, pp. 29–31.

123. Harold Ellis, *Boulainvilliers and the French Monarchy: Aristocratic Politics in Early Eighteenth-Century France* (Ithaca, N.Y., 1988), pp. 31–39. See also J. Q. C. Mackrell, *The Attack on "Feudalism" in Eighteenth-Century France* (London and Toronto, 1988), pp. 17–47.

124. [Lafiteau, Bishop of Sisteron], *Entrétiens d'Anselme et d'Isidore sur les affaires du temps* (France, 1756), pp. 108–9; and [Abbé Bertrand Capmartin de Chaupy], *Observations sur le refus que fait le Châtelet de reconnoître la Chambre royale* (France, 1754), pp. 73–74. See also Van Kley, *The Damiens Affair*, pp. 194–98.

125. *La fin mot de l'affaire*, p. 19; *Lettre de M.D.L.V. avocat au parlement* (n.p., n.d.), pp. 5, 39–40, in LP 804, no. 13; and Voltaire, *Avis important d'un gentilhomme à toute la noblesse du royaume* (1771), in *Oeuvres complètes*, 28: 393–95.

126. These references are, in order, from [Villette], *Le Soufflet du maître perruquier à sa femme*, p. 14; *Les bons citoyens, ou lettres des sénat-graphs, écrits par des gens respectables* (Rouen, 1771), pp. 5–6, in BPR, LP 810, no. 26; *Réponse à la lettre d'un magistrat à un duc et pair, sur le discours de M. le chancelier au lit de justice, du 7 décembre 1770* (n.p., n.d.), p. 10, in BPR, LP 804, no. 6.

127. *La tête leur tourne*, pp. 14–15.

128. Loyseau's formula is invoked in [Marie], *Considérations sur l'édit de décembre 1770*, p. 58; and *Examen analytique et raisonné d'un écrit qui a pour titre: Protestations des princes du sang* (n.p., n.d.), in BPR, LP 814, no. 18. For an ingeniously "patriotic" exegesis of the formula see Mey, *Maximes du droit public françois*, 2:115.

129. Van Kley, *The Damiens Affair*, pp. 194–98, 211–19; and *The Jansenists and the Expulsion of the Jesuits from France*, pp. 137–62.

130. Echeverria, *The Maupeou Revolution*, pp. 125–77. See, for example, *La tête leur tourne*, p. 14; or *Réflexions d'un maître perruquier sur les affaires de l'état*, pp. 14–16. Patriot constitutionalism also contributed to the obliteration of Bossuet's distinction by equating "absolute" with "arbitrary" or "despotic," as [Linguet's] *Nouvelles réflexions d'un citoyen sur l'édit de décembre 1770* perceptively observed at the time, p. 29.

131. This already began to happen in 1775 with the publication of Guillaume Saige's *Catéchisme du citoyen*, which effectively endowed elements of patriot constitutionalism with a Rousseauean political will. See Keith M. Baker, "French Political Thought at the Accession of Louis XVI," *Journal of Modern History*, 50 (June 1978): 279–303.

132. [Linguet], *Remontrances d'un citoyen aux parlemens de France*, pp. 20, 42–43.

133. *Réponse de H[enri] le Grand aux remontrances des parlemens* (n.p., n.d.), pp. 4–5, in BPR, LP 810, no. 7.

134. [Linguet], *Remontrances d'un citoyen aux parlemens de France*, pp. 20, 42–43; *Réponse de H[enri] le Grand aux remontrances des parlemens* (n.p., n.d), pp. 4–5, in BPR, LP 810, no. 7; and *Lettre de M.D.L.V. avocat au parlement*, p. 34.

135. [Marie], *Observations sur un écrit intitulé: Protestations des princes*, pp. 12–13.

136. *Lettre d'un avocat de Paris aux magistrats du parlement de Rouen, au sujet de l'arrêt de cette cour, du 15 avril 1771*, p. 14, in BPR, LP 810, no. 4. See also [Marie], *Considérations sur l'édit de décembre 1770*, pp. 62–65.

137. On Moreau's effort to build an archival arsenal in defense of the monarchy, see Keith Michael Baker, "Controlling French History: The Ideological Arsenal of Jacob-Nicolas Moreau," in *Inventing the French Revolution: Essays on Political Culture in the Eighteenth Century* (Cambridge, 1989), pp. 59–85.

138. This account of Hardouin's and Berruyer's apologetical efforts on behalf of "tradition" is dependent upon Robert R. Palmer's classic *Catholics and Unbelievers in Eighteenth-Century France* (Princeton, N.J., 1947), pp. 65–76. The *Nouvelles ecclésiastiques* devoted a special issue to Berruyer—and to the Bishop of Soisson's "pastoral" refutation of Berruyer's *Histoire du peuple de dieu*—on March 19, 1760, pp. 49–64, but other numbers of the clandestine journal are peppered with pejorative references to the Hardouin-Berruyer duo.

139. Pierre Bouquet, *Lettres provinciales ou examen impartial de l'origine, de la constitution, et des révolutions de la monarchie française. Par un avocat de province à un avocat de Paris* (La Haye: "chez Le Neutre, à l'enseigne de la Bonne Foi," 1772). The title is almost certainly a satirical reference to Pascal's *Lettres provinciales*, as the supposed publisher and his ensign are a satirical reference to Butard's Jansenist printshop-bookstore "at the ensign of the Truth" on the rue Saint-Jacques. In his copy of the book, (BPR, LP 812, no. 2) Le Paige noted that Bouquet was an "éleve tonsuré," by which he probably meant that Bouquet was a tonsured graduate of a Jesuit college.

140. Pidansat de Mairobert, *Journal historique*, December 10, 12, 1772, 3:384–85, 390.

141. On this book, I am dependent on an untitled and unpublished paper presented by D. Carroll Joynes at the meeting of the American Historical Association in Chicago, December 1986.

142. *Arrêt du Conseil d'état du roi, qui supprime un imprimé qui a pour titre: Lettres provinciales. Du 28 novembre 1772. Extrait des registres du Conseil d'état* (Paris, 1772), in BN, A-D 41, MSS Fr 22100, no. 184.

143. On this subject see Jeremy Popkin and Dale Van Kley, "The Pre-Revolutionary Debate: An Introductory Essay for the French Revolutionary Research Collection," in Popkin and Van Kley, eds., *The Pre-Revolutionary Debate,* section 5 of *The French Revolution Research Collection,* ed. Colin Lucas (Oxford, 1989), pp. 1–40, as well as Van Kley, "The Jansenist Constitutional Legacy in the French Prerevolution, 1750–1789," and "The Estates General as Ecumenical Council: The Constitutionalism of Corporate Consensus and the *Parlement*'s Ruling of September 25, 1788," *Journal of Modern History* 61 (March 1989): 1–52.

144. These theses are argued in greater detail in the works cited in n. 143, as well as in Van Kley, "The Jansenist Constitutional Legacy in the French Prerevolution;" and "The Estates General as Ecumenical Council: The Constitutionalism of Corporate Consensus and the *Parlement*'s Ruling of September 25, 1788." They are also indebted in various ways to the work of Keith M. Baker, in particular the article "Firing the French Constitution" in *Inventing the French Revolution,* pp. 252–305.

145. Developing this aspect of revolutionary political culture will eventually mean picking up some suggestions left dangling by Edgar Quinet in his *La Révolution,* 2 vols. (Paris, 1869), 1:124–92, 2:132–80, 2:583–95.

6

The End of Religious Establishment and the Beginning of Religious Politics: Church and State in the United States

R. Laurence Moore

The relationship between religion and politics is a perplexing subject. Even brief reflections about historical experience leave us dazed by the various patterns of conflict and accommodation that have marked the interaction between those who have ruled churches and those who have ruled states. The one thing that these historical figures have rarely done, although the formula has been often enough prescribed, is to leave one another alone.

The United States was supposed to have learned something from the turmoil of the European past and to have written a Constitution that took politics out of religion and religion out of politics. Yet what emerged was not a clear division but new patterns of church/state interaction that over time have baffled everyone, not least the members of the nation's Supreme Court.[1] Although the First Amendment to the Constitution banned a national establishment of religion, although Thomas Jefferson recommended a wall of separation between church and state, and although most states enforced a purported separation of church and state long before the Constitution's proscription was formally applied to them in the 1940s, religion and politics in America have remained closely related.[2]

In fact their association might at present be stronger than if in the beginning a state church had been given a legally defined public role. That possibility is suggested by the situation that exists in some other countries. For example, although England maintains a costly church establishment and assigns to a few bishops a privileged presence in the House of Lords, prime ministers and MPs can nod off during the occasions of ceremonial piety they are obligated to attend and otherwise ignore religion. Not having the benefit of anointed state guardians who look after "the" church, American politicians frequently are forced into assuming something close to that role.

Some observers of the American scene noticed the paradox very early in the nation's history. The critical importance of religion to public life was already obvious by the time Alexis de Tocqueville visited the United States.[3] Europeans do not encounter in America their own various patterns of church/state interaction. Nonetheless what they find is in their view a ubiquitous public presence of religion, in decidedly lowbrow forms, that carries astonishing influence over the ways in which American governments and politicians behave. Protestant evangelists have no monarchs to bless, but the cozy company they have kept with presidents in recent times is a fact suggestive of both symbolic and actual power.[4] Catholic bishops get little public money for their schools, but the votes they can influence make congressmen in their districts extremely eager to please them.[5]

The commonplace intersections between religion and politics in the United States can be demonstrated in a number of different ways. In the first place, organized churches have acted in the past and in the present as political lobbies, taking stands on everything from the abolition of slavery to nuclear disarmament.[6] Under present laws they could lose their tax exempt status for such activity, but that isn't likely. In becoming politically active, they have sometimes reconstituted themselves as ecumenical organizations or what Robert Wuthnow has termed "special purpose groups."[7] The Federal (later National) Council of Churches, which was founded in 1908, has spoken out on social issues in ways that have promoted specific and usually liberal pieces of legislation. Temperance and Sabbatarian groups created broad and well-financed organizational networks in the nineteenth century to exert political pressure, and Jerry Falwell's Moral Majority more recently made the tradition of religious partisanship popular among conservative voting blocs.[8] Religious leaders have noisily linked themselves to political action groups, and they have sometimes run for and been elected to political office. Since they are constitutionally presumed not to form a religious establishment (such a thing is after all banned), they have in the name of religious liberty (the other half of the First Amendment's religious clause) enjoyed considerable leeway in the practice of religious politics.[9]

The overt linkage between churches and politics can easily be described in historical narrative. There are many examples. A more difficult sort of analysis relates to the ways in which the culturally diffused presence of religion affects public life in the United States. Polls about religious observance and belief in various countries are difficult to interpret. Nonetheless, the majority of them do indicate that Americans are more regular in church attendance, assign religion more importance in their lives, and believe more strongly in biblical authority than most Europeans. Take, for example, a question regularly asked by international pollsters: How important is religion to your life? In a comparative survey published a decade ago 58 percent of Americans replied "very important," and only 12 percent said "not too much" or "not at all." Judged by responses to this question, Italians are the most religious Western Europeans. Yet only 36 percent of them named religion as a "very important" personal force, and 22 percent, twice the figure for Americans, consigned it to one of the categories of insignificance.[10]

These differentials between Europe and the United States were already clear by the end of the nineteenth century and were especially marked in urban working classes.[11] Among immigrant Americans, religious labels were the quickest ways to summarize and to contest cultural differences. An ethnic cohesiveness linked to religion, rather than collective class action, became the preferred strategy for survival among workers. Since they faced no state religion that could be identified with rulers, exploiters, or oppressors, they never grew as antagonistic toward religion as their counterparts in Europe. And although many of these immigrant workers who were Catholic found an enemy in a generic American Protestantism, that encounter only served to make them more Catholic, in the Irish, Polish, and Italian cases perhaps more Catholic than they had been in their homelands.[12]

To find countries that are statistically more religious than the United States, one must turn to much less economically developed areas of the world, to Latin America and to parts of Africa and Asia. The United States is one of the few highly industrialized countries where churches are generally attended for things other than baptisms, weddings, and burials. Yet the high level of popular piety depends neither upon an established church nor upon any unusually high social status accorded to religious institutions or to clerics as quasi-public officials. Churches and clerics have struggled to hold their own in American life since the early days of the republic. They have largely succeeded, but their relative authority in public life has doubtlessly declined over the *longue durée* along with the theological and biblical literacy of the American people.

This last fact suggests that the role played by American clergy in

American politics is a manifestation of, rather than the main reason for, religious and political entanglement in the United States. It also suggests that religion's impact upon political attitudes and behavior cannot always be traced to the work of ecclesiastic institutions. Peter Berger, Thomas Luckmann, John Wilson, Gerhard Lenski, and other sociologists of religion have helped us understand why studying churches does not exhaust the subject of the influence of religion.[13] Even without the contributions of sociology, the religious roots of many American political utterances were obvious. So were the millennial assumptions that underlay the American sense of national mission.[14] Robert Bellah has justly called our attention to a blurring of secular and sacred in American public rhetoric. Whether his use of the term "civil religion" can withstand critical scrutiny has been the subject of much debate.[15] But at the very least it seems true that conceptions of American nationhood, ritually trotted out to justify whatever policies American politicians want to sanctify, have purposefully blended the claim of popular origins with the claim of divine origins. Americans established no church, merely a nation under God.

Doubtlessly, one of the most persuasive demonstrations of how "invisible" or quasi-institutional forces of religion have affected American politics has come from what we used to call the "new" political historians. Their quantified correlations between religious identification and political affiliation have passed from novel into standard interpretation. The attitude of a nineteenth-century American male toward Catholics was as important as his attitude toward slavery in determining his party affiliation on the eve of the Civil War. The United States never developed religiously based political parties just as it never developed class-based political parties. Nonetheless, religious affiliation was part of the equation determining how people distinguished their political allies from their political enemies. From the Civil War until the relatively recent present, most northern white Protestants voted for the Republican party. For much of this century white southern Protestants (and black ones as well, once they could vote) joined with Catholics and Jews to form the electoral base of the Democratic party.[16] Theological differentiations had little to do with the political differentiations. What mattered was the general cultural outlook of religious groups, as well as their place in the social hierarchy.

The various facts that we have been summarizing are generally well understood and certainly much discussed. Commonly these discussions, when carried on in the context of contemporary politics, contain overtones of judgment. The influence of religion on political life is deemed by some as a baleful one, an anachronism that somehow was never properly excised, and by others as exactly what the founders wanted. From the first quarter we hear calls for a higher and thicker wall of the sort proposed by Jefferson; and from the second we hear alarmed complaints about "the naked public square."[17]

Whatever the wisdom of excluding religion from the political realm, we must pose the question of whether any strict and complete exclusion is possible. Arguably, religious and moral concerns are inseparable from the sorts of political issues that get a democratic people excited. American citizens may vote their pocketbooks, but it often takes something else to get them to work for a candidate, to contribute money to someone's campaign, and even to vote. The issues surrounding slavery once excited political activism. So did the pros and cons of temperance. Contemporary American politics will not soon escape from the passions that are stirred when policy issues get tied to debates about divinity and national destiny, about the moral sanctity of the family, or about the teaching of religion in the public schools. For the moment what presidential candidates say about God in the Pledge of Allegiance and about abortion may well be the most important stands that they take in an election because for many voters they serve as symbols of particular moral universes.

The Party Spirit of the Antebellum Religious Revivals

The line of argument pursued in this article is intended to get beyond specific issues where the moral interests of Americans have affected political campaigns. George Washington's "Farewell Address" included the remonstrance: "Of all the dispositions and habits which lead to political prosperity, Religion and morality are indispensable supports." The insertion of that thought into American political rhetoric was extremely important, but the consequences have been sufficiently noted. What requires further analysis are the cultural and social patterns, the structures of practice and experience that join religion and politics in the United States no matter what the Constitution says.

In beginning this discussion the most important thing to note is that, as forms of mass behavior, religion and politics during the period before the Civil War developed almost identical ways of organizing and motivating people. The work done by Ronald Formisano and Paul Kleppner on the origins of national parties in the United States is especially helpful on this point.[18] Despite early battles fought between Federalists and Jeffersonians, permanent party organizations were solidly institutionalized in the United States only after the mid-1830s. The first such parties in the world, they were in part the outcome of a unique political situation in which white males enjoyed close to universal suffrage. However, since most American males could vote well before they became strongly committed to party allegiances, and since the framers of the Constitution not only had made no provision for parties but had viewed them with distaste, we need to consider additional factors that facilitated the appearance of national parties during the Jacksonian era. One set of factors, which both Formisano and Kleppner single out, were the transformations wrought by the tumultuous religious revivals of the early nineteenth century, especially those that shook communities all over the United States in the 1820s and 1830s.

We must consider not only what the revivals in fact accomplished, but also what their sponsors and their equally vocal detractors thought they accomplished. Historians have made a number of claims, usually drawing distinctions between the controlled renewals of spiritual life sponsored by many churches in New England and the extreme religious enthusiasm drummed into sinners by Baptist and Methodist preachers who relentlessly pursued Americans as they moved west. Some years ago Donald Mathews made the most challenging suggestion for interpreting the revivals, which are collectively known as the Second Great Awakening. Despite the different styles of revival ministry, the Awakening "in its social aspects was an organizing process that helped to give meaning and direction to people suffering in various degrees from the social strains of a nation on the move into new political, economic and geographical areas."[19] The revivals put people into churches, provided them with a sense of continuity with the past, and shaped a sense of responsibility toward rapidly growing and changing communities.

The association of the revivals with organization, or order, was a remarkably provocative claim, because it seemed to underestimate a consequence that had been more commonly stressed. The revival spirit divided. In fact, according to revivalism's many opponents, it encouraged the total breakdown of religious unity, a possibility already feared because of the ending of tax support for religion. The argument went as follows. Churches, forced to cast about as best they could for voluntary contributions, entered into a destructive and disorderly competition with one another. They used the revivals to build membership, but in encouraging emotional license among would-be adherents, they lost control over how the spoken and written word was interpreted. Revivals shattered authoritative interpretation of Scripture and inaugurated an age of religious hucksterism and charlatanism. Joseph Smith, William Miller, the Fox sisters, Andrew Jackson Davis, and John Humphrey Noyes were only some of the regrettable products of the contentious spirit fed by uncontrolled religious enthusiasm. Excess was the specter haunting antebellum America, and the revivals were its cause.

The three decades from 1830 to 1850 did constitute an antinomian moment for America's religious communities. To be sure, the surging number of religious people who followed new dispensations, new authoritative scripture, new inward sources of prophetic power, and new laws were not all products of revival fever. The revivals were themselves only one manifestation of a more general questing for a firm basis of religious authority, something destroyed before the revivals had begun. Yet revivals embodied the potentially anarchic side of the religious quest more dramatically than anything else. They were responsible for breakdowns in habits of deference simply because they indicated that people's spiritual lives, including the lives of many who represented the learned ministry, were woefully impoverished. We have considerable evidence of revival meetings that disrupted, however briefly, the normal hierarchies of respect based on age, social rank, and gender.[20]

Seemingly, then, two broad interpretations of the revivals compete with each other. One stresses order and organization, and the other, chaos and fragmentation. Both notions are essential to an explanation of what happened. The First Amendment, both in prohibiting a national religious establishment and in guaranteeing a legal legitimacy to virtually any religious claim, encouraged a greater multiplicity of sects than had existed during the colonial period. People with different social and economic rankings, with different attitudes toward moral codes, with different ethnic and historical memories, with different plans for social advancement, institutionalized and widened their differences in the churches they chose to create and join. In the first several decades of the nineteenth century religious organizations, more than any other local institutions and sometimes in the absence of other possibilities, served to encode people's sense of distinctiveness and to cover that distinctiveness with a plausible claim of respectability.

However (and here we may appreciate the shrewdness of Donald Mathew's analysis), division in any complex society is an essential characteristic of organization. People must sort themselves out before they can live together. For that reason, the fact of religious splintering should occasion no surprise. Something like it had to take place to make sense of America's heterogeneous population. What should surprise us is the relatively low level of violence that went along with the differentiation. Not everything happened in a peaceful way. The destructive outrage that was directed against Mormons and Irish Catholics in the nineteenth century was one marked characteristic of American religious development. The price that any society pays for taking religious matters seriously is religious conflict. The only exception to note about the United States is that religious dogma contributed only moderately and usually indirectly to the high level of violence that characterized the social and economic transformations of the nineteenth century.[21] Always, of course, our measures are relative ones.

The revivals worked simultaneously in two directions. They divided antebellum Americans. They encouraged exuberant behavior that tempted women and men to cut ties with past loyalties, with friends, with communities, and sometimes with family. Old sources of authority crumbled. The habit of extending deference to church officials weakened. At the same time, the revivals softened and contained some of the very differences that they institutionalized. Churches of different denominations established codes of respectable behavior, relating both to private and to public conduct, that influenced not only members of newly emerging middle classes but also the "free" workers whom they hired for wages.[22] Men and women with different denominational loyalties settled into communities with a strong sense that the religion of their neighbors, however wrong, was best left in peace. The revivals in fact diluted many doctrinal differences that had split America's oldest Protestant denominations. The dilution did not mean that those old denominations moved toward unification or that new differences concerning values and lifestyles did not replace the old ones. It only meant that the revivals helped to establish a national framework for religious controversies, normalizing and to some extent defusing quarrels by turning them into well-publicized "media" events. For the most part, the nation's judicial structures had no role to play in mediating these controversies. Politics did.

Insofar as revivals were important to social organization, they were, broadly speaking, instruments of social control. Although the enthusiastic religious seekers who attended revivals seized the responsibility for their own salvation, the headiness of that arrogant act against Calvin's God was subsequently weighted down by the self-imposed burden of proving that they were free of sin. The God of Calvin, hard taskmaster that he was, had at least not expected his creatures to demonstrate genuine worthiness. Although antebellum Americans proved to the satisfaction of their own and subsequent generations that they were not up to the challenge of moral perfection, the revivals, as the first mass movement to sweep the young republic after the Revolutionary War, provided one set of symbols and standards to which Americans could rally. By the opposition they aroused, they also suggested other standards. But again the clarification of demarcation lines was essential to social organization – and to politics. The first enduring political party system in the United States was influenced by divisions between those who were willing to use legislation to enforce Christian cultural norms and those who opposed Christian legislation. On the latter side, except in the South, were fewer partisans of revivalism.

The effects of revivalism were not serendipitous. They were precisely what their sponsors had intended. The revivals signified that many religious leaders in the United States no longer viewed their sole task as nurturing stable congregations of God's most easily visible saints. Among Protestant Christians, missionary work emerged as an important vocation that was encouraged by both the communications and the transportation revolution of the early nineteenth century. The ministers and laypersons who organized the American Bible Society and the American Tract Society were not necessarily favorably disposed toward the "excessive" emotional behavior associated with some revivals. But they shared with revivalists an imperative: they had to evangelize people who had not yet been touched by the word of God. The Bible and Tract societies, which began in England, represented an enormous undertaking – an enterprise of producing and distributing cheap print material on a scale that had no precedent in the history of popular culture. For example, in the single year 1829 the American Bible Society printed 344,500 volumes and the American Tract Society, over six million.[23]

According to one historian, the American Bible and Tract societies created mass media in this country, pointing the way to innovations adopted in the 1830s by the penny press and large publishing houses.[24] Their work lay important groundwork for all mass movements, including political ones. It amounted to a vast publicity campaign directed at dispersed, anonymous audiences. A large success was claimed for their methods. Idle men picked up a stray tract thrown carelessly from the window of a stagecoach and found their way to Christ. Drunkards tippling in barrooms staggered home with a Bible that had been stuffed into their pockets, and "chose" salvation after reading through it in the sober hours of the next morning. We may be certain that many of these published claims were spurious. No matter. The technology and the distribution networks that made possible the creation of mass audiences stimulated alert entrepreneurs who concluded that personal contact was neither necessary nor even particularly useful in efforts to affect people's behavior. The trail opened by this discovery led eventually to Madison Avenue.

Agents of evangelism were experimenting with a possibly dangerous means of persuasion. They were trying to reach people whom they did not know, using simple and sometimes sensational printed messages. The point of these messages might appear obvious to present-day readers. Nonetheless, their creators had abdicated any direct control over how these moral homilies might be understood by casual readers. They would not have risked these anonymous crusades had they seen alternative ways to order a society of free people who were daily scattering themselves over a larger and larger geographical territory. Evangelists addressed themselves to the problem of how to maintain some central focus in a society that had no state mechanisms to protect the ideal of Christian unity. They glimpsed the troubling problems that might result in a pluralistic society of people who were forever on the road and tried to render a mass audience tractable by relying on the "self-evident" moral appeal of a "practical" Christianity.[25]

Revival preachers, who helped to create receptive audiences for mass-produced Bibles and tracts, did not abandon face-to-face persuasive techniques. But they sought to add new skills to clerical performance. They felt compelled to invent tactics that were considerably more impersonal than those that are summed up by the agrarian image of a clerical pastor tending his closely quartered sheep. They had to adjust to transience, both their own transience as they moved from community to community and that of their far-straying flocks. It is true that many revivals retained the aura of family affairs. That is, they were judged successful not by the number of new members swept into the church but by the degree of renewed faith shown by those who had long been part of the congregation. However, because of the migratory habits of antebellum Americans, preachers had to reach out to many people who had no secure social moorings, strangers who did not belong to a church and who were on their way from one place to another place.

In addressing an unsettled population, using unsettled credentials and unsettled methods, revival preachers were bound to gain a reputation from their critics as rabble-rousers. Not only were their highly publicized results viewed by many as ephemeral, but their methods for stirring emotion also, it was charged, encouraged the worst effects of social disruption. Whatever the criticism, the revival preachers had a rather different interpretation of their influence. Charles Grandison Finney, who became the most famous of them all, was as intensely concerned with the maintenance of order as any of his detractors. He was a close calculator of the effects of his preaching on crowd behavior. He employed novel methods, but made them systematic. He played to emotion, but in controlled ways.[26]

The attitude of revival preachers can be gleaned from some of the published manuals devoted to the subjects of effective preaching and the organization of revival camp meetings. (The latter was associated primarily but not exclusively with Methodism.) Many small books, which began to appear in the mid-1820s, recommended spontaneous and emotional preaching as necessary for stirring revivals. However, a reading of these books suggests that the talent for spontaneous and emotional oratory was not inbred but a learned technique. Revival preaching was a calculated method of oral performance, not the unconscious spouting of spiritual inspiration. Preachers had to work hard and carefully to achieve the desired effect of goading their listeners to choose salvation. Among other things, according to Reverend Calvin Colton, they must "endeavor to ascertain generally and particularly, as far as possible, the character and temper of the community. . . . And when they address the public mind in mass, they seek to make a particular impression, and they watch and cultivate that impression, both in public and in private."[27] Inspired messages could not by themselves alter behavior. To control a crowd, one had first of all to become a crowd psychologist.

Finney himself had a great deal to say about effective preaching. To the charge that the revivals encouraged an "unphilosophical" excitement, he answered that religious excitements were essential to counter much more dangerous worldly excitements unfriendly to religion. Ministers had to think about what they had to do to attract hearers, because "secular performers" were competing for their audiences. Good preaching, he argued, had to become theatrical. It also had to pay attention to the "conversational" style of the lawyer. "The minister ought to do as the lawyer does when he wants to make a jury understand him perfectly. He uses a style perfectly colloquial. It must be the language of common life and must rely on illustration."[28] The similarity between the style and intention of this sort of oratory and that of the political oratory of Jacksonian America requires at this point only passing notice.

In short the advice books written to instruct revival preachers constituted a law and order literature. Audiences had to be stirred because unless a preacher commanded their attention he had no way to control them. Since good sermon material was abundant, what was said almost mattered less than how it was said. The method of delivery could not be plagiarized. It had to be mastered. Beyond questions of speaking strategies, the ways in which a crowd was primed to receive a message were also important. Finney did not merely arrive in a town, announce a meeting for the same evening, and depend upon the force of his personality to win over a crowd of strangers. Local churches advertised his visits, and what his audiences heard from Finney was in considerable part what they had been told to anticipate.[29]

The attention given to building expectations was especially important in organizing camp meetings. However irregular they might have been in the beginning, they became regularized both in their occurrence and in their methods of procedure. "Practical" manuals for conducting camp meetings did not begin to appear until the middle of the century, but the texts made clear that their sponsors had been giving considerable thought all along to methods of crowd control. They also had given thought to the question of how to make permanent what in its origins was often viewed as a temporary expedient.

All of this was explicit and was in part a response to criticism. Many standard images of revival camp meetings, including engraved illustrations that have survived, suggest a carnival out of control. We read about unlettered ministers who competed with one another for the attention of listeners in the same open clearing. In many cases they shouted in order to be heard over the general din of the assemblies and sought hysterical responses because they furnished the best proof of their rhetorical powers. Meetings went on all day and all night, and the daytime spiritual orgies turned under the cover of darkness into sensual orgies. For rowdies in the community, camp meetings were an invitation to licentiousness.

Those who like to keep their history lively can be grateful that these parodied descriptions have a substantial basis in fact. However, there are other facts. Fornication is scarcely the usual consequence of spiritual rapture, not because the connection is unthinkable but because knowledge of the possibility results in cautionary practices. Reputable sponsors of camp meetings had so regularized their procedures by midcentury as to render disruptive and unauthorized behavior of any kind extremely difficult. According to one defender of camp meetings, the first word in the motto of their organization was "order." "We can do nothing," it stated, "without order."[30] The many rows of seats were carefully laid out before a central, prominently raised preacher's stand. Since camp meetings went on for as long as a week, arrangements had to made for housing. People, usually family groups, lived in tents that were erected on "uniformly laid out lots." Activity schedules were carefully worked out and announced in advance. So were the rules of behavior. Preaching and prayer sessions were programmed, not spontaneous. Late night assemblies were forbidden, as was any sort of unauthorized socializing. Rowdy behavior was not tolerated. Boisterous and disruptive persons whose conduct could not be attributed to a conversion experience (and the literature prescribed ways to manage the emotional outbursts that went along with conversion) faced forcible expulsion from the meeting area. Organizers always made arrangements with local police officials.

The illustrations that were drawn and published to depict the well-run camp meeting stressed the neatness and the regularity of the gathering. In defending their practices, organizers of the meetings took the spiritual benefits of the revivals for granted. What was emphasized instead in the manuals were the social benefits that accrued to nearby towns. These were peace, quiet, and tranquillity. By the latter part of the nineteenth century many camp meeting grounds had acquired the settled permanence of vacation resorts and real estate ventures. Annual reports dealt with railroad access, drainage, garbage, police, fire departments, boating and swimming facilities, and street grading.[31] Critics still found grounds for complaint. But their complaints now had little to do with an alleged lack of control. Experiments that had begun with the aim of organizing people whose social moorings had been loosened had done exactly that—at least among one broad type of Americans who were white and aspiring to middle-class status. The success of order and organization made it hard to remember that the experiments had originated in the breakdown of older forms of social authority and deference. The antinomian impulse had been brought back within the law, though not without changes that had dramatically affected religious life in the United States.

Justifying Political Divisions: The Dangers and Opportunities Suggested by Religious Experience

The changes had affected political life as well, for as has already been suggested, important complementarities existed between the world of religion and the world of politics. From the 1830s forward, the development of party politics in the United States was riddled with religious language. Prayer was commonly a part of a political meeting, and the nominally secular activities of politicians sometimes acquired religious names. Political speakers were referred to as itinerant preachers, and campaigning was labeled missionary work. The opposition party was composed of "heathens," and electoral victory was equated with "salvation." "Election" itself was a term that recalled Protestant theology.[32] The emotionalism of political rallies and demonstrations was expressly likened to the emotionalism of the revivals.

One can multiply examples of the vocabulary that religious and political ritual shared. Jean Baker, for example, has pointed out that nineteenth-century elections became secular holy days that aped religious observance.[33] The important question to ask however is what significance attached to these commonalities. Were public affairs, as Baker argues, replacing "spiritual matters at the center of many a white man's universe?"[34] If replacement accurately describes what was happening, the borrowing of language points not to an unbroken linkage of religious styles and habits with political styles and habits but simply to a temporarily convenient transfer of familiar words from one phenomenon to something that was displacing it. We shall return to the argument of displacement later. However, we need to demonstrate first that the commonalities of language in fact derived from structural associations between two mass activities that, however different, must be understood as parts of the same cultural patterns.

As was the case in analyzing revivalism, we might learn something from the people who sharply criticized the transformations in political behavior. The invention of American government did not initially provide for political parties. Instead, the framers stated their explicit opposition to parties and tried to devise a system of checks and balances within the government that would discourage the formation of interest groups. The separation of governmental powers further undermined the ability of any organized group to control both legislative and executive action.[35] The opponents of party included Hamilton, Jefferson, and Madison. Never mind that these were the very men who were most responsible for encouraging the first party polarities in the history of the young republic. They were adamant in their refusal to endorse the idea of a permanently organized opposition to elected officials. The word "party," which was often used as a synonym for "faction," stood for tumult, discord, and dissension. To promote a party spirit was to encourage selfishness. A man linked to a party was a man linked to particular interests, frequently economic ones. He was therefore incapable of exercising disinterested judgment to promote the common good.

These seemed to be the clear lessons of eighteenth-century English politics. To be sure, in their own governments North American colonials had gained considerable experience with partylike groupings. Although nonexistent in some colonies, party activity was regularized in others. But nowhere did parties have much more than an ad hoc existence. In general, colonials retained the habit of deferring to the judgment of men who had been elected to office and concluded, even after their own experience with revolution, that organized opposition to seated authority quickly degenerated into lawless insurrection.

Many of these lessons were tied to the colonists' experience with religious discord, although the implications of possible analogies were not entirely clear. With the establishment of government under the American Constitution, all elected politicians were committed to some version of the principle of free religious practice. They associated any effort to enforce the practice of one form of Protestant worship with tyranny. At the state level, many extended that notion to protect the civil and religious freedom of Catholics and Jews. A certain amount of religious division represented in a multiplicity of sects was indicative of social health, just as was a certain amount of political division. By the end of the eighteenth century, and despite the Alien and Sedition Acts, toleration, a concept that had gained its strongest public meaning through the struggle for religious rights, was a model that protected both religious and political opinion as well as one that rendered some organized dissent normative.[36]

But how much disagreement was healthy? Experience with religious disputes suggested that there ought to be limits. A fierce spirit of religious sectarianism, even when shorn of state sponsorship, could itself become intolerant and in that form could be as dangerous to the health of society as factionalized economic interests. What were competing religious denominations if not organized and permanent parties? True, they were not in the United States vying for state power, but history suggested that religious competition was rarely politically benign. Clerical figures picked from the European past served as leading examples of incendiary party intriguers. John Trenchard and Thomas Gordon, two English Whiggish writers well-known to America's revolutionary generation, consistently made the strongest case against "the many Mischiefs, which the Leaders and Deceivers of Parties and Factions in Religion did to the World, by throwing God's Judgments at one another, and impiously confining his Providence and Mercies to themselves; and by applying the common Phaenomena and Events of Nature to their own Advantage, and interpreting the same as Denunciations of his Wrath against their Enemies; by which unhallowed Presumption they have raised up and inflamed implacable Hatred, Animosities and Uncharitableness amongst Men of the same Nation, who are all Brethren."[37] Trenchard and Gordon were writing against an intolerant church establishment, but "disestablishment" was no guarantee against the unpleasantness they described. If in the young republic it sometimes proved useful to legiti-mate the role of political dissent by appealing to the hard-won rights of religious "dissenters," it was also plausible for those who deplored the appearance of political parties to argue their case by citing the con-sequences of too much, and too firmly organized, religious discord. The issues were inextricably related.

The Constitution, arguably, had inadvertently opened up the dangerous possibility of a society rent by an infinite succession of party-like religious quarrels. No one had justified the religious clauses of the First Amendment in those terms. Rather, its proponents had argued that the government's sponsorship of religious tolerance would remove the dangers of religious contention. They believed that contentious sects were the unhealthy products of an established church, just as they imag-ined that political parties were the products of legally privileged wealth and class. As it turned out, these lessons drawn from the past were mis-leading about the future. The increasing number of quarreling religious sects in the United States confounded the framers. And so did the in-sistence of free republican citizens on organizing political parties. By mid-century Americans had to find rationales to justify two related de-velopments that they had not initially anticipated but that had become central to the operation of their society.

A major text that guided discussions of factions, or parties, of any kind in America was Madison's Federalist Ten. Madison had reasoned that Americans could effectively nullify the dangers traditionally asso-ciated with factions by increasing the size of the nation and of represen-tative districts. The geographical dispersion of collections of self-interested men thwarted their opportunities to gain a dominant voice in legislative assemblies. But Madison failed, at least in Federalist Ten, to consider one negative consequence of his proposal. "Extending the sphere," or weakening the possibility of one "faction" gaining a majority to enact "selfish" interests, risked stripping from voters a major motivation to become politically involved. The ability of a sizable political coalition to enact selfish interests, however much those interests harm the interests of other sizable coalitions, is a powerful political stimulant. Lacking that expectation, a democratic people will not easily be moved by appeals to act for the public good. Of all the fictions concocted by a democratic and very pluralistic people, the one about the "public good" remains the most abstract.[38]

Madison recognized that politics was in part driven by factional interests, and he did not expect factions to disappear. However, since he was concerned about their dangers, he could not assign to them any positive influence. The selfish interests that they represented had to be dissolved in deliberative assemblies where goals that benefited the few gave way to goals that served the general welfare. Madison did not initially explore the possibility that a way might be found to join diverse factions in a national organization that diluted some of the worst dangers of single factions seeking power on their own. That coalition of factions could preserve a high level of commitment to political action, yet be forced in some measure to speak the language of general welfare. It would survive and gain power because the men who formed it recognized compromise and pragmatism as the highest forms of political wisdom. At the same time such a coalition would accept the reasonable satisfaction of demands made by victorious factions as a legitimate function of government and the inescapable basis of political success.

What is summarized above describes what many came to view as the achievement of America's first permanent party system and its legitimation of an organized opposition to elected governments. During the 1830s America's first generation of professional politicians decided that a national political party could be distinguished from a faction. A party served diverse and competing interests and still made possible the organization and activation of the electorate. It was a way of overcoming the lack of power felt by men who counted for nothing as individual voters. A party respected the local interests of those who contributed to its national strength. Whenever possible it avoided demands that those interests be sacrificed and committed itself to sweeping statements of principle that encompassed divergent goals. Candidates of different parties found it possible to say most of the same things about most of the issues. What was done with political power had little to do with the publicized platforms of national parties, and somehow in this way political parties promoted political enthusiasm without strong ideological divisiveness. By the end of the 1830s most Americans took parties for granted. Some reached our own contemporary conclusion that the American constitutional government was impossible without a stable, mass, two-party system.

As for religion's role in fomenting antebellum political developments, religious denominations probably inured Americans to the idea that party divisions, despite the catalogue of expressed fears, might actually serve the cause of social and political stability.[39] Indeed more – at the grass roots level of church organization, religion had taught them *how* to divide. Churches provided one important example of the mechanics of division. This observation complements what Tocqueville had noted in calling New World forms of Protestant Christianity "democratic and republican religion." They "contributed powerfully to the establishment of a republic and a democracy in public affairs and from the beginning, politics and religion contracted an alliance which has never been dissolved."[40] When Catholics came in large numbers to the United States, they were accused of failing to observe this symbiotic relation between religion and democracy. In fact the Catholic Church recognized the political and religious requirements of a divided America better than many Protestants, and in the course of the nineteenth century they wrote a franker acknowledgment of pluralism into the operation of both the political and religious institutions of the nation.

These observations are all meant to suggest why the antebellum politicians' borrowing of religious language had more than a superficial significance. When Jefferson spoke of his foes as "apostates," "political heretics," "bigots," and "votaries," when he cast himself as defender of the "true faith," he was reaching for analogies that made sense to his audience.[41] His use of language was metaphorical but not playful. The terms that described the good and bad tendencies of religion also described the good and bad tendencies of politics. The easy interchangeability of reference made it possible in antebellum America for a church building to serve as a place for a political meeting. Political meetings in churches might occasion disapproval, but largely because of the particular political views being aired rather than a fixed national consensus that politics and religion had no natural intersections. Before and after the Civil War black churches in America demonstrated just how far formal associations between religion and politics could be pushed.[42] In black communities the preacher and the politician were the same person far more frequently than in white communities. But throughout American culture preacher and politician were bound by similar conventions affecting success in public life.

The habits of mind and behavior that religious practice encouraged went beyond language. Whatever their ideals about unity and proper deference to authority, revival ministers helped to create roles of public performance that were adaptable to the roles demanded of politicians. We need to refer back to what has already been suggested about oratory. Revival ministers showed great imagination in developing the aggressive means of publicity necessary to attract constituencies. The mechanisms of organization that were used in successful revivals, as well as in the various temperance crusades, resembled what was used in political campaigns. Ministers recognized that dramatic effect was necessary to accomplish anything in mass public assemblies. The image of the revival preacher was that of a man organized for practical activity. Ann Douglas has studied the effeminization of one section of the American clergy, a development strongly related to the influence of women upon religious life.[43] That is not the whole story. The ministers who were most prominent in conducting revivals cultivated an image of very masculine doers. They were depicted as men of impressive physical size, men of endurance fit to lead military campaigns, campaigners who knew how to speak the sociable language of common folk. The importance of log cabin origins attached both to successful politicians and to revival preachers.[44]

We do not mean to suggest an equation. Political parties extended principles of organization that went beyond the patterns available to religious denominations. For example, it was political parties, rather than religious sects, that fully legitimated the wisdom and necessity of permanently organized division. There was no consistently Christian way in the nineteenth century to argue that denominational fragmentation was a good thing. Although religious leaders went about building their churches as if division and competition were inevitable, they did not celebrate either division or competition as appropriate ideals in the world of religion. The most spectacular sectarians in nineteenth-century America all justified their splinter movements as efforts to restore the one true church. In contrast, by mid-century political party builders proceeded in their work with a clear conscience, extending the principles of liberalism to argue the virtue of the institutionalized competition of self-interested *groups*. The bureaucratic apparatus of national party organizations outstripped in importance the development of a similar apparatus in major denominations. Interestingly, the disputes that led to the Civil War provoked enduring rifts in many religious denominations that predated and in some cases outlasted sectional divisions in the major political parties. The same political and cultural issues that divided the ones divided the others.[45]

The legitimation of party organization was helped of course by the fact that most political differences in the United States were gathered into two major coalitions. Denominations were less successful in consolidating factions. Some historical commentary has suggested that Catholics and Protestants in the nineteenth century formed two distinct church parties. But that was scarcely true, if only because ethnic and racial divisions within those two groups doomed unified action. Religious Americans did on many occasions learn to form common causes across denominational lines, for example with respect to missionary work and tract distribution. The temperance societies formed a sort of halfway house between political parties and religious organizations. However, direct church participation in these enterprises usually was hedged with restrictions. Paradoxically, the enduring ideal of a united Christian church made cooperation among different denominations somewhat suspect. Cooperation raised the uncomfortable suggestion that the reasons given to resist more formal merger were trivial and pigheaded. Interdenominational organizations were only partial imitations of political organizations. They never aroused the energies of rank and file Christians in the way that political parties aroused their partisans in the nineteenth and early part of the twentieth centuries.

The Common Framework of Religious and Political Life: Summing Up

To conclude: what religious arrangements in antebellum America accomplished, and what was accomplished in analogous ways by political parties, was the energizing and the control of mass behavior. The problems of social order were staggering. The American masses were composed of very different sorts of people, and their cultural differences grew wider during the course of the nineteenth century rather than narrower. A religious badge of identification was a social marker. To those who wore it, often with vehement passion, it carried a whole set of connotations about who one was and who one wasn't. What religious groups and political parties both did was to establish comprehensible boundary markers without making the boundaries absolutely impenetrable. The institutions of division thus formed were also ways to bring people into some sort of common life, no mean achievement. This imperfect accomplishment would never have happened if all religious groups had demanded a high level of theological sophistication and commitment or if political parties had on all occasions demanded a high level of ideological sophistication and commitment. The cost paid for a workable American democracy was a leveling down of political and religious concepts.

What remains striking is that the two agencies most necessary to the course of American democracy and to national memory, religious denominations and political parties, were neither foreseen nor welcomed. The critics who were most worried about potential social breakdown viewed the mass activity encouraged by the religious revivals as symptoms of what they feared rather than its cure. Yet it was the sponsors of the revivals, and of aggressive evangelical activity generally, who conducted some of the first successful experiments in ordering the national population. The religious excitement that revivals stirred was surely ephemeral, just as its critics charged. They left no lasting marks of salvation on many of the "redeemed." The social excitement and disorder were also ephemeral. The essential thing that remained was a controlled way to conquer apathy for the purpose of accomplishing desired goals.

The success of the revivals, then, served as examples to the organizers of political parties in the Jacksonian era. Methods of generating crowd enthusiasm that had been devalued in conventional wisdom wound up serving the very cause of social order they were presumed to defeat. Political parties were also experiments in mass communication. Working on the assumption that a democratic people would not by any natural habits strive for the common good, they sought to develop artificial means, "new measures," to stir commitment. The parades and the rallies that political parties sponsored carried the same overtones of carnival that one found in the religious revivals. Yet the result of the activity was the reinforcement of norms and the organization of many people who would never meet into unified armies for accomplishing social action. Americans had hardly learned to banish disorder and violence from their mechanisms of democracy. Yet the orderliness of American politics at mid-century compares favorably with the boisterous drunken brawls that aroused election fever in Jefferson's home territory in the late eighteenth century.[46] American religion and American politics had by the middle of the nineteenth century achieved consequences desirable even to those who deplored the means of attaining them.

We return finally to the question of displacement, the issue of whether religious activity and political activity go forward in their separate turns, the progress of one coming always at the expense of the other. The argument that they do is familiar even to non-Marxists, and it makes considerable sense. Religious and political identifications are strong forms of orientation, and it is difficult to imagine people who manage to give a full measure of loyalty and enthusiastic commitment to both. The plausible suggestion that people seek salvation, primarily, either through religious deliverance or through secular politics does seem to hold for many classes of people. The absolute bar to political activity mandated by some religious groups, Jehovah's witnesses for example, is a case in point. Other examples include Southern Baptists whose strong religious feelings have at least historically acted to restrain political activism. (Jerry Falwell's retreat from politics is as significant as his more publicized involvement.) Highly educated agnostics vote in far greater numbers proportionately than the general population, and so on.

However, the history of nineteenth-century America yields as much evidence against the thesis of displacement as for it. The mere citation of numbers throws it into question. In contrast to many parts of Europe, where the rise of mass political parties came at a time when religious observance was lessening, organized religion and organized politics in the United States both continued on an upward rise throughout the whole of the century. A religious identification often became part of a political identification, without churches issuing political mandates to their adherents and without professional clerics seeming to have a stake in election outcomes.

The common underpinnings of religious and political enthusiasm in antebellum America made this interconnection possible. Acting religiously and acting politically arose out of the same need to give meaning and value to opposed points of view, thereby rendering a mass democratic society orderly. Most people, if we can conclude anything from silence, sensed no conflict between their religious roles and their political roles. A different history in European countries that had formal religious parties gave prominence to more sharply articulated distinctions between "religious politics" and "secular politics." Political historians of the United States have noted that religious political activists have been more comfortable in the Whig/Republican tradition of party politics than in the Democratic tradition. However, the distinction can be overdone, since regional, racial, and class differences, as well as particular issues, have kept both parties sensitive to religious issues. American Catholics, traditionally more Democratic than Whig/Republican, have often made religious demands on politics, a fact that Protestant political activists once used with an invincible lack of self-knowledge to challenge the American loyalties of Catholics. In the full range from populist to elitist politics, and in both political parties, religious resonances often shake campaign strategies. Given the way the nation was formed, it would be astonishing if they didn't.

As between denominational religion and party politics, we need not pose questions of priority. That is, it is not necessary to insist that the religious revivals were the necessary prelude to the legitimation of permanent political parties in the United States. It is equally true to say that prior political campaigns waged between Federalists and Jeffersonians created a hospitable environment for the revivals. The whole point is that the development of American culture encouraged a reciprocal influence between religion and politics.

On the other hand, given the tendency of historians to give priority to whatever is political and the disposition of many contemporary observers to view religion as harmful to political debate, I am inclined to stress the centrality of religion in the formation of the nation's political life. The religious leaders of colonial America helped to regularize the habits that were also characteristic of colonial politicians. Those habits provided an important legacy for learning how to maintain authority in the young republic as older habits of deference were knocked down. Religious enthusiasm was prior to political enthusiasm, long prior. If Michael Walzer is correct, the very concept of a politically active citizen was formed by religion.[47] And even if he is partly wrong, ardent secularists in the United States find that they must still deal with a people who believe that American religion guarantees the success of its politics, rather than vice versa. Close to a majority of Americans are willing to say that religion is the most important thing in their life. Almost no one makes the same claim about politics, not even smart politicians. That much about national life has been consistent.

NOTES

1. The literature on church and state in the United States is enormous, more extensive probably than it is for any developed Western country. That fact in itself signals that the First Amendment did not put to rest contestations between church and state. For bibliographical help see John F. Wilson, ed., *Church and State in America: A Bibliographical Guide,* 2 volumes (New York: 1986–87) and Clarence Chisholm, et al., *Religion and Politics in the 1980s: A Selective Bibliography* (1987). Two helpful volumes appeared after I wrote this article: Mark A. Noll, ed., *Religion and American Politics* (New York, 1990); Nathan O. Hatch, *The Democratization of American Christianity* (New Haven, Conn., 1989).

2. For diametrically opposed historical interpretations of the First Amendment see Gerald V. Bradley, *Church-State Relationships in America* (New York, 1987) and Leonard W. Levy, *The Establishment Clause: Religion and the First Amendment* (New York, 1986).

3. Tocqueville's most important remarks occur in chapter 17 of the first volume of *Democracy in America*. For one extended discussion of Tocqueville's views see Cushing Strout, *The New Heavens and New Earth: Political Religion in America* (New York, 1974).

4. Marshall Frady, *Billy Graham: A Parable of American Righteousness* (Boston, 1979).

5. The political power of the Catholic Church has often been exaggerated, for political reasons. For a balanced assessment of its recent role see Mary T. Hanna, *Catholics and American Politics* (Cambridge, Mass., 1979).

6. For the recent past see Allen D. Hertzke, *Representing God in America: The Role of Religious Lobbies in American Polity* (Knoxville, 1988); Mark Silk, *Spiritual Politics: Religion and America since World War II* (New York, 1988); James L. Adams, *The Growing Church Lobby in Washington* (Grand Rapids, Mich., 1970); Luke Eugene Ebersole, *Church Lobbying in the Nation's Capitol* (New York, 1951). For a longer view see Aaron I. Abell, *American Catholicism and Social Action: A Search for Social Justice, 1865–1930* (Garden City, N.Y., 1960); John R. Bodo, *The Protestant Clergy and Public Issues, 1812–1848* (Princeton, N.J., 1954); Paul Goodman, *Towards a Christian Republic: Antimasonry and the Great Transition in New England, 1826–1838* (New York, 1988); John L. Hammond, *The Politics of Benevolence: Revival Religion and American Voting Behavior* (Norwood, N.J., 1979); Harold E. Quinley, *The Prophetic Clergy: Social Activism Among Protestant Ministers* (New York, 1974).

7. Robert Wuthnow, *The Restructuring of American Religion: Society and Faith Since World War II* (Princeton, N.J., 1988).

8. Steve Bruce, *The Rise and Fall of the New Christian Right: Conservative Politics in America, 1978–1988* (Princeton, N.J., 1988); Robert Booth Fowler, *A New Engagement: Evangelical Political Thought, 1966–1976* (Grand Rapids, Mich., 1982); Samuel S. Hill and Dennis E. Owen, *The New Religious-Political Right in America* (Nashville, 1982); Robert C. Liebman and Robert Wuthnow, eds., *The New Christian Right: Mobilization and Legitimation* (Hawthorne, N.Y., 1983).

9. An intriguing issue relates to the question of whether an unavoidable clash exists between the "free exercise" clause and the "establishment" clause of the First Amendment. See, for example, Jesse H. Choper, "Defining 'Religion' in the First Amendment," *University of Illinois Law Review*, vol. 1982, pp. 579–613 and "The Religion Clauses of the First Amendment: Reconciling the Conflict," *University of Pittsburgh Law Review* 41:673–701.

10. John M. Benson, "The Polls. A Rebirth of Religion?" *Public Opinion Quarterly* 45 (Winter 1981), 576–84. See data recorded in the yearly *Index*

to International Public Opinion (Westport, Conn., 1978/79–). For other sources of comparative statistics, consult Mark Noll, et al., *The Search for a Christian America* (Westchester, Ill., 1983); special issue of "Religion in West European Politics," *West European Politics* 5 (April 1982).

11. Eric Hobsbawm, "Religion and the Rise of Socialism," *Marxist Perspectives* 1 (Spring 1978), 14–33. The different patterns of religious observance among American working classes of course have implications for the question of "why is there no socialism in the United States." None of this discussion is meant to suggest that religion has no importance in the political life of other nations. See Peter H. Merkl and Ninian Smart, eds., *Religion and Politics in the Modern World* (1983); Richard Rose, ed., *Electoral Behavior: A Comparative Handbook* (1973); special issue on religion and politics in *Journal of International Affairs* 36 (Winter 1982).

12. Jay Dolan, *The Immigrant Church: New York's Irish and German Catholics, 1815–1865* (Baltimore, 1975); Randall M. Miller and Thomas D. Marzik, eds., *Immigrants and Religion in Urban America* (Philadelphia, 1977); Kerby A. Miller, *Emigrants and Exiles: Ireland and the Irish Exodus to North America* (New York, 1985).

13. Peter Berger, *The Sacred Canopy: Elements of a Sociological Theory of Religion* (Garden City, N.Y., 1967); Thomas Luckmann, *The Invisible Religion: The Problem of Religion in Modern Society* (New York, 1967); Gerhard Lenski, *The Religious Factor: A Sociological Study of Religion's Impact of Politics, Economics, and Family Life* (Garden City, N.Y., 1961); John Wilson, *Religion in American Society: The Effective Presence* (Englewood Cliffs, N.J., 1978).

14. Conrad E. Cherry, ed., *God's New Israel: Religious Interpretations of American Destiny* (Englewood Cliffs, N.J., 1972); James West Davidson, *The Logic of Millennial Thought: Eighteenth-Century New England* (New Haven, Conn., 1977); Winthrop Hudson, *Nationalism and Religion in America: Concepts of American Identity and Mission* (New York, 1970); James H. Moorhead, *American Apocalypse: Yankee Protestants and the Civil War, 1860–1869* (New Haven, Conn., 1978); Ernest Tuveson, *Redeemer Nation: The Idea of America's Millennial Role* (Chicago, 1968); Nathan O. Hatch, *The Sacred Cause of Liberty: Republican Thought and the Millennium in Revolutionary New England* (New Haven, Conn., 1977).

15. Bellah, "Civil Religion in America," in William G. McLoughlin and Robert N. Bellah, eds., *Religion in America* (Boston, 1968), pp. 3–23. First published in *Daedalus*, Winter 1967. For some of the debate, see John F. Wilson, *Public Religion in American Culture* (Philadelphia, 1979) and Gail Gehrig, *American Civil Religion: An Assessment* (Storrs, Conn., 1979).

16. For the most useful summary, see Robert Kelley, *The Cultural Pattern in American Politics: The First Century* (New York, 1979).

17. Richard John Neuhaus, *The Naked Public Square: Religion and De-

mocracy in America (Grand Rapids, Mich., 1984); A. James Reichley, *Religion in American Public Life* (Washington, D.C., 1985).

18. Ronald P. Formisano, *The Transformation of American Political Cultures: Massachusetts Parties, 1790–1840s* (New York, 1983); Formisano, *The Birth of Mass Political Parties, Michigan, 1827–1861* (Princeton, N.J., 1971); Paul Kleppner, *The Cross of Culture: A Social Analysis of Midwestern Politics, 1850–1900* (New York, 1970); Paul Kleppner, *The Third Electoral System, 1853–1892: Parties, Voters, and Political Cultures* (Chapel Hill, N.C., 1979); Paul Kleppner, et al., *The Evolution of American Electoral Systems* (Westport, Conn., 1981). Also consult the work of Lee Benson, *The Concept of Jacksonian Democracy: New York as a Test Case* (Princeton, N.J., 1961) and Michael Holt, *Forging a Majority: The Formation of the Republican Party in Pittsburgh, 1848–1860* (New Haven, Conn., 1969).

19. Donald G. Mathews, "The Second Great Awakening as an Organizing Process, 1780–1830," *American Quarterly* 21 (1969), 22–43. For a sociologist's discussion of issues pertaining to American religion and order, see George M. Thomas, *Revivalism and Cultural Change: Christianity, Nation Building, and the Market in the Nineteenth-Century United States* (Chicago, 1989).

20. Dickson D. Bruce, Jr., *And They All Sang Hallelujah: Plain-Folk Camp-Meeting Religion, 1840–1845* (Knoxville, 1974); Bernard Weisberger, *They Gathered at the River: The Story of the Great Revivalists and Their Impact upon Religion in America* (New York, 1958); Richard Carwardine, *Transatlantic Revivalism: Popular Evangelicalism in Britain and America, 1790–1865* (Westport, Conn., 1978); T. Scott Miyakawa, *Protestants and Pioneers: Individualism and Conformity on the American Frontier* (Chicago, 1964); John B. Boles, *The Great Revival, 1787–1805* (Lexington, Ky., 1972).

21. Richard Hofstadter and Michael Wallace, eds., *American Violence: A Documentary History* (New York, 1970).

22. See especially Paul Johnson, *A Shopkeeper's Millennium: Society and Revivals in Rochester, New York, 1815–1837* (New York, 1978).

23. Lawrance Thompson, "The Printing and Publishing Activities of the American Tract Society from 1825 to 1850," *The Papers of the Bibliographical Society of America* 35 (2d quarter, 1941), 81–114.

24. David Paul Nord, "The Evangelical Origins of Mass Media in America, 1815–1835," *Journalism Monographs* (1984).

25. For a further discussion of this general point, see R. Laurence Moore, "Religion, Secularization, and the Shaping of the Culture Industry in Antebellum America," *American Quarterly* 41 (June 1989), 216–22.

26. Garth M. Rosell, "Charles G. Finney: His Place in the Stream," in Leonard I. Sweet, *The Evangelical Tradition in America* (Macon, Ga., 1984).

27. Calvin Colton, *History and Character of American Revival of Religion* (London, 1832).

28. Finney, *Lectures on Revivals of Religion* (New York, 1835), pp. 11, 192, 204.

29. Historians argue whether revival techniques have changed much from the antebellum period to the present. The point of view of this author is that techniques of course change but that revivalists have consistently been in the forefront of exploiting whatever media techniques were available. Indeed, with respect to media they have been innovators. For some individual studies see William G. McLoughlin, *Modern Revivalism* (New York, 1959); McLoughlin, *Billy Sunday Was His Real Name* (Chicago, 1953); McLoughlin, *Billy Graham, Revivalist in a Secular Age* (New York, 1960); David E. Harrell, *Oral Roberts: An American Life* (Bloomington, Ind., 1985); Jeffrey K. Hadden, *Televangelism: Power and Politics on God's Frontier* (New York, 1988); J. D. Cardwell, *Mass Media Christianity: Televangelism and the Great Commission* (Lanham, Md., 1984).

30. Rev. A. P. Mead, *Manna in the Wilderness; or, The Grove and Its Altar, Offerings, and Thrilling Incidents, Containing a History of the Origin and Rise of Camp Meetings, and a Defence of this Remarkable Means of Grace* (Philadelphia, 1860).

31. Rev. B. W. Gorham, *Camp Meeting Manual: A Practical Book for the Camp Ground in Two Parts* (Boston, 1854); Rev. E. H. Stokes, compiler, *Ocean Grove: Its Origins and Progress, as Shown in the Annual Reports Presented by the President* (Philadelphia, 1874–87); Ellen Weiss, *City in the Woods: Life and Design of an American Camp Meeting on Martha's Vineyard* (New York, 1987).

32. Joe L. Kincheloe, Jr., "Similarities in Crowd Control Techniques of the Camp Meeting and Political Rally: The Pioneer Role of Tennessee," *Tennessee Historical Quarterly* 37 (Summer 1978), 155–69.

33. Jean H. Baker, *Affairs of Party: The Political Culture of Northern Democrats in the Mid-Nineteenth Century* (Ithaca, N.Y., 1983), pp. 270–74.

34. Ibid., p. 269.

35. On this general subject see Richard Hofstadter, *The Idea of a Party System: The Rise of Legitimate Opposition in the United States, 1780–1840* (Berkeley, Calif., 1969).

36. Any number of books are useful for judging the extent of political and religious dissent in the early national period. For example, Joseph Charles, *The Origins of the American Party System* (Williamsburg, Va., 1956); Leonard Levy, *Jefferson and Civil Liberties: The Darker Side* (Cambridge, Mass., 1963); James Morton Smith, *Freedom's Fetters: The Alien and Sedition Laws and American Civil Liberties* (Ithaca, N.Y., 1966); William Lee Miller, *The First Liberty: Religion and the American Republic* (New York, 1985).

37. David L. Jacobson, ed., *The English Libertarian Heritage, from the Writings of John Trenchard and Thomas Gordon* (Indianapolis, 1965), pp. 272–73. For background on eighteenth-century English politics and American attitudes toward party, consult Isaac Kramnick, *Bolingbroke and His Circle: The Politics of Nostalgia in the Age of Walpole* (Cambridge, Mass., 1968); Bernard Bailyn, *The Origins of American Politics* (New York, 1968); Caroline Robbins, *The Eighteenth-Century Commonwealthman* (Cambridge, Mass., 1959).

38. On the general question of political fictions, see Edmund S. Morgan, *Inventing the People: The Rise of Popular Sovereignty in England and America* (New York, 1988).

39. Formisano has discussed the way in which religious division in the early republic directly stimulated the formation of a political geography: *Transformation of Political Culture*, pp. 150–70; *Birth of Mass Political Parties*, pp. 104 ff. Another important addition to the study of religious attitude and political party formation is Paul Goodman, *Towards a Christian Republic: Antimasonry and the Great Transition in New England, 1826–1836* (New York, 1988).

40. Alexis de Tocqueville, *Democracy in America*, Phillips Bradley, ed., (New York, 1945), vol. 1, p. 311.

41. Hofstadter, *Idea of a Party System*, p. 125.

42. Eric Foner, *Reconstruction: America's Unfinished Revolution, 1863–1877* (New York, 1988), pp. 90–95, 281–91; Clarence G. Walker, *A Rock in a Weary Land: The African Methodist Episcopal Church during Civil War and Reconstruction* (Baton Rouge, La., 1982); James M. Washington, *Frustrated Fellowship: The Black Baptist Quest for Social Power* (Macon, Ga., 1986).

43. Ann Douglas, *The Feminization of American Culture* (New York, 1977).

44. The stereotype of the strong-willed and strong-armed man of God is richly present in the *Autobiography of Peter Cartwright*, which was first published in 1856. Cartwright, one of the most famous of the Methodist circuit riders, was converted during an early wave of revivals in 1801. His career as a preacher fed naturally into a minor political career in Illinois. Twice elected to the lower house of the Illinois General Assembly, he lost a bid to Congress in 1846 to the Whig nominee Abraham Lincoln.

45. On the sectional splits of major denominations, see C. C. Goen, *Broken Churches, Broken Nations: Denominational Schisms and the Coming of the American Civil War* (Macon, Ga., 1986).

46. Morgan, *Inventing the People*, pp. 174–208.

47. Michael Walzer, *The Revolution of the Saints: A Study of the Origins of Radical Politics* (Cambridge, Mass., 1965).

PART III

Models for Religious History

7

Unrethinking the Sixteenth-Century Wars of Religion

John Bossy

The "innovative approach to religious history" I propose to write about is an interpretation of an area of the history of Christianity which has been influential over the past thirty years, but seems to me now to have been a failure. This is not to say that it has been a waste of time, that it did not reveal things which other approaches would not have done, or that nothing can be rescued from it. But I do offer it as something of a cautionary tale, and an illustration of two truths, one of them fairly obvious, the other more arcane. The first is that, if a historian attempts to use his position as narrator of the past to speak rather directly to something in the condition of the present, his work will not survive unscathed a change in that condition. The second is that the temptation to say something clever (which would be a rough British translation of "innovative") is one that a historian who wants to tell the truth will quite often need to resist.

My topic is the history of Western Europe during the post-Reformation age of the wars of religion, and especially during the late sixteenth century. The approach I have in mind is sociological, or rather one of the various forms which sociological interpretation of the period has taken: what one might very roughly call the American form. I begin with a layman's observation about the contemporary world. Many of the violent conflicts which get into the papers have something to do with matters of faith. There are obvious cases involving Islam: the history of Iran since the downfall of the Shah, cases in India, Africa, and elsewhere. The conflicts arising from the establishment of the state of Israel are the most obvious of all. In European Christianity, the ecumenical and secular consensus which looks impressive in the Netherlands or Germany does not seem to have made much headway in Poland or Ireland; one might also think it was losing ground to something harder edged.

What seems as interesting as the actual facts of what is going on in the world, is the surprise, bafflement, or ill-temper with which these events have usually been greeted by the average educated person in the West and indeed in the East: "puzzlement and discomfort," says Thomas Kselman.[1] It is not what either of them had been brought up to expect, nor what the pundits were predicting twenty years ago. They had been encouraged to think that conflicts, particularly conflicts in countries with a colonial or semicolonial past, were conflicts of liberation. They had also been told that conflicts which appeared to be about religion were actually about something else: conflicts of liberation, of class interest, conflicts, it might be sometimes allowed, of national allegiance. Although sociology was not the only contributor to this frame of mind, it was likely, in the 1960s and 1970s, to be expressed in sociological terms: terms perhaps Marxist, perhaps existentialist, the more academic concepts of secularization and modernization. The language in which what might seem to be religious conflict was described, often enough by participants as well as by their interviewers from the media, was the language of liberation, revolution, and their opposites, of left and right. It seemed unsophisticated, improper, and sometimes against the law to refer to these things by the names that most naturally came to mind. Lebanese Christians and Muslims were referred to, respectively, as right-wingers and left-wingers; in Northern Ireland, the Social Democratic and Labour Party or SDLP was a political party concerned with human rights whose voters just happened, as the BBC grudgingly conceded, to be "mainly Catholic."

Perhaps I am exaggerating, and it may be that the tendency always to peer inside the overtly religious for its sociological essence is mainly a thing of the past. Perhaps the Iranians have taught us once again to recognize a war of religion when we see one. I speak as a reader of the papers, not as a historian of the contemporary world. But a reader of the papers who is also a historian of early modern Europe may be excused for getting the feeling that he has been here before. For a very long time, indeed to some degree ever since they occurred, it has been doubted whether Europe's wars of religion were actually religious wars. During the century or so in which modern historiography was establishing itself, one of the standard strategies of historical description was to explain that what appeared to be confessional conflicts, in France, the Netherlands, Germany, England, or elsewhere, were actually political ones: something to do with the rise of the modern state.[2] In the climate of the 1960s it was natural that the way forward for the early modern historian should seem to lie in the submission of confessional conflicts to some kind of social or sociological analysis, on the assumption that they would be found to have something to do with the rise of modern society. In the 1990s it seems equally natural that historians and the public in general should ask themselves whether this was a profitable line to have taken.

It was tempting to offer at this point a naive narration of events in Western Europe between, say, 1559 and 1598, composed on the assumption that people at the time meant what they said and that wars of religion were wars of religion.[3] But narration is long and essays are short. So I shall take the story as known and proceed directly to the historians. I begin with a historian who is neither an American nor a sociologist. In 1955 a young English historian of German extraction, Helmut Koenigsberger, published a short piece in the *Journal of Modern History*. Entitled "The Organization of Revolutionary Parties in France and the Netherlands during the Sixteenth Century,"[4] it said that, in the three large-scale confessional movements falling within the field (the Calvinist movements in France and the Netherlands, and the Catholic League in France), we were to see something new and formidable in European history. They were, as he described them, a sort of antibody secreted by the growth of monarchical authority in sixteenth-century Europe. Hitherto opposition had been led by members of the aristocracy and had been sectional or regional in character, dependent on personal loyalties. These new movements were indeed led by members of the aristocracy (kings of Navarre, princes of Condé or Orange, dukes of Guise) and in that sense fell into a traditional mold. Where they differed was that the confessional cause they stood for enabled these leaders to recruit a national following and to employ weapons of propaganda and (especially) of organization on a scale hitherto unknown in Europe. The Calvinist or Catholic movements which they led, or did their best to lead, were not in any sense popular movements or representations of national feeling against a generally hated establishment in church and state. They succeeded, insofar as they did succeed, by the efficiency of their organization and the ruthlessness with which they were prepared to use violence and terror—and only in circumstances where the authority of the state had for one reason or another disintegrated. They appealed to a wider audience not so much by the persuasiveness of the version of Christianity they presented as by recruiting the social and economic grievances of the urban masses, whom they provided with objects on which "to vent the anger of their poverty and the despair of their unemployment in barbarous massacres and fanatical looting."[5] They were therefore, in both an ideological and a social sense, "revolutionary parties," and though the regimes they established did not last (or not in a revolutionary form), they left an indelible mark on European history as the true ancestors of the Jacobin, Bolshevik, and National Socialist movements of modern Europe. Since Koenigsberger was a historian of German background writing in the early 1950s, it is not surprising that the National Socialist model looms very heavily over the essay, as in the passage I have quoted. The main personal influence was that of Herbert Butterfield, and it was certainly a manifesto against a whig interpretation of the wars of religion.

Koenigsberger's piece became a classic of our subject, and I wish to make only two remarks about it, one explanatory and one critical. It was rescued from being simply a journalistic "point-of-view" piece by its principal historiographical source, the scholarly work done on the revolt of the Netherlands by a revisionist school of Dutch historians led by Pieter Geyl and H. A. Enno van Gelder; van Gelder's *Revolutionnaire Reformátie,* which had appeared in the middle of the war in 1943, seems to have served as a model for Koenigsberger's larger description.[6] The critical remark concerns an example of something we shall be seeing more of: what I shall call categorical anachronism. A rather strict analogy of revolution, applied to the actions of people who could not have envisaged what they were doing in quite that way, led Koenigsberger into difficulty. Here he is discussing the decline and fall of the Catholic League in France during the early 1590s. Having fallen out with their aristocratic leadership from the House of Lorraine, "the revolutionary leaders in Paris were left with only one ally—the Catholic autocrat Philip II of Spain. It was the *reductio ad absurdum* of revolution, and it was its end."[7] That is a blow that lands nowhere. Nobody on the popular or clerical side of the League, so far as I know, ever had the slightest qualm about looking to Philip for any kind of support he could get: to appeal to the most powerful Catholic prince in Christendom was simply the obvious thing for a body of beleaguered Catholics to do. If they had had qualms it would certainly not have been on the grounds that Philip II was an autocrat, assuming that that was what he was; since they did not have them (they were doing their best to make Philip's daughter Isabella queen of France), they cannot have been revolutionaries in more than a very remote sense. The absurdity is really not in the history of the League, but in Koenigsberger's description of it, as I think he would now recognize.

That said, the piece still reads well after thirty-odd years, and it has been very influential. It figures prominently in the acknowledgments of two of the historians I want to deal with, and ought to have figured in those of the third. This is a tribute to its quality, since it was not in any obvious way a sociological piece. Perhaps it is simply that it was published in the United States at an appropriate time and appealed by its fairly comparative and theoretical mode and by making the wars of religion a matter of contemporary concern. Those who followed him adopted Koenigsberger's model, though they turned its antirevolutionary values upside down.

Looked at after twenty years (it appeared in 1965), Michael Walzer's *The Revolution of the Saints* is more redolent of the sixties than almost any other history book I can think of; Christopher Hill's *The World Turned Upside Down* is certainly more so, but it appeared in the 1970s and does not fall within my topic.[8] Among the works of political and social science which one encounters in Walzer's footnotes, one cannot help noticing the name of Herbert Marcuse flitting about in a shadowy way from time to time, though formally the patron saint of the book is Max Weber.[9] It is a book with a high theoretical profile, but it seems useful to speak of it first as an empirical account of some aspects of Calvinism, mainly in England. Walzer picked up from Koenigsberger the notion of Calvin as a party ideologist rather than a theologian, and he gave an arresting account of Calvin's doctrine which absolutely avoided cliché. Calvin, he said, conceived the Fall of Man as a radical drama of social alienation and the restitution of man as a work of social reconstruction in obedience to God's commands.[10] This obedience transcended all given social institutions and political institutions which, in other accounts, Calvin was thought to have considered authoritative: the domestic family and the French monarchy were two of them. The revolutionary implications of the doctrine, bungled by the Huguenots through excessive deference to their aristocratic supporters, were properly grasped by some "British" Protestant exiles in Geneva. I say "British" because they included John Knox. These launched, in England, a "long revolution," carried on by a Puritan clergy or intelligentsia. During the next eighty years, they and their successors beavered away to undermine existing authorities and institutions. They expounded the essentials of a new godly commonwealth, persuaded a portion of the English gentry and bourgeoisie to identify themselves with it, and inspired them with a militancy and a taste for godly warfare under which the old regime collapsed and that of Oliver Cromwell emerged.

This was of course not an innocent narrative, as even the simplest reader will have figured out after noticing the subtitle Walzer gave to the book: "A Study in the Origins of Radical Politics." In its larger context the book claimed to reveal how England (and possibly Europe and the world) passed from a "traditional" to a nontraditional state, underwent "modernization." This conception, and much of his incidental discussion, Walzer had borrowed from Weber: he claimed to be following Weber in offering Calvinist Christianity as the agent of transition to modernity, and differing from him in seeing the locus of the Calvinist breakthrough in the political, not the economic world. Walzer claimed Weber's authority for his characterization of what he called "the traditional world" or "traditional society," though he also frequently described it as "feudal," which does not seem a very Weberian term. The principal characteristic of this traditional society was universal hierarchy and nonparticipatory politics; he also mentioned extended kinship, personalized relations, the organic analogy, natural law, and the reign of custom.

All these, as Walzer told the story, were demolished by the innovative voluntarism of God's will embodied in the saints, and now one could see exactly what he meant by describing Calvinism as an "ideology." It was, to be precise, "an ideology of the transition period" and was for this reason bound to decay when the transition to modernity had been achieved and liberalism, capitalism, and other forms of rational conduct had been made possible. There was rather a surprise towards the end of the book, since Walzer balked at saying that Calvin or Calvinism was the creative agent of the transition, as most of it had seemed to imply. The transition was going on anyway, "traditional society" was breaking down, and the "function" of Calvinist Christianity was to make it possible for Englishmen to live with and make sense of it: to "meet the human needs that arise whenever traditional controls give way and hierarchical status and corporate privilege are called into question." In this retrospective light, Calvin's account of the Fall of Man, which in chapter two had seemed powerful and creative, turned out to look like a fairly transparent rationalization of "social" facts; the whole impressive construction threatened to subside into a more modish version of the transition from feudalism to capitalism. With that concession, Walzer offered his analysis of the modernization process as a model which would be found to apply to the French and Russian Revolutions, though not like Koenigsberger's to National Socialism.[11]

This is not the place for an adequate discussion of the merits and defects of Walzer's analysis; in any case the task has been done with great fairness and sensitivity by Patrick Collinson in a chapter of *The Religion of Protestants.* [12] Collinson's verdict, which is a very careful negative, arises, it seems to me, from restoring the distinction between matters of the polity and matters of salvation which Walzer's and Weber's notion of society had intentionally confused. I shall only add a comment on one small and possibly marginal point in the book, because it illustrates a family resemblance, in the shape of categorical anachronism, between Koenigsberger, Walzer, and my next author. It comes at the end of a section where Walzer has been discussing the Huguenots, and ascribing their failure to draw revolutionary conclusions to their noble status and, more hazardously for the general theory, to a fear of the "radicalism" of the Catholic League. "A man," he says, "who still possessed a village could hardly be a whole-hearted member of a Calvinist congregation, nor would he dare explore the logic of Calvinist thought." He was, that is, *a priori* disqualified from embracing a doctrine of social alienation and social reconstruction. In the inaccurate sense in which Walzer was using the word, I should think that Admiral Coligny "possessed" several villages; the godly husband of the godly Lady Brilliana Harley, who said that "hierarchy must down," possessed, and rather vigorously, at least one. [13] The impossibility, and the logic, were in the historian's construction and not in the facts of the case. So, I may add, was the "still," with its intimation of access to the universal laws of historical development.

Overconfidence in the creative powers of the mind may not have been a general characteristic of the sixties, but it was one of the features *The Revolution of the Saints* shared with my next example. I can say something about this, because I wrote it myself. It was a piece called "The Character of Elizabethan Catholicism," and it had appeared in *Past and Present* in 1962, some three years before Walzer published his book. I do not think Walzer had read it when he wrote, but his passage about the Huguenots, which I have just quoted, could have appeared in it practically unchanged. I expounded, on behalf of the Catholic gentry of Elizabethan England, the religious and other implications of "possessing a village," which I knitted together into a binding ideology of conservative loyalism. Having done that, I borrowed roughly the conception of Calvinism Walzer was to use; rather like Koenigsberger (whom, again, I am sure I had not read at the time), I applied it to the contemporary version of Catholicism represented by Elizabethan priests. They too emerged as "alienated intellectuals," or "clerks" as I described them, agents of transcendental alteration battering at the foundations of tradition, including their own. The piece worked hard, and rather successfully I think, at redescribing these missionaries of the Counter-Reformation according to a model of entrepreneurial activism which might have come from Weber but had actually come from Sartre. As with all decent ideologies, this one worked out in the end as a political practice and theory: to use the then chic term, a *praxis* of political activism floated on a populist or bourgeois political theory borrowed from the Catholics of Leaguer France. That made two ideologies, one seigneurial and conservative, one entrepreneurial and progressive. I concluded in Hegelian mode by explaining the domestic difficulties of late Elizabethan Catholicism as a conflict between the two of them: roughly speaking, a failure of nerve on the part of the clergy permitted their own ideology to be swallowed up in a more self-conscious version of that of the Catholic gentry.[14]

This was an elegant solution and satisfying in various ways: it satisfied the editorial board of *Past and Present,* whom it had been designed to impress. On the right hand, it delivered, in the end, the appropriate picture of the English Catholic community as an engine of reaction. On the left, it enabled the alienated intellectuals of Elizabethan Catholicism to make their contribution to the great processes of English revolution: even though, after the Gunpowder Plot of 1605, this contribution had floated loose from its moorings in the Catholic community, which had been at some pains to push it off. Taken as a whole, to use a phrase which I cannibalized from the Ph.D. thesis out of which the piece had emerged, the history of Elizabethan Catholicism was "a progress from inertia to inertia in three generations." Connoisseurs of Sartre will give that word "inertia" a good deal of moral weight. The implication was that a successful explosion on 5 November 1605 would have been an authentic expression of existential ethics and a milestone on one of the *chemins de la liberté.*[15]

This also, you may think, was absurd, in more ways than one. It was not rubbish, but it concealed two forms of categorical anachronism, one like Koenigsberger's and one like Walzer's. I quote the last sentence of the first part of the piece, where the *Weltanschauung* of the Elizabethan Catholic gentry is described, rather wittily I thought, as "a sort of natural economy in religion." "Whether they continued to conform outwardly [to the Church of England], or took the plunge into recusancy, they could provide themselves with no practical object but the preservation within their households of a conscience conceived as passive."[16] The sentence is in exactly the same form as Walzer's about the Huguenot nobility and invites exactly the same objections. It is not true: even if we exclude political activists like Robert Catesby, the Gunpowder plotter, as fellow-travelers of clerical ideology, we still have to reckon with, for example, their contemporaries and neighbors who provided themselves with the practical object of launching the iron industry in the west Midlands. And it is disingenuous in form: a logical, or ideological, or sociological contradiction that is a necessity of the argument, or perhaps a necessity of the argument's being as compulsory as it is being claimed to be, is being slipped in among the facts and presented as having been found there. I sympathize with critics who have objected to the second phase of the argument, which features the entrepreneurial clergy, as leading me to the implausible or empirically unsound conclusion that Elizabethan Catholicism was a creation *ex nihilo;*[17] the temptation to be innovative or clever is certainly one that this twenty-seven-year-old historian might have resisted more strongly than he did. His reinterpretation of the founding events of the post-Reformation English Catholic community as a chapter in the history of progressive ideology — which did, I think, say something worthwhile about the subject, as Walzer did about his — may in the end turn out to have said more about the history of his feelings, a not untypical history of the sixties. Perhaps it also, in its tenderness for terrorism, says something about the history of the world since then.

It may be that, so far, I have confused sociological history with what one might call liberation history, of which my next example is a fairly extreme case. It looks, at first sight, rather antisociological, and came out only in 1981; however we categorize it, its affinity with Koenigsberger and Walzer seems obvious, and unless I am mistaken it shares with my own piece a good deal of input from Sartre. Donald Kelley's *The Beginning of Ideology: Consciousness and Society in the French Reformation* is a narrative account of the early history of French Protestantism; it is also a sort of exemplary tale of personal liberation, and Kelley is a great deal more open about this than I was.[18] He starts off, attractively to me, by saying that he wants to break the mold of vulgar or inattentive materialism in which historians tend to write, to get rid of Freud, Marx, and talk about modernization, and to restore subjective consciousness to sixteenth-century history. The plan of the book, by conventional standards eccentric, seems an interesting experiment in itself, and well designed to shake out tendentious abstraction and restore to us real people and real life; he gives himself room for memorable descriptions of Beza, Dolet, Ramus, Hotman, and Condé at the crises of their individual lives. By placing their experiences of conversion in the context, not of a problematic traditional society, but of what he calls a "primal dialectic" of relations between children and parents, he seems to me to have made Walzer's point more successfully than Walzer did and, despite some worrying language, to have put his finger close to a neuralgic area of sixteenth-century reality, especially French.[19] My own conjecture would be rather the opposite of his, that the unwillingness of the Roman Church to alter its anarchistic theology of marriage before the very end of the Council of Trent persuaded a lot of respectable French parents that domestic authority would be better preserved under an alternative regime; but child psychology is no doubt a more promising field of investigation for the peculiarly autonomous souls Kelley was writing about, and perhaps for Huguenots in general. After this cheering start, and much enlightenment by the way, it is a sad comedown to be offered at the end of the book the dry bread of "identification . . . socialization . . . intellectualization . . . legitimation . . . publication . . . organization" in the guise of a structural analysis of the French Protestant movement. I appreciate that he is trying to be systematically descriptive without being reductive; but, rather as with Walzer, his language works against him, dragging him to take seriously a dud piece of sociologizing abstraction from the sixties called "On the Etiology of Internal Wars," and to suppose that there is something to be learnt about Huguenots from the literature of relative deprivation.[20]

There seem to be two reasons for this disappointing outcome. One of them is a general point about society which I shall come to in a moment. The other is that what Kelley is really interested in here is not Protestants, but ideology – which, I imagine, has something to do with his describing himself in his blurb as a "lapsed Protestant." "The ideological process," he says, "is not dependent upon a particular content"; which seems to mean that you can have what is worthwhile in Protestantism without actually having to be a Protestant yourself. As a statement about one's private life, that seems fair enough, and I imagine that most of my authors might have said something similar. But as a guide to writing a history book about Protestants, there must be something the matter with it, which the end of the book seems to show. As he describes it, the *dénouement* of a saga beginning with traumatic individual conversion and entering collective history via persecution, proselytizing, and civil war is not the victory, defeat, or survival of the cause of true religion; not the St. Bartholomew Massacre or the Edict of Nantes or its revocation. It is the "sublimation" (I use Kelley's own word) of this cause into "ideology." The ideology, you will not be surprised to learn, was expressed in statements of progressive political theory and is historically meaningful because it managed to enunciate a prophetic message about "the human condition," or life in general. The message is, roughly, self-determination.[21] If Theodore Beza or François Hotman had actually *been* lapsed Protestants, this would be a sensible view to take; as they were not, Kelley's commentary on their distinguished history seems, in the end, gratuitous. I think it is a test of this that it would not have been possible to write the last five sentences consistently in the past historic tense.

A strange thing about *The Beginning of Ideology,* on which those who know more about American academe than I do may be able to shed some light, is that Kelley took almost no notice of the work of the best American historian of the Huguenots, Robert Kingdon. Walzer, in twenty-five pages of a book really about something else, managed to make relevant to his theme the substance of Kingdon's first book, *Geneva and the Coming of the Wars of Religion in France,* published in 1956. Sixteen years after Walzer, Kingdon having published a sequel in the meantime, Kelley gave no substantive reference to and made no actual use of either. He was missing something. In the second of Kingdon's books, *Geneva and the Consolidation of the French Protestant Movement,*[22] we find that between 1562 and 1572, in such time as it could spare from fighting a civil war, the French Protestant community was racked by a severe dispute between most of its pastors, led by Beza, and some of its most intelligent laymen, including the celebrated logician Peter Ramus. The dispute was about the constitution of a reformed church: the pastors were presbyterians and the laymen congregationalists. There is plenty of stimulating matter in Kingdon's narrative. It casts doubt on the common idea, refurbished by Koenigsberger, that Calvinism succeeded by organization. It evokes Walzer's notion of a conflict between the Huguenot clergy and nobility, but suggests that, if there was one, the nobility lost it. It might be thought to show how much deeper was the Huguenots' commitment to their idea of the church than to the political arguments which they offered in self-defense after the trauma of the 1572 massacres. But the church, as such, is not a category in Kelley's description, which is the most amazing categorical anachronism of all. After telling us about his lapsedness, he also tells us in the blurb of his book that he is now going to give up sixteenth-century history: he has gone to edit the *Journal of the History of Ideas* instead.

I sum up what seems to have been the message of the body of historians of the wars of religion during the past thirty years, which I have represented, I hope not unfairly, by my four examples. It has been the message of the media. People do not really fight about religion. If they seem to be doing so, they must really be fighting about something else. Social analysis has been the normal method for finding out what that something else was, and it has generally turned out to be some form of Weber's breakthrough to modernity. Since that, or something like it, has been supposed to be what was substantially going on under the accidents of the wars of religion, statements about Christianity have been interpreted as ideological, that is, as saying something different from what they purported to say. Despite the talent and ingenuity which have gone into this effort of reinterpretation, because of that talent and ingenuity, it has led with seeming inevitability to conclusions at variance with historical truth and common sense. Do I wish to say, in the graphic phrase used by Jonathan Clark of a similar phase of British historiography, that the social or sociological interpretation of the wars of religion has "hit the buffers"?[23] Well, yes, that is roughly what I do want to say. I think there is no doubt that a crash has occurred, and should like to conclude by enquiring more generally why it should have done and what we can do to rescue something from it.

On the reasons I shall be brief, because I have implied most of them already and talked about one of them elsewhere. There seem to be two. One is a rather important fact about society, the other an accidental fact (at least I think it is an accidental fact) about the discipline of sociology as applied to our subject.

The fact about society is that there is good reason to suppose that no such thing existed in the sixteenth century. I suspect that there was no such thing because there was no such concept: we (meaning the historians I have mentioned) could not have got Shakespeare or Montaigne to agree or disagree with what we were saying, because they could not have understood it. They had, and used, the word, but meant something different by it. They would also have failed to see our problem, since they had a perfectly satisfactory system for referring to everything we might want to mean by society. There was nothing we could refer to which they would not recognize as falling under the heading "Commonwealth," or under the heading "Church" or "Christianity." All the features ascribed by Weber or Walzer to "traditional society" – degree, custom, personalized relations and so on – fell quite adequately into one or other of these categories, if they did not fall into both at once. Perhaps I say that too confidently: Luther invented a three-category model, though I do not think it worked. But it seems to me enough to substantiate what I have been saying about categorical anachronism. Society is a third leg which they did not need and I do not think we need: a sixteenth-century historian who straps it on takes the risk of falling on his face.[24]

The fact about sociology is that sociologists of religion, so far as my reading goes, seem unable to talk about wars of religion. One can see how this would be with Durkheim or somebody writing in Durkheim's tradition: if you think that the sacred is the social, the social the collective, and the collectivity coterminous with the commonwealth, you seem to be unable to conceive of a war of religion at all, at least within the boundaries of a state. With Weber and Weberians I think that there is a different problem: you have opposites and contraries, but opposites and contraries do not make war. For a war you need enemies, which are something different, and I do not see where a strict Weberian is going to find them. To massacre for modernization is irrational; to massacre against modernization is rational, but Weber's and Walzer's traditionalists do not sound as if they would have the gumption to do it. It is true that one Weberian, the late Benjamin Nelson, did discover enemies and enmity in his *The Idea of Usury*. But I think he found them by violating some Weberian instincts in order to reformulate a classic Weberian problem, the connection between the Reformation and social ethics or human relations. Arguably he did this when he decided that a question in Society had to be treated as a question in Christianity; surely he did it when he conceded that, if one was to talk intelligibly about society in the sixteenth century, one would have to use the word in the sense in which people used it at the time: companionship, fellowship, relationship, participation of persons with one another. He found enmity because he found friendship, otherhood because he found brotherhood. I do not think he has been much followed; he was certainly not followed by Walzer.[25]

Nevertheless Nelson's case seems to me rather exemplary and will serve to launch me in the direction of some positive (I hesitate to say "innovative") conclusions. For I do not wish to say that the founding fathers of the sociology of religion have nothing to say to an early modern historian. By affirming that ideas of the holy, or moral passion, are something to do with states of human relations, they have told historians something we needed to be told. But we can use this message without burdening ourselves or our readers with the encumbrance of "Society" with a capital *S*. In this spirit, I have three thoughts to offer as a contribution to the rescuing or redemptive process.

First: If I exclude talk about Society from useful discussion of the wars of religion, I do not exclude as irrelevant all topics which have been or might be considered social. I think it was entirely appropriate for Walzer and myself to suppose that a relevant matter was some constitutional state of unease or hostility between laity and clergy: the thought was often expressed at the time and seems to stand up to close description. It was also relevant and appropriate for us to have talked about clientage, fidelity, deference in connection with people's choices of faith and community. When I talked about "seigneurial Catholicism" in England and others talked about "seigneurial Protestantism" in France, we were not committing a categorical anachronism, though we probably overdid it.[26] But we did not need to shelter these conceptions under the umbrella "Society:" they were quite adequately accommodated in the mansions of Church and Commonwealth. The same will be true of the questions about males and females which have risen to the surface more recently.

Second: There is a rich seam to be mined by following Benjamin Nelson's example and translating Society into society. The supreme symbol and embodiment of Christian society in this, proper, sense is the Eucharist, and (though they have not been mainly dealing with our period, but with times and situations somewhat earlier) we have an international team of distinguished examples of how to go about this central topic: Henri de Lubac on the doctrine of the Body of Christ, Mervyn James on the Corpus Christi celebrations of fifteenth-century English towns, Bernd Moeller on the "sacred society" of German cities before and during the Reformation.[27] Their "society," at least as I understand it, is not given, but to be worked for, achieved, and if possible embodied, if only on festal occasions.

Third: In my own field, we are lucky enough to have a model in what I am reasonably sure has been the most important contribution to understanding the wars of religion made in our time. I doubt if I am telling much of a secret by revealing that it was made by Natalie Davis, and was called "The Rites of Violence."[28] It was, in the first place, a product of its time, and a fellow-passenger with the books and essays I have talked about. It was published in 1973, written in Berkeley, California, and at least partly inspired by Belfast. It was indebted to E. P. Thompson. It revealed reading in the social sciences (Charles Tilly on "isomorphy," somebody else on "conditions for guilt-free massacre.") It talked about roles, goals, and legitimation. It appeared in *Past and Present*. In her last sentence the author spoke darkly about "changing our central values." All circumstances, you might think, of a classic text of liberation history.

This was indeed exactly what it was, though in a sense of its own. She cleared out an immense heap of historians' garbage: clapped-out constructions put up by supposedly social historians of Christian violence from the pogroms of Spanish Jews in the fourteenth century to the Gordon Riots in the eighteenth. And first and best of all, she cleared out Society. You may not believe this, but it is true. She used the word only once in the piece and in a proper sense of something you could envisage as an ideal or for the future: compare her fellow-worker Phyllis Mack, who, writing at the same time at much the same length on much the same subject (the iconoclastic riots of 1566 in the Netherlands), used it twenty-four times, not counting synonyms.[29] She used the word "social" once or twice, but with enough relatedness to carry it ("social resentment"); and I think this was a hangover from her unpublished thesis on Lyon, from which she borrowed a table. She made a very careful, and occasional, choice of alternatives: "social body," "religious community," or "community." She used "community" in two cases, once to mean "religious community," and once about the modern world. It seems to me that she very distinctly avoided using the word "Society" in her last sentence, about central values; it reads as if the word had been on the tip of her tongue. I used to think that this avoidance had been accidental; now, rightly or wrongly, it strikes me as an intentional act of self-discipline and genuine liberation.

What it did for her was to enable her to record what was actually there. It enabled her to convey with a vernal freshness the sounds and sights and smells, frightful as they frequently were, of France in the age of the St. Bartholomew massacres. That was not, in my view, a trivial matter: you cannot smell Society. It enabled her to embark on the restitution of proper categories: sacred and profane, magistracy and ministry, male and female, not to mention Catholic and Protestant. It enabled historians of, roughly, innovative and traditional attitudes to communicate with one another.

I end with an anecdote. One of the sources of Christian violence which Natalie Davis talks about is the Old Testament. She quotes, at the beginning of the piece, two famous passages as they were conveyed by Catholic preachers to the people of Paris during the 1560s: the injunction from Deuteronomy, chapter 13, to slay those who departed to serve alien gods and the account of the slaying of Jezebel by Jehu from the Second Book of Kings, chapter 9. While I was refreshing my memory of Davis's essay, I found in the mail a short piece by Patrick Collison on the captivity of Mary, Queen of Scots. In interpreting a comment by her jailer, the godly Sir Amyas Paulet, on the "foolish pity" which would be shown in sparing Mary's life, Collison cited the same two passages. They are not pretty, but the coincidence gave pleasure.[30] I was also thinking of what Davis had said about the intimacy between modes of murder and destruction and modes of Christian, or Catholic, worship; about water and fire. I thought of *Little Gidding*, and the death of water and fire; then of the Elizabethan Puritan's dogged answer to the charge that he and his brethren were sowing discord in the Church of England: "Can ye put fire and water together, but there will be a rumble?"[31]

Historians should probably keep to themselves their views about the connection between what they write and absolute morality or the contemporary world. They will not be judged by that. But when they have done their job as faithfully as they can, there may be a case for their coming clean. Professor Collinson deplores the lack of "foolish pity" in the public affairs of our time. Professor Davis says, a little nervously, that "the rites of violence are not the *rights* of violence in any absolute sense."[32] What I say is that a historian may do his job properly and take what view he likes of the conduct of his subjects, except to forgive them because they knew not what they did.

NOTES

1. Thomas A. Kselman, *Miracles and Prophecies in Nineteenth-century France* (New Brunswick, N.J., 1983), p. 3.

2. The origins of this frame of mind can be traced in A. G. Dickens and John M. Tonkin, *The Reformation in Historical Thought* (Oxford, 1985), part 2.

3. J. H. Elliott, *Europe Divided, 1559–1598* (London, 1968), has rightly become the classic account. Since I was not very welcoming, when it appeared, to Marvin O'Connell's volume on *The Counter-Reformation* (New York, 1974), in The Rise of Modern Europe series, I should now say that I think there is a lot to be said for its prudence, humanity, and sense of connection. His

final quotation from *Don Quixote*—"Let us proceed fairly and softly, and not look for this year's birds in last year's nests"—might serve as a motto for us all. To the two principal theaters of the wars of religion there are extremely satisfying guides in J. H. M. Salmon, *Society in Crisis: France in the Sixteenth Century* (London, 1975), though I deplore its title, and in Geoffrey Parker, *The Dutch Revolt* (London, 1977).

4. *Journal of Modern History* 27 (1955), pp. 335–51; reprinted in his *Estates and Revolutions* (Ithaca, N.Y., 1971), pp. 224–53, which I use.

5. Art. cit., p. 251.

6. Art. cit., pp. 234f. I have not seen *Revolutionnaire Reformatie*, but see J. W. Smit, "The Present Position of Studies Regarding the Revolt of the Netherlands," in *Britain and the Netherlands*, vol. 1, ed. J. S. Bromley and E. H. Kossman (London, 1960), pp. 17–24. Cf. P. Geyl, *The Revolt of the Netherlands, 1555–1609* (English trans., 2nd ed., London, 1958), pp. 119–44; and L. J. Rogier, *Geschiedenis van het Katholicisme in Noord-Nederland in de 16e en de 17e Eeuw* (3 vols., Amsterdam, 1945–1947). Van Gelder seems to have changed his mind later.

7. Art. cit., p. 249.

8. Michael Walzer, *The Revolution of the Saints: A Study in the Origins of Radical Politics* (Cambridge, Mass., 1965; I use the paperback edition, New York, 1968); Christopher Hill, *The World Turned Upside Down: Radical Ideas during the English Revolution* (London, 1972). On the term "radical" I share the reservations of Jonathan Clark, *English Society* (see below, n. 23), pp. xiii, 3, 277–348.

9. Walzer, *Revolution of the Saints*, pp. 57, 304.

10. Ibid., pp. 27ff.

11. Ibid., pp. 1–21, 300–320, quotation from p. 312.

12. Patrick Collinson, *The Religion of Protestants: The Church in English Society, 1559–1625* (Oxford, 1982), ch. 4, "Magistracy and Ministry," pp. 141–88. The book was originally the Ford Lectures for 1979.

13. Walzer, *Revolution of the Saints*, p. 92; Collinson, *Religion of Protestants*, pp. 164–70.

14. John Bossy, "The Character of Elizabethan Catholicism," *Past and Present*, no. 21 (1962), pp. 39–59; reprinted in T. Aston, ed., *Crisis in Europe 1560–1660* (London, 1965), pp. 223–46, which I use.

15. Art. cit., p. 246, cf. 236–38; J.-P Sartre, *Critique de la raison dialectique* 1 (Paris, 1960), 1:231–77. I do not think I can have read this when I thought of the phrase, but I had certainly read Francis Jeanson, *Sartre par lui-même* (Paris, 1955), pp. 165ff.

16. Art. cit., pp. 226, 229.

17. Christopher Haigh, "The Continuity of Catholicism in the English Reformation," *Past and Present*, no. 93 (1981), pp. 37–69; Patrick McGrath, "Elizabeth Catholicism: A Reconsideration," *Journal of Ecclesiastical History*

35 (1984): 417. I found a more historical context for my argument in H. O. Evennett, *The Spirit of the Counter-Reformation* (Cambridge, 1968; paperback Notre Dame, Ind.: 1970), and it was accordingly modified in my *The English Catholic Community, 1570–1850* (London, 1975); it was still excessive, but I do not think I should be doing a service to Elizabethan history if I withdrew it entirely.

18. Donald R. Kelley, *The Beginning of Ideology: Consciousness and Society in the French Reformation* (Cambridge, 1981), preface and p. 277 (on Koenigsberger).

19. Ibid., pp. 10, 70 ff.; cf. my *Christianity in the West, 1400–1700* (Oxford, 1985), pp. 23–25.

20. Kelley, *Beginning of Ideology*, p. 327, and epilogue, pp. 337–44.

21. Ibid., pp. 299 ff., 322, 327.

22. Robert M. Kingdon, *Geneva and the Coming of the Wars of Religion in France* (Geneva, 1956); *Geneva and the Consolidation of the French Protestant Movement* (Madison, Wisc., 1967), especially pp. 37–122; Walzer, *Revolution of the Saints*, pp. 68, 70.

23. J. C. D. Clark, "On Hitting the Buffers: The Historiography of England's Ancien Regime," *Past and Present*, no. 117 (1987), pp. 195–207. I record my general sympathy with this line and with Clark's *English Society, 1688–1832* (Cambridge, 1985), about which I like most things except the title. Even that I probably ought to swallow on the principles expounded in the piece cited in the next note.

24. The argument is elaborated in my "Some Elementary Forms of Durkheim," *Past and Present*, no. 95 (1982), pp. 3–18; cf. the more learned argument to the same effect by Stuart Clark, "French Historians and Early Modern Popular Culture," *Past and Present*, no. 100 (1983), pp. 62–99. It goes back, via D. Z. Phillips, *Religion without Explanation* (Oxford, 1976), to Wittgenstein.

25. Benjamin Nelson, *The Idea of Usury: from Tribal Brotherhood to Universal Otherhood* (2nd ed., Chicago/London, 1969), *passim;* I tried to follow him myself in "The Mass as a Social Institution, 1200–1700," *Past and Present,* no. 100 (1983), see pp. 37 ff.

26. Bossy, "The Character of Elizabethan Catholicism," p. 224; cf. Menna Prestwich, ed., *International Calvinism, 1541–1715* (Oxford, 1985), p. 80.

27. Henri de Lubac, *Corpus Mysticum: l'Eucharistie et l'Église au Moyen Âge* (2nd ed., Paris, 1949); M. E. James, "Ritual, Drama and Social Body in the Late Mediaeval English Town," *Past and Present,* no. 98 (1983), pp. 3–29, reprinted in his *Society, Politics and Culture* (Cambridge, 1986), pp. 16–47; Bernd Moeller, *Imperial Cities and the Reformation* (English trans., Philadelphia, 1972), pp. 41–115.

28. Natalie Z. Davis, "The Rites of Violence: Religious Riot in 16th-Century France," *Past and Present,* no. 59 (1973), pp. 53–91, reprinted in her

Society and Culture in Sixteenth-Century France (London, 1975), pp. 152–87, which I use.

29. Phyllis Mack, "The Wonderyear: Reformed Preaching and Icono-clasm in the Netherlands," in J. Obelkevich, ed., *Religion and the People, 800–1700* (Chapel Hill, N.C., 1979), pp. 191–220; cf. her *Calvinist Preaching and Iconoclasm in the Netherlands* (Cambridge, 1978), published under the name Phyllis Mack Crew. Of these, the first seems to me a classic example of the destruction of historical sense by talk about society (see pp. 206, 208, 211); cf. Parker, *The Dutch Revolt*, pp. 74 ff., 288, n. 7, for something more like real life. The book, where the argument is greatly watered down, conveys a lot of valuable descriptive knowledge. The discussion about Davis's article between herself and Janine Estèbe in *Past and Present*, no. 67 (1975), pp. 127–35, gives quite a good idea of what was at stake in the piece.

30. Davis, "The Rites of Violence," pp. 152–53; Patrick Collinson, *The English Captivity of Mary, Queen of Scots* (Sheffield, 1987), p. 5.

31. Davis, "The Rites of Violence," pp. 178 ff., 185 f.; T. S. Eliot, "Little Gidding," lines 74–77, from *Four Quartets;* Collinson, "The Godly: Aspects of Popular Protestantism," in *Godly People: Essays on English Protestantism and Puritanism* (London, 1983), p. 5. It has been gratifying to see, after this essay was written, that the last chapter of Collinson's latest book, *The Birthpangs of Protestant England* (London, 1988) is entitled "Wars of Religion." It describes a "war in the streets" less bloody than what occurred on the streets of France, but leading in the end to a civil war which English historians are belatedly coming to acknowledge as a war of religion (pp. 127–55, especially pp. 132 f., 136, 152 f.).

32. Collinson, *English Captivity of Mary, Queen of Scots*, p. 4; Davis, "The Rites of Violence," p. 187.

8

Historiographical Heresy: Catholicism as a Model for American Religious History

Jon Butler

Historians usually doubt the value of historical models to guide research. Most see their craft as implicitly nominal. They eschew philosophies of history and frequently denigrate the influence of ideology in shaping books and articles. They make sense of this event and that circumstance; if a model emerges here, in the current study, it probably will be of little use there, in the next one.

It may be difficult, however, to find a more strongly "modeled" field than that of American religious history. From the 1840s forward, when the Presbyterian missionary in Europe, Robert Baird, wrote histories that celebrated American religion as one means of proselytizing there, Puritan themes have dominated the field—Calvinism, evangelicalism, declension, rising secularism, laicization, democracy, and American exceptionalism. Other concerns are handled as variations on the Puritan model and others which don't fit at all are simply described as aberrations. Few know the power of this Puritan Ur-text better than do historians of non-Puritan groups. Scholars who write about Catholicism, Eastern Orthodoxy, Judaism, and native American religion have often felt adrift or alienated as they attempt to fit their subjects into the Puritan and Protestant model. Their subjects emerge as "legitimate" only when they surrender their distinctive non-Puritan characteristics. James Hennesey exemplified the pattern recently when he described American Catholicism as a "Square Peg in a Round Hole." It is a wonderful phrase that simultaneously connotes Catholicism's seeming distance from the Puritan model and the frustration of its historians endlessly seeking a proper "fit."[1]

Recent events demonstrate how poorly the Puritan model comprehends modern American religious development. The early healing career of Oral Roberts and the continuing importance of shrines among Catholics point up the breadth of the desire for direct supernatural intervention manifested in divine healing in American religion. The refusal of many followers to abandon Jim Bakker and Jimmy Swaggart after the public revelations of their peccadillos reveals a commitment to joy and forgiveness that would have astonished even nineteenth-century Arminians, much less seventeenth-century Calvinists. The importance of Robert Schuller's "Crystal Cathedral" in Orange County, California, points up the influence of place, not just grace, in American Protestantism. Contests for control of the Southern Baptist Convention suggest how thoroughly a love of authority rests uneasily alongside the evangelicals' seeming antiauthoritarianism. And a continuing evangelical anger about the Supreme Court decision in *Engle v. Vitale* (1966) outlawing compulsory school prayer demonstrates how thinly voluntarism can run in the American Protestant tradition.

These complexities of American religion simply are not well encompassed by the Puritan model of American religious history. In fact, obeisance to the Puritan myth produces misshapen judgments about the American religious experience, as R. Laurence Moore has so eloquently pointed out in his recent book, *Religious Outsiders and the Making of Americans*. Historians who are overly concerned by "fit" and "accommodation" look too uncritically at the shape of the interpretative house into which they and their subjects are being squeezed. The Puritan model, rather than explaining the rich complexity of the developing American religious tradition, is too often startled by it. Too much importance is assigned to seventeenth-century Puritanism, for example, too little to eighteenth- and nineteenth-century religious movements that owed few debts to Puritanism. As penance, we cannot merely go back to the "facts," as though they can speak for themselves. Rather, we must develop more complex, more sophisticated, and above all, more accurate models of religious practice and development. Only in doing so can we better understand the remarkable produce of the spiritual cornucopia that has so consistently typified American religion from colonization to the present.

Of course, it may seem only cheeky to suggest that Catholicism provides a beginning model for American religious history. Catholicism seems foreign rather than native, institutional rather than individual, hierarchical rather than democratic, and liturgical rather than evangelical. Yet it is the very richness and complexity of Catholicism that advances its promise as a model for understanding the American religious experience.

Out of the rich complexity of the Catholic tradition, six themes seem particularly suited to better understanding the substance and dynamics of American religious development. One is ethnic heterogeneity. Religious history is, above all else, the history of people, and in the Catholic as well as American experience, people come in an astonishing variety of shapes, colors, and cultures. They usually exhibit another characteristic as well: a remarkable spiritual heterogeneity that frequently defies institutional efforts to shape an orthodox laity. A third theme concerns a strong interest in demonstrations of divine intervention, not merely in the past, but also in the present. In some regards, this is one of the important themes that uplifts the specifically religious from that which might be considered philosophical or ethical: supernatural activity perceptible to modern men and women. A fourth theme concerns moral behavior or, more precisely, its sources. Vagaries in lay religious practice lead us to ask about the sources of moral behavior in societies where many people know little about religion and where churches are well aware that they hold no monopoly on moral instruction. A fifth theme concerns the importance of place—sacred place. Among Protestants as among Catholics faith often has distinctly physical *and* aesthetic dimensions that typically (but not exclusively) are expressed through architecture, decor, and other aspects of the physical environment. The final theme is one for which Catholicism is almost notorious both within and without its constituency: institutional authority. If religious history properly centers on faith practiced by the laity, while church history centers on faith as taught by churches, it is nonetheless crucial to understand how institutions attempt to shape lay faith, a point often lost in the Protestant model that stresses individualism and antiauthoritarianism in American religion.

Two caveats before we begin, however. First, the model suggested here constitutes only a beginning suggestion, not a finished product. Both Catholicism and the American religious tradition are sufficiently complex to make it absurd to select several themes from either, then claim that they constitute the heart, essence, or achievement of either or both traditions. Second, the model is based on a sense of what is admirable in Catholic religious history, not on its typical practice. Catholic history is no more free from the foibles of the historian's craft than is any other history, and achievement lags behind promise there as often as it does elsewhere, hence, the aphorism: do what we say, not what we do. Still, Catholic history at its best may touch important issues in American religious development more effectively than does the traditional Puritan-centered model.

Catholicism's relevance to American religious history generally has been advanced dramatically by the renewed attention to immigration and ethnicity in American history. Moreover, it has become impossible to write about immigration without writing about religion, and about a multiplicity of religions. Timothy L. Smith is probably overly optimistic when he describes the immigrant experience as a "theologizing experience." Yet immigrants and religion formed positive unions, not only among Catholic Chicanos, Puerto Ricans, Cubans, and Poles, but among Lutheran Swedes, Danes, Norwegians, and Germans.[2]

Certainly, it is impossible to discuss either immigration or immigrant religion without reference to Catholicism. Whether in monographic studies (such as Jay Dolan's *Immigrant Church* and Robert Orsi's *Madonna of 115th Street*), general histories of American Catholicism (such as those by John Tracy Ellis, Hennesey, and Dolan) or general histories of American immigration (including Thomas Archdeacon's recent survey), Catholicism stands at the very center of the American immigrant experience. This would be true even if American Catholicism had not blossomed beyond its antebellum Irish and German origins. But it is more so because Catholicism was the recipient and beneficiary of so many immigrant experiences stretching across so many decades. Moreover, unlike Turner's frontier, this immigrant and ethnic experience remains open. The reception of immigrants from Mexico, Puerto Rico, or southeast Asia has emerged as a vital social issue for Catholics and all Americans. Sadly, the measure of this continuing openness is most reluctantly seen in the re-emergence of anti-immigrant groups, such as the American Immigration Control Foundation, that promote consciousness about America's long history of immigration restriction and that openly fuel the fires of religious prejudice, particularly against Catholic immigrants from Latin America and non-Christian immigrants from Asia.[3]

The value of the immigration perspective, so obvious in nineteenth- and twentieth-century American history, is crucial in more subtle ways to understanding seventeenth-century Puritanism. Even New Englanders had to *become* Americans, and if it was their genius to turn Old World flight into New World errand, sometimes transforming themselves and their environment as Perry Miller argued, the Puritans had to get there first. Equally important, the persistence and character of English immigration after 1660 holds a critical, yet largely unexplored, key to understanding Puritanism's decline in America. Although we know virtually all there is to know about astonishing numbers of individual immigrants from Old to New England who came between 1621 and 1650, we know next to nothing about those who came after 1650. Were they connected to dissenting congregations in England? Did they come in family groups as did their predecessors? Is it possible that their emigration looked much more like the astonishingly secular and individualist immigration which characterized the Chesapeake Bay region between 1607 and 1670? Did this immigration combine with internal changes in New England to shape the declension that the Mathers bemoaned so after 1680? In short, it is possible that the immigration process, which created New England Puritanism, subsequently played a major role in unraveling it?[4]

The eighteenth-century American experience magnifies the centrality of immigration to American Protestant development. Marilyn Westerkamp and Leigh Eric Schmidt detail the importance of Scottish and Scots-Irish ecclesiastical and liturgical traditions in shaping Presbyterian denominational and liturgical development. They describe the vital Scottish tradition of "sacramental piety," whose communal emotionalism virtually created the American revival tradition, a tradition often mistakenly credited to the Puritans. Studies by Daniel Thorpe of Moravian settlement in North Carolina and by Mechal Sobel of African interchange with Virginia colonists stress the pluralism of both tidewater and frontier society and suggest that "acculturation" was something experienced by established settlers as well as newcomers. Even if the interchange among Virginia blacks and whites was not as equal as Sobel suggests, its existence clearly shaped both southern society and southern religion.[5]

The influence of ethnicity also extends far beyond the Catholic experience. Ethnicity is an elusive concept. Its most supple and persuasive formalizations stress a sense of "peoplehood" centering on both national and religious identity. Two contrasting examples demonstrate how thoroughly this sense of peoplehood affects religion. The Huguenots, who left France in the 1680s to escape religious persecution and became the first major continental Europeans to settle in Britain's mainland colonies, illustrate the result of group fragmentation. Huguenots gained extraordinary material prosperity in America. They also disappeared quickly as an ethnic as well as a religious group by taking non-Huguenot spouses and by leaving the Huguenot churches. By 1750 only two independent Huguenot congregations still existed in the colonies, in New York City and Charleston, and many of their "members" also belonged to non-Huguenot congregations and supported the old Huguenot congregations as a charity. In contrast, the experience of Scottish settlers in New Jersey demonstrates how Presbyterianism flourished by synthesizing themes of national identity, Presbyterian catechizing, and an accelerating revival tradition. As a result, a religiously fractured people at home in the 1680s emerged in New Jersey and in America as homogeneously Presbyterian by 1750, creating in the process the seemingly indelible "Scottish Presbyterian."[6]

Mormonism further illustrates the importance of a sense of ethnicity—peoplehood—in nineteenth-century American religion. Jan Shipps has demonstrated that as Mormons erected and ran their intricate theological maze they created the processes that gave birth to a powerful group and religious identity. Kenneth Winn has also shown how Mormons shifted their political identity and national loyalty and thereby shaped their religious progress. Between 1830 and 1850 they changed from a group evidencing enthusiastic "republican" principles aligned with classical Jeffersonian values to a group distinguished by deep alienation, anger, and hostility bordering on outright rebellion. This shift followed their experience of virulent anti-Mormon violence and the assassination of Joseph Smith in Carthage, Illinois, in 1844, again pointing up the role of external pressures in creating group identity. Of course, like the Catholicism with which nativists so often linked it in the 1840s, Mormonism might be considered an aberration in American religion. But, surely, the point of recent studies has been to lift this veil. In these works Mormonism emerges as a quintessentially American religion that survived and prospered when its distinctive theology meshed with its enveloping sense of peoplehood—of ethnicity—in a unique American environment where support as well as hostility shaped the movement.[7]

Heterodoxy also is crucial to understanding Americans and Catholics. Ironically, anti-Catholic literature in America long stressed Catholic homogeneity; Catholicism was dangerous because it brooked no dissent. In fact, few historians understand the persistence of heterodoxy —doctrinal as well as ethnic—better than historians of Catholicism. Catholic historians take it for granted that they will deal with diversity, eclecticism, even chaos in the history of the church. In the fourteenth as well as the fourth century, orthodoxy was a goal, not an achievement, and the same has been true in the twentieth century. Moreover, especially in the United States, ethnic variety has almost certainly guaranteed remarkably different understandings of Catholic faith and the relationship of faith to society. The tensions also range far beyond ethnicity. From antebellum contests over the "trustee" issue, to the liturgical and theological disputes spawned by Vatican II, American Catholics and their historians have long since learned that the church best resembles a well-worn umbrella sheltering an extraordinary variety of opinions and practices on both ecclesiastical and spiritual issues.[8]

In contrast, historians of American Protestantism tend to stress homogeneity as the model for their groups, as did Perry Miller in *The New England Mind* and *Orthodoxy in New England*. The consequence is serious. Such a homogeneous model is frequently unable to explain discord and division within religious groups and, when forced to do so, resorts to invoking external causes as the culprit. Witness the difference in historians' treatment of Anne Hutchinson and Dorothy Day. Neither were representative of Puritans or Catholics. But only Protestants would assume that they needed to be. Hutchinson is treated largely as an aberration within the history of Puritanism. Indeed, what may still be the best study of the movement—Emery Battis's *Saints and Sectaries*—actually explains it away as a product of menopausal hysteria. Only Philip Gura's recent book, *A Glimpse of Sion's Glory,* enables the historian to predict the rise of Hutchinson and her followers by emphasizing the diversity and radicalism within New England Puritan ranks, especially before 1660. Day can be and is treated as a unique figure who also occupied a historically understandable place within the broad spectrum of modern Catholic belief and practice. In her autobiography Day described how, in a church with many traditions in thought and practice, she selected some and rejected others and did so consciously rather than accidentally. This point is central to the historians who have grappled with Day's career. Mel Piehl, Nancy Robert, and, most recently, James Fisher, all treat Day as important not because she brought heterodoxy to Catholicism but because she so thoroughly reshaped one of modern Catholicism's many competing constituencies, Catholic liberalism.[9]

The ability of the Catholic historical model to handle religious heterodoxy also enables historians to better probe interaction between "popular" and "official" religion and to grapple with the problem of religious syncretism. Historians of Catholicism have had to deal with the conversion of the Roman Empire, the problems of "paganism," non-Christian belief and practice, and Christianization. They have also long acknowledged limitations in lay understanding and practice of Christianity. It is not surprising, therefore, that the initial historical work on popular religion—religion as it was understood and practiced by laypeople—emerged among scholars of European Catholicism. Medievalists had long felt compelled to explain the extraordinary visual images present in Europe's cathedrals. Gabriel Le Bras, the French "religious sociologist" (his term), sought to put social science in the service of Christianization; after all, he reasoned, how could the Church bring the gospel to the masses if it knew so little about them, including religious yearnings only partially understood or tapped by the church? Lucien Febvre and many other historians active with the Annales School began probing early modern religion in their drive to uncover the textures of daily life.[10]

The contrast in the reception of several recent books reveals the resistance of the Protestant model to the vagaries of popular religion. Even the critics of Jean Delumeau's *Catholicism between Luther and Voltaire: A New View of the Counter-Reformation* viewed it as a logical consequence of Catholic concern about erratic lay religious practice from ancient to modern times, however much they disagreed with Delumeau's formulation of the dynamics between church and laity. Reaction to two books on popular Protestantism has been much more hostile, however, one in a subtle way, the other directly. Keith Thomas's *Religion and the Decline of Magic* has received nothing but extraordinary praise. Yet twenty years after its publication, its findings remain largely unintegrated into synoptic histories of English Puritanism or Tudor-Stuart culture. The subject of magic and popular religion still is foreign territory in British religious history, and the only substantial attempt to provide an integrated approach to the topic is David D. Hall's book on American Puritans, *Worlds of Wonder, Days of Judgment: Popular Religious Belief in Early New England*. Gerald Strauss's *Luther's House of Learning* also received considerable praise, but often won biting criticism as well, some of it verging on the vicious. German historians seem to have been angered by Strauss's suggestion that the gap between Lutheran church teachings and lay behavior might have been immense. Surely, such findings can be traced to peculiar conditions in the unrepresentative dioceses he studied and perhaps to Strauss's gullibility in believing self-serving negative reports from Lutheran bishops.[11]

In America, where one might think popular or lay religion would draw the special attention from historians, particularly given the rhetoric about voluntarism and laicization in American Protestantism, work has progressed slowly. It is no accident that the most successful study of popular religion in America is Robert Orsi's *Madonna of 115th Street.* Orsi reveals the tensions that existed between faith as perceived by New York's Irish Catholic hierarchy and its late nineteenth-century Sicilian immigrants even as he demonstrates how the immigrant community worked out a popular faith that exercised an enormous influence over Italians in Harlem from the 1890s to the 1950s. If he does not tell us what happened to that faith amid post-World War II suburbanization, we are left with a rich portrait that prepares us to anticipate future tensions.

Popular religion has emerged as important in Mormon history as well, though with a somewhat peculiar twist. Charges of fortune-finding and magic lodged against Joseph Smith have informed Mormon history and anti-Mormon agitation since 1830, though for many years Mormon authorities regularly denied them. But recently, Mormon historians have accommodated such views even as incontrovertible evidence of magical practice has mounted. In his recent biography of Smith, Richard Bushman acknowledges many of the practices, then notes that since they were so common, they scarcely detracted from Smith's legitimacy. This approach begs the question of the precise relationship between folk supernaturalism and organized religion. But it also has the distinct advantage of acknowledging an interrelationship between folk supernaturalism and Mormon religious thinking at the movement's creation and thereby substantiates the need to inquire about their interrelationship in later decades.[12]

"Popular" Protestantism has been treated with surprising hesitancy. Charles Hambrick-Stowe's *The Practice of Piety* details the literature seventeenth-century New England ministers wrote for their listeners but provides relatively little information on readers' reactions. Hall's *Days of Wonder, Days of Judgment* offers the clearest attempt to reconcile tensions between the formal religion taught by ministers and the religion practiced by the laity in and out of pews. Hall doesn't deny differences as thoroughly as does George Selement, who actually argues that the laity's religion *was* the religion of the pulpit. But Hall does argue for an incorporation of lay views on the supernatural—particularly on the matter of wonders and miracles—even as he warns against exaggerating lay and clerical differences. Finally, David Harrell's study of twentieth-century Pentecostalism in *All Things are Possible* demands that readers take the groups seriously, including their miracle working and their remarkable rejection of race segregation in worship as early as the 1940s.[13]

The prospect of multi-directional relations between institutional religion and the laity also propels us toward a badly needed study of the sources of moral concepts and behavior. This topic is implicit in all religious history but seldom is studied. Though secular and religious historians regularly root morality in religion, no historical study yet demonstrates the accuracy or the context of this formulation. Histories of moral doctrine and moral philosophy remain high intellectual history. Books which appear to study morality in society, including such well-known works as Norbert Elias's *The Civilizing Process* and many Puritan studies, more often examine prescriptive literature than social practice. Since morality (and "immorality") is not confined to the churched in any society—not even in New England—we are left with a puzzling question: How does the laity, churched and unchurched, come to morality? In what way does religion, organized and folk, underwrite moral behavior? For example, are the rudimentary concepts of morality that proscribe homicide, assault, theft, and adultery rooted essentially in social processes that transcend formal religious training, while moral concepts that channel seemingly more flexible social behavior, such as marriage and child-rearing or views on slavery, women's rights, or abortion, are more likely influenced by formal religious training? If so, to what extent do these views overlap and what happens when they do, or when they conflict?[14]

Questions about the sources of popular morality go to the heart of questions about religion's influence on society. Ironically, until recently the Protestant model of religious history has tended to reflect a strikingly authoritarian sense of causality, especially in Puritan studies. Since New England moral concepts and behavior derived from Puritan principles taught by Puritan ministers, we can uncover the source of moral behavior in New England by studying what the ministers taught. But why should we assume that New Englanders refrained from homicide, fornication, assault, and thievery because their legal codes donned Old Testament garb, particularly when disagreement existed on so many issues there? Virginians, who were never accused of being too puritanical, also executed murderers, punished fornication, and forbade thievery and assault. Does religion account for their action?[15]

A Catholic model helps with these questions because it emphasizes highly variegated interrelationships between organized religion and the laity. For historians, at least, one meaning of the term "lapsed Catholic" points to the powerful subliminal role of church teaching even among those who have long since abandoned active membership. Similarly, there is an implicit usefulness in the variegated Catholic concept of sin, mortal and venial, particularly when one remembers the conceptual ambiguities that stalk the clerical-lay boundary on both sides. It is the very malleability – even confusion – resident in the Catholic understanding of lay behavior that upholds its promise for understanding complex interrelationships between formal religious teaching and moral behavior in the laity.[16]

The importance of place in Catholic practice and, hence, in the Catholic model of religious history opens up the question of aesthetics in expressing and determining religious practice. Catholicism has always attached considerable importance to place. The miracle that occurs at each Mass sacralizes the site of the Mass. A place thereby becomes *the* place, and its existence, in turn, increases the expectation of miracles. In contrast, Protestant models of religion and religious history tend to dismiss the importance of place. As a result, historians of Protestantism frequently have found themselves bereft of a coherent approach to aesthetics in Protestant faith. Protestantism centers itself on grace, not place. This conviction is built on Protestant criticism of the Mass and its liturgy and paraphernalia. A Protestantism brought into being through often violent iconoclasm, resulting in the destruction of Catholic church buildings, statues, and relics, not surprisingly accords little formal importance to the physical expression of faith and grace. This criticism has also tended to equate ritual with liturgy. This is what makes sense of the radical critique of state-church Protestantism, such as the Anabaptist critique of Swiss Calvinism or the Puritan critique of Anglicanism. Both railed against their opponents' ritual by tagging it "Catholic liturgy," even as they denied the existence of a ritual or liturgical element in their own worship, saying it was merely biblical and properly modeled on the "true" worship of the early church.[17]

A Catholic historical model returns us to the importance of place in American religion. In its positive form, this emphasis involves the sacralization of space. From the provision of chapels in early Maryland to the development of the first shrines in antebellum America to the construction of the great American basilicas and cathedrals in America between 1840 and 1940, Catholics have demonstrated that the sacralization of space in America has been as important as the sacralization of space in Europe and elsewhere.[18]

Protestants have not followed far behind, though the record of their efforts remains more obscure, in part, because their historians have not known quite what to do with it. In the 1680s Anglicans became particularly aware that without places of worship, Christianity was waning in America, and their Society for the Propagation of the Gospel in Foreign Parts remedied that deficiency by providing both ministers and buildings for English residents of America (only later for native Americans or Africans). The crypt at the First Presbyterian Church of Newburyport, Massachusetts, holding the body of the eighteenth-century evangelist George Whitefield, became the site for innumerable visitations between Whitefield's death in 1770 and the 1830s. The visitors, apparently mostly Protestant clergymen, slowly stripped Whitefield of all his clothes, taking pieces as relics, and regularly held his skull up to view in the course of their visit. Thus, when the Freewill Baptist minister David Marks viewed Whitefield's body in 1834, he reported that the skeleton was strewn about the casket, which was itself filled with dirt. Mormons also sacralized the American landscape, at least upstate New York, by making it the site of sacred occurrences recounted in the *Book of Mormon.* Add to this the importance other groups attached to place, from the "Mother Church" of Christian Science to Robert Schuller's "Crystal Cathedral," and the centrality of place for Protestants becomes more apparent than Protestant history allows.[19]

Ironically, iconoclasm also bespeaks the importance of place. The Puritan iconoclasm that castigated Anglican liturgy and underwrote seventeenth-century New England worship also underwrote eighteenth-century evangelical revolts. The Virginia Baptists described by Rhys Isaac in *The Transformation of Virginia, 1740–1790* opted for a deliberately plain style to distinguish their worship from the colony's ostentatious Anglican churches. Yet this Baptist worship was rich in ritual. Its ministers cultivated plainness in dress, plainness in speech, and plainness in church architecture. Inexorably, plainness became a principal ritual mark of Baptist worship, and artlessness constituted the Baptists' major aesthetic achievement. Aesthetic "simplicity" so successfully rationalized complex Baptist evangelical doctrines that for generations it constituted the Baptist "style" in America, a strategy also adopted in the twentieth century by the Jehovah's Witnesses, among others. In contrast, other Gilded Age Protestants perfected neoromanesque and baroque church architecture in massive urban church buildings. Especially favored by Episcopalians, who also renewed Anglo-Catholic liturgy, it found a more perplexing reception among urban Methodists and Baptists who seem to have been persuaded that "timeless" ritual or "traditional" church architecture might ease the tension with a Gilded Age materialism they imbibed but could not master.[20]

Government policy often acknowledges the importance of place in American religion. Local officials sometimes try to restrict the construction of places of worship because they believe that buildings sanction religious practice and solidify group identity. From the 1830s to the 1980s they have frequently used incorporation laws and zoning laws to prevent "unorthodox" religious groups from constructing religious facilities, hoping at the least that the groups would go somewhere else but knowing that the failure to erect church buildings would retard, if not squash, local growth.[21]

The importance of place also makes sense of violent iconoclasm. American anti-Catholic mobs never were reticent about vandalizing Catholic churches, shrines, and convents; violence distinguished their behavior from the 1640s through the 1940s and followed a long tradition of physical destructiveness in English anti-Catholicism. Nor has such destructiveness been limited to anti-Catholicism. Anti-Mormon rioters took considerable pleasure in destroying Mormon temples in the 1840s, much less in murdering Joseph Smith, and anti-Semitic agitators have long eagerly vandalized Jewish synagogues, and more recently Islamic mosques.[22]

Finally, the importance of place in religion is suggested by the fear that church officials commonly voice about mobility. This fear is not merely modern. As early as the 1760s the Philadelphia Baptist Association began keeping statistics on the number of members "dismissed by letter," meaning the number of church members moving elsewhere carrying a letter testifying to good standing in their old congregation, and the number "received by letter," meaning the number of persons who used the letters in seeking admittance to a new congregation. The former usually outnumbered the latter by a margin of two to one. Between 1781 and 1800, for example, the association dismissed 1011 members with letters but received only 505; between 1801 and 1807 the disparity increased, 780 members dismissed with letters but only 359 admitted. Modern observers are no less sensitive to the phenomenon. Harvey Cox openly complained in *The Secular City* that "high mobility [plays] havoc with traditional religion. It separates people from the holy places. It mixes them with neighbors whose gods have different names and who worship them in different ways." Sociologists Robert Wuthnow and Kevin Christiano find Cox's fears largely supported. Residential mobility clearly suppresses active worship among both Catholics and Protestants, though not equally, and does so whether tested on a local or even a regional basis.[23]

For Catholics, of course, sacred places also are often the sites of healing miracles as well as the miracle of the Mass. This theme is so pervasive that any scholar who attempted to write the church's history without reference to saints, shrines, and miracles certainly would qualify for the judgment a court once attached to the notorious eighteenth-century New England revivalist James Davenport: *non compos mentis*. Claims for miracles have been as common in American Catholicism as in Catholicism elsewhere. Reports of miracles first occurred among missionaries working with native Americans in California, Maryland, and New France. The first claim for miracles among European Catholics in America occurred in Washington, D.C., in the 1810s and subsequent claims surrounded the work of Mother Ann Seton in Philadelphia. Postbellum America witnessed increasing numbers of shrines devoted to healing, such as the shrine of Saint Jude in Chicago, described by Robert Orsi elsewhere in this volume.[24]

Protestant models of religious history tend to leave historians bereft of ways of handling miracles, even Protestant ones, except as aberrations. Not all Protestants have eschewed miracles. George Fox's *Book of Miracles* recounted many attempts to heal the sick and raise the dead that won Fox considerable notoriety and many followers. Hints at efforts at spiritual healing appear in the trial of Anne Hutchinson—not surprising since she had acted as a midwife—and popped up again in the 1690s when the New England "Rogerenes" advocated healing by prayer and rejected physical medicines, then again in the mid-eighteenth century when a Connecticut Valley minister, John Blunt (or Blount), was disciplined by a Northampton, Massachusetts, ministerial meeting for his efforts at faith healing.[25]

"Prayer bids" submitted by Jonathan Edwards's parishioners in Northampton suggest a continuing concern with healing, if not miracles. The Tennent family of New Jersey and Pennsylvania directly evidenced miracles in their lives and bodies. These included being raised from the dead, being saved from perjury convictions by witnesses who were prompted by dreams to testify in court, and, for no explainable reason, losing all the toes on one foot while sleeping—all of which were interpreted by the Tennents and by their parishioners as miraculous events. Witch beliefs—Cotton Mather called their enactment "diabolical miracles"—did not die at Salem but persisted into the next century. The South Carolina jurist Nicholas Trott inveighed against witches before the Charleston grand jury in 1707 (to no avail), and Philadelphia residents stoned a suspected witch to death in the city streets as the Constitutional Convention was meeting, to the considerable embarrassment of the city's newspapers.[26]

These Protestant miracles in the century of the Enlightenment explain both how and why miracles fascinated nineteenth-century American Protestants. An interest in divine interventionism, including the miraculous, was not unique to Catholicism or an aberration in American religion but part and parcel of the American Protestant experience. From the 1790s into the 1820s, Methodist itinerants regularly recruited followers by publicly reporting their apparitions and conversations in dreams with angels, biblical figures, Christ, even God. Little wonder that Joseph Smith was not surprised to see the angel Moroni in upstate New York in the 1820s or to receive from him golden plates containing new religious revelations. Little wonder too that well-churched Protestants, rather than the unchurched and otherwise indifferent, were the most likely patrons of spiritualist seances or later found themselves attracted to Pentecostalism, then to Christian Science, a movement which both modernized and Protestantized spiritual healing by regularizing it as a "science." In this context, the persistence of healing evangelists in modern America, symbolized in the success of A. A. Allen's "healing cloth" ministry in Miracle Valley, Arizona, in the 1950s and the development of the charismatic movement among both Protestants and Catholics in the 1960s and 1970s, becomes all the more predictable, perhaps even inevitable.[27]

Finally, a Catholic model of religious history opens up the analysis of power and authority in American religion. Protestants have frequently viewed Catholicism as epitomizing the perverse and evil exercise of power and authority in religion. This theme has distinguished much writing on Catholic ecclesiastical authority from antebellum nativism to Paul Blanshard's modern intellectual anti-Catholicism. For Catholic historians, the machinations of ecclesiastical politics very nearly consumed their work. Well into the 1970s, American Catholic history *was* the history of bishops, archbishops, and ecclesiastical power. Only recently has this tradition been challenged by historians who have sought to emphasize faith in the laity rather than power in the hierarchy, though they recognize that the questions are not mutually exclusive.[28]

Protestant models of religious authority are largely mono-phenomenal and mono-causal and lead, inevitably, to premature proclamations of democracy and laicization in American religion. The historiography of Puritanism offers an example. The interpretations of James Truslow Adams and Thomas Jefferson Wertenbaker found in New England only two kinds of politics, both of which were connected to religion: evil conspiracies that produced repression and liberal crusades that opened up New England society. Critics of these interpretations, beginning with

Samuel Eliot Morrison and continuing well beyond Perry Miller, challenged their predecessors, but often only obliquely. They stressed the Puritans' intelligence, intellectuality, and even their humanism even as they slid past the problem of authority. Miller, for example, emphasized the intellectual origins of Puritan orthodoxy and had little interest in probing the exercise of authority and role of coercion shaping seemingly homogenous New England communities.[29]

Recent community studies have presented a highly mixed picture of early New England. Though society appears to have been highly ordered in Sudbury and Andover but more tumultuous in Plymouth, Boston, and Salem, few historians address the broadest questions of authority explicitly. If anything, pointed questions about authority seem rather to have faded. As a result, the most formidable recent challenge to the revisionist-humanist interpretation of Puritan culture is, oddly, John Demos's book on witchcraft, *Entertaining Satan: Witchcraft and the Culture of Early New England.* Demos depicts a crabbed, unpleasant, dangerous society, not an intellectual, much less humanistic or modern one. Its intolerance turned even minor social infractions into witchcraft accusations and led to continuing executions of convicted witches long after witch trials had declined in England. Tellingly, perhaps, this cultural and religious aspect of Demos's work has been almost thoroughly overlooked; historians and readers concentrate on witchcraft to the exclusion of its ramifications for the concept of authority and the exercise of power in New England society.[30]

Not all historians of Protestantism beg the question of authority. Robert Doherty's and Larry Ingle's studies of the Hicksite schism among early nineteenth-century Friends are models of sensitive analysis, though they also disagree about the event. Literature published in the 1960s and 1970s on antebellum abolitionism drew the question of values, racism, and elitism into sharp relief and questioned the easy equation of evangelical religion, antislavery, and democracy. Recent studies of post–World War II religion—from Robert Wuthnow's *Restructuring of American Religion* to James Davison Hunter's *Evangelicalism: The Coming Generation*—tackle the relationship between political frustration and evangelical attachment.[31]

Especially with regard to evangelical revivalism, historians usually assume democracy in American religion rather than analyze it. In history, this habit consigns religions that seem undemocratic and clerically dominated to a distinctly un-American status. In social policy, its implications are less innocuous. The new religious groups that manifest distinctly hierarchical and authoritarian ecclesiastical structures—Hare Krishna and the various "Jesus cults" among them—find themselves investigated by Congress and subject to the extension of laws relating to parental control of children; "brainwashing" allegedly destroys freedom of the will and renders adult members "children," thereby placing the new groups beyond the protection of the First Amendment.[32]

Power and authority exist within every religious group, just as they exist within every society. Though the Catholic model of religious history sometimes overemphasizes the personal power of church officials, it nonetheless offers a malleable framework for exploring the interrelationship of authority and power within churches. Such a complex model would be particularly helpful in understanding the position of the clergy in American religion, for example. The most sensitive renderings of the clergy's position have appeared in the literature on Puritanism, particularly in David Hall's book *The Faithful Shepherd*. Other histories, cultural as well as religious, assume the "decline" of ministerial authority after 1700. Yet there is much to question here. Ministerial ranks increased enormously in America between 1790 and 1850; church membership also increased, both numerically and relatively. A larger percentage of Americans belonged to churches in 1850 than in 1800 or in 1700. Granted that the character of ministerial authority changed, did their authority also decline? Only local studies of ministerial authority will answer this question.[33]

Authority exercised in the great American denominations that emerged after 1700 also remains only casually studied. The riddle of American Methodism, "popular" yet notorious for its ecclesiastical hierarchicalism, remains unsolved, though it has attracted attention from many historians, both secular and religious. Indeed, Nathan Hatch's recent book, *The Democratization of American Christianity*, deepens the mystery. By highlighting the expansive democratic rhetoric of early national and antebellum societies, Hatch actually heightens the contrast with ecclesiastical practices in the Protestant denominations, most of which bore more resemblance to Methodist practice than they cared to admit publicly. New religious groups also exhibit a love of authority even when they are born out of a strident antiauthoritarianism. Mario DePillis has pointed out that Mormonism's appeal often rested on its remarkable authoritarianism through which Mormon followers would escape the disputes that afflicted "orthodox" Christianity.[34]

Coercion at the federal level also proves to be more than a nineteenth-century phenomenon. As late as the 1970s and 1980s Christian Science authorities in Boston sustained church orthodoxy through a private federal law. After Mary Baker Eddy's death, the church constrained dissent through strong internal coercion, and in 1971 it won congressional passage of Private Law 92-60 to secure a unique copyright extension on Eddy's 1906 edition of *Science and Health with Key to the Scriptures* and all previous editions. From 1971 until 1987 it used this extension to prevent publication by dissident reformers of Baker's original writings. The church's monopoly on Christian Science texts ended in 1987 when the U.S. District Court of Appeals in Washington, D.C. upheld a lower court decision that overturned the private law as unconstitutional.[35]

Similarly, the long contest for control of the Southern Baptist Convention's ecclesiastical hierarchy in the 1980s suggests that the lure of authority and power, not merely the principle of participation, makes "democratization" especially appealing. The conservative victors' promises to restructure denominational boards and dismiss "liberal" ministers and professors point up the appeal of majoritarianism, even in a denomination whose colonial predecessors spent much of their time evading censure by New England and Virginia authorities.[36]

The lure of coercion that fuels the contest in the Southern Baptist Convention also distinguishes support for the "school prayer" amendment. American liberals often misunderstand the controversy because they assume that for everyone coercion is antithetical to prayer. But the object of the school prayer amendment is power, not piety. Its backers often concede that the prayers would be superficial. They persist, however, because coercion is the prize. Convinced that the United States was, is, or ought to be a Christian society, backers of school prayer see no conflict in forcing nonbelievers and the religiously indifferent into a public obeisance to "religion," by which they mean Christianity or at least the Judeo-Christian heritage. The object is not prayer and pious contemplation but a coerced public acknowledgment of society's dependence on "God." Prayer is a means; power is the object.[37]

Ethnicity, spiritual heterogeneity, morality, sacred place, miracle, coercion. These themes alone do not explain the American religious past or predict its future. All are endemic to the history of Catholicism, though they are neither synonymous with it nor encompass it. All also are surprisingly endemic to the history of American Protestantism and to the history of other religious expression in America. There, they exist in different configurations than they do within Catholicism. Indeed, Protestants, Catholics, and others have so long arranged their own configuration of these and other important elements in the making of the

American religious tradition that historians might despair of models at all. Yet the function of historical models is not to find duplicates but to produce supple, comprehensive guides to historical analysis. However ironic, it ought to be no surprise that sophisticated history in a two-thousand-year-old church might serve as the foundation for a more general model of religious development in a nation sometimes distinguished by virulent anti-Catholicism but also exhibiting a history of religious complexity easily equal to that of its European and Asian precedessors.

NOTES

The author wishes to thank Eric Monkkonen for his extensive criticisms and comments.

1. James Hennesey, "Square Peg in a Round Hole: On Being Roman Catholic in America," *Records of the American Catholic Historical Society of Philadelphia* 81 (December 1973): 167–95.

2. Timothy L. Smith, "Religion and Ethnicity in America," *American Historical Review* 83 (1978): 1155–85; Randall Miller, ed., *Immigrants and Religion in Urban America* (Philadelphia, 1977).

3. Jay P. Dolan, *The Immigrant Church: New York's Irish and German Catholics, 1815–1865* (Baltimore, 1975); Robert A. Orsi, *The Madonna of 115th Street: Faith and Community in Italian Harlem, 1880–1950* (New Haven, Conn., 1985); Marcus Hansen, *The Atlantic Migration, 1607–1860: A History of the Continuing Settlement of the United States* (Cambridge, Mass., 1940); James J. Hennesey, *American Catholics: A History of the Roman Catholic Community in the United States* (New York, 1981); Thomas J. Archdeacon, *Becoming American: An Ethnic History* (New York, 1983). The literature on immigration, ethnicity, and religion is massive and beyond recounting here. Suffice it to say that every issue of the *Journal of Immigration History* contains articles and reviews detailing the involvement.

4. David Grayson Allen, *In English Ways: The Movement of Societies and the Transferal of English Local Law and Custom to Massachusetts Bay in the Seventeenth Century* (Chapel Hill, N.C., 1981); Henry A. Gemery, "Emigration from the British Isles to the New World, 1630–1700," *Research in Economic History* 5 (1980): 179–231; Henry A. Gemery, "European Emigration to North America, 1700–1820: Numbers and Quasi-Numbers," *Perspectives in American History* n.s. 1 (1984): 283–342; Clifford K. Shipton, "Immigration to New England, 1680–1740," *Journal of Political Economy* 44 (1936): 225–39.

5. Marilyn Westerkamp, *Triumph of the Laity: Scots-Irish Piety and the Great Awakening, 1625–1760* (New York, 1988); Leigh Eric Schmidt, *Holy Fairs:*

Scottish Communions and American Revivals in the Early Modern Period (Princeton, N.J., 1990); Mechal Sobel, *The World They Made Together: Black and White Values in Eighteenth-Century Virginia* (Princeton, N.J., 1988); Daniel B. Thorpe, *The Moravian Community in Colonial North Carolina: Pluralism on the Southern Frontier* (Knoxville, 1989).

6. Jon Butler, *The Huguenots in America: A Refugee People in New World Society* (Cambridge, Mass., 1983); Ned Landsman, *Scotland and Its First American Colony, 1683-1765* (Princeton, N.J., 1985). Also see William Petersen, "Concepts of Ethnicity," *Harvard Encyclopedia of American Ethnic Groups* (Cambridge, Mass., 1980), 234-42. Before their emigration in the 1680s, Scots were frequently divided among numerous religious groups, including the Church of Scotland, Presbyterians (among whom there were many divisions), and Quakers, while many expressed no interest in organized religion.

7. Jan Shipps, *Mormonism, The Story of a New Religious Movement* (Urbana, Ill., 1985); Kenneth Winn, *Exiles in a Land of Liberty: Mormons in America, 1830-1846* (Chapel Hill, N.C., 1989). Also see Nathan O. Hatch, *The Democratization of American Christianity* (New Haven, Conn., 1989).

8. On the trustee issue see Patrick Carey, *People, Priests, and Prelates: Ecclesiastic Democracy and the Tensions of Trusteeism* (Notre Dame, Ind., 1987). For a conservative evaluation of Catholic practice in the 1960s, see Gary Wills, *Bare Ruined Choirs: Doubt, Prophecy, and Radical Religion* (Garden City, N.Y., 1972). John Van Engen's essay in this volume deals with the issue of heterodoxy in the medieval period.

9. Philip Gura, *A Glimpse of Sion's Glory: Puritan Radicalism in Seventeenth-Century New England* (Middletown, Conn., 1984); Emery Battis, *Saints and Sectaries: Anne Hutchinson and the Antinomian Controversy in the Massachusetts Bay Colony* (Chapel Hill, N.C., 1962); Nancy L. Roberts, *Dorothy Day and the Catholic Worker* (Albany, N.Y., 1984); Mel Piehl, *Breaking Bread: The Catholic Worker and the Origin of Catholic Radicalism in America* (Philadelphia, 1982); Dorothy Day, *The Long Loneliness: The Autobiography of Dorothy Day* (New York, 1952).

10. Gabriel Le Bras, *Introduction à l'Histoire de la Pratique Religieuse en France*, 2 vols. (Paris, 1942-1945); Le Bras, *Etudes de Sociologie Religieuse*, 2 vols. (Paris, 1955-1956); Fernand Boulard, *Problèmes Missionaires de la France Rurale*, 2 vols. (Paris, 1945).

11. Jean Delumeau, *Catholicism between Luther and Voltaire: A New View of the Counter-Reformation*, trans. Jeremy Moiser (Philadelphia, 1977); Keith Thomas, *Religion and the Decline of Magic* (New York, 1971); David D. Hall, *Worlds of Wonder, Days of Judgment: Popular Religious Belief in Early New England* (New York, 1989); Gerald Strauss, *Luther's House of Learning: Indoctrination of the Young in the German Reformation* (Baltimore, 1978); James M. Kittelson, "Successes and Failures in the German Reformation: The Report from Strasbourg," *Archiv für Reformationsgeschichte* 73 (1982): 153-75.

12. Richard Bushman, *Joseph Smith and the Beginnings of Mormonism* (Urbana, Ill., 1985); also see D. Michael Quinn, *Mormonism and the Magic World View* (Salt Lake City, 1987).

13. George Selement, "The Meeting of Elite and Popular Minds at Cambridge, New England, 1638–1645," *William and Mary Quarterly*, 3d ser., 41 (1984): 32–48; David D. Hall, "Toward a History of Popular Religion in New England," ibid., 49–55; David D. Hall, *Worlds of Wonder, Days of Judgment*.

14. The major Puritan studies which do examine social behavior also are not comparative: Emil Oberholtzer, *Delinquent Saints: Disciplinary Action in the Early Congregational Churches of Massachusetts* (New York, 1956); Roger Thompson, *Sex in Middlesex: Popular Mores in a Massachusetts County, 1649–1699* (Amherst, Mass., 1986); Norbert Elias, *The Civilizing Process*, trans. Edmund Jephcott (New York, 1978); Elias, *Power and Civility*, trans. Jephcott (New York, 1982).

15. Philip Greven, *The Protestant Temperament: Patterns of Child-Rearing, Religious Experience, and the Self in Early America* (New York, 1977), studies the effects of different forms of Protestantism on child rearing and personality. On matters of crime and the law see Michael Hindus, *Prison and Plantation: Crime, Justice, and Authority in Massachusetts and South Carolina, 1767–1878* (Chapel Hill, N.C., 1980).

16. For an excellent discussion of the "Catholic Ethos," including the problem of sin, in American Catholicism, see Dolan, *American Catholic Experience: A History from Colonial Times to the Present* (New York, 1987), chap. 8.

17. Keith Thomas, *Religion and the Decline of Magic*.

18. This sacralization of space in American Catholicism is not well studied, but for an early tourist guide to modern shrines that gives some historical information, see Ralph L. Woods and Henry F. Woods, *Pilgrim Places in North America: A Guide to Catholic Shrines* (New York, 1939).

19. David Marks described his visit to Whitefield's tomb in *Memoirs of the Life of David Marks, Minister of the Gospel*, ed. Marilla Marks (Dover, N.H., 1846), p. 335.

20. Rhys Isaac, *The Transformation of Virginia, 1740–1790* (Chapel Hill, N.C., 1982); R. Jackson Lears, *No Place of Grace: Antimodernism and the Transformation of American Culture, 1880–1920* (New York, 1981).

21. The wide variety of restrictive laws against new religious groups, including the use of law to prevent construction of religious buildings, is described in Thomas Robbins, et. al., eds., *Cults, Culture, and the Law: Perspectives on New Religious Movements* (Chico, Calif., 1985).

22. John Phillips, *The Reformation of Images: Destruction of Art in England, 1535–1660* (Berkeley, Calif., 1973); Ray Billington, *The Protestant Crusade, 1800–1860* (Chicago, 1964); Winn, *Exiles in a Land of Liberty* updates Billington on anti-Mormonism.

23. The Baptist statistics have been gleaned from the yearly statistical

digests printed in *The Minutes of the Philadelphia Baptist Association, from A.D. 1707, to A.D. 1807,* ed. A. D. Gillette (Philadelphia, 1851). Harvey Cox quoted in Robert Wuthnow and Kevin Christiano, "The Effects of Residential Migration on Church Attendance in the United States," Wuthnow, ed., *The Religious Dimension: New Directions in Quantitative Research* (New York, 1979), pp. 257–76.

24. The history of the Catholic miraculous tradition in America has yet to be written, but for a start see Robert Emmett Curran, S.J., "'The Finger of God Is Here': The Advent of the Miraculous in the Nineteenth-Century American Catholic Community," *Catholic Historical Review* 73 (1987): 41–61.

25. *George Fox's "Book of Miracles,"* ed. Henry J. Cadbury (Cambridge, Mass., 1948); Michael MacDonald, *Mystical Bedlam: Madness, Anxiety, and Healing in Seventeenth-Century England* (New York, 1981); John Boles and Anna Williams, *The Rogerenes* (Boston, 1904), pp. 273, 289; *The Diary of Isaac Backus,* ed. William McLoughlin, 3 vols. (Providence, R.I., 1980), 1:59.

26. Stephen J. Stein, "'For Their Spiritual Good': The Northampton, Massachusetts, Prayer Bids of the 1730s and 1740s," *William and Mary Quarterly,* 3d ser., 37 (1980): 261–85. No discussion of the miraculous in early America should proceed without reading the superb article by D. P. Walker, "Valentine Greatrakes, the Irish Stroker and the Question of Miracles," in *Mélanges sur la littérature de la Renaissance à la mémoire de V.-L. Saulnier* (Geneva, 1984), pp. 343–56. Also see Increase Mather, *An Essay for the Recording of Illustrious Providences . . .* (Boston, 1684), pp. 177, 253, 319; Mather, *Cases of Conscience Concerning Evil Spirits Personating Men* (Boston, 1693; London, 1862), p. 257. On the Tennents, see [Elias Boudinot,] *Memoirs of the Life of William Tennent, . . . An Account of His Being Three Days in a Trance and Apparently Living* (Trenton, N.J., 1810). Alexander Archibald offered a naturalistic explanation for the events in *Biographical Sketches of the Founder and Principal Alumni of the Log College* (Philadelphia, 1851), pp. 150–52; Nicholas Trott, "A Charge Delivered at the General Sessions . . . 1705/06," in L. Lynn Hogue, "An Edition of 'Eight Charges Delivered at so Many Several General Sessions . . . (1703–1707) by Nicholas Trott'" (Ph.D. dissertation, University of Tennessee, 1972), pp. 133–63; Francis Le Jau to Philip Stubs, April 15, 1707, in *The Carolina Chronicle of Dr. Francis Le Jau, 1706–1717,* ed. Frank J. Klingberg (Berkeley, 1956), p. 25.

27. On miracles in modern America, see David Harrell, *All Things Are Possible: The Healing and Charismatic Revivals in Modern America* (Bloomington, Ind., 1975).

28. Paul Blanshard wrote frequently about Catholicism and politics, his first and most famous book being *American Freedom and Catholic Power* (Boston, 1949). The most thoroughgoing example of the "new Catholic history" is, of course, Dolan's *American Catholic Experience.*

29. James Truslow Adams, *The Founding of New England* (Boston, 1921);

Thomas Jefferson Wertenbaker, *The Puritan Oligarchy: The Founding of American Civilization* (New York, 1947). Characteristically, Miller and Thomas Johnson, in their edited source book, *The Puritans,* revised edition (New York, 1963), entitled their chapter on politics, "The Theory of the State and of Society," thereby avoiding the problem of practice.

30. Darrett B. Rutman, *Winthrop's Boston: Portrait of a Puritan Town* (Chapel Hill, N.C., 1965); Sumner Chilton Powell, *Puritan Village: The Formation of a New England Town* (Middletown, Conn., 1964); Kenneth A. Lockridge, *A New England Town: The First Hundred Years, Dedham, Massachusetts, 1636–1736* (New York, 1970); Philip Greven, *Four Generations: Population, Land, and Family in Colonial Andover, Massachusetts* (Ithaca, N.Y., 1970); John Demos, *A Little Commonwealth: Family Life in Plymouth Colony* (New York, 1970); John P. Demos, *Entertaining Satan: Witchcraft and the Culture of Early New England* (New York, 1982). On the problems of New England as a model of American cultural development see Jack P. Greene, *Pursuits of Happiness: The Social Development of Early Modern British Colonies and the Formation of American Culture* (Chapel Hill, N.C.: 1988).

31. Robert Doherty, *The Hicksite Separation: A Sociological Analysis of a Religious Schism in Early Nineteenth-Century America* (New Brunswick, N.J., 1967); H. Larry Ingle, *Quakers in Conflict: The Hicksite Reformation* (Knoxville, 1986); James Hunter Davison, *Evangelicalism: The Coming Generation* (Chicago, 1987); Robert Wuthnow, *The Restructuring of American Religion: Society and Faith since World War II* (Princeton, N.J.: 1988).

32. On cults and their perceived danger to American society see Robbins, et al., *Cults, Culture, and the Law;* Florence Kaslow and Marvin B. Sussman, eds., *Cults and the Family* (New York, 1982); Lowell D. Streiker, *The Gospel Time Bomb: Ultrafundamentalism and the Future of America* (Buffalo, N.Y., 1984); Willa Appel, *Cults in America: Programmed for Paradise* (New York, 1983); David G. Bromley and Anson D. Shupe, Jr., *Strange Gods: The Great American Cult Scare* (Boston, 1981).

33. David Hall, *The Faithful Shepherd: The New England Ministry in the Seventeenth Century* (Chapel Hill, N.C., 1972). On the "decline" of ministerial status in the eighteenth and nineteenth centuries see James W. Schmotter, "Ministerial Careers in Eighteenth-Century New England: The Social Context, 1700–1760," *Journal of Social History,* 9 (1975): 249–67; Donald M. Scott, *From Office to Profession: The New England Ministry, 1750–1850* (Philadelphia, 1978); Burton Bledstein, *The Culture of Professionalism: The Middle Class and the Development of Higher Education in America* (New York, 1976), 173–76, 197. Several helpful Catholic models might include two books on Chicago Catholicism: Charles Shanabruch, *Chicago's Catholics: The Evolution of an American Identity* (Notre Dame, Ind., 1981), and Edward R. Kantowicz, *Corporation Sole: Cardinal Mundelein and Chicago Catholicism* (Notre Dame, Ind., 1983).

34. See Jon Butler, *Awash in a Sea of Faith: Christianizing the American*

People (Cambridge, Mass., 1990), chap. 9; Mario DePillis, "The Quest for Religious Authority and the Rise of Mormonism," *Dialogue* 1 (1966–67): 68–88; Leonard J. Arrington and Davis Bitton, *The Mormon Experience: A History of the Latter-Day Saints* (New York, 1979), pp. 39–40.

35. *United Christian Scientists, et al.* v. *Christian Science Board of Directors,* First Church of Christ, Scientist [Boston], *Federal Register,* 2d ser. (Saint Paul, 1988), vol. 829 F. 2d, 1152–1170.

36. Nathan O. Hatch, *The Democratization of American Christianity;* on formal church-state relations see the recent bibliography edited by John F. Wilson, *Church and State in America: A Bibliographical Guide,* 2 vols. (Westport, Conn., 1986–1987).

37. An interesting sample of the discussion regarding school prayer and other forms of government support for religion, largely meaning Christianity, can be found in the booklet *Religion and the Constitution,* American Enterprise Forum, no. 62 (Washington, D.C., 1984), in which backers of school prayer, such as Illinois Representative Henry Hyde, consistently cite nineteenth-century congressional practice in aiding Christianity to support their point. As one of the participants notes (p. 11), "fundamentalist Christians" often are opposed to school prayers and particularly to silent prayer on the intriguing ground of blasphemy.